W9-AWI-266

The First Anthology

30 Years of
The New York Review of Books

EDITED BY
Robert B. Silvers, Barbara Epstein,
and Rea S. Hederman

THE NEW YORK REVIEW OF BOOKS
NEW YORK

The First Anthology
30 Years of The New York Review of Books

A **New York Review** Book

Copyright © 1993 NYREV, Inc., and the authors.
All rights including translation into other languages
reserved by the publishers in the United States,
Great Britain, Mexico, and all countries participating
in the Universal Copyright Convention, and the
Pan American Copyright Convention.
Nothing in this publication may be reproduced
without the permission of the publisher.
Inquiries to The New York Review of Books
250 West 57th Street
New York, NY 10107

Illustrations by David Levine
Designed by Andrea Barash

Library of Congress Catalog Card Number: 93-85356

ISBN 0-940322-01-3

Printed in the USA

Second Printing

Table of Contents

Contributors

Editors' Note

For thirty years we resisted an anthology from the *New York Review*. To choose among the thousands of articles we have published since the first experimental issue in the winter of 1963 always seemed too painful. For each piece that seemed likely, five or six others came immediately to mind. Finally, in the autumn of 1992, as we contemplated our thirtieth anniversary year, our publisher Rea Hederman undertook to choose about two dozen articles for our first anthology. Having come to the paper in 1984 (while promising not to interfere with our unique editorial freedom to publish what we want), he was not encumbered by any reluctance to choose among the large number of articles whose claims seem to us undeniable and for which our admiration is as intense as ever.

During two months Rea Hederman assembled a list of four hundred pieces, which was reduced to forty, and then to most of those published here. The result was pleasing, less painful than we expected. We could then put some other articles in and take some out. The result, of course, can be no more than a hint of what the paper has done since Jason Epstein suggested that the *New York Times* strike of 1963 offered a chance to start a new kind of book review. And naturally we miss here such contributors as (to mention only those who have died) F. W. Dupee, Paul Goodman, H. L. A. Hart, Irving Howe, George Lichtheim, Mary McCarthy, Arnaldo Momigliano, J. Robert Oppenheimer, Philip Rahv, Leonard Schapiro, I. F. Stone, Frances Yates, and Edmund Wilson. One could easily make another, equally interesting anthology from the articles of these writers alone. Now that we are in an anthological mood, perhaps we will.

—*Robert Silvers*
Barbara Epstein

Lyndon Baines Johnson

A Day at the White House by Dwight Macdonald was originally published July 15, 1965.

DWIGHT MACDONALD

A Day at the
White House

"PRESIDENT AND MRS. JOHNSON are planning the most extensive arts festival ever held in the White House," reported the *New York Times* on May 27th. It would last thirteen hours, there would be exhibitions of current American painting, sculpture, and photography; programs of American plays, movies, ballet, and music; and readings by two novelists, Saul Bellow and John Hersey, two poets, Robert Lowell and Phyllis McGinley, and one popular biographer, Catherine Drinker Bowen. The Johnsonian consensus: Bellow and Lowell balanced against Hersey and McGinley, with Miss Bowen added to the democratic, or kitschy, side of the scale to make it all the more consensual. As the drunk said about the books in Jay Gatsby's library: "Absolutely real—have pages and everything.... See! It's a bona-fide piece of printed matter.... This fella's a regular Belasco! What thoroughness! What realism! Knew when to stop, too—didn't cut the pages. But what do you expect?" Our President, too, is a regular Belasco for realistic stage settings and, like Gatsby, he knows when, and where, to stop: just beyond Miss Bowen. He doesn't cut the pages. But what do you expect? A consensus is a consensus.

A week later, the consensus was broken by Robert Lowell, who wrote a letter to the President that appeared on the front page of the June 3 *Times*:

> .... Although I am very enthusiastic about most of your domestic legislation and intentions, I nevertheless can only follow our present foreign policy with the greatest dismay and distrust.... We are in danger of imperceptibly becoming an explosive and suddenly chauvinistic nation, and we may even be drifting on our way to the last clear ruin.
>
> I know it is hard for the responsible man to act; it is also painful for the private and irresolute man to dare criticism. At this anguished, delicate and perhaps determining moment, I feel I am serving you and our country best by not taking part in the White House Festival of the Arts.

In the same issue of the *Times*, statements appeared by Bellow and Hersey explaining why they had decided not to join Lowell. Neither expressed disagreement with his "dismay and distrust" (though Bellow seemed to accept Vietnam, criticizing only the Dominican occupation; I'm told he had first written a much stronger letter but then, like his Herzog, didn't send it; there was to be plenty of Herzogian behavior by others at the Festival). Bellow reasoned—logically enough if one doesn't accept Lowell's premise that our recent foreign policy is so shameful and disastrous as to make it an overriding consideration even in lending support to a presidential arts festival—that it was not "a political occasion which demands agreement with Mr. Johnson on all the policies of his administration." "Moreover," he concluded, "Mr. Johnson is not simply this country's principal policy-maker. He is an institution. When he invited me to Washington, I accepted in order to show my respect for his intentions and to honor his high office." This makes no sense to me. President Harding had "intentions" and he was also "an institution" to whose "high office" honor was, on this reasoning, due. But I don't think Bellow, had he been anachronistically invited to the White House then, would have accepted, any more than Emerson and Thoreau would have agreed to read from their works if President Polk had staged an arts festival during the Mexican War.

Mr. Hersey said he was "deeply troubled by the drift toward reliance on military solutions in our foreign policy" but that he felt he could "make a stronger point by standing in the White House, I would hope in the presence of the President, and reading from a work of mine entitled *Hiroshima.*"

The day Lowell's letter appeared in the *Times* I was asked to sign a telegram to the President supporting his position, which I gladly did because I agreed with its content and admired its personal, unrhetorical style. The statement appeared in the next morning's *Times* (June 4) and the same morning I received a telegram: "THE PRESIDENT AND MRS. JOHNSON INVITE YOU TO THE WHITE HOUSE FESTIVAL OF THE ARTS TO BEGIN AT 10 AM ON JUNE 14TH AND CONTINUE THROUGH THE EVENING..." After some thought and consultation, I decided that while the most consistent course, morally and intellectually, would be to refuse—also, if I may say so, the easiest—it might be more fruitful to accept, so that at least one critical observer would be there to report on what happened. So I wired my acceptance to the Festival's impresario, Dr. Eric Goldman—professor of history at Princeton and President Johnson's chief cultural adviser—stating that, as he probably knew by then, I supported Lowell's stand and should feel free to comment publicly on the Festival. On these terms, I sacrificed, not for the first time, consistency, and possibly even good taste, in the interest of a larger objective.

IT TURNED OUT to be worth it. For one thing, I secured a copy of a document of primary importance, whose significance none of the newspaper reports, including Howard Taubman's copious account in the *Times*, seems to have grasped: the guest list.[1] I've seen no mention, for instance, that there were *two* guest lists, one for the first sitting, from 10 AM on, and the other for the second, from 7 PM on. Each contained roughly 175 persons, but the first group was invited for the major part of the Festival while the second came in only for a cocktail party on the lawn followed by the President's speech of welcome, a buffet supper, and two hours of ballet and jazz. The most enjoyable part of the day in fact, but still they were placed below the salt. The only rationale of this discrimination I can detect is that all the artists without exception—all the painters, sculptors, and photographers— were relegated to the second sitting. A mistake, if one purpose of the Festival was, as a White House "source" suggested, to bring together the patron and the artist. But further examination of the guest list shows the aims to have been different. "Does anyone know exactly why this particular group of people is here or why this Festival is being held in the first place?" Mildred Dunnock asked. (*She* was there to give two soliloquies from *Death of a Salesman*—but, still, why?) Asked the same question later, Jack Valenti, a presidential assistant, answered: "This is a wonderful thing to show the White House's great interest in the arts. It doesn't matter why, just that it was." Theirs not to reason why...So one purpose was to give the Johnson administration a cultural image, a consensus of artists and writers reciprocating "the White House's great interest in the arts" by turning out for the Festival.

But the main purpose was to impress not the actual producers of art or thought with the "White House's great interest" but rather our cultural fuglemen ("a trained soldier stationed in front of a military company as a

---

[1] How many others besides Lowell declined, and for what reasons, I don't of course know. Two refusals because of our present foreign policy have been made public: those of the photographer Paul Strand, and the sculptor Alexander Calder. And two have not: those of Jack Levine, the painter, and Robert Brustein, the drama critic—both have authorized me to state the fact. As for the rest of the absentees, who include practically the entire literary establishment, from Edmund Wilson to Thornton Wilder, all that can be said is that they were not there.

guide for the others in their exercises"), that is, directors and patrons of art museums, presidents of symphony orchestras (i.e., the money holders or raisers—no directors or composers of any note were present, not Stravinsky or Copland or Thomson or Carter or Stokowski or Barber or Harris or Bernstein or Menotti), organizers of local "arts councils," and various pundits from TV, newspapers, and big-circulation magazines. Whether this purpose was achieved or not I don't know, but that it was paramount an examination of the guest list shows.

Excluding the *ex officio* invitees who were asked because they were reading or acting or dancing or playing music or because their pictures or sculptures or movies or plays were on view—eighty would be a generous estimate, most of them in the below-the-salt 7 PM sitting—there were present at either 10 AM or 7 PM the following who might be considered to have some direct connection with arts and letters: Alfred H. Barr, James Johnson Sweeney, Ralph Ellison, Reed Whittemore (this year's poet in residence at the Library of Congress), Thomas Hess (editor of *Art News*), José Limon, Russell Lynes, Paul Horgan, Pauline Kael (movie critic), Harold Taylor, Henry Geldzahler (Metropolitan Museum of Art), Frank Getlein (art critic), and myself. Adding, to be generous, ten or so newspaper critics (if there can be such a creature) and the art editor of *Time*, this comes to twenty-five participants who were some kind of artist or writer (and who were invited as part of the audience). Add five senators and congressmen (who seem to have been selected for political rather than cultural reasons— Javits, Lindsay, Morse, Robert Kennedy, Paul Douglas, and Fulbright are not on the list while Congressmen Brademas, Farnsley, and Thompson are, also Senators Cooper and Yarborough) and another five names I've at least heard of: Earl Warren, Sol Hurok, Abe Fortas, Irv Kupcinet (a Chicago columnist and TV impresario—*Kup's show*—whose iridescent jacket livened things up), and the Hon. William Walton, chairman of the Washington Commission of Fine Arts and one of the few Kennedy intimates who were present.[2] Adding these ten to the artists and intellectuals mentioned above, we get 113 names or about one third of the participants,

---

[2] Arthur Schlesinger, Jr., for instance, was not invited, although he had ridiculed Lowell's letter and described Lewis Mumford's speech, as president of the American Academy of Arts and Letters, criticizing our current foreign policy, as "an anxious blast of a somewhat inchoate sort." Schlesinger, who was once a professor of history, added that the reactions of the audience reminded him of the "wild, unleashed emotionalism" of Hitler's Nuremberg rallies. What more could one ask? But Lyndon Johnson is a hard man; no invitation.

active or passive, in the Festival. What of the other two thirds? A good number, perhaps thirty, are not identified nor do their names wake any resonance in my ear. No doubt Fred Lazarus and Mrs. Irma Lazarus, both of Cincinnati, Mrs. R. Max Brooks of Austin, Texas, and Dr. Abdul Hamid, the rector of the University of Kabul, all had some reason for being there. Likewise the large New York City contingent of names unknown to me, such as Paul Leaf, Mr. and Mrs. Wright Rumbough, Jr., Lansdell K. Christie, and Orrin Christy, Jr.

There is no doubt, however, as to the identity of the great majority of participants. They were patrons, bureaucrats, or entrepreneurs of culture: Dempster Christenson, Pres., Sioux Falls-Augustana Sym. Orch., S. Dak.; R. Phillips Hanes, Jr., Pres., Arts Council of America, Winston-Salem, NC; John D. Rockefeller III, Chr. Bd. Trustees, Lincoln Center, NYC; Mrs. Hugh Bullock, Pres., the Academy of American Poets, NYC; Hon. Roger Stevens, Chr., National Council on the Arts, Washington, DC; Col. Eben Henson, Pres., Kentucky Council of the Performing Arts, Danville, Ky.; and J. Paul Hewitt, Chr., Louisiana Commission on Culture and the Performing Arts, which seems to take care of everything.

I ENTERED THE WHITE HOUSE on the dot of ten and was greeted cordially by an attractive young matron who gave me a smile, and a luxurious program with the President's seal embossed on its laid-paper cover, and a large card with my name (misspelled "McDonald") inscribed in bold calligraphy over a pale blue vignette of the White House. She pressed the gummy back side to my chest—rather like being decorated—and it stuck there all through that long day's journey into night. I was then briefed on my next move ("Straight up the stairs, sir, then sharp *right*") by one of the pleasant young officers who chivvied us about all day like respectful sheepdogs. Their crisp, incredibly clean white uniforms were accented only by brass buttons, silver shoulder-bars, and one of those military shoulder corsages of gold cords and tassels looped over the left shoulder.

The first familiar face I saw, on emerging from the labyrinthine corridors, was Saul Bellow's. He didn't look happy. We greeted each other in a Stanley-Livingstone mood, two exiles meeting among all those strange natives. Nor was the mood dissipated for me, when we instantly began to argue, violently, about The Lowell Problem. Arguments are part of the New York ambience I'm used to and, for a few moments, I felt at home at The White House Festival of the Arts. Our argument—can't really call it a "dialogue," not even a "discussion"—was cut short by one of the military sheepdogs who began to arrange us in line to be presented to the First Lady. ("You must be pleased to see so many able-bodied young men not fighting in Vietnam," a museum director observed to me.) We filed past Mrs. Johnson, murmuring our names to an officer-footman who repeated them to her, whereupon she smiled and shook hands with every appearance of delight. Since the President didn't appear until eight o'clock that evening when he gave a brief speech of welcome, after which he disappeared without any handshakes or, from where I sat, smiles, I cannot report on him as a host. But his wife was a charming hostess, agreeable and indefatigable.

"10:25–10:30 AM. East Room. Mrs. Johnson opens the Festival with brief remarks," stated the program and so it came to pass. Logistically, the Festival was a great success. "A festival is a time for feasting and there is a rich feast indeed before us," she began, optimistically. "The arts will be presented in many forms, all of which are warmly welcome in this house. For as Aristotle told us long ago, in part the arts imitate nature but in part they also 'complete what nature cannot elaborate.'" She omitted the last sentence—I quote from the text given to the press—perhaps feeling, as a sensible woman, that her ghost-writer had overestimated the capacity of her audience for a willing suspension of disbelief. But she did include the next three sentences, which perfectly sum up the consensual approach to culture: "There is something here for the taste of everyone. Each of us will like or dislike particular things. All contribute to the enormous vigor and diversity of the creative life in America." Well, maybe, but only an omnivorous Walt Whitman could have swallowed what was served up to us at the Festival. My difficulty is that I like or dislike particular things; intensely; and regardless of the enormous vigor and diversity of the creative life. She concluded, as per script: "You have earned the gratitude of every American for the beauty, the meaning and the zest you are contributing to our lives." That "you" was disturbing, surrounded as I was by patrons of symphony orchestras, the president of the American Watercolor Society, and John D. Rockefeller III. I was reminded, *proportions gardées*, of Henry Wallace's postwar tour of Siberia in which he innocently saluted his audiences, composed of guards and officials in charge of forced-labor camps, as free-spirited pioneers taming the wild frontier in the best American tradition. "Men born in wide free spaces will not brook injustice and will not even temporarily live in slavery," Mr. Wallace declaimed to the stupefied prison-wardens of Irkutsk.

Mark Van Doren, the *compère* of the literary session, now rose, looking very solemn, and began by noting with regret "the absence of Lowell":

...I have been troubled as to whether I should speak of it at all; I do so now, after several previous attempts, merely as honoring the scruple of a fine poet who, in his own terms, was "conscience-bound" to stay away.

Originally, Mr. Van Doren had planned to say a great deal more—his "merely" above is accurate—and a typescript had been given out to the press. Some of it may be of interest:

> ...Surely it is no secret that many share his concern—I do, for one—and perhaps it is true that all of us, without exception, are somewhat uneasy. But the main point I wish to make is that Mr. Lowell, by acting and speaking as he did, honored an ancient tradition in the arts.... He spoke out of his deepest conviction.... Nothing prevents a poet from being a citizen, too; and if Mr. Lowell thought that his duty as a citizen was to be absent from this place, it is not for us who are present to doubt that he was as serious as he was sensitive, or that it was difficult for him to stay away. History will show whether his dismay and distrust were justified; meanwhile, however, he himself has made history, and it seems fitting to record that simple fact.

Why did Van Doren omit, when he came to give the talk, all the politics and most of the praise for Lowell? Howard Taubman quotes Van Doren as saying he "had decided to shorten his comments after a talk with Bellow and Hersey," while Drew Pearson writes that "Eric Goldman diplomatically persuaded Van Doren to eliminate most of the criticism."

After Catherine Drinker Bowen had read, with spirit, an amusing extract from her biography of the late Justice Holmes, Saul Bellow, looking even more solemn than Mr. Van Doren, read, with less spirit, an extract from *Herzog* which was more amusing than Miss Bowen's passage and, in every way, much the best writing we heard that morning.

Next came Phyllis McGinley, a pleasant-looking matron in a flowered hat who was introduced by Mr. Van Doren with the admonition that light verse can be fine poetry, too, and in Miss McGinley's case, was: "She is nothing less than a poet." The warning was wasted on me, since I am fond of light verse. The trouble was that Miss McGinley's seemed on the heavy side. After "Apologia," a soggy pastiche of Housman and Millay, she swung into her big number, lasting eight or nine minutes, "In Praise of Diversity," an updated "Essay on Man":

> *Counting no blessing but the flaw*
> *That difference is the moral law.*

(Could I have got that down right?) I don't think Pope would have rhymed "sexes" with "Texas" or "beginning" with "original sinning" or "knee" with "courtesy." Pop Pope, you might say. That this work was originally composed for recitation at a Columbia commencement is something to think about. Ever the obliging poetaster, Miss McGinley inserted, for the occasion, six new lines which take a firm, positive stand in favor of both and indeed all sides:

> Applaud both dream and commonsense,
> Born equal; then with all our power,
> Let us, for once, praise Presidents
> Providing Dream its festival hour.
> And while the pot of culture's bubblesome,
> Praise poets, even when they're troublesome.

John Hersey next rose to read passages from *Hiroshima*, not in the presence of the President, but with Mrs. Johnson in the first row. He prefaced them, speaking slowly and emphatically.

> I read these passages on behalf of the great number of citizens who have become alarmed in recent weeks by the sight of fire begetting fire.
> Let these words be a reminder. The step from one degree of violence to the next is imperceptibly taken and cannot easily be taken back. The end point of these little steps is horror and oblivion.
> We cannot for a moment forget the truly terminal dangers, in these times, of miscalculation, of arrogance, of accident, of reliance not on moral strength but on mere military power. Wars have a way of getting out of hand.

Mr. Hersey is a reserved, gentlemanly fellow—also the newly appointed master of a Yale college—and it must have pained him to make such ungracious comments about her husband's policies in the presence of his hostess. But he evidently shared Lowell's "dismay and distrust" to such an extent that he insisted on making a statement that was impolite, irrelevant, and necessary.

From 11:20 to 12:10 the program advised "viewing of the works of art." There was a lot of viewing of the works of art: again from 5 to 7 and, at the very end: "10:30 PM: Mrs. Johnson closes the Festival and guests will view the art." Fortunately, the art proved to be, with the exception of Duke Ellington's band, the best thing at the Festival: a broad representation of every kind of contemporary American painting and sculpture that was selected with sophisticated taste, all the more remarkable because it was assembled in three weeks from thirty museums. The photographic exhibition, however, was disappointing: poor examples of such masters as Stieglitz, Evans, and Abbott and too many chestnuts like Capa's "Death of a Loyalist Militiaman."

Luncheon was, as the card said, "hosted" by the National Art Gallery, to which we were transported in special buses, landing at the "rarely used Presidential entrance," also called "the VIP entrance." After lunch, George F. Kennan, former ambassador to the Soviet Union and Yugoslavia, now of the Institute of Advanced Studies at Princeton, and also president of the National Institute of Arts and Studies, addressed on the subject of "The Arts and American Society." Fair enough. Mr. Kennan is an admirable man, an original and independent political thinker who writes well and has—or so I thought—a cultural background more common in the past among establishment figures than today. Like Adlai Stevenson. And like Stevenson, he was disappointing. What I could hear of his speech—the echoes in the stone-walled Garden Court were deafening—was not promising: "Beauty is open-ended.... The artist is an odd ball...the help-ing hand of the Maecenas...he [the artist] must do what he can to shield the public from artistic frivolity and charlatanism." (But frivolity I think an essential trait of any artist, and Baudelaire, writing of Poe, said truly: "A lit-tle charlatanism is permitted to genius.")

Reading the text confirmed my suspicions. The central theme is that the artist must be tolerant of the public, and vice versa, because each needs the other. An American Civil Liberties Union approach: "These rules of mutual forbearance are the prerequisites, then, as I see them, for a success-ful relationship between American society and the arts." I don't think many practicing artists would feel elated by this solution, but luckily none were present.

There was also the curious matter, especially for such a stiff-necked character as Mr. Kennan, of a page and a half of additional remarks that was given out to the press just before lunch, but which he failed to deliver. They were addressed to what by that time had become The Lowell-Hersey-Van Doren Problem:

> I do not wish to aggravate feelings that are already tense [he began, or rather had intended to begin]....The worker in the vineyard of the arts has, God knows, no obligation to agree with the government in matters of political policy, or to conceal his disagreement...[BUT] government is made up, in overwhelming majority, of honorable and well-meaning peo-ple charged with preserving the intactness of our national life, without which it is hard to picture any national culture at all....[BUT] People in government...will have to bear in mind...first of all, that in the moral spirit of this country, of which the arts are one of the great interpreters and custodians, we have a very special and precious thing—the very soul of the nation.... Secondly, that artists and writers feel themselves today—more,

I think, than ever before—a responsible part of the public conscience of the nation, and are recognized in this capacity by many others, particularly among the youth, and finally, this being so, and for their own sake as well, that there is reason to view with concern the anguish many of them feel over these problems, and to respect their need and their longing to be permitted to identify with the methods and the tone of American diplomacy no less than with its objectives.

Why Mr. Kennan decided at the last minute not to pronounce in public words he had already given to the press I do not know. The Washington *Evening Star* (which quotes most of the above) suggests that Kennan himself was of two minds even after he had non-said his additional remarks: "He told at least one reporter he had no objection to their being quoted anyhow, even though undelivered, and told another reporter he didn't want them quoted at all. Then he went off to catch a plane for Yugoslavia, where he is to make a speech today, leaving behind with White House cultural adviser Eric Goldman a brief 'clarifying' statement that didn't seem to clarify anything."

Back to the White House for an hour of music, which I don't pretend to judge, but I'm told the Louisville Symphony Orchestra played well and Roberta Peters was in good voice when she sang Gershwin's "Summertime." Then to the East Room again (3:45–4:15 PM) where Helen Hayes introduced gracefully (all too) ten-minute excerpts from two "classics" (*The Glass Menagerie* and *Death of a Salesman*) and two recent plays by young writers: Frank Gilroy's *The Subject Was Roses* and Millard Lampell's *Hard Travelin'*. The last was the only one that came off: written with style and pace, and well played by Moses Gunn and Tom Ligon. Miss Hayes was fluttery and exalted. The First Lady of the American Stage. She wondered why plays had become so "grimly realistic" since "the joy and fun of my salad days." But she soon cheered up: the new playwrights "sometimes draw the picture a little *too* dark" but "Oh what power they put into their words!" There was also some Kennanesque talk about the role of art in "helping people to understand themselves."

Back to the dining room to view a half-hour of "The Motion Picture," very brief film clips from movies by Hitchcock, Wyler, Kazan, Stevens, and Zinneman which, except for the famous taxicab scene between Marlon Brando and Rod Steiger from *On the Waterfront*, were mediocre or worse. They consulted six film critics—but not me, possibly because they suspected I would have recommended giving the whole thirty minutes to Kubrick's *Dr. Strangelove*. The chief interest was provided by Charlton Heston, the "narrator," a fine figure of a man bursting with health and ideas. "The salt shaker is essential to the American movie," he began. I'm not sure just what he meant; not *cum grano salis* as I'd hoped, but probably the literal object since he went on "Bogart with a toothpick, Chaplin with a cane, these are hard to beat.... Film has been described as the most uniquely American of all the arts." From this seed Mr. Heston nurtured a healthy growth of chauvinism until finally all the great directors abroad were getting their stuff, really, by copying the ungreat directors in Hollywood. His introductions to the film clips were also memorable: "We know what Hitchcock can do with Janet Leigh and a bathtub.... His style is subjective because his ideas don't exist as persuasion but as experience." (That's what my notes say.) "To define Stevens's style is to trace the melodic line of Mozart."

After a two-hour recess, we assembled at seven for the home stretch: a cocktail party in the garden with Mrs. Johnson circulating amiably and unweariedly, the President's speech from the stage that had been erected to be used later, after an al fresco supper on the lawn, for a ballet performance "hosted" by Gene Kelly and then an hour of Duke Ellington's band.

The President's speech had its Hestonesque moments. But the passage which scared me was:

> Every President has known that our people look to this city, and this House, not only to follow but to lead, not only to listen but to teach, not only to obey their will but to help design their purpose. The Presidency is...a wellspring of moral leadership. [I think he left out "moral" but let's hope my ear was wrong.] We are using this great power to help move toward justice for all our people, not simply because American freedom depends on it. And we are trying to stimulate creation, not because of our personal tastes or desires but because American greatness will rest on it. This is the true meaning of this occasion.

I don't like that "leadership," moral or not, nor do I want my purpose to be designed by anybody else, not even McGeorge Bundy. And I'd be much easier in mind if the President's attempt to "stimulate creation" grew from his own "personal tastes or desires," however unsympathetic I might find them, and not from his hope to use our arts and letters as underpinning for "American greatness," for which I don't give a damn.

The President didn't look any happier than Saul Bellow did. Perhaps both realized they'd somehow gotten into a false position. "Some of them insult me by staying away and some of them insult me by coming," the President grumbled to a reporter. There was a bad moment when he departed from the text to growl briefly but ominously at his guests. Also at

Dr. Eric Goldman (who looked most unfestive throughout his festival—the only really happy-looking people, in fact, were Duke Ellington and his bandsmen). The text reads: "You have been asked to come not because you are the greatest artists of the land, although some of you may be [but] because you have distinguished yourselves in the world of American art." In delivering the speech, the President gave a twist to this tepid encomium: "You have been asked to come not because you are the greatest artists of the land, although in the judgment of those who made up this guest list, you may have been." Tom Donnelly, who writes a sophisticated column in the Washington *Daily News*, interpreted this: "The President was thus indicating his displeasure with certain of his guests and certain of his list-makers." Other indications were his failure to receive his guests formally or to talk to them informally (or at all) and his quick exit from the party as soon as he'd got through his speech. Poor Dr. Goldman, caught like Polonius ("wretched, rash, intruding fool!") between the fell and incensed points of mighty antagonists. He had to invite a few artists and intellectuals to leaven the dough, no pun intended, of all those patrons and kultur-apparatchiks, but it turned out badly and his boss is a man who doesn't easily accept opposition, or defeat.

The President's "forward" policies in Vietnam and the Dominican Republic have not only, in a few months, alarmed and disgusted the intelligentsia (the academic community, writers and artists, and the better-educated part of the professional classes) so much as to split them off from him, but they have also produced another split, between the intelligentsia and the rest of the country, which is getting as marked as it was during the McCarthy era. Johnson's popularity, according to the pollsters, is greater today than it ever was. But not among the kind of people who were invited to the White House Festival of the Arts—or, more accurately, among perhaps a third of them, the artists, writers, and intellectuals that Dr. Goldman simply had to include. For example, I circulated a two-sentence "Statement to the Press" while I was there: "We wish to make it clear that, in accepting the President's kind invitation, we do not mean to repudiate the courageous stand taken by Robert Lowell nor to endorse the Administration's foreign policy. We quite share Mr. Lowell's dismay at our country's recent action in Vietnam and the Dominican Republic." Tom Hess and I showed this to perhaps forty of our fellow guests. We got only nine signatures—among them Willem DeKooning, Herbert Ferber, Isamu Noguchi, and Reed Whittemore—but it was significant that nobody refused to sign because he favored the President's foreign policy. "I'm an artist, I don't know anything about politics," they said; or "Okay—but this isn't the time or place"; or, most frequent, "We're here as guests, it's rude, in bad taste." Charlton Heston, with whom I had an eyeball-to-eyeball confrontation in the Rose Garden—he's really *tall*—told me, in the nicest possible way, that it was "arrogant" for mere intellectuals to question our President's decisions since he "must" know far more than we do. Mary McGrory, in the New York *Post*, reported that Ralph Ellison "turned him [me] down cold," complaining to her: "It's adolescent, he's boring from within at the White House." His objections, however, although delivered *fortissimo*, were tactical rather than political: he felt that circulating such a "stupid" document might frivolously imperil the *rapprochement* between the White House and Culture, or us, that was symbolized by the Festival. But the symbol was obsolete before any of us checked in at the East Gate on June 14, as the extraordinary effect of Robert Lowell's letter showed. Rarely has one person's statement of his moral unease about his government's behavior had such public resonance. I think it was because the letter was so personal, so unexpected, and yet so expressive of a widespread mood of "dismay and distrust." Herzen writes, in his memoirs, of the effect on the Russian intelligentsia, stifled under Nicholas I, who had his own methods of getting a national consensus, of the publication of Tchaadayev's *Philosophical Letters to a Lady*, another individualistic and unexpected protest: "It was a shot that rang out in the dark night.... It forced us all to awake."

After Watts by Elizabeth Hardwick *was originally published March 31, 1966,*
as a review of Violence in the City—an End or a Beginning? A Report by the
Governor's Commission on the Los Angeles Riots.

ELIZABETH HARDWICK

After Watts

THE DISASTER AND THEN, after a period of mourning or shock, the Report. Thus we try to exorcise our fears, to put into some sort of neutrality everything that menaces our peace. The Reports look out upon the inexplicable in private action and the unmanageable in community explosion; they investigate, they study, they interview, and at last, they recommend. Society is calmed, and not so much by what is found in the study as by the display of official energy, the activity underwritten. For we well know that little will be done, nothing new uncovered—at least not in this manner; instead a recitation of common assumptions will prevail, as it must, for these works are rituals, communal rites. To expect more, to anticipate anguish or social imagination, leads to disappointment and anger. The Reports now begin to have their formal structure. Always on the sacred agenda is the search for "outside influence," for it appears that our dreams are never free of conspiracies. "We find," one of the Reports goes, "no evidence that the Free Speech Movement was organized by the Communist Party, or the Progressive Labor Movement, or any other outside group." Good, we say, safe once more, protected from the ultimate.

It is also part of the structure of a Report that it should scold us, but scold in an encouraging, constructive way, as a mother is advised to reprimand her child. For, after all, are we to blame? To blame for riots, assassinations, disorderly students? The Reports say, yes, we are to blame, and then again we aren't. Oswald, friendless and Watts, ignored. Well, we should indeed have done better—and they should have done better, too.

WATTS—A STRIP OF PLASTIC and clapboard decorated by skimpy palms. It has about it that depressed feeling of a shimmering timeless afternoon in the Caribbean: there, just standing about, the melancholy bodies of young black boys—and way off, in the distance, the looming towers of a Hilton. Pale stucco, shacky stores, housing projects, laid out nicely, not tall, like rows of tomato vines. Equable climate, ennui, nothingness. Here? Why here? we demand to know. Are they perhaps, although so recently from little towns and rural counties of the South, somehow longing for the sweet squalor of the Hotel Theresa, the battered seats of the Apollo Theatre? This long, sunny nothingness, born yesterday. It turns out to be an exile, a stopover from which there is no escape. In January there was a strange quiet. You tour the streets as if they were a battlefield, our absolutely contemporary Gettysburg. Here, the hallowed rubble of the Lucky Store, there once stood a clothing shop, and yonder, the ruins of a supermarket. The standing survivors told the eye what the fallen monuments had looked like, the frame, modest structures of small, small business itself more or less fallen away from all but the most reduced hopes. In the evening the owners lock and bolt and gate and bar and then drive away to their own neighborhoods, a good many of those also infested with disappointments unmitigated by the year-round cook-out. Everything is small but with no hint of neighborliness.

The promise of Los Angeles, this beckoning openness, newness, freedom. But what is it? It is neither a great city nor a small town. Sheer impossibility of definition, of knowing what you are experiencing exhausts the mind. The intensity and diversity of small-town Main Streets have been stretched and pulled and thinned out so that not even a Kresge, a redecorated Walgreen's, or the old gray stone of the public library, the spitoons and insolence of the courthouse stand to keep the memory intact. The past resides in old cars, five years old, if anywhere. The Watts riots were a way to enter history, to create a past, to give form by destruction. Being shown the debris by serious, intelligent men of the district was like being on one of those cultural tours in an underdeveloped region. Their pride, their memories were of the first importance. It is hard to find another act in American history of such peculiarity—elation in the destruction of the lowly symbols of capitalism.

And now, how long ago it all seems. How odd it is to go back over the old newspapers, the astonishing photographs in *Life* magazine, the flaming buildings, the girls in hair curlers and shorts, the loaded shopping carts, "Get Whitey," and "Burn, baby, burn," and the National Guard, the crisis, the curfew, and Police Chief Parker's curtain line, "We're on top and they are on the bottom." In the summer of 1965 "as many as 10,000 Negroes took to the streets in marauding bands." Property damage was forty million; nearly four thousand persons were arrested; thirty-four were killed. A commission headed by John A. McCone produced a report called "Violence in the City—an end or a beginning?" (Imagine the conferences about the title!) It is somewhat dramatic, but not unnerving since its cadence whispers immediately in our ear of the second-rate, the Sunday Supplement, the *Reader's Digest*.

THE WATTS REPORT is a distressing effort. It is one of those bureaucratic documents, written in an ambivalent bureaucratic prose, and it yields little of interest on the surface and a great deal of hostility below the surface. (Bayard Rustin in *Commentary* shows brilliantly how the defects of Negro life are made to carry the blame for Negro behavior in a way that exonerates the conditions that produced the defects.) In our time, moral torpor and evangelical rhetoric have numbed our senses. The humble meters of the McCone Report are an extreme example of the distance a debased rhetoric puts between word and deed. A certain squeamishness calls the poor Negroes of Watts the "disadvantaged" and designates the police as "Caucasians." "A dull, devastating spiral of failure" is their way of calling to mind the days and nights of the Watts community.

The drama of the disadvantaged and the Caucasians opens on a warm night and a drunken driver. Anyone who has been in Watts will know the beauty and power of the automobile. It is the lifeline, and during the burning and looting, car lots and gasoline stations were exempt from revenge. Watts indeed is an island; even though by car it is not far from downtown Los Angeles, it has been estimated that it costs about $1.50 and one-and-a-half to two hours to get out of Watts to possible employment. One might wonder, as he reads the opening scene, why the police were going to tow the drunken driver's car away, rather than release it to his mother and brother who were trying to claim it? For this is a deprivation and frustration not to be borne in the freeway inferno. Without a car you are not truly alive; every sort of crippling, disabling imprisonment of body and mind attends this lack. The sight of the "Caucasians" and the hot night and the hatred and deprivation burst into revolutionary ecstasy and before it was over it extended far beyond Watts, which is only the name for a small part of the community, into a much larger area of Negro residence.

And what is to be done, what does it mean? Was it gray, tired meat and shoes with composition soles at prices a little starlet might gasp at? Of course we know what the report will say, what we all say; all that is true and has nevertheless become words, rhetoric. It's jobs and headstarts and housing and the mother at the head of the family and reading levels and dropouts. The Report mentions some particular aggravations: the incredible bungling of the poverty program in Los Angeles; the insult of the repeal of the Rumford Fair Housing Act; the civil rights program of protest. The last cause is a deduction from the Byzantine prose of the report which reads: "Throughout the nation, unpunished violence and disobedience to law were widely reported, and almost daily there were exhortations, here and elsewhere, to take extreme and even illegal remedies to right a wide variety of wrongs, real and supposed." *Real* and *supposed*; in another passage the locution "many Negroes felt and *were encouraged* to feel" occurs. These niceties fascinate the student of language. They tell of unseen strange encouragements, of what nature we are not told.

Still, the Watts Report is a mirror: the distance its bureaucratic language puts between us and the Negro is the reflection of reality. The demands of those days and nights on the streets, the smoke and the flames, are simply not to be taken in. The most radical reorganization of our lives could hardly satisfy them, and there seems to be neither the wish nor the will to make the effort. The words swell as purpose shrinks. Alabama and California are separated by more than miles of painted desert. The civil rights movement is fellowship and Watts is alienation, separation.

> "What can violence bring you when the white people have the police and the power? What can it bring you except death?"
> "Well, we are dying a little bit every day."

THE FINAL WORDS of the report seem to struggle for some faint upbeat and resolution but they are bewildered and fatigued. "As we have said earlier in this report there is no immediate remedy for the problems of the Negro and other disadvantaged in our community. The problems are deep and the remedies are costly and will take time. However, through the implementation of the programs we propose, with the dedication we discuss, and with the leadership we call for from all, our Commission states without dissent, that the tragic violence that occurred during the six days of August will not be repeated."

How hard it is to keep the attention of the American people. Perhaps that is what "communications" are for: to excite and divert with one thing after another. And we are a nation preeminent in communications. The Negro has been pushed out of our thoughts by the Vietnam War. Helicopters in Southeast Asia turned out to be far easier to provide than the respect the Negro asked for.

> "The army? What about the army?"
> "It's the last chance for a Negro to be a man...and yet it's another prison, too."

The months have gone by. And did the explosion in Watts really do what they thought afterward? Did it give dignity and definition? Did it mean anything in the long run? We know that only the severest concentration will keep the claims of the Negro alive in America, because he represents all the imponderables of life itself. Anxiety and uncertainty push us on to something else—to words which seem to soothe, and to more words. As for Watts itself: the oddity of its simplicity can scarcely be grasped. Its defiant lack of outline haunts the imagination. Lying low under the sun, shadowed by overpasses, it would seem to offer every possibility, every hope. In the newness of the residents, of the buildings, of the TV sets, there is a strange stillness, as of something formless, unaccountable. The gaps in the streets are hardly missed, where there is so much missing. Of course it is jobs and schools and segregation, yes, yes. But beyond that something that has nothing to do with Negroes was trying to be destroyed that summer. Some part of new America itself—that "dull, devastating spiral of failure" the Mc-Cone Commission imagines to belong only to the "disadvantaged" standing friendless in their capsule on the outskirts of downtown Los Angeles.

Ford Madox Ford

On Two Poets by Robert Lowell was originally published May 12, 1966. It appeared in slightly different form as "Ford Madox Ford" and "Sylvia Plath's 'Ariel'" in Robert Lowell: Collected Prose, edited by Robert Giroux. Copyright © 1987 by Caroline Lowell. Reprinted by permission of Farrar, Straus & Giroux, Inc.

ROBERT LOWELL

On Two Poets

I

Ford Madox Ford

I FIRST MET FORD IN 1937, a year or so after the publication of *Buckshee*, and two years before his death. Reading these poems is like stepping back in time to Ford in his right setting, France, to a moment when both he and Europe between the wars were, imperceptibly, miraculously, a little younger, hopeful, and almost at a pause in the onrush. When I knew Ford in America, he was out of cash, out of fashion, and half out of inspiration, a half-German, half-English exile in love with the French, and able to sell his books only in the United States. Propped by his young wife, he was plodding from writers' conference to writers' conference, finally ending up as writer in residence at Olivet College in Michigan. He seemed to travel with the leisure and full dress of the last hectic Edwardian giants—Hudson, James, and Hardy. He cried out, as if wounded, against the eminence, pomp, and private lives of Tennyson, Carlyle, and Ruskin, the false gods, so he thought, of his fathers. He was trailed by a legend of personal heroism and slump, times of great writing, times of space-filling, past triumph and past humiliation, Grub Street drudgery, and aristocratic indolence. He was the friend of all good writers, and seemed to carry a concealed pistol to protect them and himself against the shoving noncreative powers of editors, publishers, businessmen, politicians, college presidents, literary agents—his cronies, his vultures.

Always writers and writing! He was then at work on his last book, *The March of Literature*, and rereading the classics in their original tongues. At each college stop he picked up armloads of Loeb classics, and reams of unpublished manuscript. Writers walked through his mind and his life— young ones to be discovered, instructed, and entertained, contemporaries

to be assembled, telegraphed, and celebrated, the dead friend to be resur-
rected in anecdote, the long, long dead to be freshly assaulted or defended.
Ford was large, unwieldy, wheezy, unwell, and looked somehow like a
British version of the Republican elephant. His conversation, at least
as finished and fluent as his written reminiscences, came out in ordered,
subtly circuitous paragraphs. His marvelous, altering stories about the
famous and colorful were often truer than fact. His voice, always *sotto voce*,
and sometimes a muffled Yorkshire gasp, made him a man for small gather-
ings. Once I watched an audience of three thousand walk out on him, as he
exquisitely, ludicrously, and inaudibly imitated the elaborate periphrastic
style of Henry James. They could neither hear nor sympathize.

LARGENESS IS THE KEY WORD for Ford. He liked to say that genius is memory. His own was like an elephant's. No one admired more of his elders, or
discovered more of his juniors, and so went on admiring and discovering
till the end. He seemed to like nothing that was mediocre, and miss nothing that was good. His humility was edged with a mumbling insolence. His
fanatical life-and-death dedication to the arts was messy, British, and
amused. As if his heart were physically too large for his body, his stamina,
imperfection, and generosity were extreme.

Ford's glory and mastery are in two or three of his novels. He also never
stopped writing and speaking prose. He had a religious fascination in the
possibilities of sentence structure and fictional techniques. About poetry,
he was ambivalent. He had a flair for quoting beautiful unknown or forgotten lines, yet called poetry something like "the less civilized medium,"
one whose crudity and barbarism were decked out with stiff measures and
coarse sonorities. Like Boris Pasternak, he preferred Shakespeare's prose to
his blank verse, and thought no poetry could equal the novels of Flaubert.

He himself wrote poetry with his left hand—casually and even con-
temptuously. He gives sound and intense advice to a beginning poet: "Forget about Piers Plowman, forget about Shakespeare, Keats, Yeats, Morris,
the English Bible, and remember only that you live in our terrific, untidy,
indifferent empirical age, where not a single problem is solved and not a
single Accepted Idea from the poet has any more magic..." Yet he himself as
a poet was incurably of the nineteenth century he detested, and to the end
had an incurable love for some of its most irritating and overpoetic conventions. His guides were always "Christabel," the Browning of "My Last
Duchess," the Rossettis, Morris, and their successors, the Decadents. He is
Pre-Raphaelite to the heart. Their pretty eloquence, their passionate sim-

plicities, their quaint neo-Gothic, their vocabulary of love and romance, their keyed-up Christianity, their troubadour heresies, and their terribly over-effective rhythms are always peeping through Ford's railway stations and straggling free verse. For Ford and his ablest contemporaries, Hardy, Hopkins, Housman, Yeats, de la Mare, Kipling, and Pound, the influence and even the inspiration of the Pre-Raphaelites was unavoidable. Each, in his way, imitated, innovated, modified, and revolted. Ford's early imitations have a true Pre-Raphaelite brio, but he is too relaxed and perhaps too interested in life to have their finest delicacy, conviction, and intensity. His revolt is brave and resourceful, but the soul of the old dead style remains to hamper him. Even in prose, except for *The Good Soldier* and *Parade's End*, he had difficulty in striking the main artery; in poetry, he almost never struck it. His good phrases and rhythms grow limp or hopped up with impatient diffidence, and seldom reach their destination. The doggerel bounce and hackneyed prettiness of lines like

> *The poor saint on his fountain*
> *On top of his column*
> *Gazes up sad and solemn*

(to choose a bad example) keeps breaking in on passages that are picturesque and lovely. His shorter poems are brisk, his longer diffuse.

POUND'S FAMOUS COMMAND that *poetry must be at least as well-written as prose* must have been inspired by Ford, though I doubt if Ford believed this a possibility or really had much fondness for a poetry that wasn't simple, poetic, and pastoral. I heard someone ask him about Pound's influence on Yeats's later style. "Oh," Ford said, "I used to tell Ezra that he mustn't write illiterate poetic jargon. Then he'd go to Yeats and say the same thing." This was tossed off with such flippant finality that I was sure it was nonsense. Years later, however, Pound told me the same story. He said too that Ford actually lived the heroic artistic life that Yeats talked about. There must be more to the story. Ford had no gift like Yeats for combining a conversational prose idiom with the grand style. I think he must often have felt the mortification of seeing the shining abundance of his novels dwindle away in his poetry to something tame, absent-minded, and cautious. He must have found it hard to get rid of his jingling, hard to charge his lines, hard to find true subjects, and harder still to stick to them when found. Even such an original and personal poem as "On Heaven" is forever being beguiled from the road. Yet a magnificence and an Albigensian brightness hover over these rambling steps: Ford and Pound were companions on the great road from twelfth-century Toulouse to twentieth-century London.

Buckshee is Ford, the poet, at his best. It too is uneven and rambling—uneven, rambling, intimate, and wonderful. Gardening in Provence, or hearing a night bell strike two in Paris, Ford ruminates with weary devotion on his long labors, and celebrates his new young marriage—zero minutes out of time, when time was short, and the air stiff with Nazi steel and propaganda! In his last years, Ford's political emotions were to the left, but his memory, pace, and tastes were conservative. He didn't like a place without history, a patina of dust, "Richelieu's Villa Latina with its unvarying status quo ante." Above all he hated a world ruled by the "maniacal monotone of execration." I remember how he expressed his despair of the America he was part of, and humorously advised me to give up eating corn lest I inherit the narrow fierceness of the Red Indian. In "Coda," the last and supreme poem in this sequence, he is back in Paris, his great threatened love and symbol for civilization. In his dark apartment, he watches the lights of a taxi illuminate two objects, the "pale square" of his wife's painting, *Spring in Luxemburg,* and the galleys of his manuscript, momentarily lit up like Michelangelo's scroll of the Fates. Then he says to his wife, the painter:

> *I know you don't like Michelangelo*
> *But the universe is very large having room*
> *Within it for infinities of gods.*

Buckshee coughs and blunders a bit in getting off, but in *"Champêtre,"* *"Temps de Sécheresse,"* and "Coda," Ford finds the unpredictable waver of his true inspiration. In these reveries, he has at last managed to work his speaking voice, and something more than his speaking voice, into poems—the inner voice of the tireless old man, the old master still in harness, confiding, tolerant, Bohemian, newly married, and in France.

II

Sylvia Plath

(1932–1963)

IN THE POEMS WRITTEN in the last months of her life, and often rushed out at the rate of two or three a day, Sylvia Plath becomes herself, becomes something imaginary, newly, wildly, and subtly created—hardly a person at all, or a woman, certainly not another "poetess," but one of those super-real, hypnotic great classical heroines. This character is feminine, rather than female, though almost everything we customarily think of as feminine is turned on its head. The voice is now coolly amused, witty, now sour, now fanciful, girlish, charming, now sinking to the strident rasp of the vampire—a Dido, Phaedra, or Medea who can laugh at herself as "cow-heavy and floral in my Victorian nightgown." Though lines get repeated, and sometimes the plot is lost, language never dies in her mouth.

Everything in these poems is personal, confessional, felt, but the manner of feeling is controlled hallucination, the autobiography of a fever. She burns to be on the move, a walk, a ride, a journey, the flight of the queen bee. She is driven forward by the pounding pistons of her heart. The title *Ariel* summons up Shakespeare's lovely, though slightly chilling and androgynous spirit, but the truth is that this *Ariel* is the author's horse. Dangerous, more powerful than man, machinelike from hard training, she herself is a little like a racehorse, galloping relentlessly with risked, outstretched neck, death hurdle after death hurdle topped. She cries out for that rapid life of starting pistols, snapping tapes, and new world records broken. What is most heroic in her, though, is not her force, but the desperate practicality of her control, her hand of metal with its modest, womanish touch. Almost pure motion, she can endure "God, the great stasis in his vacuous night," hospitals, fever, paralysis, the iron lung, being stripped like a girl in the booth of a circus sideshow, dressed like a manikin, tied down like Gulliver by the Lilliputians . . . apartments, babies, prim English landscapes, bee-hives, yew trees, gardens, the moon, hooks, the black boot, wounds, flowers with mouths like wounds, Belsen's lampshades made of human skin, Hitler's homicidal iron tanks clanking over Russia. Suicide, father-hatred, self-loathing—nothing is too much for the macabre gaiety of her control. Yet it is too much; her art's immortality is life's disintegration. The surprise, the shimmering, unwrapped birthday present, the transcendence "into the red eye, the cauldron of morning," and the lover, who are always waiting for her, are Death, her own abrupt and defiant death.

> He tells me how badly I photograph.
> He tells me how sweet
> The babies look in their hospital
> Icebox, a simple
> Frill at the neck,
> Then the flutings of their Ionic
> Death-gowns,
> Then two little feet.

THERE IS A PECULIAR, haunting challenge to these poems. Probably many, after reading *Ariel*, will recoil from their first overawed shock, and painfully wonder why so much of it leaves them feeling empty, evasive, and inarticulate. In her lines, I often hear the serpent whisper, "Come, if only you had the courage, you too could have my rightness, audacity, and ease of inspiration." But most of us will turn back. These poems are playing Russian roulette with six cartridges in the cylinder, a game of "chicken," the wheels of both cars locked and unable to swerve. O for that heaven of the humble copyist, those millennia of Egyptian artists repeating their lofty set patterns! And yet Sylvia Plath's poems are not the celebration of some savage and debauched existence, that of the "damned" poet, glad to burn out his body for a few years of continuous intensity. This poetry and life are not a career; they tell that life, even when disciplined, is simply not worth it.

It is poignant, looking back, to realize that the secret of Sylvia Plath's last irresistible blaze lies lost somewhere in the checks and courtesies of her early laborious shyness. She was never a student of mine, but for a couple of months seven years ago she used to drop in on my poetry seminar at Boston University. I see her dim against the bright sky of a high window, viewless unless one cared to look down on the city outskirts' defeated yellow brick and square concrete pillbox filling stations. She was willowy, long-waisted, sharp-elbowed, nervous, giggly, gracious — a brilliant, tense presence embarrassed by restraint. Her humility and willingness to accept what was admired seemed at times to give her an air of maddening docility that hid her unfashionable patience and boldness. She showed us poems, that later, more or less unchanged, went into her first book, *The Colossus*.

They were somber, formidably expert in stanza-structure, and had a flair for alliteration and Massachusetts's low-tide dolor.

> *A mongrel working his legs to a gallop*
> *Hustles the gull flock to flap off the sand-spit.*

Other lines showed her wit and directness.

> *The pears fatten like little Buddhas.*

Somehow none of it sank very deep into my awareness. I sensed her abashment and distinction, and never guessed her later appalling and triumphant fulfillment.

Lesbos
(From *Ariel*)

Viciousness in the kitchen!
The potatoes hiss.
It is all Hollywood, windowless,
The fluorescent light wincing on and off like a terrible migraine,
Coy paper strips for doors—
Stage curtains, a widow's frizz.
And I, love, am a pathological liar,
And my child—look at her, face down on the floor,
Little unstrung puppet, kicking to disappear—
Why she is schizophrenic,
Her face red and white, a panic,
You have stuck her kittens outside your window
In a sort of cement well
Where they crap and puke and cry and she can't hear.
You say you can't stand her,
The bastard's a girl.
You who have blown your tubes like a bad radio
Clear of voices and history, the staticky
Noise of the new.
You say I should drown the kittens. Their smell!
You say I should drown my girl.
She'll cut her throat at ten if she's mad at two.
The baby smiles, fat snail,
From the polished lozenges of orange linoleum.
You could eat him. He's a boy.
You say your husband is just no good to you.
His Jew-Mama guards his sweet sex like a pearl.
You have one baby, I have two.
I should sit on a rock off Cornwall and comb my hair.
I should wear tiger pants, I should have an affair.
We should meet in another life, we should meet in air,
Me and you.

Meanwhile there's a stink of fat and baby crap.
I'm doped and thick from my last sleeping pill.

The smog of cooking, the smog of hell
Floats our heads, two venomous opposites,
Our bones, our hair.
I call you Orphan, orphan. You are ill.
The sun gives you ulcers, the wind gives you T.B.
Once you were beautiful.
In New York, in Hollywood, the men said: "Through?
Gee baby, you are rare."
You acted, acted, acted for the thrill.
The impotent husband slumps out for a coffee.
I try to keep him in,
An old pole for the lightning,
The acid baths, the skyfuls off to you.
He lumps it down the plastic cobbled hill,
Flogged trolley. The sparks are blue.
The blue sparks spill,
Splitting like quartz into a million bits.

O jewel! O valuable!
That night the moon
Dragged its blood bag, sick
Animal
Up over the harbor lights.
And then grew normal,
Hard and apart and white.
The scale-sheen on the sand scared me to death.
We kept picking up handfuls, loving it,
Working it like dough, a mulatto body,
The silk grits.
A dog picked up your doggy husband. He went on.

Now I am silent, hate
Up to my neck,
Thick, thick.
I do not speak.
I am packing the hard potatoes like good clothes,
I am packing the babies,
I am packing the sick cats.

O vase of acid,
It is love you are full of. You know who you hate.
He is hugging his ball and chain down by the gate
That opens to the sea
Where it drives in, white and black,
Then spews it back.
Every day you fill him with soul-stuff, like a pitcher.
You are so exhausted.
Your voice my ear-ring,

Flapping and sucking, blood-loving bat.
That is that. That is that.
You peer from the door,
Sad hag. "Every woman's a whore.
I can't communicate."

I see your cute decor
Close on you like the fist of a baby
Or an anemone, that sea
Sweetheart, that kleptomaniac.
I am still raw.
I say I may be back.
You know what lies are for.

Even in your Zen heaven we shan't meet.

A Buddhist Poet in Vietnam by Thich Nhat Hanh was originally published June 9, 1966.
All three poems reprinted here appear in Call Me By My True Names: The Collected
Poems of Thich Nhat Hanh, *published by Parallax Press, Berkeley, California.*

THE FEW POEMS published here are not typical of my own poetry or of Vietnamese poetry generally. The tradition of poetry in Vietnam is very old and complex. It draws on early Chinese poetry, on the French Romantic and symbolist poets of the nineteenth and twentieth centuries, and, in my own case, on Zen Buddhist writers. Much of my poetry could be called "philosophical" and friends have found it in some ways similar to the work of Tagore: at least, it is extremely difficult to translate it into English.

But the poems published here are different. They are popular poems in free verse and when I write them I feel I am trying to speak very simply for the majority of Vietnamese who are peasants and cannot speak for themselves; they do not know or care much about words like communism or democracy but want above all for the war to end so they may survive and not be maimed or killed. I wrote the poems first for myself; when I read them over I can regain once more the state of intense feeling in which I composed them. But they have now been read and heard by many Vietnamese; and they have been denounced by both sides fighting in the war. A few days after they were published last year government police came to seize them from the bookstores, but by then they had all been sold. They were attacked by the Hanoi radio and by the radio of the National Liberation Front. They have since been read in public along with the peace poems of other Buddhists and they have been sung with guitar accompaniment at student meetings, much as songs of protest are sung in the United States.

I risk my life publishing these poems. Other Buddhists who have protested the war have been arrested and exiled, and now they are being killed in Danang. It was because of this great risk that the Buddhists who demonstrated this spring were reluctant to advocate openly an end to the war through negotiations: instead they called for elections and democracy. We have been placed in an impossible dilemma. If we openly call for peace, we are identified with the Communists and the government will try to suppress us. If we criticize the Communists, we find ourselves allied with those Vietnamese who have been the paid propagandists of the Americans for years and whose words against communism are soiled and discredited because they have been paid to say them. To be honorably anti-Communist has been to remain silent, and, being silent, we have been called innocent of the dangers of communism; but we are not. We are very well aware of the restrictions on Buddhism in the North. We have studied what has happened in China. We know there is no place for spirituality in Marxism. We are ready to undertake a peaceful political struggle with the Communists if only the destruction of the war can be stopped. We are confident that the

South Vietnamese can protect themselves from Communist domination if they are allowed to carry on their political life in peace.

The tragedy of American policy is that it has made such a peaceful political struggle all the more difficult. For the Americans could have helped to reconstruct the country peacefully if they had cooperated with, and strengthened, the Buddhists and others who had the respect of the people. Instead they tried to divide the Buddhists and prevent them from becoming an organized force. This was disastrous. Catholicism came to Vietnam with the French, and the Catholic leaders backed by the United States were suspect from the first; the Buddhist tradition is closely linked with nationalism and it is unthinkable to the broad mass of the people that the Buddhists would betray them to a foreign power. At the same time, Vietnamese Buddhism is syncretic in character; there are Catholic priests who are closer to us on the question of peace than some Buddhist priests who are old and have lost courage. (A few months ago, eleven Catholic priests issued a strong statement calling for peace. They were attacked by the Catholic leaders.)

NOW THE UNITED STATES has become too afraid of the Communists to allow a peaceful confrontation with them to take place; and when you are too afraid you cannot win. Sending 300,000 American troops to Vietnam and bombing the countryside have only caused the Communists to grow stronger. American military operations have killed and wounded more innocent peasants than Vietcong, and the Americans are blamed and hated for this. The peasants are not violently antagonistic to the Vietcong: the strong anti-Communists are mostly people in the cities who fear loss of their property, cars, businesses, and homes, and rely on the foreign army to protect them. The American soldiers, moreover, are not well educated and do not understand the Vietnamese: Every GI will make a small mistake that offends a Vietnamese every day, even when he is not drunk or in search of women—at least 300,000 mistakes a day. And the continual roaring overhead of planes on their way to drop bombs makes people sick and mad.

So it is understandable that the people in the villages distrust those who are connected with the government and the Americans. Along with others, I have organized a Buddhist School of Youth for Social Service at Cholon to train teams of young people to work at "community develop-ment" in the villages. About two hundred have already been trained. We have refused to accept money from the government or the American Military Assistance Group. That would have been ruinous. Instead 1,200 Buddhists each contributed the small sum of fifty piastres to start the school in a Buddhist convent. We went into the villages carrying no weapons, owning nothing of our own but our robes, and have been welcomed. The peasants we have worked with tell us that the government officials assigned to "assist" them kept thousands of piastres a month for themselves and did nothing for them. They have come to dislike the Vietcong and they fear the Americans, whose artillery bombardments have fallen upon them.

If the United States wants to escalate the war, nothing that the Vietnamese can do will matter. A change of government will make no difference. The war will go on. The Buddhist leader Thich Tri Quang believes that we may attain peace indirectly by means of political maneuvering and through elections. He is a man of action, and of courage and intelligence, whose life is good: he is not bound by money. But there are other Buddhists who have chosen a less "activist" political role who have high prestige and whose views will also be influential. There is, for example, the group of young monks and writers who publish the magazines *Giu Thom Que Me* (To Help the Motherland) and *Thien My* and other publications of the La Boi publishing house in Saigon, and who are trying to create a new Buddhist ideology emphasizing ways of helping the people who live on the land.

I DOUBT MYSELF that much will be gained by indirect political maneuvering against the government and the Catholics, so long as the United States is determined to continue the war. Underlying the struggles with the government in Danang and other cities is the unstated question whether the war will go on; and this the United States will decide. I believe that the most effective thing we can do is to follow the open and direct way of advocating peace, however dangerous this may be, by telling the world that we do not accept this war; that the Communists grow stronger each day it is fought; that a cease-fire must be arranged with the Vietcong as soon as possible; that we would then welcome the help of Americans in the peaceful reconstruction of Vietnam. Only America can stop this war which is destroying not only our lives, but our culture and everything of human value in our country.

Condemnation

Listen to this:
Yesterday six Vietcong came through my village.
Because of this my village was bombed—completely destroyed.
Every soul was killed.
When I come back to the village now, the day after,
There is nothing to see but clouds of dust and the river, still flowing.
The pagoda has neither roof nor altar.
Only the foundations of houses are left.
The bamboo thickets are burned away.

Here in the presence of the undisturbed stars,
In the invisible presence of all the people still alive on earth,
Let me raise my voice to denounce this filthy war,
This murder of brothers by brothers!
I have a question: Who pushed us into this killing of one another?

Whoever is listening, be my witness!
I cannot accept this war.
I never could, I never shall.
I have to say this a thousand times before I am killed.

I feel I am like that bird which dies for the sake of its mate.
Dripping blood from its broken beak, and crying out:
Beware! Turn around to face your real enemies—
Ambition, violence, hatred, greed.

Men cannot be our enemies—even men called "Vietcong"!
If we kill men, what brothers will we have left?
With whom shall we live then?

Our Green Garden

Fires spring up like dragon's teeth at the ten points of the universe.
A furious acrid wind sweeps them toward us from all sides.
Aloof and beautiful, the mountains and rivers abide.

All around, the horizon burns with the color of death.
As for me, yes, I am still alive,
But my body and the soul in it writhe as if they too had been set afire.
My parched eyes can shed no more tears.

Where are you going this evening, dear brother, in what direction?
The rattle of gunfire is close at hand.
In her breast, the heart of our mother shrivels and fades like a dying
    flower.
She bows her head, the smooth black hair now threaded with white.
How many nights, night after night, has she crouched wide-awake,
Alone with her lamp, praying for the storm to end?

Dearest brother, I know it is you who will shoot me tonight,
Piercing our mother's heart with a wound that can never heal.
O terrible winds that blow from the ends of the earth
To hurl down our houses and blast our fertile fields!

I say farewell to the blazing, blackening place where I was born.
Here is my breast! Aim your gun at it, brother, shoot!
I offer my body, the body our mother bore and nurtured.
Destroy it if you will,
Destroy it in the name of your dream,
That dream in whose name you kill.

Can you hear me invoke the darkness:
"When will these sufferings end,
O darkness, in whose name you destroy?"

Come back, dear brother, and kneel at our mother's feet.
Don't make a sacrifice of our dear green garden

To the ragged flames that are carried into the dooryard
By wild winds from far away.

Here is my breast. Aim your gun at it, brother, shoot!
Destroy me if you will
And build from my carrion whatever it is you are dreaming of.

Who will be left to celebrate a victory made of blood and fire?

Peace

They woke me this morning
To tell me my brother had been killed in battle.
Yet in the garden, uncurling moist petals,
A new rose blooms on the bush.
And I am alive, can still breathe the fragrance of roses and dung.
Eat, pray, and sleep.
But when can I break my long silence?
When can I speak the unuttered words that are choking me?

—Nhat Hanh

Alexander Herzen

The Great Amateur by Isaiah Berlin was originally published March 14, 1968.
Copyright © 1968 Isaiah Berlin.

ISAIAH BERLIN

The Great Amateur

ALEXANDER HERZEN, like Diderot, was an amateur of genius whose opin-
ions and activities changed the direction of social thought in his country.
Like Diderot too, he was a brilliant and irrepressible talker. He talked
equally well in Russian and French to his intimate friends and in the
Moscow salons, and later in his life in Russian, German, French, in Paris,
Nice, London, Geneva—always in an overwhelming flow of ideas and images; the loss to posterity (as with Diderot) is probably immense; he had no
Boswell, no Eckermann, to record his conversation, nor would he have suffered such a relationship. His prose is essentially a form of talk, with the
vices and virtues of talk: eloquent, spontaneous, liable to the heightened
tones and exaggerations of the born storyteller unable to resist long digressions which themselves carry him into a network of intersecting tributaries
of memory or speculation, but always returning to the main stream of the
story or the argument. Above all, his prose has the vitality of spoken
words—it appears to owe nothing to the carefully composed formal sentences of the French *philosophes* whom he admired or to the terrible philosophical style of the Germans from whom he learned. We hear his voice —
almost too much—in the essays, the pamphlets, the autobiography, as
much as in the letters and scraps of notes to his friends.

Civilized, imaginative, self-critical, Herzen was a marvelously gifted
social observer; the record of what he saw is unique, even in the articulate
nineteenth century. He had an acute, easily stirred, and ironical mind, a
fiery and poetical temperament, and a capacity for vivid, often lyrical, writing—qualities that combined and reinforced one another in the succession
of sharp vignettes of men, events, ideas, personal relationships, political situations, and descriptions of entire forms of life in which his writings
abound. He was a man of extreme refinement and sensibility, great intellectual energy and biting wit, easily irritated *amour propre*, and a taste for
polemical writing; he was addicted to analysis, investigation, exposure; he
saw himself as an expert "unmasker" of appearances and conventions, and

dramatized himself as a devastating discoverer of their social and moral core. Tolstoy, who had little sympathy with Herzen's opinions, and was not given to excessive praise of his contemporaries among men of letters, especially among his countrymen, said toward the end of his life that he had never met anyone with "so rare a combination of scintillating brilliance and depth." These gifts make a good many of Herzen's essays, political articles, day-to-day journalism, casual notes and reviews, and especially letters written to intimates or to political correspondents, irresistibly readable even today, when the issues with which they were concerned are for the most part dead and of interest mainly to historians.

Although much has been written about Herzen, and not only in Russian, the task of his biographers has not been made easier by the fact that he left an incomparable memorial to himself in his own greatest work—translated by Constance Garnett as *My Past and Thoughts*—a literary masterpiece worthy of being placed by the side of the novels of his contemporaries and countrymen, Tolstoy, Turgenev, Dostoevsky. Nor were they altogether unaware of this. Turgenev, an intimate and lifelong friend (the fluctuations of their personal relationship were important in the lives of both; this complex and interesting story has never been adequately told) admired him both as a writer and as a revolutionary journalist. The celebrated critic Vissarion Belinsky discovered, described, and acclaimed his extraordinary literary gift when they were both young and relatively unknown. Even the angry and suspicious Dostoevsky excepted him from the virulent hatred with which he regarded the pro-Western Russian revolutionaries, recognized the poetry of his writing, and remained well-disposed toward him until the end of his life. As for Tolstoy, he delighted both in his society and his writings: half a century after their first meeting in London he still remembered the scene vividly.[1]

It is strange that this remarkable writer, in his lifetime a celebrated European figure, the admired friend of Michelet, Mazzini, Garibaldi, and

---

[1] P. Sergeyenko, in his book on Tolstoy, says that Tolstoy told him in 1908 that he had a very clear recollection of his visit to Herzen in his London house in March 1861. "Lev Nikolaevich remembered him as a not very large, plump little man, who generated electric energy. 'Lively, responsive, intelligent, interesting,' Lev Nikolaevich explained (as usual illustrating every shade of meaning by appropriate movements of the hands) 'Herzen at once began talking to me as if we had known each other for a long time. I found his personality enchanting. I have never met a more attractive man. He stood head and shoulders above all the politicians of his own and of our time.'" (P. Sergeyenko, *Tolstoi i ego sovremenniki*, Moscow, 1911, pp. 13–14.)

Victor Hugo, long canonized in his own country not only as a revolutionary but as one of its greatest men of letters, is, even today, not much more than a name in the West. The enjoyment to be obtained from reading his prose—for the most part still untranslated—makes this a strange and gratuitous loss.

ALEXANDER HERZEN was born in Moscow on April 6, 1812, some months before the great fire that destroyed the city during Napoleon's occupation after the battle of Borodino. His father, Ivan Alexandrovich Yakovlev, came of an ancient family distantly related to the Romanov dynasty. Like other rich and well-born members of the Russian gentry, he had spent some years abroad, and, during one of his journeys, met, and took back to Moscow with him, the daughter of a minor Württemberg official, Luise Haag, a gentle, submissive, somewhat colorless girl, a good deal younger than himself. For some reason, perhaps owing to the disparity in their social positions, he never married her according to the rites of his own Church. Yakovlev was a member of the Orthodox Church, she remained a Lutheran.[2] He was a proud, independent, disdainful man, and had grown increasingly morose and misanthropic. He retired before the war of 1812, and at the time of the French invasion was living in bitter and resentful idleness in his house in Moscow. During the French occupation he was recognized by Marshal Mortier, whom he had known in Paris, and agreed—in return for a safe conduct enabling him to take his family out of the devastated city—to carry a message from Napoleon to the Emperor Alexander. For this indiscretion he was sent back to his estates and only allowed to return to Moscow somewhat later.

In his large and gloomy house in the Arbat he brought up his son Alexander, to whom he had given the surname Herzen, as if to stress the fact that he was the child of an irregular liaison, an affair of the heart. Luise Haag was never accorded the full status of a wife, but the boy had every attention lavished upon him. He received the normal education of a young Russian nobleman of his time, that is to say, he was looked after by a host of nurses and serfs, and taught by private tutors, German and French, carefully chosen by his neurotic, irritable, devoted, suspicious father. Every care was taken to develop his gifts. He was a lively and imaginative child and absorbed knowledge easily and eagerly. His father loved him after his fash-

---

[2] There is evidence, although it is not conclusive, that she was married to him according to the Lutheran rite, not recognized by the Orthodox Church.

ion: more, certainly, than his other son, also illegitimate, born ten years earlier, whom he had christened Yegor (George). But he was, by the 1820s, a defeated and gloomy recluse, unable to communicate with his family or indeed anyone else. Shrewd, honorable, and neither unfeeling nor unjust, a "difficult" character like old Prince Bolkonsky in Tolstoy's *War and Peace*, Ivan Yakovlev emerges from his son's recollections a self-lacerating, grim, shut-in, half-frozen human being, who terrorized his household with his whims and his sarcasm. He kept all doors and windows locked, the blinds permanently drawn, and, apart from a few old friends and his own brothers, saw virtually nobody. In later years his son described him as the product of "the encounter of two such incompatible things as the eighteenth century and Russian life"—a collision of cultures that had destroyed a good many among the more sensitive members of the Russian gentry in the reigns of Catherine II and her successors.

The boy escaped with relief from his father's oppressive and frightening company to the rooms occupied by his mother and the servants; she was kind and unassuming, crushed by her husband, frightened by her foreign surroundings, and seemed to accept her almost oriental status in the household with uncomplaining resignation. As for the servants, they were serfs from the Yakovlev estates, trained to behave obsequiously to the son and probable heir of their master. Herzen himself, in later years, attributed the deepest of all his social feelings, concern for the freedom and dignity of human individuals (which his friend, the critic Belinsky, diagnosed so accurately), to the barbarous conditions that surrounded him in childhood. He was a favorite child, and much spoiled; but the facts of his irregular birth and of his mother's status were brought home to him by listening to the servants' gossip and, on at least one occasion, by overhearing a conversation about himself between his father and one of his old army comrades. The shock was, according to his own testimony, profound. It was probably one of the determining factors of his life.

He was taught Russian literature and history by a young university student, an enthusiastic follower of the new Romantic movement, which, particularly in its German form, had then begun to dominate Russian intellectual life. He learned French (which his father wrote more easily than Russian) and German (which he spoke with his mother) and European, rather than Russian, history—his tutor was a French refugee who had emigrated to Russia after the French Revolution. The Frenchman did not reveal his political opinions, so Herzen tells us, until one day, when his pupil asked him why Louis XVI had been executed; to this he replied in an altered voice, "Because he was a traitor to his country," and, finding the boy responsive, threw off his reserve and spoke to him openly about the liberty and equality of men. Herzen was a lonely child, at once pampered and cramped, lively and bored; he read voraciously in his father's large library, especially French books of the Enlightenment. He was fourteen when the leaders of the Decembrist conspiracy were hanged by the Emperor Nicholas I. He later declared that this event was the critical turning point of his life; whether this was so or not, the memory of these aristocratic martyrs in the cause of Russian constitutional liberty later became a sacred symbol to him, as to many others of his class and generation, and affected him for the rest of his days. He tells us that a few years after this, he and his intimate friend Nick Ogaryov, standing on the Sparrow Hills above Moscow, took a solemn "Hannibalic" oath to avenge these fighters for the rights of man and to dedicate their own lives to the cause for which they had died.

In due course he became a student at the University of Moscow, read Schiller and Goethe, and somewhat later the French utopian socialists, Saint-Simon, Fourier, and other social prophets whose works were smuggled into Russia in defiance of the censorship, and became a convinced and passionate radical. He and Ogaryov belonged to a group of students who read forbidden books and discussed dangerous ideas. For this he was, together with most other "unreliable" students, duly arrested and, probably because he declined to repudiate the views imputed to him, condemned to imprisonment. His father used all his influence to get the sentence mitigated, but could not save his son from being exiled to the provincial city of Vyatka, near the borders of Asia, where he was not indeed kept in prison, but put to work in the local administration.

To his astonishment, he enjoyed this new test of his powers; he displayed administrative gifts and became a far more competent and perhaps even enthusiastic official than he was later prepared to admit, and helped to expose the corrupt and brutal governor, of whom he painted an unfavorable and repulsive portrait. In Vyatka he became involved in a passionate love affair with a married woman, behaved badly, and suffered agonies of contrition. He read Dante, went through a religious phase, and began a long and passionate correspondence with his first cousin Natalie, who, like himself, was illegitimate, and lived as a companion in the house of a rich and despotic aunt. As a result of his father's ceaseless efforts, he was transferred to the city of Vladimir, and with the help of his young Moscow friends, arranged the elopement of Natalie. They were married in Vladimir against their relations' wishes. He was in due course allowed to return to Moscow and was appointed to a government post in Petersburg.

WHATEVER HIS AMBITIONS at the time, he remained indomitably independent and committed to the radical cause. As a result of an indiscreet letter, opened by the censors, in which he had criticized the behavior of the police, he was again sentenced to a period of exile, this time to Novgorod. Two years later, in 1842, he was once more permitted to return to Moscow. He was by then regarded as an established member of the new radical intelligentsia, and, indeed, as an honored martyr in its cause, and began to write in the progressive periodicals of the time. He always dealt with the same central theme: the oppression of the individual; the humiliation and degradation of men by political and personal tyranny; the yoke of social custom, the dark ignorance, and savage, arbitrary misgovernment which maimed and destroyed human beings in the brutal and odious Russian Empire.

Like the other members of his circle, the young poet and novelist Turgenev, the critic Belinsky, the future political agitators Bakunin and Katkov (the first in the cause of revolution, the second of reaction), the literary essayist Annenkov, his own intimate friend Ogaryov, Herzen plunged into the study of German metaphysics and French socioligical theory and history—the works of Kant, Schelling, and, above all, Hegel: Saint-Simon, Augustin-Thierry, Leroux, Mignet, and Guizot. He composed arresting historical and philosophical essays, and stories dealing with social issues; they were published, widely read and discussed, and created a considerable reputation for the author. He adopted an uncompromising position. A leading representative of the dissident Russian gentry, he owed his socialist beliefs less to a reaction against the cruelty and chaos of the laissez faire economy of the bourgeois West—for Russia, then in its early industrial beginnings, was still a semifeudal, socially and economically primitive, society—than to a direct response to the agonizing social problems in his native land: the poverty of the masses, serfdom, and lack of individual freedom at all levels, and a lawless and brutal autocracy.[3] In addition, there was the wounded national pride of a powerful and semibarbarous society, whose leaders were aware of its backwardness, and suffered from mingled

---

3 The historical and sociological explanation of the origins of Russian socialism and of Herzen's part in it cannot be attempted here. It has been treated in a number of (untranslated) Russian monographs, both pre- and postrevolutionary; the best, most detailed, and original study of this topic is *Alexander Herzen and the Birth of Russian Socialism* by Martin Malia.

admiration, envy, and resentment of the civilized West. The radicals believed in reform along democratic, secular, Western lines; the Slavophiles retreated into mystical nationalism, and preached the need for return to native, "organic" forms of life and faith that, according to them, had been all but ruined by Peter's reforms which had merely encouraged a sedulous and humiliating aping of the soulless, and, in any case, hopelessly decadent West. Herzen began as an extreme "Westerner," but he preserved his links with his Slavophile adversaries. He regarded the best among them as romantic reactionaries, misguided nationalists, but honorable allies against the Tsarist bureaucracy, and later tended systematically to minimize his differences with them, perhaps from a desire to see all Russians who were not dead to human feeling ranged in a single vast protest against the evil regime.

In 1847 Ivan Yakovlev died. He left the greater part of his fortune to Luise Haag and her son, Alexander Herzen. With immense faith in his own powers, and burning with a desire (in Fichte's words that expressed the attitude of a generation) "to be and do something" in the world, Herzen decided to emigrate. Whether he wished or expected to remain abroad during the rest of his life is uncertain, but so it turned out to be. He left in the same year, traveling in considerable state, accompanied by his wife, his mother, and two friends as well as servants; he slowly crossed Germany, and toward the end of 1847 reached the coveted city of Paris, the capital of the civilized world. He plunged at once into the life of the exiled radicals and socialists of many nationalities who played a central role in the fermenting intellectual and artistic activity of that city. By 1848, when a series of revolutions broke out in country after country in Europe, he found himself with Bakunin and Proudhon on the extreme left wing of revolutionary socialism. When rumors of his activities reached the Russian government, he was ordered to return immediately. He refused. His fortune in Russia and that of his mother were declared confiscated. Aided by the efforts of the banker James de Rothschild who had conceived a liking for the young Russian "baron" and was in a position to bring pressure on the Russian government, Herzen recovered the major portion of his fortune, and thereafter experienced no financial want. This gave him a degree of independence not then enjoyed by many exiles, as well as the financial means for supporting other refugees and radical causes.

SHORTLY AFTER HIS ARRIVAL in Paris, before the revolution, he contributed a series of impassioned articles to a Moscow periodical controlled by his friends, in which he gave an eloquent and violently critical account of the conditions of life and culture in Paris, and, in particular, a devastating analysis of the degradation of the French bourgeoisie, an indictment not surpassed even in the works of his contemporaries Marx and Heine. His Moscow friends for the most part received this with disfavor: they regarded his analyses as characteristic flights of a highly rhetorical fancy, irresponsible extremism, ill-suited to the needs of a misgoverned and backward country compared to which the progress of the middle classes in the West, whatever its shortcomings, was a notable step forward toward universal enlightenment. These early works—*The Letters from Avenue Marigny* and the *Italian Sketches* that followed—possess qualities which became characteristic of all his writings: a rapid torrent of descriptive sentences, fresh, lucid, direct, interspersed with vivid and never irrelevant digressions, variations on the same theme in many keys, puns, neologisms, quotations real and imaginary, verbal inventions, gallicisms which irritated his nationalistic Russian friends, mordant personal observations, and cascades of vivid images and incomparable epigrams, which, so far from either tiring or distracting the reader by their virtuosity, add to the force and swiftness of the narrative. The effect is one of spontaneous improvisation, of exhilarating conversation by an intellectually gay, brilliant, and unusually honest man endowed with singular powers of observation and expression. The mood is one of ardent political radicalism imbued with a typically aristocratic (and even more typically Muscovite) contempt for everything narrow, calculating, self-satisfied, commercial, anything cautious, petty, or tending toward compromise and the *juste milieu*, of which Louis Philippe and Guizot are held up as particularly repulsive incarnations.

Herzen's outlook in these essays is a combination of optimistic idealism—a vision of a socially, intellectually, and morally free society, the beginnings of which, like Proudhon, Marx, and Louis Blanc, he saw in the French working class; faith in the radical revolution which alone could create the conditions for their liberation. But with this went a deep distrust (something that his allies did not share) of all general formulae as such, of the programs and battle cries of all the political parties, above all, of the great, official, historic goals—progress, liberty, equality, national unity, historical rights, human solidarity—principles and slogans in the name of which men had been, and doubtless would soon again be, violated and slaughtered, and their forms of life condemned and destroyed.

Like the more extreme of the left-wing disciples of Hegel, in particular like the anarchist Max Stirner, Herzen saw danger in the great magnificent abstractions the mere sound of which precipitated men into violent and meaningless slaughter—new idols, it seemed to him, on whose altars human blood was to be shed tomorrow as irrationally and uselessly as the blood of the victims of yesterday or the day before, sacrificed in honor of older divinities—church or monarchy or the feudal order or the sacred customs of the tribe, that were now discredited as obstacles to the progress of mankind.

Together with this skepticism about the meaning and value of abstract ideals as such, in contrast with the concrete, short-term, immediate goals of identifiable living individuals—specific freedoms, reward for the day's work—Herzen spoke of something even more disquieting—a haunting sense of the ever widening, unbridgeable gulf between the humane values of the relatively free and civilized elites (to which he knew himself to belong) and the actual needs, desires, and tastes of the vast voiceless masses of mankind, barbarous enough in the West, wilder still in Russia or the plains of Asia beyond. The old world was crumbling visibly, and it deserved to fall. It would be destroyed by its victims—the slaves who cared nothing for the art and science of their masters; and indeed, Herzen asks, why should they care? Was it not erected on their suffering and degradation? Young and vigorous, filled with a just hatred of the old world built on their fathers' bones, the new barbarians will raze to the ground the edifices of their oppressors, and with them all that is most sublime and beautiful in Western civilization. Such a cataclysm might be not only inevitable but justified, since this civilization, noble and valuable in the eyes of its beneficiaries, has offered nothing but suffering, a life without meaning, to the vast majority of mankind. Yet he does not pretend that this makes the prospect, to those who, like him, have tasted the ripest fruits of civilization, any less dreadful.

IT HAS OFTEN been asserted by both Russian and Western critics that Herzen arrived in Paris a passionate, even utopian social idealist, and that it was the failure of the Revolution of 1848 which brought about his disillusionment and a new, more pessimistic realism. This does not seem sufficiently borne out by the evidence.[4] Even in 1847, the skeptical note, in particular, pessimism about the degree to which human beings can be transformed, and the still deeper skepticism about whether such changes, even if they

---

[4] The clearest formulation of this familiar and almost universal thesis is to be found in Mr. E. H. Carr's treatment of Herzen in *The Romantic Exiles* and elsewhere. Mr. Malia's book almost alone avoids it.

were achieved by fearless and intelligent revolutionaries or reformers, ideal images of whom floated before the eyes of his Westernizing friends in Russia, would in fact lead to a juster and freer order, or on the contrary to the rule of new masters over new slaves—that ominous note is sounded clearly before the great debacle. Yet, despite this, Herzen (unlike Heine who was prey to not dissimilar doubts), remained a convinced, ultimately optimistic revolutionary. The spectacle of the workers' revolt and its brutal suppression in Italy and in France haunted Herzen all his life. His first-hand description of the events of 1848–1849, in particular of the drowning in blood of the July revolt in Paris, is a masterpiece of "committed" historical and sociological writing. So, too, are his sketches of the personalities involved in these upheavals, and his reflections upon them. Most of these essays and letters remain untranslated.

Herzen could not and would not return to Russia. He became a Swiss citizen, and to the disasters of the revolution was added a personal tragedy—the seduction of his adored wife Natalie by the most intimate of his new friends, the radical German poet Georg Herwegh, a friend of Marx and Wagner, the "iron lark" of the German Revolution as he was called half ironically by Heine. Herzen's progressive, somewhat Shelleyan, views on love, friendship, equality of the sexes, and the irrationality of bourgeois morality, were tested by this crisis and broken by it. He went almost mad with grief and jealousy: his love, his vanity, his deeper assumptions about the basis of all human relationships, suffered a traumatic shock from which he was never fully to recover. He did what few others have ever done: described every detail of his own agony, every step of his altering relationship with Natalie, with Herwegh and Herwegh's wife (as they seemed to him in retrospect). He noted every communication that occurred between them, every moment of anger, despair, affection, love, hope, hatred, contempt; every tone and *nuance* in his own moral and psychological condition are raised to high relief against the background of his public life in the world of exiles and conspirators, French, Italian, German, Russian, Austrian, Hungarian, Polish, who move on and off the stage on which he himself is always the central, self-absorbed, tragic hero. The account is not unbalanced—there is no obvious distortion—but it is wholly egocentric.

All his life Herzen perceived the external world clearly, and in proportion, but through the medium of his own self-romanticizing personality, with his own impressionable, ill-organized self at the center of his universe. No matter how violent his torment, he retains full artistic control of the tragedy which he is living through, but also writing. It is, perhaps, this artistic egotism, which all his work exhibits, that was in part responsible both for Natalie's suffocation and for the lack of reticence in his description of what took place: Herzen takes wholly for granted the reader's understanding, and still more, his undivided interest in every detail of his own, the writer's, mental and emotional life. Natalie's letters and desperate flight to Herwegh show the measure of the increasingly destructive effect of Herzen's self-absorbed blindness upon her frail and *exalté* temperament. We know comparatively little of Natalie's relationship with Herwegh: she may well have been physically in love with him, and he with her: the inflated literary language of the letters conceals more than it reveals; what is clear is that she felt unhappy, trapped, and irresistibly attracted to her lover. If Herzen sensed this, he perceived it very dimly.

He appropriated the feelings of those nearest him as he did the ideas of Hegel or George Sand: that is, he took what he needed, and poured it into the vehement torrent of his own experience. He gave generously, if fitfully, to others; he put his own life into them, but for all his deep and lifelong belief in individual liberty and the absolute value of personal life and personal relationships, scarcely understood or tolerated wholly independent lives by the side of his own; his description of his agony is scrupulously and bitterly detailed and accurate, never self-sparing, eloquent but not sentimental, and remorselessly egocentric. It is a harrowing document. He did not publish the story in full during his lifetime, but now it forms part of his memoirs.

SELF-EXPRESSION—the need to say his own word—and perhaps the craving for recognition by others, by Russia, by Europe, were primary needs of Herzen's nature. Consequently, even during this, the darkest period of his life, he continued to pour out a stream of letters and articles in various languages on political and social topics; he helped to keep Proudhon going, kept up a correspondence with Swiss radicals and Russian émigrés, read widely, made notes, conceived ideas, argued, worked unremittingly both as a publicist and as an active supporter of left-wing and revolutionary causes. After a short while Natalie returned to him in Nice, only to die in his arms. Shortly before her death, a ship on which his mother and one of his children, a deaf-mute, were traveling from Marseilles sank in a storm. Their bodies were not found. Herzen's life had reached its lowest ebb. He left Nice and the circle of Italian, French, and Polish revolutionaries to many of whom he was bound by ties of warm friendship, and with his three surviving children went to England. America was too far away and, besides, seemed to him too dull. England was no less remote from the scene of his defeats, political and personal, and yet still a part of Europe. It was then the country most hospitable to political refugees, civilized, tolerant of eccentricities or indifferent to them, proud of her civil liberties and her sympathy with the victims of foreign oppression. In 1851 he went to London.

He and his children wandered from home to home in London and its suburbs, and there, after the death of Nicholas I had made it possible for him to leave Russia, his most intimate friend, Nicholas Ogaryov, joined them. Together they set up a printing press, and began to publish a periodical in Russian called *The Polar Star*—the first organ wholly dedicated to uncompromising agitation against the Imperial Russian regime. The earliest chapters of *My Past and Thoughts* appeared in its pages. The memory of the terrible years 1848–1851 obsessed Herzen's thoughts and poisoned his bloodstream: it became an inescapable psychological necessity for him to seek relief by setting down this bitter history. This was the first section of his memoirs to be written. It was an opiate against the appalling loneliness of a life lived among uninterested strangers[5] while political reaction seemed to envelop the entire world, leaving no room for hope. Insensibly he was drawn into the past. He moved further and further into it and found it a source of liberty and strength.

This is how the book which he conceived on the analogy of *David Copperfield* came to be composed.[6] He began to write it in the last months of 1852. He wrote by fits and starts. The first two parts were probably finished by the end of 1853. In 1854 a selection which he called *Prison and Exile*—a

---

[5] Herzen had made no genuine friends in England, although he had associates, allies, and admirers. One of these, the radical journalist W. J. Linton, to whose *English Republic* Herzen had contributed articles, described him as "short of stature, stoutly built, in his last days inclined to corpulence, with a grand head, long chestnut hair and beard, small, luminous eyes, and rather ruddy complexion. Suave in his manner, courteous, but with an intense power of irony, witty, . . . clear, concise and impressive, he was a subtle and profound thinker, with all the passionate nature of the 'barbarian,' yet generous and humane" (*Memories*, London, 1895, pp. 146–147). And in his *European Republicans*, published two years earlier, he spoke of him as "hospitable and taking pleasure in society, . . . a good conversationalist, with a frank and pleasing manner," and said that the Spanish radical Castelar said that Herzen, with his fair hair and beard, looked like a Goth, but possessed the warmth, vivacity, "verve and inimitable grace" and "marvellous variety" of a Southerner. Turgenev and Herzen were the first Russians to move freely in European society. The impression that they made did a good deal, though perhaps not enough, to dispel the myth of the "Slav soul," which took a long time to die. Perhaps it is not altogether dead yet.

[6] "Copperfield is Dickens's *Past and Thoughts*," he said in one of his letters in the early Sixties; humility was not among his virtues.

title perhaps inspired by Silvio Pellico's celebrated *I Miei Prigioni*, was published in English. It was an immediate success; encouraged by this, he continued. By the spring of 1855, the first five parts of the work were completed; they were all published by 1857. He revised Part IV, added new chapters to it, and composed Part V; he completed the bulk of Part VI by 1858. The sections dealing with his intimate life—his love and the early years of his marriage, were composed in 1857: he could not bring himself to touch upon them until then. This was followed by an interval of seven years. Independent essays such as those on Robert Owen, the actor Shchepkin, the painter Ivanov, Garibaldi (*Camicia Rossa*), were published in London[7] between 1860 and 1864; but these, although usually included in the memoirs, were not intended for them. The first complete edition of Parts I–IV appeared in 1861. The final sections—Part VIII and almost the whole of Part VII—were written, in that order, in 1865–1867.

Herzen deliberately left some sections unpublished: the most intimate details of his personal tragedy appeared posthumously—only a part of the chapter entitled *Oceano Nox* was printed in his lifetime. He omitted also the story of his affairs with Medvedeva in Vyatka and with the serf girl Katerina in Moscow—his confession of them to Natalie cast the first shadow over their relationship, a shadow that never lifted; he could not bear to see it in print while he lived. He suppressed, too, a chapter on "The Germans in Emigration" which contains his unflattering comments on Marx and his followers, and some characteristically entertaining and ironical sketches of some of his old friends among the Russian radicals. He genuinely detested the practice of washing the revolutionaries' dirty linen in public, and made it clear that he did not intend to make fun of allies for the entertainment of the common enemy. The first authoritative edition of the memoirs was compiled by Mikhail Lemke in the first complete edition of Herzen's works, which was begun before, and completed some years after, the Russian Revolution of 1917. It has since been revised in successive Soviet editions. The fullest version is that published in the new exhaustive edition of Herzen's works, a handsome monument of Soviet scholarship—which at the time of writing is still incomplete.

The memoirs formed a vivid and broken background accompaniment to Herzen's central activity: revolutionary journalism, to which he dedicated his life. The bulk of it is contained in the most celebrated of all Russian periodicals published abroad, *Kolokol—The Bell*—edited by Herzen

---

7 In *The Bell*: see below.

and Ogaryov in London and then in Geneva from 1857 until 1867, with the motto *vivos voco*. *The Bell* had an immense success. It was the first systematic instrument of revolutionary propaganda directed against the Russian autocracy, written with knowedge, sincerity, and mordant eloquence. The journal gathered round itself all that was uncowed not only in Russia and the Russian colonies abroad, but also among Poles and other oppressed nationalities. It began to penetrate into Russia by secret routes and was regularly read by high officials of state, including, it was rumored, the Emperor himself. The copious information that reached Herzen and his friends in clandestine letters and personal messages, describing various misdeeds of the Russian bureaucracy, was used to expose specific scandals — cases of bribery, miscarriage of justice, tyranny, and dishonesty by officials and influential persons. *The Bell* named names, offered documentary evidence, asked awkward questions, and exposed repulsive aspects of Russian life.

Russian travelers visited London in order to meet the mysterious leader of the mounting opposition to the Tsar. Generals, high officials, and other loyal subjects of the Empire were among the many visitors who thronged to see him, some out of curiosity, others to shake his hand, to express sympathy or admiration. He reached the peak of his fame, both political and literary, after the defeat of Russia in the Crimean War and the death of Nicholas I. The open appeal by Herzen to the new Emperor to free the serfs and initiate bold and radical reforms "from above," and (after the first concrete steps toward this had been taken in 1859) his paean of praise to Alexander II under the title of "Thou hast conquered, O Galilean," helped to create the illusion on both sides of the Russian frontier that a new liberal era had at last dawned, in which a degree of understanding—perhaps of actual cooperation—could be achieved between Tsardom and its opponents. This state of mind did not last long. But Herzen's credit stood very high—higher than that of any other Russian in the West. In the late Fifties and early Sixties, he was the acknowledged leader of all that was generous, enlightened, civilized, humane in Russia.

MORE THAN BAKUNIN and even Turgenev, whose novels formed a central source of knowledge about Russia in the West, Herzen counteracted the legend, ingrained in the minds of progressive Europeans (of whom Michelet was perhaps the most representative), that Russia was nothing but the government jack-boot on the one hand, and the dark, silent, sullen mass of brutalized peasants on the other—an image that was the byproduct of the widespread sympathy for the principal victim of Russian despotism, the martyred nation, Poland. Some among the Polish exiles spontaneously conceded this service to the truth on Herzen's part, if only because he was one of the rare Russians who genuinely liked and admired individual Poles, worked in close sympathy with them, and identified the cause of Russian liberation with that of all her oppressed subject nationalities. It was, indeed, this unswerving avoidance of chauvinism that was among the principal causes of the ultimate collapse of *The Bell* and Herzen's own political undoing.

After Russia, Herzen's deepest love was for Italy and the Italians. The closest ties bound him to the Italian exiles, Mazzini, Garibaldi, Saffi, and Orsini. Although he supported every liberal beginning in France, his attitude toward her was more ambiguous. For this there were many reasons. Like Tocqueville (whom he personally disliked), he had a distaste for all that was centralized, bureaucratic, hierarchical, subject to rigid forms or rules. France was to him the incarnation of order, discipline, the worship of the state, of unity, and of the despotic, abstract formulae that flattened all things to the same rule and pattern—something that had a family resemblance to the animating principle of the great slave states—Prussia, Austria, Russia. With it he constantly contrasts the decentralized, uncrushed, untidy, "truly democratic" Italians, whom he believes to possess a deep affinity with the free Russian spirit embodied in the peasant commune with its sense of natural justice and human worth. To this ideal even England seemed to him to be far less hostile than legalistic, calculating France: in such moods he comes close to his romantic Slavophile opponents. Moreover, he could not forget the betrayal of the revolution in Paris by the bourgeois parties in 1848, the execution of the workers, the suppression of the Roman revolution by the troops of the French Republic, the vanity, weakness, and rhetoric of the French radical politicians—Lamartine, Marrast, Ledru-Rollin, Felix Pyat.

HIS SKETCHES of the lives and behavior of leading French exiles in England are masterpieces of amused, half-sympathetic, half-contemptuous description of the grotesque and futile aspects of every political emigration condemned to sterility, intrigue, and a constant flow of self-justifying eloquence before a foreign audience too remote or bored to listen. Yet he thought well of individual members of it: he had for a time been a close ally of Proudhon, and, despite their differences, he continued to respect him; he regarded Louis Blanc as an honest and fearless democrat, was on good terms with Victor Hugo, and he liked and deeply admired Michelet. In later years he visited at least one Paris political salon—admittedly, it was that of a Pole—with evident enjoyment: the Goncourts met him there and left a vivid description in their journal of his appearance and his conversation.[8]

Although he was half-German himself, or perhaps because of it, he felt, like his friend Bakunin, a strong aversion from what he regarded as the incurable philistinism of the Germans, and what seemed to him a peculiarly unattractive combination of craving for blind authority with a tendency to squalid internecine recriminations in public, more pronounced than among other émigrés. Perhaps his hatred of Herwegh, whom he knew to be a friend both of Marx and of Wagner, as well as Marx's onslaughts on Karl Vogt, the Swiss naturalist to whom Herzen was devoted, played some part in this. At least three of his most intimate friends were pure Germans; Goethe and Schiller meant more to him than Russian writers; yet there is something genuinely venomous in his account of the German exiles, quite different from the high-spirited sense of comedy with which he describes the idiosyncrasies of the other foreign colonies gathered in London in the Fifties and Sixties—a city, if we are to believe Herzen, equally unconcerned with their absurdities and their martyrdom.

---

8 See entry in the *Journal* for 8th February, 1865—"Dinner at Charles Edmond's (Chojecki)...A Socratic mask with the warm and transparent flesh of a Rubens portrait, a red mark between the eyebrows as from a branding iron, greying beard and hair. As he talks there is a constant ironical chuckle which rises and falls in his throat. His voice is soft and slow, without any of the coarseness one might have expected from the huge neck; the ideas are fine, delicate, pungent, at times subtle, always definite, illuminated by words that take time to arrive, but which always possess the felicitous quality of French as it is spoken by a civilized and witty foreigner.

"He speaks of Bakunin, of his eleven months in prison, chained to a wall, of his escape from Siberia by the Amur River, of his return by way of California, of his arrival in London, where, after a stormy, moist embrace, his first words to Herzen were 'Can one get oysters here?'"

Herzen delighted the Goncourts with stories about the Emperor Nicholas, after the fall of Eupatoria during the Crimean War, walking in the night in his empty palace, with the heavy, unearthly steps of the stone statue of the Commander in *Don Juan*. This was followed by anecdotes about English habits and manners—"a country which he loves as the land of liberty"—to illustrate its absurd, class-conscious, unyielding traditionalism, particularly noticeable in the relations of masters and servants. The Goncourts quote a characteristic epigram made by Herzen to illustrate the difference between the French and the English characters. They go on to report the story of how James de Rothschild managed to save Herzen's property in Russia.

As for his hosts, the English, they seldom appear in his pages. Herzen had met Mill, Carlyle, and Owen. He was on reasonably good terms with several editors of radical papers (some of whom, like Linton and Cowen, helped him to propagate his views, and to preserve contact with revolutionaries on the continent as well as with clandestine traffic of propaganda to Russia), and one or two radically inclined members of Parliament, including a minor minister. In general, however, he seems to have had even less contact with Englishmen than his contemporary and fellow exile, Karl Marx. He admired England. He admired her constitution; the wild and tangled wood of her unwritten laws and customs brought the full resources of his romantic imagination into play. The entertaining passages of *My Past and Thoughts* in which he compared the French and the English, or the English and the Germans, display acute and amused insight into the national characteristics of the English. But he could not altogether like them: they remained for him too insular, too indifferent, too unimaginative, too remote from the moral, social, and aesthetic issues which lay closest to his own heart, too materialistic and self-satisfied. His judgments about them, always intelligent and sometimes penetrating, are distant, acid, and tend to be conventional. A description of the trial in London of a French radical who had killed a political opponent in a duel in Windsor Great Park is wonderfully executed but remains a piece of genre painting, a gay and brilliant caricature. The French, the Swiss, the Italians, even the Germans, certainly the Poles, are closer to him. He cannot establish any genuine personal *rapport* with the English. When he thinks of mankind he does not think of them.

Apart from his central preoccupations, he devoted himself to the education of his children, which he entrusted in part to an idealistic German lady, Malwida von Meysenbug, afterward a friend of Nietzsche and Romain Rolland. His personal life was intertwined with that of his intimate friend Ogaryov, and of Ogaryov's wife who became his mistress. In spite of this the mutual devotion of the two friends remained unaltered — the memoirs reveal little of the curious emotional consequences of this relationship.

For the rest, he lived the life of an affluent, well-born man of letters, a member of the Russian and, more specifically, Moscow gentry, uprooted from his native soil, unable to achieve a settled existence or even the semblance of inward or outward peace, a life filled with occasional moments of hope and even exultation, followed by long periods of misery, corrosive self-criticism, and, most of all, overwhelming, omnivorous, bitter nostalgia. It may be this, as well as objective reasons, that caused him to idealize the Russian peasant, and to dream that the answer to the central "social" question of his time—that of growing inequality, exploitation, dehumanization of both the oppressor and the oppressed—lay in the preservation of the Russian peasant commune. He perceived in it the seeds of the development of a nonindustrial, semi-anarchist, "free" socialism. Only such a solution, plainly influenced by the views of Fourier, Proudhon, and George Sand, seemed to him to avoid the crushing, barrack-room discipline demanded by Western Communists from Cabet to Marx; and from the equally suffocating, and, it seemed to him, far more vulgar and philistine ideals contained in moderate, half-socialist doctrines, with their faith in the progressive role of developing industrialism preached by the forerunners of social democracy in Germany and France and of the Fabians in England. At times he modified his view: toward the end of his life he began to recognize the historical significance of the organized urban workers. But all in all, he remained faithful to his belief in the Russian peasant commune as an embryonic form of a life in which the quest for individual freedom was reconcilable with the need for collective activity and responsibility. He retained to the end a romantic vision of the inevitable coming of a new, just, all-transforming social order.

Herzen is neither consistent nor systematic. His style during his middle years has lost the confident touch of his youth, and conveys the consuming nostalgia that never leaves him. He is obsessed by a sense of the power of blind accident, although his faith in the values of life for its own sake, of art, of social freedom, of personal relationships, remains unshaken. Almost all traces of Hegelian influence are gone. "The absurdity of facts offends us . . . it is as though someone had promised that everything in the world will be exquisitely beautiful, just and harmonious. We have marvelled enough at the deep abstract wisdom of nature and history; it is time to realise that nature and history are full of the accidental and senseless, of muddle and bungling." This is highly characteristic of his mood in the Sixties; and it is no accident that his exposition is not ordered, but is a succession of fragments, episodes, isolated vignettes, a mingling of *Dichtung* and *Wahrheit*, facts and poetic license.

His moods alternate sharply. Sometimes he believes in the need for a great, cleansing, revolutionary storm, even were it to take the form of a barbarian invasion likely to destroy all the values that he himself holds dear. At other times he reproaches his old friend Bakunin, who joined him in London after escaping from his Russian prisons, for wanting to make the revolution too soon; for not understanding that dwellings for free men cannot be constructed out of the stones of a prison; that the average European of the nineteenth century is too deeply marked by the slavery of the old order to be capable of realizing true freedom, that it is not the liberated slaves who will build the new order, but new men brought up in liberty. History has its own tempo; patience and gradualism—not the haste and violence of a Peter the Great—can alone bring about a permanent transformation. At such moments he wonders whether the future belongs to the free, anarchic peasant, or to the bold and ruthless planner; perhaps it is the industrial worker who is to be the heir to the new, unavoidable, collectivist economic order.[9] Then again he returns to his early moods of disillusionment and wonders whether men in general really desire freedom: perhaps only a few do so in each generation, while most human beings only want good government, no matter at whose hands; and he echoes de Maistre's bitter epigram about Rousseau: "Monsieur Rousseau has asked why it is that men who are born free are nevertheless everywhere in chains; it is as if one were to ask why sheep, who are born carnivorous, nevertheless everywhere nibble grass." Herzen develops this theme. Men desire freedom no more than fish desire to fly. The fact that a few flying fish exist does not demonstrate that fish in general were created to fly, or are not fundamentally quite content to stay below the surface of the water, forever away from the sun and the light. Then he returns to his earlier optimism and the thought that somewhere—in Russia—there lives the unbroken human being, the peasant with his faculties intact, untainted by the corruption and sophistication of the West.

But this Rousseau-inspired vision, as he grows older, begins to fade. His sense of reality is too strong. For all his efforts and the efforts of his socialist friends, he cannot deceive himself entirely. He oscillates between pessimism and optimism, skepticism and suspicion of his own skepticism, and is kept morally alive only by his hatred of all injustice, all arbitrariness, all mediocrity as such—in particular by his inability to compromise to any degree with either the brutality of reactionaries or the hypocrisy of bourgeois liberals. He is preserved by this, buoyed up by his belief that such evils will destroy themselves, by his love for his children and his devoted friends, and by his unquenchable delight in the variety of life and the comical absurdities of human character.

---

[9] This is the thesis in which orthodox Soviet scholars claim to discern the beginnings of a belated approach to the doctrines of Marx.

On the whole, he grew more pessimistic. He began with an ideal vision of mankind, largely ignored the chasm which divided it from the present—whether the Russia of Nicholas, or the corrupt constitutionalism in the West. In his youth he glorified Jacobin radicalism and condemned its opponents in Russia—blind conservatism, Slavophile nostalgia, the cautious gradualism of his friends Granovsky and Turgenev, as well as Hegelian appeals to patience and rational conformity to the inescapable rhythms of history, which seemed to him designed to ensure the triumph of the new bourgeois class. His attitude, before he went abroad, was boldly optimistic. There followed, not indeed a change of view, but a cooling-off, a tendency to a more sober and critical outlook. All genuine change, he began to think in 1847, is necessarily slow; the power of tradition (which he at once mocks and admires in England) is very great; men are less malleable than was believed in the eighteenth century, nor do they truly seek liberty, only security and contentment; communism is but Tsarism stood on its head, the replacement of one yoke by another; the ideals and watchwords of politics turn out, on examination, to be empty formulae to which devout fanatics happily slaughter hecatombs of their fellows. He no longer feels certain that the gap between the enlightened elite and the masses can ever, in principle, be bridged (this becomes an obsessive refrain in later Russian thought), since the awakened people may, for unalterable psychological or sociological reasons, despise and reject the gifts of a civilization which will never mean enough to them. But if all this is even in small part true, is radical transformation either practicable or desirable? From this follows Herzen's growing sense of obstacles that may be insurmountable, limits that may be impassable, his empiricism, skepticism, the alternations of hope and gloom, the latent pessimism, and intermittent despair of the middle Sixties.

THIS IS THE ATTITUDE[10] which some Soviet scholars interpret as the beginning of an approach on his part toward a quasi-Marxist recognition of the inexorable laws of social development—in particular the inevitability of industrialism, and of the central role to be played by the proletariat. This is not how the majority of Herzen's Russian left-wing critics interpreted his views in his lifetime, or in the half century that followed. To them, rightly or wrongly, these doctrines seemed symptomatic of retreat, vacillation, and betrayal. For in the Fifties and Sixties, a new generation of radicals grew up in Russia, then a backward country in the painful process of the earliest,

---

[10] See footnote 9 on page 61.

most rudimentary beginnings of slow, sporadic, inefficient industrialization. These were men of mixed social origins, filled with contempt for the feeble liberal compromises of 1848, will no illusions about the prospects of freedom in the West, determined on more ruthless methods; accepting as true only what the sciences can prove, prepared to be hard, and if need be, unscrupulous and cruel, in order to break the power of their equally ruthless oppressors; bitterly hostile to the aestheticism, the devotion to civilized values, of the "soft" generation of the Forties.

Herzen realized that the criticism and abuse showered upon him as an obsolete aristocratic dilettante by these "nihilists" (as they came to be called after Turgenev's novel *Fathers and Sons,* in which this conflict is vividly presented for the first time) was not altogether different from the disdain that he had himself felt in his own youth for the aristocratic and ineffective reformers of Alexander I's reign; but this did not make his position easier to bear. That which was ill-received by the tough-minded revolutionaries pleased Tolstoy, who said more than once that the censorship of Herzen's works in Russia was a characteristic blunder on the part of the government; the government, in its anxiety to stop young men from marching toward the revolutionary morass, seized them and swept them off to Siberia or prison long before they were even in sight of it, while they were still on the broad highway; Herzen had trodden this very path; he had seen the chasm and warned against it, particularly in his "Letters to an Old Comrade." Nothing, Tolstoy argued, would have proved a better antidote to the "revolutionary nihilism" which Tolstoy condemned, than Herzen's brilliant analyses. "Our young generation would not have been the same if Herzen had been read by them during the last twenty years." Suppression of his books, Tolstoy went on, was both a wicked, and from the point of view of those who did not desire a violent revoultion, an idiotic policy.

At other times, Tolstoy was less generous. In 1860, six months before they met, he had been reading Herzen's writings with mingled admiration and irritation: "Herzen is a man of scattered intellect, and morbid *amour-propre*," he wrote in a letter, "but his breadth, ability, goodness, elegance of mind are Russian." From time to time various correspondents record the fact that Tolstoy read Herzen, at times aloud to his family, with the greatest admiration. In 1896, during one of his angriest, most antirationalist moods, he said, "What has Herzen said that is of the slightest use?"—as for those who maintained that the generation of the Forties could not say what it wanted to say because of the rigid Russian censorship, Herzen wrote in perfect freedom in Paris, and yet managed to say "nothing useful."

What irritated Tolstoy most was Herzen's socialism. In 1908 he complained that Herzen was "a narrow socialist," even if he was "head and shoulders above the other politicians of his age and ours." The fact that he believed in politics as a weapon was sufficient to condemn him in Tolstoy's eyes. From 1862 onward, Tolstoy had declared his hostility to faith in liberal reform and improvement of human life by legal or institutional change. Herzen fell under this general ban. Moreover, Tolstoy seems to have felt a certain lack of personal sympathy for Herzen and his public position—even a kind of jealousy. When, in moments of deep discouragement and irritation, Tolstoy spoke (perhaps not very seriously) of leaving Russia forever, he would say that whatever he did, he would not join Herzen or march under his banner: "he goes his way, I shall go mine."

He greatly underrated Herzen's revolutionary temperament and instincts. However skeptical Herzen may have been of specific revolutionary doctrines or plans in Russia—and no one was more so—he believed to the end of his life in the moral and social need and the inevitable coming, soon or late, of a revolution in Russia—a violent transformation followed by a just, that is a socialist, order. He did not, it is true, close his eyes to the possibility, even the probability, that the great rebellion would extinguish values to which he was himself dedicated—in particular, the freedom without which he and others like him could not breathe. Nevertheless, he recognized not only the inescapable necessity but the historic justice of the coming cataclysm. His moral tastes, his respect for human values, his entire style of life, divided him from the tough-minded younger radicals of the Sixties, but he did not, despite all his distrust of political fanaticism, whether on the right or on the left, turn into a cautious, reformist, liberal constitutionalist. Even in his gradualist phase he remained an agitator, an egalitarian, and a socialist to the end. It is this in him that both the Russian populists and the Russian Marxists—Mikhailovsky and Lenin—recognized and saluted.

It was not prudence or moderation that led him to his unwavering support of Poland in her insurrection against Russia in 1863. The wave of passionate Russian nationalism which accompanied its suppression lost him sympathy even among Russian liberals. The circulation of *The Bell* declined. The new, "hard" revolutionaries needed his money, but made it plain that they looked upon him as a liberal dinosaur, the preacher of antiquated humanistic views, useless in the violent social struggles to come. He left London in the late Sixties and attempted to produce a French edition of *The Bell* in Geneva. When this periodical, too, failed, he visited his friends in Florence, returning to Paris early in 1870, before the outbreak of the Franco-Prussian War. There he died of pleurisy, broken both morally and physically, but not disillusioned; still writing with concentrated intelligence and force. His body was taken to Nice, where he is buried beside his wife. A life-sized statue still marks his grave.

HERZEN'S IDEAS have long since entered into the general texture of Russian political thought—liberals and radicals, populists and anarchists, socialists and Communists, have all claimed him as an ancestor. But what survives today of all that unceasing and feverish activity, even in his native country, is not a system or a doctrine, but a handful of essays, some remarkable letters, and the extraordinary amalgam of memory, observation, moral passion, psychological analysis, and political description, wedded to a major literary talent, which has immortalized his name. What remains is, above all, a passionate and inextinguishable temperament and a sense of the life and ferment of nature, an infinity of unpredictable possibilities, which he felt with an intensity which not even his uniquely rich and flexible prose could fully express.

He believed that the ultimate goal of life was life itself; that the day and the hour were ends in themselves, not a means to another day or another experience. He believed that remote ends were a dream, that faith in them was a fatal illusion; that to sacrifice the present, or the immediate and foreseeable future, to these distant ends must always lead to cruel and futile forms of human sacrifice. He belived that values were not found in an impersonal, objective realm, but were literally created by human beings and changed with the generations of men, but were nonetheless binding upon those who lived in their light; that suffering was inescapable, and infallible knowledge neither attainable nor needed. He believed in reason, scientific method, individual action, empirically discovered truth. But he tended to suspect that faith in general formulae, laws, prescription in human affairs was an attempt, sometimes catastrophic, always irrational, to escape from the uncertainty and unpredictable variety of life to the false security of our own symmetrical fantasies. He was fully conscious of what he believed. He had obtained his knowledge at the cost of painful, and, at times, unintended, self-analysis, and he described what he saw in language of exceptional vitality, precision, and poetry. His purely personal credo remained unaltered from his earliest days: "Art, and the summer lightning of individual happiness: these are the only real goods we have," he declared in a self-revealing passage of the kind that so deeply shocked the stern young Russian revolutionaries in the Sixties. Yet even they and their descendants did not and do not reject his artistic and intellectual achievement.

Herzen was not, and had no wish to be, an impartial observer. No less than the poets and the novelists of his nation, he created a style, an outlook, and, in the words of Gorky's tribute to him, "an entire province, a country astonishingly rich in ideas,"[11] where everything is immediately recognizable as being his and his alone, a country into which he transplanted all that he touched, in which things, sensations, feelings, persons, ideas, private and public events, institutions, entire cultures, were given shape and life by his powerful and coherent historical imagination, and have stood up, untouched by the forces of decay, in the solid world which his memory, his intelligence, and his artistic genius recovered and reconstructed. *My Past and Thoughts* is the Noah's ark in which he saved himself, and not himself alone, from the destructive flood in which many idealistic radicals of the Forties were drowned. Genuine art transcends its immediate purpose and lives on. The structure that Herzen built in the first place, perhaps, for his own personal salvation, built out of material provided by his own predicament—out of exile, solitude, despair—survives intact. Written abroad, concerned largely with European issues and figures, these reminiscences are a great, perhaps the greatest, most lasting monument to the civilized, sensitive, morally preoccupied, and gifted Russian society to which Herzen belonged, and for which alone he wrote; their vitality and fascination have not declined in the hundred years that have passed since the first chapters saw the light.

[11] *Istoriya Rosskoy Literatury*, p. 206. (Moscow, 1939).

Reflections on Violence by Hannah Arendt was originally published February 27, 1969.

HANNAH ARENDT

Reflections on Violence

I

THESE REFLECTIONS WERE PROVOKED by the events and debates of the last few years, as seen against the background of the twentieth century. Indeed this century has become, as Lenin predicted, a century of wars and revolutions, hence a century of that violence which is currently believed to be their common denominator. There is, however, another factor in the present situation which, though predicted by nobody, is of at least equal importance. The technical development of implements of violence has now reached the point where no political goal could conceivably correspond to their destructive potential or justify their actual use in armed conflict. Hence, warfare—since times immemorial the final merciless arbiter in international disputes—has lost much of its effectiveness and nearly all of its glamour. "The apocalyptic" chess game between the superpowers, that is, between those that move on the highest plane of our civilization, is being played according to the rule: "If either 'wins' it is the end of both."[1] Moreover the game bears no resemblance to whatever war games preceded it. Its "rational" goal is mutual deterrence, not victory.

Since violence—as distinct from power, force, or strength—always needs *implements* (as Engels pointed out long ago),[2] the revolution in technology, a revolution in tool-making, was especially marked in warfare. The very substance of violent action is ruled by the question of means and ends, whose chief characteristic, if applied to human affairs, has always been that the end is in danger of being overwhelmed by the means, which it both justifies and needs. Since the end of human action, in contrast with the products of fab-

---

[1] Wheeler, "The Strategic Calculators," in Nigel Calder, *Unless Peace Comes* (Viking, 1968), p. 109.
[2] *Herrn Eugen Dührings Umwälzung der Wissenschaft* (1878), Part II, Ch. 2.

rication, can never be reliably predicted, the means used to achieve political goals are more often than not of greater relevance to the future world than the intended goals. Moreover, all violence harbors within itself an element of arbitrariness; nowhere does Fortuna, good or ill luck, play a more important role in human affairs than on the battlefield; and this intrusion of the "Random Event" cannot be eliminated by game theories but only by the certainty of mutual destruction. It seems symbolic of this all-pervading unpredictability that those engaged in the perfection of the means of destruction have finally brought about a level of technical development where their aim, namely warfare, is on the point of disappearing altogether.[3]

No one concerned with history and politics can remain unaware of the enormous role violence has always played in human affairs; and it is at first glance rather surprising that violence has so seldom been singled out for special consideration.[4] (In the last edition of the *Encyclopedia of the Social Sciences* "violence" does not even rate an entry.) This shows to what extent violence and its arbitrary nature were taken for granted and therefore neglected; no one questions or examines what is obvious to all. Whoever looked for some kind of sense in the records of the past was almost bound to look upon violence as a marginal phenomenon. When Clausewitz calls war "the continuation of politics with other means," or Engels defines violence as the accelerator of economic development,[5] the emphasis is on political or economic continuity, on continuing a process which is determined by what preceded violent action. Hence, students of international relations have held until very recently that "it was a maxim that a military resolution in discord with the deeper cultural sources of national power could not be stable," or that, in Engels's words, "wherever the power structure of a country contradicts its economic development" political power with its means of violence will suffer defeat.[6]

---

3 As General André Beaufre points out ("Battlefields of the 1980s," in Calder, *Unless Peace Comes*, p. 3): Only "in those parts of the world not covered by nuclear deterrence" is war still possible, and even this "conventional warfare," despite its horrors, is actually already limited by the ever-present threat of escalation into nuclear war. The chief reason why warfare is still with us is neither a secret death wish of the human species nor an irrepressible instinct of aggression nor, finally and more plausibly, the serious economic and social dangers inherent in disarmament, but the simple fact that nothing to substitute for this final arbiter in international affairs has yet appeared on the political scene.

4 There exists, of course, a large literature on war and warfare, but it deals with the implements of violence, not with violence as such.

5 See Engels, *Herrn Eugen Dührings Umwälzung der Wissenschaft*, Part II, Ch. 4.

6 Wheeler, "The Strategic Calculators," p. 107 and Engels, *Herrn Eugen Dührings*, Part II, Ch. 4.

Today all these old verities about the relation of war and politics or about violence and power no longer apply. We know that "a few weapons could wipe out all other sources of national power in a few moments,"[7] that biological weapons are devised which would enable "small groups of individuals...to upset the strategic balance" and be cheap enough to be produced by "nations unable to develop nuclear striking forces,"[8] that "within a very few years" robot soldiers will have made "human soldiers completely obsolete,"[9] and that, finally, in conventional warfare the poor countries are much less vulnerable than the great powers precisely because they are "underdeveloped" and because technical superiority can "be much more of a liability than an asset" in guerrilla wars.[10]

What all these very uncomfortable novelties add up to is a reversal in the relationship between power and violence, foreshadowing another reversal in the future relationship between small and great powers. The amount of violence at the disposal of a given country may no longer be a reliable indication of that country's strength or a reliable guarantee against destruction by a substantially smaller and weaker power. This again bears an ominous similarity to one of the oldest insights of political science, namely that power cannot be measured by wealth, that an abundance of wealth may erode power, that riches are particularly dangerous for the power and well-being of republics.

The more doubtful the outcome of violence in international relations, the more it has gained in reputation and appeal in domestic affairs, specifically in the matter of revolution. The strong Marxist flavor in the rhetoric of the New Left coincides with the steady growth of the entirely non-Marxian conviction, proclaimed by Mao Tse-tung, "Power grows out of the barrel of a gun." To be sure, Marx was aware of the role of violence in history, but this role was to him secondary; not violence but the contradictions inherent in the old society brought about its end. The emergence of a new society was preceded, but not caused, by violent outbreaks, which he likened to the labor pangs that precede, but of course do not cause, the event of organic birth.

In the same vein, Marx regarded the state as an instrument of violence at the command of the ruling class; but the actual power of the ruling class

---

7 Wheeler, "The Strategic Calculators," p. 107.
8 Nigel Calder, "The New Weapons," in *Unless Peace Comes*, p. 239.
9 M.W. Thring, "Robots on the March," in *Unless Peace Comes*, p. 169.
10 Vladimir Dedijer, "The Poor Man's Power," in *Unless Peace Comes*, p. 29.

did not consist of nor rely on violence. It was defined by the role the ruling class played in society, or more exactly, by its role in the process of production. It has often been noticed, and sometimes deplored, that the revolutionary Left, under the influence of Marx's teachings, ruled out the use of violent means; the "dictatorship of the proletariat"—openly repressive in Marx's writings—came after the revolution and was meant, like the Roman dictatorship, as a strictly limited period. Political assassination, with the exception of a few acts of individual terror perpetuated by small groups of anarchists, was mostly the prerogative of the Right, while organized armed uprisings remained the specialty of the military.

ON THE LEVEL OF THEORY, there were a few exceptions. Georges Sorel, who at the beginning of the century tried a combination of Marxism with Bergson's philosophy of life—which on a much lower level of sophistication shows an odd similarity with Sartre's current amalgamation of existentialism and Marxism—thought of class struggle in military terms; but he ended by proposing nothing more violent than the famous myth of the general strike, a form of action which we today would rather think of as belonging to the arsenal of nonviolent politics.

Fifty years ago, even this modest proposal earned him the reputation of being a fascist, his enthusiastic approval of Lenin and the Russian Revolution notwithstanding. Sartre, who in his preface to Fanon's *The Wretched of the Earth* goes much further in his glorification of violence than Sorel in his famous *Reflections on Violence*—further than Fanon himself whose argument he wishes to bring to its conclusion—still mentions "Sorel's fascist utterances." This shows to what extent Sartre is unaware of his basic disagreement with Marx on the question of violence, especially when he states that "irrepressible violence . . . is man recreating himself," that it is "mad fury" through which "the wretched of the earth" can "become men."

These notions are all the more remarkable since the idea of man creating himself is in the tradition of Hegelian and Marxian thinking; it is the very basis of all leftist humanism. But according to Hegel, man "produces" himself through thought,[11] whereas for Marx, who turned Hegel's "idealism" upside down, it was labor, the human form of metabolism with nature, that fulfilled this function. One may argue that all notions of man-creating-himself have in common a rebellion against the human condition

---

11 It is quite suggestive that Hegel speaks in this context of "*Sichselbstproduzieren.*" See *Vorlesungen über die Geschichte der Philosophie*, edited by Hoffmeister, p. 114.

itself—nothing is more obvious than that man, be it as a member of the species or as an individual, does *not* owe his existence to himself—and that therefore what Sartre, Marx, and Hegel have in common is more relevant than the specific activities through which this nonfact should have come about. Still, it is hardly deniable that a gulf separates the essentially peaceful activities of thinking or laboring and deeds of violence. "To shoot down a European is to kill two birds with one stone... there remains a dead man and a free man," writes Sartre in his preface. This is a sentence Marx could never have written.

I quote Sartre in order to show that this new shift toward violence in the thinking of revolutionaries can remain unnoticed even by one of their most representative and articulate spokesmen.[12] If one turns the "idealistic" *concept* of thought upside down one might arrive at the "materialistic" *concept* of labor; one will never arrive at the notion of violence. No doubt, this development has a logic of its own, but it is logic that springs from experience and not from a development of ideas; and this experience was utterly unknown to any generation before.

THE PATHOS AND THE *ELAN* of the New Left, their credibility as it were, are closely connected with the weird suicidal development of modern weapons; this is the first generation that grew up under the shadow of the atom

---

12 The New Left's unconscious drifting away from Marxism has been duly noticed. See especially recent comments on the student movement by Leonard Schapiro in *The New York Review* (December 5, 1968) and *La Révolution introuvable* by Raymond Aron (Paris, 1968). Both consider the new emphasis on violence as a kind of backsliding either to Marxian utopian socialism (Aron) or to the Russian anarchism of Nechaev and Bakunin (Schapiro), who "had much to say about the importance of violence as a factor of unity, as the binding force in a society or group, a century before the same ideas emerged in the works of Jean-Paul Sartre and Frantz Fanon." Aron writes in the same vein: "*Les chantres de la révolution de mai croient dépasser le marxisme;... ils oublient un siècle d'histoire*" (p. 14). To a non-Marxist such a reversion would of course hardly be an argument; but for Sartre, who for instance writes, "revisionism is reversion to pre-Marxism and *therefore* untenable" (my italics), it must constitute a formidable objection.

Sartre himself, in his *Critique of Dialectical Reason*, gives a kind of Hegelian explanation for his espousal of violence. His point of departure is that "need and scarcity determined the Manicheistic basis of action and morals" in present history, "whose truth is based on scarcity [and] must manifest itself in an antagonistic reciprocity between classes." Under such circumstances, violence is no longer a marginal phenomenon. "Violence and counterviolence are perhaps contingencies, but they are contingent necessities, and the imperative consequence of any attempt to destroy this inhumanity is that in destroying in the

bomb, and it inherited from the generation of its fathers the experience of a massive intrusion of criminal violence into politics—they learned in high school and in college about concentration and extermination camps, about genocide and torture, about the wholesale slaughter of civilians in war, without which modern military operations are no longer possible even if they remain restricted to "conventional" weapons.

The first reaction was a revulsion against violence in all its forms, an almost matter-of-course espousal of a politics of nonviolence. The successes of this movement, especially with respect to civil rights, were very great, and they were followed by the resistance movement against the war in Vietnam which again determined to a considerable degree the climate of opinion in this country. But it is no secret that things have changed since then, and it would be futile to say that only "extremists" are yielding to a glorification of violence, and believe, with Fanon, that "only violence pays."[13]

The new militants have been denounced as anarchists, red fascists, and, with considerably more justification, "Luddite machine smashers."[14] Their

adversary the inhumanity of the contra-man, I can only destroy in him the humanity of man, and realize in me his inhumanity. Whether I kill, torture, enslave . . . my aim is to suppress his freedom—it is an alien force, *de trop*." His model for a condition in which "each one is one too many. . . . Each is *redundant* for the other," are the members of a bus queue who obviously "take no notice of each other except as a number in a quantitative series." He concludes, "They reciprocally deny any link between each of their inner worlds." From this, it follows that praxis "is the negation of alterity, which is itself a negation"—a highly welcome conclusion since the negation of a negation is an affirmation.

The flaw in the argument seems to me obvious. There is all the difference in the world between "not taking notice" and "denying," between "denying any link" with somebody and "negating" his otherness; and there is still a considerable distance to travel from this theoretical "negation" until any sane person will arrive at killing, torturing, and enslaving.

All the above quotations are drawn from R.D. Laing and D.G. Cooper, *Reason and Violence: A Decade of Sartre's Philosophy, 1950–1960* (London, 1964), Part III. This seems fair since Sartre in his foreword to the book says: "*J'ai lu attentivement l'ouvrage que vous avez bien voulu me confier et j'ai eu le grand plaisir d'y trouver un exposé très clair et très fidèle de ma pensée.*"

13 Page 61. I am using Frantz Fanon's *The Wretched of the Earth* (1961) because of its great influence on the present student generation. Fanon himself, however, is much more doubtful about violence than his admirers. It seems that only the first chapter of the book, "Concerning Violence," has been widely read. Fanon knows of the "unmixed and total brutality [which], if not immediately combated, invariably leads to the defeat of the movement within a few weeks." Grove Press edition, 1968, p. 147.

14 Nathan Glazer, in an article on "Student Power at Berkeley" in *The Public Interest* (Special Issue, *The Universities*, Fall 1968) writes: "The student

behavior has been blamed on all kinds of social and psychological causes, some of which we shall have to discuss later. Still, it seems absurd, especially in view of the global character of the phenomenon, to ignore the most obvious and perhaps the most potent factor in this development, for which moreover no precedent and no analogy exist—the fact that, in general, technological progress seems in so many instances to lead straight to disaster, and, in particular, the proliferation of techniques and machines which, far from only threatening certain classes with unemployment, menaces the very existence of whole nations and, conceivably, of all mankind. It is only natural that the new generation should live with greater awareness of the possibility of doomsday than those "over thirty," not because they are younger but because this was their first decisive experience in the world. If you ask a member of this generation two simple questions: "How do you wish the world to be in fifty years?" and "What do you want your life to be like five years from now?" the answers are quite often preceded by a "Provided that there is still a world," and "Provided I am still alive."

TO BE SURE, the recent emphasis on violence is still mostly a matter of theory and rhetoric, but it is precisely this rhetoric, shot through with all kinds of Marxist leftovers, that is so baffling. Who could possibly call an ideology Marxist that has put its faith, to quote Fanon, in "the classless idlers," believes that "in the lumpenproletariat the rebellion will find its urban spearhead," and trusts that the "gangsters light the way for the people"?[15] Sartre in his great felicity with words has given expression to the new faith. "Violence," he now believes, on the strength of Fanon's book, "like Achilles' lance, can heal the wounds that it has inflicted." If this were true, revenge

---

radicals...remind me more of the Luddite machine smashers than the Socialist trade unionists who achieved citizenship and power for workers," and he concludes from this impression that Zbigniew Brzezinski (in an article about Columbia in *The New Republic*, June 1, 1968) may have been right in his diagnosis: "Very frequently revolutions are the last spasms of the past, and thus are not really revolutions but counterrevolutions, operating in the name of revolutions." Isn't this bias in favor of marching forward at any price rather odd in two authors who are generally considered to be conservatives? And isn't it even more odd that Glazer should remain unaware of the decisive differences between manufacturing machinery in early nineteenth-century England and the hardware developed in the middle of the twentieth century, much of which is for destruction and not for production and can't even be smashed by the rebels for the simple reason that they know neither where it is located nor how to smash it?

[15] Fanon, *The Wretched of the Earth*, pp. 130, 129, and 69, respectively.

would be the cure-all for most of our ills. This myth is more abstract, further removed from reality than Sorel's myth of a general strike ever was. It is on a par with Fanon's worst rhetorical excesses, such as, "Hunger with dignity is preferable to bread eaten in slavery." No history and no theory are needed to refute this statement; the most superficial observer of the processes in the human body knows its untruth. But had he said that bread eaten with dignity is preferable to cake eaten in slavery, the rhetorical point would have been lost.

If one reads these irresponsible and grandiose statements of these intellectuals—and those I quoted are fairly representative, except that Fanon still manages to stay closer to reality than most of them—and if one looks at them in the perspective of what we know about the history of rebellions and revolutions, it is tempting to deny their significance, to ascribe them to a passing mood, or to the ignorance and nobility of sentiment of those who are exposed to unprecedented events without any means to handle them mentally, and who therefore have revived thoughts and emotions which Marx had hoped to have buried forever. For it is certainly nothing new that those who are being violated dream of violence, that those who are oppressed "dream at least once a day of setting" themselves up in the oppressor's place, that those who are poor dream of the possessions of the rich, that the persecuted dream of exchanging "the role of the quarry for that of the hunter," and the last of the kingdom where "the last shall be first, and the first last."[16]

The great rarity of slave-rebellions and of uprisings among the disinherited and downtrodden is notorious; on the rare occasions when they occurred it was precisely "mad fury" that turned dreams into nightmares for everybody, and in no case, so far as I know, was the force of mere "volcanic" outbursts, as Sartre states, "equal to that of the pressure put on" the oppressed. To believe that we deal with such outbursts in the National Liberation movements, and nothing more, is to prophesy their doom—quite apart from the fact that the unlikely victory would not result in the change of the world (or the system) but only of its personnel. To think, finally, that there is such a thing as the "Unity of the Third World" to which one could address the new slogan in the era of decolonization, "Natives of all underdeveloped countries unite!" (Sartre) is to repeat Marx's worst illusions on a greatly enlarged scale and with considerably less justification.

16 Fanon, *The Wretched of the Earth*, pp. 37ff. and 53.

THERE STILL REMAINS THE QUESTION why so many of these new preachers of violence have remained unaware of their decisive disagreement with the teachings of Karl Marx, or, to put it another way, why they cling with such stubborn tenacity to concepts which are not only refuted by actual events but are clearly inconsistent with their own politics. For although the one positive political slogan the new movement has put forth, the claim for "participatory democracy," which has echoed around the globe and which constitutes the most significant common denominator of the rebellions in the East and the West, derives from the best in the revolutionary tradition—the council system, the always defeated but only authentic outgrowth of all revolutions since the eighteenth century—it cannot be found in nor does it agree, either in word or in substance, with the teachings of Marx and Lenin, both of whom aimed at a society in which the need for public action and participation in public affairs would have "withered away," along with the state itself.

(It is true that a similar inconsistency could be charged to Marx and Lenin themselves. Didn't Marx support and glorify the Paris Commune of 1871, and didn't Lenin issue the famous slogan of the Russian Revolution, "All power to the *soviets*"? But Marx thought of the Commune not as a new form of government but as a necessarily transitory organ of revolutionary action, "the political form at last discovered under which to work out the economic emancipation of labor," a form which, according to Engels, was identical with "the dictatorship of the Proletariat." The case of Lenin is more complicated. Still, it was Lenin who emasculated the *soviets* and finally gave all power to the Party.)

Because of its curious timidity in theoretical matters, which contrasts oddly with its bold courage in practice, the slogan of the New Left has remained in a declamatory stage, to be invoked like a charm against both Western representative democracy, which is about to lose even its merely representative function to the huge party machines that "represent" not the party membership but its functionaries, and the Eastern one-party bureaucracies, which rule out participation on principle. I am not sure what the explanation of these inconsistencies will eventually turn out to be; but I suspect that the deeper reason for this loyalty to a typical nineteenth-century doctrine has something to do with the concept of Progress, with the unwillingness to part with this notion that has always united liberalism, socialism, and communism, but has nowhere reached the level of plausibility and sophistication we find in the writings of Karl Marx. (For inconsistency has always been the Achilles' heel of liberal thought; it combined an unswerving loyalty to Progress with a no less strict refusal to look upon History in Marxian and Hegelian terms, which alone could justify this belief.)

THE NOTION THAT there is such a thing as Progress for mankind as a whole, that it is the law which rules all processes in the human species, was unknown prior to the eighteenth century and became an almost universally accepted dogma in the nineteenth. The same idea both informed Darwin's biological discoveries, whereby mankind owed its very existence to an irrepressible forward movement of Nature, and gave rise to the new philosophies of History, which, since Hegel, have understood progress expressly in terms of organic development. Marx's idea, borrowed from Hegel, that every old society harbors the seeds of its successors as every living organism harbors the seeds of its offspring is indeed not only the most ingenious but the only possible conceptual guarantee for the sempiternal continuity of Progress in History.

To be sure, a guarantee which in the final analysis rests on not much more than a metaphor is not the most solid basis to erect a doctrine upon, but this, unhappily, Marxism shares with a great many other doctrines in philosophy. Its great advantage becomes clear as soon as one compares it with other concepts of History—such as the rise and fall of empires, the eternal recurrence of the same, the haphazard sequence of essentially unconnected events—all of which can just as well be documented and justified, but none of which will guarantee a continuum of linear time and hence a continuous progress in history. And the only competitor in the field, the ancient notion of a Golden Age at the beginning, from which everything else is derived, implies the rather unpleasant certainty of continuous decline.

There are, however, a few melancholy side effects in the reassuring idea that we need only march into the future, which we can't help doing anyhow, in order to find a better world. There is, first of all, the simple fact that this general future of mankind has nothing to offer the individual life, whose only certain future is death. And if one leaves this out of account and thinks only in generalities, there is the obvious argument against progress that, in the words of Herzen, "Human development is a form of chronological unfairness, since latecomers are able to profit by the labors of their predecessors without paying the same price,"[17] or, in

---

[17] Alexander Herzen is quoted here from Isaiah Berlin's introduction to Franco Venturi, *Roots of Revolution* (Grosset and Dunlap, 1966).

the words of Kant, "It will always remain bewildering...that the earlier generations seem to carry on their burdensome business only for the sake of the later...and that only the last should have the good fortune to dwell in the [completed] building."[18]

However, these disadvantages, which were only rarely noticed, are more than outweighed by the enormous advantage that Progress not only explains the past without breaking up the time continuum, but can also serve as a guide for action into the future. This is what Marx discovered when he turned Hegel upside down: he changed the direction of the historian's glance; instead of looking toward the past, he now could confidently look into the future. Progress gives an answer to the troublesome question: And what shall we do now? The answer, on the lowest level, says: Let us develop what we have into something better, greater, etc. (The liberals' at first glance irrational faith in growth, so characteristic of all our present political and economic theories, depends on this notion.) On the more sophisticated level of the Left, it tells us to develop present contradictions into their inherent synthesis. In either case we are assured that nothing altogether new and unexpected can happen, nothing but the "necessary" results of what we already know.[19] How reassuring that, in Hegel's words, "nothing else will come out but what was already there."[20]

I don't need to add that all our experiences in this century, which has constantly confronted us with the totally unexpected, stand in flagrant contradiction to these notions and doctrines, whose very popularity seems to consist in offering a comfortable, speculative or pseudo-scientific, refuge from reality. But since we are concerned here primarily with violence I must warn against a tempting misunderstanding. If we look upon history as a continuous chronological process, violence in the shape of war and revolution may appear to constitute the only possible interruptions of such processes. If this were true, if only the practice of violence would make it possible to interrupt automatic processes in the realm of human affairs, the preachers of violent actions would have won an important point, although, so far as I know, they never made it. However, it is the function of all action, as distinguished from mere behavior, to interrupt what otherwise

---

[18] Kant, "Idea for a Universal History with Cosmopolitan Intent," Third Principle.

[19] For an excellent discussion of the obvious fallacies in this position, see Robert A. Nisbet, "The Year 2000 and All That," in *Commentary*, June 1968, and the ill-tempered critical remarks in the September issue.

[20] Hegel, *Vorlesungen über die Geschichte der Philosophie*, pp. 100ff.

would have proceeded automatically and therefore predictably. And the distinction between violent and nonviolent action is that the former is exclusively bent upon the destruction of the old and the latter chiefly concerned with the establishment of something new.

II

IT IS AGAINST the background of these experiences that I propose to raise the question of violence in the political realm. This is not easy; for Sorel's remark sixty years ago, that "The problems of violence still remain very obscure,"[21] is as true today as it was then. I mentioned the general reluctance to deal with violence as a separate phenomenon in its own right, and I must now qualify this statement. If we turn to the literature on the phenomenon of power, we soon find out that there exists an agreement among political theorists from Left to Right that violence is nothing more than the most flagrant manifestation of power. "All politics is a struggle for power; the ultimate kind of power is violence," said C. Wright Mills, echoing, as it were, Max Weber's definition of the state as the "rule of men over men, based on the means of legitimate, i.e. allegedly legitimate, violence."[22]

The agreement is very strange; for to equate political power with "the organization of violence" makes sense only if one follows Marx's estimate of the state as an instrument of suppression in the hands of the ruling class. Let us therefore turn to authors who do not believe that the body politic, its laws and institutions, are merely coercive superstructures, secondary manifestations of some underlying forces. Let us turn, for instance, to Bertrand de Jouvenel, whose book *Power* is perhaps the most prestigious and, anyway, the most interesting recent treatise on the subject. "To him," he writes, "who contemplates the unfolding of the ages war presents itself as an activity of States *which pertains to their essence.*"[23] But would the end of warfare, we are likely to ask, mean the end of States? Would the disappearance of violence in the relationships between States spell the end of power?

The answer, it seems, would depend on what we understand by power. De Jouvenel defines power as an instrument of rule, while rule, we are told,

---

[21] Georges Sorel, *Reflections on Violence*, "Introduction to the First Publication" (1906) (Collier Books, 1961) p. 60.

[22] C. Wright Mills, *The Power Elite* (Oxford University Press, 1956), p. 171. Max Weber, in the first paragraph of *Politics as a Vocation* (1921). Weber seems to have been aware of his agreement with the Left. He quotes in this context Trotsky's remark in Brest-Litovsk, "Every state is based on violence" and he adds, "This is indeed true."

[23] Bertrand de Jouvenel, *Power: The Natural History of its Growth* (1945, 1952), p. 122.

owes its existence to "the instinct of domination."[24] As he writes, "To command and to be obeyed: without that, there is no Power—with it no other attribute is needed for it to be.... The thing without which it cannot be: that essence is command." If the essence of power is the effectiveness of command, then there is no greater power than that which grows out of the barrel of a gun. Bertrand de Jouvenel and Mao Tse-tung thus seem to agree on so basic a point in political philosophy as the nature of power.

THESE DEFINITIONS COINCIDE with the terms which, since Greek antiquity, have been used to define the forms of government as the rule of man over man—of one or the few in monarchy and oligarchy, of the best or the many in aristocracy and democracy, to which today we ought to add the latest and perhaps most formidable form of such dominion, bureaucracy, or the rule by an intricate system of bureaux in which no men, neither one nor the best, neither the few nor the many, can be held responsible, and which could be properly called the rule by Nobody. Indeed, if we identify tyranny as the government that is not held to give account of itself, rule by Nobody is clearly the most tyrannical of all, since there is no one left who could even be asked to answer for what is being done. It is this state of affairs which is among the most potent causes for the current worldwide rebellious unrest.

Moreover, the force of this ancient vocabulary has been considerably strengthened by more modern scientific and philosophical convictions concerning the nature of man. The many recent discoveries of an inborn instinct of domination and an innate aggressiveness in the human animal were preceded by very similar philosophic statements. According to John Stuart Mill "the first lesson of civilization [is] that of obedience," and he speaks of "the two states of the inclinations ... one the desire to exercise power over others; the other ... disinclination to have power exercised over themselves."[25] If we would trust our own experiences in these matters, we should know that the instinct of submission, an ardent desire to obey and be ruled by some strong man, is at least as prominent in human psychology as the will-to-power, and politically perhaps more relevant.

A German saying that whoever wants to command must first learn how to obey points to the psychological truth in these matters, namely, that the will-to-power and the will-to-submission are interconnected; conversely, a strong disinclination to obey is usually accompanied by an equally strong

24 *Power*, p. 93.
25 John Stuart Mill, *Considerations on Representative Government* (1861).

repugnance to dominate and command. It is indeed bitter to obey, but from this it does not follow that to rule others is a pleasure. Historically speaking, the ancient institution of slave economy would be inexplicable on these grounds. For its express purpose was to liberate the citizens from the burden of household affairs and to permit them to enter the public life of the community where all were equals; if it were true that nothing is sweeter than to give commands and to rule others, the master would never have left his household.

HOWEVER, THERE EXISTS another tradition and another vocabulary no less old and time-honored than the one mentioned above. When the Athenian city-state called its constitution an isonomy or the Romans spoke of the *civitas* as their form of government, they had in mind another concept of power, which did not rely upon the command-obedience relationship. It is to these examples that the men of the eighteenth-century revolutions turned when they ransacked the archives of antiquity and constituted a republic, a form of government, where the rule of law, resting on the power of the people, would put an end to the rule of man over man, which they thought was "a government fit for slaves." They too, unhappily, still talked about obedience—obedience to laws instead of men; but what they actually meant was the support of the laws to which the citizenry had given its consent.[26]

Such support is never unquestioning, and as far as reliability is concerned it cannot match the indeed "unquestioning obedience" that an act of violence can exact—the obedience every criminal can count on when he snatches my pocketbook with the help of a knife or robs a bank with the help of a gun. It is the support of the people that lends power to the institutions of a country, and this support is but the continuation of the consent which brought the laws into existence to begin with. (Under conditions of representative government the people are supposed to rule those who govern them.) All political institutions are manifestations and materializations of power; they petrify and decay as soon as the living power of

---

[26] The sanctions of the laws, which, however, are not their essence, are directed against those citizens who—without withholding their support—wish to make an exception from the law for themselves; the thief still expects the government to protect his newly acquired property. It has been noted that in the earliest systems of law there were no sanctions whatsoever. (See de Jouvenel, *Power*, p. 276.) The punishment of the lawbreaker was banishment or outlawry; by breaking the law, the criminal had put himself outside the community constituted by it.

the people ceases to uphold them. This is what Madison meant when he said, "all governments rest on opinion," a statement that is no less true for the various forms of monarchies than it is for democracies. The strength of opinion, that is, the power of the government, is "in proportion to the number with which it is associated"[27] (and tyranny, as Montesquieu discovered, is therefore the most violent and the least powerful among the forms of government).

Indeed, it is one of the most obvious distinctions between power and violence that power always stands in need of numbers, whereas violence relying on instruments up to a point can manage without them. A legally unrestricted majority rule, that is, a democracy without a constitution, can be very formidable indeed in the suppression of the rights of minorities and very effective in the suffocation of dissent without any use of violence. Undivided and unchecked power can bring about a "consensus" that is hardly less coercive than suppression by means of violence. But that does not mean that violence and power are the same.

It is, I think, a rather sad reflection on the present state of political science that our language does not distinguish between such key terms as power, strength, force, might, authority, and, finally, violence—all of which refer to distinct phenomena. To use them as synonyms not only indicates a certain deafness to linguistic meanings, which would be serious enough, but has resulted in a kind of blindness with respect to the realities they correspond to. Behind the apparent confusion lies a firm conviction that the most crucial political issue is, and always has been, the question of Who rules Whom? Only after one eliminates this disastrous reduction of public affairs to the business of dominion will the original data concerning human affairs appear or rather reappear in their authentic diversity.

It must be admitted that it is particularly tempting to think of power as a matter of command and obedience, and hence to equate power with violence, when discussing what is only one of power's special provinces, namely, the power of government. Since in foreign relations as well as in domestic affairs violence is used as a last resort to keep the power structure intact against individual challengers—the foreign enemy, the native criminal—it looks indeed as though power, relying on violence, were the velvet glove which may or may not conceal an iron hand. However, upon closer inspection the assumption loses much of its plausibility. For our purpose, it is perhaps best illustrated by the phenomenon of revolution.

[27] *The Federalist*, No. 49.

III

SINCE THE BEGINNING of the century, theoreticians have told us that the chances of revolution have significantly decreased in proportion to the increased destructive capacities of weapons at the unique disposition of governments. The history of the last seventy years, with its extraordinary record of successful and unsuccessful revolutions, tells a different story. Were people mad who even tried against such overwhelming odds? How can an even temporary success be explained? The fact is that the gap between state-owned means of violence and what people can muster by themselves—from beer bottles to Molotov cocktails and guns—has always been so enormous that technical improvements make hardly any difference. Textbook recommendations of "how to make a revolution" in an orderly progress from dissent to conspiracy, from resistance to armed uprising, are all based on the mistaken notion that revolutions are being "made." In a contest of violence against violence the superiority of the government has always been absolute; but this superiority lasts only so long as the power structure of the government is intact—that is, so long as commands are obeyed and the army or police forces are prepared to risk their lives and use their weapons.

When this is no longer the case the situation changes abruptly. Not only is the rebellion not put down, the arms themselves change hands—sometimes, as in the Hungarian Revolution, within a few hours. (We should understand this after years of futile fighting in Vietnam where, prior to the full-scale Russian aid, the National Liberation Front for a long time fought us with weapons that were made in the United States.) Only after the disintegration of the government in power has permitted the rebels to arm themselves can one speak of an "armed uprising," which often does not take place at all or occurs when it is no longer necessary. Where commands are no longer obeyed, the means of violence are of no use. Hence obedience is not determined by commands but by opinion, and, of course, by the number of those who share it. Everything depends upon the power behind the violence. The sudden dramatic breakdown of power, which ushers in revolutions, reveals in a flash how civil obedience—to the laws, to the rulers, to the institutions—is but the outward manifestation of support and consent.

WHERE POWER HAS DISINTEGRATED revolutions are possible but not necessary. We know of many instances when utterly impotent regimes were permitted to continue in existence for long periods of time—either because there was no one to test their strength and to reveal their weakness or because they were lucky enough not to be engaged in war and suffer defeat. For disintegration often becomes manifest only in direct confrontation; and even then, when power is already in the street, some group of men, prepared for such an eventuality, is needed to pick it up and assume responsibility.

We have recently witnessed how the relatively harmless, essentially non-violent French students' rebellion was sufficient to reveal the vulnerability of the whole political system, which rapidly disintegrated before the astonished eyes of the young rebels. Without knowing it they had tested the system; they intended no more than to challenge the ossified university system, and down came the system of governmental power together with that of the huge party bureaucracies *"une sorte de désintégration de toutes les hiérarchies."*[28] It was a textbook case of a revolutionary situation which did not develop into a revolution because there was nobody, least of all the students, who was prepared to seize power and the responsibility that goes with it.

Nobody except, of course, De Gaulle. Nothing was more characteristic of the seriousness of the situation than his appeal to the army, his ride to see Massu and the generals in the dark of the night, a walk to Canossa if there ever was one in view of what had happened only a few years before. But what he sought and received was support, not obedience, and the means to obtain it were not commands but concessions.[29] If commands had been enough he would never have had to leave Paris.

No government exclusively based upon the means of violence has ever existed. Even the totalitarian ruler needs a power basis, the secret police and its net of informers. Only the development of robot soldiers, which would eliminate the human factor completely and, conceivably, permit one man

---

28 Raymond Aron, *La Révolution introuvable*, p. 41.

29 The price De Gaulle had to pay for the army's support was public rehabilitation of his enemies—amnesty for General Salan, return of Bidault, return also of Colonel Lacheroy, sometimes called "the torturer in Algeria." Not much seems to be known about the negotiations. One is tempted to think that the recent rehabilitation of Pétain, again glorified as the "victor of Verdun" and, more importantly, the incredible, blatant lying statement immediately after, which blamed the Communist Party for what the French now call *les événements*, were part of the bargain. God knows, the only reproach the government could have addressed to the Communist Party and the trade-unions was that they lacked the power to prevent *les événements*.

with a push button at his disposal to destroy whomever he pleases could change this fundamental ascendancy of power over violence. Even the most despotic domination we know of, the rule of master over slaves, who always outnumbered him, did not rest upon superior means of coercion as such but upon a superior organization of power, that is, upon the organized solidarity of the masters.[30]

Single men without others to support them never have enough power to use violence. Hence, in domestic affairs, violence functions indeed as the last resort of power against criminals or rebels—that is, against individuals who, as it were, refuse to be overpowered by the consensus of the majority. And even in actual warfare, we have seen in Vietnam how an enormous superiority in the means of violence can become helpless if confronted with an ill-equipped but well organized opponent who is much more powerful. This lesson, to be sure, could have been learned since the beginnings of guerrilla warfare, which is at least as old as the defeat of Napoleon's still unvanquished army in Spain.

TO SWITCH FOR A MOMENT to conceptual language: Power is indeed of the essence of all government, but violence is not. Violence is by nature instrumental; like all means, it always stands in need of guidance and justification through the end it pursues. And what needs justification through something else cannot be the essence of anything. The end of war is peace; but to the question, And what is the end of peace?, there is no answer. Peace is an absolute, even though in recorded history the periods of warfare have nearly always outlasted the periods of peace. Power is in the same category; it is, as the saying goes, "an end in itself." (This, of course, is not to deny that governments pursue policies and employ their power to achieve prescribed goals. But the power structure itself precedes and outlasts all aims, so that power, far from being the means to an end, is actually the very condition that enables a group of people to think and act according to means and ends.) And since government is essentially organized and institutionalized power, the current question, What is the end of government?, does not make much sense either. The answer will be either question-begging—to enable men to live together—or dangerously utopian: to promote happiness or to realize a classless society or some other nonpolitical

---

[30] In ancient Greece, such an organization of power was the polis whose chief merit, according to Xenophon, was that it permitted the "citizens to act as bodyguards to one another against slaves." *Hiero*, IV, 3.

ideal, which if tried out in earnest can only end in the worst kind of government, that is, tyranny.

Power needs no justification as it is inherent in the very existence of political communities; what, however, it does need is legitimacy. The common usage of these two words as synonyms is no less misleading and confusing than the current equation of obedience and support. Power springs up whenever people get together and act in concert, but it derives its legitimacy from the initial getting together rather than from any action that then may follow. Violence needs justification and it can be justifiable, but its justification loses in plausibility the farther away its intended end recedes into the future. No one will question the use of violence in self-defense because the danger is not only clear but present, and the end to justify the means is immediate.

IV

POWER AND VIOLENCE, though they are distinct phenomena, usually appear together. Up to now, we have discussed such combinations and found that, wherever they are so combined, power is the primary and predominant factor. The situation, however, is entirely different when we deal with them in their pure states—as for instance in cases of foreign invasion and occupation. The difficulties of achieving such domination are very great indeed, and the occupying invader will try immediately to establish Quisling governments, that is to find a native power base with which to support his dominion. The head-on clash between Russian tanks and the entirely nonviolent resistance of the people in Czechoslovakia is a textbook case of a confrontation of violence and power in their pure states.

But while this kind of domination is difficult, it is not impossible. Violence, we must remember, does not depend on numbers or opinion but on implements, and the implements of violence share with all other tools that they increase and multiply human strength. Those who oppose violence with mere power will soon find out that they are confronted not with men but with men's artifacts, whose inhumanity and destructive effectiveness increase in proportion to the distance that separates the opponents. Violence can always destroy power; out of the barrel of a gun grows the most effective command, resulting in the most instant and perfect obedience. What can never grow out of it is power.

In a head-on clash between violence and power the outcome is hardly in doubt. If Gandhi's enormously powerful and successful strategy of nonviolent resistance had met with a different enemy—Stalin's Russia, Hitler's Germany, even prewar Japan, instead of England—the outcome would not have been decolonization but massacre and submission. However, England in India or France in Algeria had good reasons for their restraint. Rule by sheer violence comes into play where power is being lost; it is precisely the shrinking power of the Russian government, internally and externally, that became manifest in its "solution" of the Czechoslovak problem—just as it was the shrinking power of European imperialism that became manifest in the alternative of decolonization or massacre.

TO SUBSTITUTE VIOLENCE for power can bring victory, but its price is very high; for it is not only paid by the vanquished, it is paid by the victor in his own power. The much-feared boomerang effect of the "government of sub-ject races" (Lord Cromer) upon the home government during the imperial-ist era meant that rule by violence in far-away lands would end by affecting the government of England, that the last "subject race" would be the Eng-lish themselves. It has often been said that impotence breeds violence, and psychologically this is quite true. Politically, loss of power tempts men to substitute violence for power—we could watch this process on television during the Democratic Convention in Chicago[31]—and violence itself results in impotence.

Nowhere is the self-defeating factor in the victory of violence over power more evident than in the use of terror for purposes of maintaining domination, about whose weird successes and eventual failures we know perhaps more than any generation before us. Terror is not the same as vio-lence; it is rather the form of government that comes into being when vio-lence, having destroyed all power, does not abdicate but, on the contrary, remains in full control. It has often been noticed that the effectiveness of terror depends almost entirely on the degree of social atomization, the dis-appearance of every kind of organized opposition, which must be achieved before the full force of terror can be let loose. This atomization—an outra-geously pale, academic word for the horror it implies—results finally in a total loss of power.

The decisive difference between totalitarian domination, based on ter-ror, and tyrannies and dictatorships, established by violence, is that only the former turns not only against its enemies but against its friends and supporters as well, being afraid of all power, even the power of its friends. The climax of terror is reached when the police state begins to devour its own children, when yesterday's executioner becomes today's victim. And this is also the moment when power disappears entirely. There exist now a

---

[31] It would be interesting to know if, and to what extent, the alarming rate of unsolved crimes is matched not only by the well-known spectacular rise in crim-inal offenses but also by a definite increase in police brutality. The recently pub-lished *Uniform Crime Report for the United States* (Federal Bureau of Investiga-tion, US Department of Justice, 1967) gives no indication how many crimes are actually solved—as distinguished from "cleared by arrest"—but does mention in the summary that police solutions of serious crimes declined in 1967 by 8 per-cent. Only 21.7 percent (or 21.9 percent) of all crimes are "cleared by arrest," and of these only 75 percent could be turned over to the courts and only about 60 percent of those were found guilty! Hence, the odds in favor of the criminal are so high that the constant rise in criminal offenses seems only natural. What-ever the causes for the spectacular decline of police efficiency, the decline of police power is evident and with it the likelihood of increased brutality.

great many plausible reasons to explain the de-Stalinization of Russia—none, I believe, so compelling as the realization by the Stalinist functionaries themselves that a continuation of the regime would lead, not to an insurrection, against which terror is indeed the best safeguard, but to a paralysis of the whole country.[32]

To sum up: politically speaking, it is not enough to say that power and violence are not the same. Power and violence are opposites; where the one rules absolutely, the other is absent. Violence appears where power is in jeopardy, but left to its own course its end is the disappearance of power. This implies that it is not correct to say that the opposite of violence is nonviolence: to speak of nonviolent power is actually redundant. Violence can destroy power; it is utterly incapable of creating it. Hegel's and Marx's great trust in the dialectical "power of negation," by virtue of which opposites do not destroy but smoothly develop into each other because contradictions promote and do not paralyze development, rests on a much older philosophical prejudice, the prejudice that evil is no more than a privative modus of the good, that good can come out of evil, that, in short, evil is but the temporary manifestation of a still hidden good. Such time-honored opinions have become dangerous. They are shared by many who have never heard of the names Hegel or Marx, for the simple reason that they inspire hope and dispel fear—a treacherous hope used to dispel legitimate fears. By this, I don't mean to equate violence with evil; I only want to stress that violence can't be derived from its opposite, which is power, and that in order to understand it for what it is, we shall have to examine its roots and causes.

---

[32] Solzhenitsyn, in *The First Circle*, shows in detail how attempts at rational economic development were wrecked by Stalin's methods, and one hopes that this book will put to rest the myth that terror and the enormous loss in human lives were the price that had to be paid for rapid industrialization of the country. Rapid progress was made after Stalin's death, and what is striking in Russia today is that the country is still backward not only in comparison with the West but with most of the satellite countries. In Russia itself, there seems to be not much illusion left on this point, if there ever was any. The younger generation, especially the veterans of the Second World War, knows very well that only a miracle saved Russia from defeat in 1941, and that this miracle was the brutal fact that the enemy turned out to be even worse than the native ruler. What then turned the scales was that police terror abated under the pressure of the national emergency; the people, left to themselves, could again gather together and generate enough power to defeat the foreign invader. When they returned from prisoner-of-war camps or from occupation duty they were promptly sent to long years in labor and concentration camps in order to break them from the habits of freedom. It is precisely this generation that tasted freedom during the war and the terror afterward that is challenging the tyranny of the present regime.

V

THAT VIOLENCE OFTEN SPRINGS from rage is a commonplace, and rage can indeed be irrational and pathological, but so can every other human affect. It is no doubt possible to create conditions under which men are dehuman-ized—such as concentration camps, torture, famine, etc.—but this does not mean that they become animal-like; and, under such conditions, not rage and violence but their conspicuous absence is the clearest sign of de-humanization. For rage is by no means an automatic reaction to misery and suffering as such; no one reacts with rage to a disease beyond the pow-ers of medicine or to an earthquake, or, for that matter, to social conditions which seem to be unchangeable. Only where there is reason to suspect that conditions could be changed and are not, does rage arise. Only when our sense of justice is offended do we react with rage.

To resort to violence in view of outrageous events or conditions is enor-mously tempting because of the immediacy and swiftness inherent in it. It goes against the grain of rage and violence to act with *deliberate* speed; but this does not make it irrational. On the contrary, in private as well as pub-lic life there are situations in which the very swiftness of a violent act may be the only appropriate remedy. The point is not that this will permit us to let off steam—which indeed can be equally well done by pounding the table or by finding another substitute. The point is that under certain cir-cumstances violence, which is to act without argument or speech and with-out reckoning with consequences, is the only possibility of setting the scales of justice right again. (Billy Budd striking dead the man who bore false witness against him is the classic example.) In this sense, rage and the violence that sometimes, not always, goes with it belong among the "nat-ural" human emotions, and to cure man of them would mean nothing less than to dehumanize or emasculate him.

RAGE AND VIOLENCE turn irrational only when they are directed against substitutes, and this, I am afraid, is precisely what not only the psychiatrist and polemologists, concerned with human aggressiveness, commend, but what corresponds, alas, to certain moods and unreflected attitudes in soci-ety at large. We all know, for example, that it has become rather fashionable among white liberals to react against "black rage" with the cry, We are all guilty, and black militants have proved only too happy to accept this "confession" and to base on it some of their more fantastic demands.

Where all are guilty, however, no one is; confessions of collective guilt are always the best possible safeguard against the discovery of the actual culprits. In this particular instance, it is in addition a dangerous and obfuscating escalation of racism into some higher, less tangible regions: The real rift between black and white is not healed when it is being translated into an even less reconcilable conflict between collective innocence and collective guilt. It is racism in disguise and it serves quite effectively to give the very real grievances and rational emotions of the Negro population an outlet into irrationality, an escape from reality.

Moreover, if we inquire historically into the causes that are likely to transform the *engagés* into the *enragés*, it is not injustice that ranks first but hypocrisy. Its momentous role in the later stages of the French Revolution, when Robespierre's war upon hypocrisy transformed the "despotism of liberty" into the Reign of Terror, is too well known to be repeated here; but it is important to remember that this war had been declared long before by the French moralists, who saw in hypocrisy the vice of all vices and found it the one ruling supreme in "good society," which somewhat later was called bourgeois society.

There are not many authors of rank who glorified violence for violence's sake; but these few—Sorel, Pareto, Fanon—were motivated by a much deeper hatred for bourgeois society and were led to a much more radical break with its moral standards than the conventional Left, which was chiefly inspired by compassion and a burning desire for justice. To tear the mask of hypocrisy from the face of the enemy, to unmask him, his devious machinations and manipulations that permit him to rule without using violent means, that is, to provoke action even at the risk of annihilation so that the truth may come out—these are still among the strongest motives in today's violence on the campuses and in the streets. And this violence again is not irrational. Since men live in a world of appearances, hence depend upon manifestation, hypocrisy's conceits—as distinguished from temporary ruses, followed by disclosure in due time—cannot be met with what is recognized as reasonable behavior. Words can be relied upon only so long as one is sure that their function is to reveal and not to conceal. It is the semblance of rationality, rather than the interests behind it, that provokes rage. To respond with reason when reason is used as a trap is not "rational"; just as to use a gun in self-defense is not "irrational."

Although the effectiveness of violence, as I remarked before, does not depend on numbers—one machine-gunner can hold hundreds of well-organized people at bay—it is nonetheless the case that its most dangerously attractive features come to the fore in collective violence. It is perfectly true, as Fanon writes, that in military as well as revolutionary action "individualism is the first [value] to disappear"[33]; in its stead, we find a kind of group coherence which is more intensely felt and proves to be a much stronger, though less lasting, bond than all the varieties of friendship, civil or private:[34] "the practice of violence binds men together as a whole, since each individual forms a violent link in the great chain, a part of the great organism of violence which has surged upward."[35]

THESE WORDS OF FANON point to the well-known phenomenon of brotherhood on the battlefield, where often the noblest, most selfless deeds are daily occurrences. Of all equalizers, death seems to be the most potent one in the few extraordinary situations in which it is permitted to play a political role. The experience of death, whether the experience of dying or the inner awareness of one's own mortality, is perhaps the most antipolitical experience there is, in so far as it is usually faced in complete loneliness and impotence, signifying that we shall leave the company of our fellow men and with it that being-together and acting in concert which make life worthwhile.

But death faced collectively and in action changes its countenance; now it is as though nothing is more likely to intensify our vitality than its proximity. Something we are usually hardly aware of, that our own death is accompanied by the potential immortality of the group to which we belong and, in the final analysis, of the species, moves into the center of our experience, and the result is that it is as though Life itself, the immortal life of the species, nourished as it were by the sempiternal dying of its individual members, is "surging upward," is actualized in the practice of violence.

It would be wrong, I think, to speak here of mere emotions. What is important is that these experiences, whose elementary force is beyond doubt, have never found an institutional, political expression. No body

33 Fanon, *The Wretched of the Earth*, p. 47.
34 J. Glenn Gray, *The Warriors: Reflections on Men in Battle* (Harper Torchbook, 1969), is most perceptive and instructive on this point. It should be read by everyone interested in the practice of violence.
35 Fanon, *The Wretched of the Earth*, p. 93.

politic I know of was ever founded on the equality before death and its actualization in violence.[36] But it is undeniably true that the strong fraternal sentiments, engendered by collective violence, have misled many good people into the hope that a new community together with a "new man" will arise out of it. The hope is an illusion for the simple reason that no human relationship is more transitory than this kind of brotherhood, which can be actualized only under conditions of immediate danger to life.

This, however, is but one side of the matter. Fanon concludes his praising description of the experiences in the practice of violence by remarking that in this kind of struggle the people realize "that life is an unending contest," that violence is an element of life. Doesn't it follow that praise of life and praise of violence are the same? Sorel, at any rate, thought along these lines sixty years ago. The bourgeoisie, he argued, had lost the "energy" to play its role in the antagonism of classes; only if the proletariat could be persuaded to use violence in order to reaffirm class distinctions and awaken the fighting spirit of the bourgeoisie could Europe be saved.[37]

HENCE LONG BEFORE Konrad Lorenz discovered the life-promoting function of aggressiveness in the animal kingdom, violence was praised as a manifestation of the life force, and specifically of its creativity. Sorel, inspired by Bergson's *élan vital*, aimed at a philosophy of creativity designed for "producers" and polemically directed against the consumer society and its intellectuals; both groups, he felt, were parasites.

Fanon, who had an infinitely more intimate experience of the practice of violence than any of its other glorifiers, past or present, was greatly influenced by Sorel's equation of violence, life, and creativity, and we all know to what extent this old combination has survived in the rebellious state of

---

[36] It is also noteworthy that death as an equalizer plays hardly any role in political philosophy, although human mortality—the fact that men are "mortals," as the Greeks used to say—was understood as the strongest motive for political action in prephilosophic political thought. It was the certainty of death that made men seek immortal fame in deed and word and that prompted them to establish a body politic which was potentially immortal. Hence, politics was precisely a means to escape from equality before death into a distinction which would assure some measure of deathlessness. Hobbes is the only political philosopher in whose work death in the form of fear of violent death plays a crucial role. But it is not equality before death that is decisive for Hobbes, but equality of ability to kill and the resulting equality of fear that persuades men in the state of nature to bind themselves into a Commonwealth.

[37] Sorel, *Reflections on Violence*, Ch. 2, "On Violence and the Decadence of the Middle Classes."

mind of the new generation—their taste for violence again is accompanied by a glorification of life, and it frequently understands itself as the necessarily violent negation of everything that stands in the way of the will-to-live. And this seemingly so novel biological justification of violence is again not unconnected with the most pernicious elements in our oldest tradition of political thought. According to the traditional concept of power, which, as we saw, was equated with violence, power was expansionist by nature, it has, as de Jouvenel has argued, "an inner urge to grow," it was creative because "the instinct of growth is proper to it."[38]

Just as in the realm of organic life everything either grows or declines and dies, so in the realm of human affairs power supposedly can sustain itself only through expansion; otherwise it shrinks and dies. "That which stops growing begins to rot," said a Russian in the entourage of Catherine the Great, "The people erect scaffolds, not as the moral punishment of despotism, but as the *biological* penalty for weakness" (my italics). Revolutions, therefore, we are told, were directed against the established powers "only to the outward view." Their true "effect was to give Power a new vigor and poise, and to pull down the obstacles which had long obstructed its development."[39] When Fanon is speaking of the "creative madness" present in violent action, he is still thinking along the lines of this tradition.[40]

Nothing, I think, is more dangerous theoretically than this tradition of organic thought in political matters, in which power and violence are interpreted in biological terms. In the way these terms are understood today, life and life's alleged creativity, are their common denominator so that the precedence of violence is justified on the ground of creativity. The organic metaphors with which our entire present discussion of these matters, especially the riots, is shot through—the notion of a "sick society," of which the riots are symptoms as fever is a symptom of disease—can only promote violence in the end. Thus the debate between those who propose violent means to restore "law and order" and those who propose nonviolent reforms begins to sound ominously like a discussion between two physicians who debate the relative advantages of surgical as opposed to medical treatment of their patient. The sicker the patient is supposed to be, the more likely that the surgeon will have the last word.

38 *Power*, pp. 114 and 123 respectively.
39 de Jouvenel, *Power*, pp. 187–188.
40 Fanon, *The Wretched of the Earth*, p. 45.

Moreover, so long as we talk about these matters in nonpolitical, biological ways, the glorifiers of violence will have the great advantage to appeal to the undeniable fact that, in the household of nature, destruction and creation are but two sides of the natural process, so that collective violent action, quite apart from its inherent attraction, may appear as natural a prerequisite for the collective life of mankind as the struggle for survival and violent death for the continuing life in the animal kingdom.

No doubt, the danger of being carried away by the deceptive plausibility of organic metaphors is particularly great where the racial issue is involved. Racism, white or black, is fraught with violence by definition because it objects to natural organic facts—a white or black skin—which no persuasion and no power can change; all one can do, when the chips are down, is to exterminate their bearers. Violence in interracial struggle is always murderous, but it is not "irrational"; it is the logical and rational consequence of racism, by which I do not mean some rather vague prejudices on either side but an explicit ideological system.

Prejudices, as distinguished from both interests and ideologies, may yield under the pressure of power—as we have seen during the years of a successful civil rights movement that was entirely nonviolent. But while boycotts, sit-ins, and demonstrations were adequate in eliminating discriminatory laws and ordinances, they proved utter failures and became counterproductive when confronted with social conditions—the stark needs of the black ghettos on one side, the overriding interests of the lower-income groups with respect to housing and education on the other. All this mode of action could do, and did, was to bring these conditions into the open, into the street, where the basic irreconcilability of interests was dangerously exposed.

BUT EVEN TODAY'S violence, black riots, and the much greater potential violence of the white backlash are not yet manifestations of racist ideologies and their murderous logic. The riots, as has recently been stated, are "articulate protests against genuine grievances";[41] "indeed restraint and selectivity—or... rationality are certainly among [their] most crucial features."[42]

---

[41] Robert M. Fogelson, "Violence as Protest," in *Urban Riots: Violence and Social Change*, Proceedings of the Academy of Political Science, Columbia University, 1968.

[42] "Violence as Protest." See also the excellent article "Official Interpretation of Racial Riots" by Allan Silver in the same collection.

And much the same is true for the backlash phenomena. It is not irrational for certain interest groups to protest furiously against being singled out to pay the full price for ill-designed integration policies whose consequences their authors can easily escape.[43] The greatest danger is rather the other way round: since violence always needs justification, an escalation of the violence in the streets may bring about a truly racist ideology to justify it, in which case violence and riots may disappear from the streets and be transformed into the invisible terror of a police state.

Violence, being instrumental by nature, is rational to the extent that it is effective in reaching the end which must justify it. And since when we act we never know with any amount of certainty the eventual consequences of what we are doing, violence can remain rational only if it pursues short-term goals. Violence does not promote causes, it promotes neither History nor Revolution, but it can indeed serve to dramatize grievances and to bring them to public attention. As Conor Cruise O'Brien once remarked, "Violence is sometimes needed for the voice of moderation to be heard." And indeed, violence, contrary to what its prophets try to tell us, is a much more effective weapon of reformers than of revolutionists. (The often vehement denunciations of violence by Marxists did not spring from humane motives but from their awareness that revolutions are not the result of conspiracies and violent action.) France would not have received the most radical reform bill since Napoleon to change her antiquated education system without the riots of the French students, and no one would have dreamed of yielding to reforms of Columbia University without the riots during the spring term.

Still, the danger of the practice of violence, even if it moves consciously within a nonextremist framework of short-term goals, will always be that the means overwhelm the end. If goals are not achieved rapidly, the result will not merely be defeat but the introduction of the practice of violence into the whole body politic. Action is irreversible, and a return to the status quo in case of defeat is always unlikely. The practice of violence, like all action, changes the world, but the most probable change is a more violent world.

43 Stewart Alsop in a perceptive column, "The Wallace Man," in *Newsweek*, October 21, 1968, makes the point: "It may be illiberal of the Wallace man not to want to send his children to bad schools in the name of integration, but it is not at all unnatural. And it is not unnatural either for him to worry about the 'molestation' of his wife, or about losing his equity in his house, which is all he has." Alsop also quotes the most effective statement of George Wallace's demagoguery: "There are 535 members of Congress and a lot of these liberals have children, too. You know how many send their kids to the public schools in Washington? Six."

FINALLY, THE GREATER the bureaucratization of public life, the greater will be the attraction of violence. In a fully developed bureaucracy there is nobody left with whom one could argue, to whom one could present grievances, on whom the pressures of power could be exerted. Bureaucracy is the form of government in which everybody is deprived of political freedom, of the power to act; for the rule by Nobody is not no-rule, and where all are equally powerless we have a tyranny without a tyrant. The crucial feature in the students' rebellions around the world is that they are directed everywhere against the ruling bureaucracy. This explains, what at first glance seems so disturbing, that the rebellions in the East demand precisely those freedoms of speech and thought that the young rebels in the West say they despise as irrelevant. Huge party machines have succeeded everywhere to overrule the voice of the citizens, even in countries where freedom of speech and association is still intact.

The dissenters and resisters in the East demand free speech and thought as the preliminary conditions for political action; the rebels in the West live under conditions where these preliminaries no longer open the channels for action, for the meaningful exercise of freedom. The transformation of government into administration, of republics into bureaucracies, and the disastrous shrinkage of the public realm that went with it, have a long and complicated history throughout the modern age; and this process has been considerably accelerated for the last hundred years through the rise of party bureaucracies.

What makes man a political being is his faculty to act. It enables him to get together with his peers, to act in concert, and to reach out for goals and enterprises which would never enter his mind, let alone the desires of his heart, had he not been given this gift—to embark upon something new. All the properties of creativity ascribed to life in manifestations of violence and power actually belong to the faculty of action. And I think it can be shown that no other human ability has suffered to such an extent by the Progress of the modern age.

For progress, as we have come to understand it, means growth, the relentless process of more and more, of bigger and bigger. The bigger a country becomes in population, in objects, and in possessions, the greater will be the need for administration and with it, the anonymous power of the administrators. Pavel Kohout, the Czech author, writing in the heyday of the Czech experiment with freedom, defined a "free citizen" as a "Citizen-Co-ruler." He meant nothing else but the "participatory democracy" of which we have heard so much in recent years in the West. Kohout added that what the world, as it is today, stands in greatest need of may well be "a new example" if "the next thousand years are not to become an era of supercivilized monkeys."[44]

THIS NEW EXAMPLE will hardly be brought about by the practice of violence, although I am inclined to think that much of its present glorification is due to the severe frustration of the faculty of action in the modern world. It is simply true that the riots in the ghettos and the rebellions on the campuses make "people feel they are acting together in a way that they rarely can."[45] We don't know if these occurrences are the beginnings of something new—the "new example"—or the death pangs of a faculty that mankind is about to lose. As things stand today, when we see how the superpowers are bogged down under the monstrous weight of their own bigness, it looks as though the "new example" will have a chance to arise, if at all, in a small country, or in small, well-defined sectors in the mass societies of the large powers.

For the disintegration processes, which have become so manifest in recent years—the decay of many public services, of schools and police, of mail delivery and transportation, the death rate on the highways, and the traffic problems in the cities—concern everything designed to serve mass society. Bigness is afflicted with vulnerability, and while no one can say with assurance where and when the breaking point has been reached, we can observe, almost to the point of measuring it, how strength and resiliency are insidiously destroyed, leaking, as it were, drop by drop from our institutions. And the same, I think, is true for the various party systems—the one-party dictatorships in the East as well as the two-party systems in England and the United States, or the multiple party systems in Europe—all of which were supposed to serve the political needs of modern mass societies, to make representative government possible where direct democracy would not do because "the room will not hold all" (John Selden).

Moreover, the recent rise of nationalism around the globe, usually understood as a worldwide swing to the right, has now reached the point where it may threaten the oldest and best established nation states. The Scotch and the Welsh, the Bretons and the Provençals, ethnic groups

---

44 See Günter Grass, Pavel Kohout, *Briefe über die Grenze* (Hamburg, 1968), pp. 88 and 90 respectively.

45 Herbert J. Gans, "The Ghetto Rebellions and Urban Class Conflict," in *Urban Riots.*

whose successful assimilation had been the prerequisite for the rise of the nation state, are turning to separatism in rebellion against the centralized governments of London and Paris.

Again, we do not know where these developments will lead us, but we can see how cracks in the power structure of all but the small countries are opening and widening. And we know, or should know, that every decrease of power is an open invitation to violence—if only because those who hold power and feel it slipping from their hands have always found it difficult to resist the temptation of substituting violence for it.

Igor Stravinsky

Eau de Vie: An Interview on Beethoven by Igor Stravinsky with Robert Craft was originally published October 22, 1970.

IGOR STRAVINSKY *with* ROBERT CRAFT

Eau de Vie:
An Interview on
Beethoven

ROBERT CRAFT: You have shared some of your views on the Beethoven sonatas and quartets but not those on the symphonies.

IGOR STRAVINSKY: Because we have no perspective on music *that* popular. And while negative criticism does not interest me, the affirmative is too difficult—in the sense of Professor Popper's argument that the hypotheses of science can be proved false but not true. And, finally, because the symphonies are public statements, the sonatas and quartets—especially the later examples—private or at least more intimate ones, to which I am more drawn.

Except the Adagio of the Ninth. Which I say because I have been so deeply moved by it lately, a confession that seems to make me guilty of the Affective Fallacy. But in fact I have always tried to distinguish between the musical object and the emotion it induces, partly on the grounds that the object is active, the emotion reactive, hence a translation. Not that I ever believed in separations of the sort; or believe now in those fashionable leucotomies of "sensibility" and "intellect," the so-called "new" and "old" brains. My point was simply that your feelings and my feelings are much less interesting than Beethoven's art. And that in the first place Beethoven was not conveying his "emotion" but his musical ideas; nor do these necessarily "translate" whatever emotions he may have had at the time, though they may have trans*ferred* them. In other words, I stood (and stand) exactly opposite Diderot, who asked that a painting "move" him, "break" his "heart," let him "tremble" and "weep," but only "delight" his "eyes afterward." In short, never mind the *art*.

CRAFT: What constitutes an idea? What are you aware of first?

STRAVINSKY: Intervals, intervallic combinations. Rhythm, being design (and structure), tends, if not to come later, at least to be subject to change, which intervallic ideas rarely are. In my own case, both generally occur together. One indispensable attribute of the composer's imagination, I might add, is the ability to recognize the potential of his idea; to see at once, for example, whether it is overcomplex and requires disentanglement, or too loose and requires concentration. Force of habit probably plays a larger part in this than the composer himself realizes.

I have never seen the sketches of the first movement of Beethoven's Fifth Symphony but cannot believe that interval and rhythm were conceived separately; certainly they cannot be regarded as other than perfectly congruent in the finished composition. (Or as the "Two Natures" theologians maintained, "without separation or confusion.") The most remarkable aspect of the movement, nevertheless, is the rhythmic. First of all, the *ir*regular durations are confined to the *unsounding* music, the varying-in-length silences. Second, the *sounding* music is articulated by only three—and these even-multiple—rhythmic units: halves, quarters, and eighths (no iambs! no triplets!). And third—the most surprising delimitation of all—the movement is without syncopation.

Beethoven follows these conditions so strictly, moreover, that one almost suspects him of imposing them for the "game." But far from restricting his invention, it is *as* prodigal as ever and more radical. In the wind and string dialogue from m. 196, for instance, thirty-two half notes succeed each other with no *rhythmic* relief, whatever the other kinds (the melodic-harmonic movement, the weight-shifting instrumentation, the changing phrase lengths). And not only is the passage not rhythmically monotonous, it has as much tension as any in *Le Sacre du printemps*.

The second movement, for comparison, falls so thumpingly *on* the beats in the wrong sense—inevitability—that rhythmic tension scarcely exists. Besides, Beethoven does not always resist the temptation to overextend (cf. the woodwind music mm. 129–143). After the first movement, the symphony is a little hard to take.

CRAFT: Which symphonies can you take all the way?

STRAVINSKY: Two, Four, Eight. But Six not at all; the music is always "beautiful," of course, but no more than that. No doubt the tonal and metrical regularity suit the simplicity of the "scene"; but does the "scene" matter? The "brook," though Danubian in length, lacks incident (rapids, whirlpools, falls), and to me few episodes in the great composer's work are less welcome than the return of the second theme at m. 113. Yet thematic structures of the *Pastorale* are found in earlier and later symphonies as well; in the Adagio of the Fourth (m. 34), for example; and in the Andante of the Fifth (the theme itself, but most conspicuously in its thirty-second-note variation); and, most surprisingly, at the final climax of the Adagio of the Ninth (m. 147).

The first movement of the Second Symphony is the most relentlessly brilliant in all the nine, besides which it establishes many of the features of Beethoven's symphonic style: the hammer-blow upbeats, the sudden pauses, sudden harmonic turns, sudden extensions and truncations, and sudden reversals—or withholdings—of expected volumes. The other movements, too, are models for later symphonies, the Larghetto for the Andante of the Fifth (cf. from m. 230, especially), the Scherzo and finale for their counterparts in the Fourth. But apart from Haydn in Number One, the symphonies rarely disturb the ghosts of predecessors; at the same time one of these rarities is the episode at "A" in this finale; it might have occurred in a Mozart opera overture.

CRAFT: And the *Eroica*?

STRAVINSKY: The first movement is always so mangled by demigod conductors that I seldom get through it. And the same can be said of the Funeral March, which the conductor may have come to praise but usually only succeeds in burying. Finally, the let-down of the last movement—this not the conductor's fault—is all the worse for following the most marvelous Scherzo Beethoven ever wrote.

The Fourth (together with the Eighth) is the most evenly sustained of the symphonies. Yet as a rule the first tempo is taken so slowly that an accelerando is needed to accommodate the chords at the end of the Introduction. Obviously one measure of the Introduction must approximate two measures of the Allegro (just as the sixteenths at the end of the Introduction to the First Symphony should equal the sixteenths of the Allegro— i.e., should be played as sixty-fourths). Weber's incomprehension before this symphony is all the odder, incidentally, in that the clarinet cantabile in the second movement is so close to his music.

CRAFT: And the Ninth as an entity?

STRAVINSKY: The Allegro contains many new things (the Wagnerian bass at m. 513, for one), but the principal theme ends with a bump, and the dotted-note figure is stiff-necked (cf. the eight fortissimo measures immediately before the *da capo*). The Scherzo, though the best part of the Huntley-Brinkley program, is—like the Scherzo of the Seventh—too long. Moreover, it is *always* wrongly played. The duple and triple measures should be approximately equal. If this were not already obvious from the *stringendo* lead-in, it would have to be from the Presto, which is a more reliable indicator than the metronome, and which, unlike it, could hardly be a misprint. In short, the relationship is roughly the same as the one obtaining between the duple and triple meters in the Scherzo of the *Eroica*.

But as for the great untouchable finale, one still hardly dares to tell the truth, and that though the composer himself seems to have recognized it (according to Sonnleithner and others). Part of the truth is that some of the music is very banal—the last Prestissimo, for one passage, and, for another, the first full-orchestra version of the theme, which is German-band music of the *Kaisermarsch* class. The banality weighs heavily, too, perhaps disproportionately so. Another part of the truth is that the voices and orchestra do not mix. The imbalances are a symptom. I have not heard a live performance since 1958, when I conducted a piece of my own on a program with it; but I have *never* heard a balanced one. The "wrong" notes stick out wrongly in the "apocalyptic" first chord despite recording engineers, nor can all of their periphonic faking rescue the string figuration in the "*Seid umschlangen, Millionen!*" the failure not being electronic but musical. Yet the largest mistake is in the "message," hence, if you will pardon the expression, in the "medium." The message of the voices is a finitude greatly diminishing the message of the wordless music. And the first entrance of the voice is a shocking intrusion; the singer could hardly be more out of place if he were Pagliacci.

CRAFT: And the Adagio?

STRAVINSKY: I lack the wherewithal to argue "rightness," as I said. Nor can I even affirm it so precisely as the deaf man's nephew. "How well you have brought in the Andante, uncle," he remarked in a conversation book, and with far wider meaning than he knew, for the shape of the Adagio and its counterparts, and the lilt of the three-meter with its over-the-bar suspensions, were to become properties—sometimes stage properties—of the "old," meaning a new Vienna. The so-called Viennese style, some part of a common language of composers as different as Brahms, Strauss, Wolf, and Mahler, was not merely forecast but invented in this movement. Mahler particularly; the evocation of him in the wind serenade centerpiece is truly uncanny—except that Beethoven was always the most observant messenger from the future, from the only future *I* care about anyway. But enough. Go and listen. The whole movement is a sublimely sustained melody by the composer who more than any other, "Doth refine and exalt Man to the height he would beare."

Oliver Sacks

The Megrims by W.H. Auden was originally published June 3, 1971, as a review of Migraine
by Oliver Sacks, University of California Press.

W. H. AUDEN

The Megrims

There screen'd in shades from day's detested glare,
Spleen sighs for ever on her pensive bed,
Pain at her side, and megrim at her head.
—Pope

DR. SACKS'S PRIMARY PURPOSE in writing this book was, no doubt, to enlighten his fellow practitioners about a complaint of which most of them know all too little. As Dr. Gooddy says in his foreword:

> The common attitude is that migraine is merely a form of mainly non-disabling headache which occupies far more of a busy doctor's time than its importance warrants.... Some tablets and the current inelegant cliché of "learning to live with it" are advised by the physician, who hopes he will not be on duty the next time the patient comes for advice.... Many doctors are only too pleased when a patient, in desperation, takes himself off to the practitioners of "fringe medicine," almost hoping that the results will be both disastrous and very costly.

I am sure, however, that any layman who is at all interested in the relation between body and mind, even if he does not understand all of it, will find the book as fascinating as I have.

It has been estimated that migraine afflicts at least 10 percent of the human race and the true percentage may well be higher, since probably only those who suffer severe attacks consult a doctor. Even if, like myself, one has had the good fortune never to have experienced an attack, we all have known some relative or friend who has had them, so that we can compare their character traits and symptoms with Dr. Sacks's detailed descriptions.

Unlike contagious diseases and genetic disabilities such as hemophilia on the one hand, and hysteria on the other, migraine is a classic example of a psychosomatic illness in which physiological and psychological factors play an equal role. As physical organisms we are pretty much the same, that is to say, our bodies have a limited repertoire of symptoms. This makes it possible to diagnose a case of migraine, to distinguish it from, say, epilepsy or asthma. But as conscious persons who can say I, each of us is unique. This means that no two cases of migraine are identical; treatment that succeeds with one patient can fail with another.

> A migraine is a physical event which may also be from the start, or later become, an emotional or symbolic event. A migraine expresses both physiological and emotional needs: it is the prototype of a psychophysiological reaction. Thus the convergence of thinking which its understanding demands must be based simultaneously, both on neurology and on psychiatry.... Finally, migraine cannot be conceived as an exclusively human reaction, but must be considered as a form of biological reaction specifically tailored to human needs and human nervous systems.

The first part of Dr. Sacks's book consists of a series of detailed clinical observations. He distinguishes between three types of migraine, common migraine, popularly called "a sick headache," classical migraine, in which, as in epileptic attacks, there is frequently a distortion of the visual field, and migrainous neuralgia, or "cluster headache," so called because attacks are closely grouped. These descriptions, interesting as I found them, I do not feel qualified to discuss.

I will mention two curious observations Dr. Sacks makes. He tells us that the "Nightmare Song" in Iolanthe mentions no fewer than twelve migraine symptoms, and that the visions of the medieval nun Hildegard of Bingen were clearly visual auras caused by classical migraine.

PART TWO IS DEVOTED to the questions, "What circumstances trigger off a migraine attack?" and "Is there a migraine personality?" The evidence is bewilderingly diverse. Thus, migraine often runs in families, but Dr. Sacks believes this is probably learned from the family environment, not genetically inherited, for many patients have no such family history.

Though classical migraine commonly attacks young people and males, this is not invariable, and the first attack of common migraine may occur after the age of forty, among women, for example, during their menopause. Classical migraine and cluster headache tend to occur for no discernible reason at regular intervals, varying from two to twelve weeks; common migraine seems more dependent upon external and emotional situations. Some cases resemble allergies: an attack can be caused by bright lights, loud noises, bad smells, inclement weather, alcohol, amphetamines. Others suggest a hormonal origin: migraine is not uncommon among women during their menstrual periods, but very rare during pregnancy.

Such a diversity naturally produces an equal diversity of theories as to the basic cause of migraine. The somatically oriented physician looks for a chemical or neurological solution, the psychiatrist for an exclusively psychological answer. Dr. Sacks thinks that both are only half-right. Of the psychological theories the two most accepted are those of Wolff (1963) and Fromm-Reichmann (1937).

> Migraineurs are portrayed by Wolff as ambitious, successful, perfectionistic, rigid, orderly, cautious, and emotionally constipated, driven therefore, from time to time, to outbursts and breakdowns which must assume an indirect somatic form. Fromm-Reichmann is also able to arrive at a clear-cut conclusion: migraine, she states, is a physical expression of unconscious hostility against consciously beloved parents.

Dr. Sacks's experiences with his patients have led him to conclude that while many are, as Wolff says, hyperactive and obsessional, there are others who are lethargic and sloppy, and that while, as Fromm-Reichmann says, most migraine attacks are a somatic expression of violent emotions, usually rage, this may be a reaction to an intolerable life situation of which the patient is quite aware, and may also be self-punitive.

> We find, in practice, that sudden rage is the commonest precipitant, although fright (panic) may be equally potent in younger patients. Sudden elation (as at a moment of triumph or unexpected good fortune) may have the same effect.... Nor should one claim that all patients with habitual migraine are "neurotic" (except in so far as neurosis is the universal human condition), for in many cases the migraines may replace a neurotic structure, constituting an alternative to neurotic desperation and assuagement.

IN PART THREE, Dr. Sacks discusses the physiological, biological, and psychological factors in migraine. His theories about its biological basis I found particularly interesting and suggestive. Among all animals are to be found two possible reactions to a situation of threat or danger, fight-or-flight and immobilization. He quotes Darwin's description of the second:

> The picture of passive fear, as Darwin portrays it, is one of passivity and prostration, allied with splachnic and glandular activity ("...a strong tendency to yawn...death-like pallor...beads of sweat stand out on the skin. All the muscles of the body are relaxed. The intestines are affected. The sphincter muscles cease to act, and no longer retain the contents of the body...."). The general attitude is one of cringing, cowering, and sinking. If the passive reaction is more acute, there may be abrupt loss of postural tone or of consciousness.

He believes that, despite the association between migraine and rage, it is from this passive reaction, tailored to human nature, that migraine is biologically derived. This seems to me very plausible. Before he invented weapons, primitive man must have been one of the most defenseless of all the creatures, being devoid of fangs or claws or tusks or hooves or venom, and a relatively slow mover. It seems unlikely, therefore, that aggression or rage can have been a basic biological instinct in man as it is in the predator carnivores. Human aggression must be a secondary modification of what was originally a feeling of terror and helplessness. As Coleridge said: "In all perplexity there is a portion of fear, which disposes the mind to anger."

Dr. Sacks concludes his chapter on psychological approaches to migraine by saying that three kinds of psychosomatic linkage may occur.

> . . . first, an inherent physiological connection between certain symptoms and effects; second, a fixed symbolic equivalence between certain physical symptoms and states of mind, analogous to the use of facial expressions; third, an arbitrary, idiosyncratic symbolism uniting physical symptoms and phantasies, analogous to the construction of hysterical symptoms.

THE LAST PART is devoted to the problems of therapy. As in all cases of functional disorders, the personal relation between doctor and patient is of prime importance. "Every sickness is a musical problem," said Novalis, "and every cure a musical solution." This means, as Dr. Sacks says, that, whatever method of treatment a physician may choose or be forced to choose, there is only one cardinal rule:

> . . . one must always listen to the patient. For if migraine patients have a common and legitimate complaint besides their migraines, it is that they have not been listened to by physicians. Looked at, investigated, drugged, charged: but not listened to.

Dr. Sacks recognizes that there are drugs, notably Ergotomine Tartrate and Methysergide, which can relieve the pain of an acute attack, and which it would be heartless to refuse a patient, unless he has other physiological conditions which counterindicate their use, but he regards them as somewhat dangerous palliatives which cannot effect a permanent cure.

His own bias, he tells us, is toward psychotherapy, but he is modest in his claims. He does not think, for example, that the only solution to migraine is depth analysis, for which few patients have either the money or the time. Further, he admits that some patients find a psychotherapeutic approach unacceptable.

> Severely affected patients should be seen on a regular basis, at intervals— approximately of two to ten weeks. The early interviews must be long and searching, in order to expose for both patient and physician the general situation and specific stresses which are involved, while establishing the

foundations of the physician's authority and the patient-physician relationship; later consultations may be briefer and more limited in scope and will chiefly be concerned with the discussion of current problems as these are experienced by the patient and expressed in his migraines. Cursory medical attention is disastrous, and an important cause of allegedly "intractable" migraine.

He also recommends the keeping of two calendars, a migraine calendar and a calendar of daily events, which may reveal unsuspected circumstances as provocative of attacks.

"Cure," in his opinion, means finding for each particular patient the best *modus vivendi for him*. This can mean, in certain cases, allowing the patient to "keep" his headaches.

The attempt to dislodge severe habitual migraines in a pathologically unconcerned or hysterical personality may force the patient to face intense anxieties and emotional conflicts which are even less tolerable than the migraines. The physical symptoms, paradoxically, may be more merciful than the conflicts they simultaneously conceal and express.

Such patients would agree with Marx: "The only antidote to mental suffering is physical pain."

Honoré de Balzac

Balzac at Thirty by V. S. Pritchett was originally published February 22, 1973.

V. S. PRITCHETT

Balzac at Thirty

LIKE DICKENS, BALZAC contained his age, and again like Dickens he had an immediate sense of his public. When later on he was criticized for potboiling he said hotly that an artist who has no private means and who is not supported by some sinecure in his government has to pay attention to popular taste and the demands of editors. The young Balzac first reached a large public with a very hot boiler. There was a passing craze for revaluations—what were called *physiologies*; and in 1829 Balzac dashed off a *Physiologie du mariage*—"by a Bachelor." He was thirty. The book was not only wittily topical; it drew on something central and quite serious in Balzac's nature. The cynical bachelor did really think that marriage ought to be made more agreeable among the rising middle classes. The book made him notorious if not famous, and established him in the minds of a large number of women readers. They might be angry, they might be admiring, they wrote hundreds of arguing, confessional, or ecstatic letters to the writer who was so much on their side and who had the gift of intimacy. For the rest of his life women were his chief correspondents.

For if there was one thing the "celestial" Balzac family knew all about it was domestic love. Not the cold campaigns of seduction in *Les Liaisons dangereuses*; not the crystalizing of the varieties of the passion which Stendhal had examined in *De l'amour* only a few years before, for Balzac lacked that psychological fineness; but love in the married state, love in the household. Indeed he might have quoted Sterne:

> Love, you see, is not so much a Sentiment as a Situation, into which a man enters, as my brother Toby would do, in a *corps*—no matter whether he loves the service or no—being once in it, he acts as he did....

He had listened to his father's "utterances" drawn from *Tristram Shandy* and Rabelais, as the father sat at home with a restless wife who had presented him with another man's child. He had seen one sister die early in a marriage that had become wretched. His first two mistresses, Mme de

Berny and the Duchesse d'Abrantès, were married women, both older than his mother and more than twenty years older than himself—so that at this time he could be said to be a young man with three mothers, all on the worst of terms with one another. He had listened to the unhappy life stories of the tender Mme de Berny, who had been brought up as a girl at the court of Versailles; and in the company of the duchesse heard confidences of the somewhat businesslike attitude to love at Napoleon's court. The duchesse had even been the mistress of Metternich. One can hear these voices mixed with his in the *Physiologie*.

BALZAC HAD the journalist's talent for having it all ways. Blatantly imitating Stendhal, he spiced his confection with anecdotes and aphorisms, and with satirical gambols, like his praise of the female headache:

> *O migraine, protectrice des amours, impôt conjugale, bouclier sur lequel viennent expirer tous les désirs maritaux. . . . Honte au médecin que te trouverait un préservatif.*

That might have come from Molière. The book is genial, frank in its sexuality, and has a streak of the vulgar. Its conclusion is very moral: a plea for sincere love. The fact is that the roving bachelor liked even his loose women to be settled among their household goods. The hope for the married woman lies in the art of becoming the mistress-wife. *La Physiologie du mariage* owed its success to Balzac's adroit perception of a change in women's attitudes since the eighteenth century. In its defense of married women in their virtues, sufferings, or in their delinquencies, it caught a tide that was running for female emancipation which had become powerful.

For the Napoleonic wars had made love sudden and short, and marriages desperate and unstable; but now two impulses appeared in the mind of the "new" middle-class woman. In one she was tempted by a longing to revive the illicit intrigues of the aristocracy of the *ancien régime*; but, with inborn respectability, she required a moral veil to be cast over what went on under the system of the arranged marriage and the dowry. She required an appropriate hypocrisy: vice was eager to pay its tribute to virtue. (In *La Cousine Bette*, Balzac notes the change when Mme Marneffe, the new courtesan, puts on sentimental, religious, and moral airs, and always speaks of her "fall" as she skillfully bleeds her lovers.)

The second impulse was more elevated. It was directed to a mystical emancipation; concentrated in the Saint-Simonist movement and particularly in the figure of Enfantin, who held that "the definite moral law can only be revealed by Man *and* Woman, and that its application must be the result of their harmonious association." Another cult, directed to the emancipation of women, was called *Evadaisme*—the word combines the names Adam and Eve. The status of women was raised, according to this doctrine, by putting Eve's name first. The leader of this cult was called Le Mapah. He wrote innumerable pamphlets, one of which contains the verse quoted by Enid Starkie in her book on Petrus Borel:

> *Mary is no longer the Mother. She is the wife.*
> *Jesus Christ is no longer the son. He is the husband.*
> *The old world (confession) is coming to an end.*
> *The new world (expansion) is about to begin.*

The noisy man-woman who wore trousers, smoked cigars, and was popularly known as the *lionne* appeared in the imitations of George Sand and was a byproduct of this new theology. If Balzac's common sense leaves such speculations aside in the *Physiologie* he had his own quasi-scientific interest in androgynous beings.

In the meantime Balzac had found a public. He turned to writing *feuilletons* for the new reviews like *La Revue de Paris*, *Le Charivari*, which published Daumier's drawings, and the gossipy *Caricature*. And in one series of stories, *La Femme de trente ans*, he strengthened his hold on his readers. He had shrewdly noted one more change in social wishes. The conventional notion was that after her marriage by the time she was twenty, a woman ceased to be interesting; yet at thirty she was still young. Women who had been forced into marriage and were isolated, betrayed, took lovers, and were abandoned, were forced to come to terms with circumstance: it is Mme de Berny's story. The joke that went around Paris was that a clever new writer of light novelettes had extended the age of love for women by ten years.

THE BALZAC WE KNOW begins to appear. His hand as a writer of "black" romance is seen in the terrible drama of *El Verdugo*, in which a Spanish father tells his son to execute the whole family to save it from the dishonor of being executed by the French invaders. But after this Balzac abandons fashionable romance for the daily life he knows best. In the collection of stories he eventually assembled under the title of *Scènes de la vie privée*, there are stories of the sentiments: the wife deceived by her husband; the woman abandoned by her lover; the old age of a woman whom marriage has deceived and whose lover is in conflict with her daughter. And, more important and coherent, there is the portrait of Gobseck, the money lender; the delightful study of a rebellious girl—from an incident in the early life of his sister Laure—in the *Bal de Sceaux*; *Le Curé de Tours* with its portrait of the innocent old Abbé who is destroyed by making an enemy of his landlady; and *Colonel Chabert*.

The last two are very fine short stories, and although Balzac came to despise the form in time, he showed an absolute mastery in it. He moved with discursive ease among stories that depended on exact observation of circumstance, moved on to the changes of feeling and behavior of men and women brought up under different dispensations: the old survivors of the *ancien régime* in their châteaux in Touraine; the people who had known the Revolution and the wars; and the people of the restored monarchy. Again and again we hear his explaining voice, with his sudden eager phrase "*voici pourquoi*—that is why" such and such an event emerged from the circumstances he has set out.

"That is why" is at the heart of his stories. His characters are items of social history, but warm and alive. He had, up till now, spent his time listening to everyone—above all listening to women, lawyers, returned soldiers. He had met many veterans at the house of his brother-in-law at St. Cyr, and there were thousands in Paris anyway. The story of Colonel Chabert comes from one of those encounters, and its content is worth examining for it already shows Balzac as more than a raconteur or conventional realist. The story opens with a minute but vivacious description of a lawyer's office and its bumptious, slangy clerks—"puddle jumpers"—who are shooting pellets of bread at an old man dressed in a coachman's coat passing in the street below. Balzac is a master of office slang.

The old man comes into the office and stands, monosyllabic, before the mocking clerks, who treat him as an idiot. His skin is transparent, he is a motionless, shabby, living corpse with the air of a tragic idiot.

"I am Colonel Chabert," he says.

"Which Colonel Chabert?" the clerk says.

"The one who was killed at Eylau," he replies.

We are at once in the middle of a terrifying story of how the Colonel has groped back to life from under the bodies of a mass grave on the battlefield and has managed after a year or two to crawl back to France. He is a man who is officially "dead" and therefore has no identity. He has come to the lawyers to establish that he is living and to trace his wife who has married again and, of course, has inherited his money. The struggle to recover an inheritance is a theme to which Balzac continually returned. Where Balzac shows his mastery is in setting the central part of the story in a lawyer's office, for this establishes that the dead man's return to life is really a return to a world dominated by greed; and it enables Balzac to make two reflections that bear not only on the surface of the tale, but on its moral theme.

Of the lawyer's dirty office, with its clerks who jeer at the poor wretches who come to get justice or revenge there, he writes:

> After the second-hand clothes shop, a lawyer's office is the most horrifying of street markets our society has to offer. It is on a par with the gambling house, the courts, the lottery office and the brothel. What is the explanation? Because perhaps they place dramas of the human soul in a scene which is utterly indifferent to their hopes.

IN HOW MANY SCENES in Balzac are we struck by the indifference of the environment which has been realistically recorded. But in his comments on the Colonel's decision to return to beggary because of his contempt for the vulgar meanness of his wife, the honest lawyer seems to be speaking for Balzac's pessimism. In our society, the lawyer says, the priest, the doctor, and the lawyer are the people who stand apart because they are bound to lose all respect for the world as it is.

> I have seen a father die penniless in a garret abandoned by his daughters to whom he gave 40,000 francs a year. I have seen wills put on the fire; mothers robbing their children, wives reducing their husbands to madness, so that they can live in peace with their lovers. I have seen women corrupting the tastes of their legitimate children so that these destroy themselves, in order that the mother can give everything to a love child.

Such tales are pure Balzac — one notices for example the plot of *Le Père Goriot* in that list — and one begins to see that he is himself the observant lawyer of the passions before he is their psychologist. But upon his definitions he always imposes something else: the quality of dramatic vision. This visionary insight turns Colonel Chabert into something more than a wronged soldier. Coming back from the dead, he *looks* dead to this world, a ghost, a creature to be mocked and disbelieved. His false death becomes a resource — a fierce decision to remain a ghost rather than to accept life as it is now lived by others.

In all Balzac's characters there is not only the physical man or woman shown exactly in feature and in the clothes they wear, but there is also this gleam of a vision, sordid or strange, by which they live. Like the characters of Dickens, they live by a self-imagination. Balzac was an exhaustive user of his life. He will tell a story; in the next he will reverse it, playing variations on his themes. At the time when he was telling these tales of circumstance, he turned from time to time to the visionary or allegorical stories, and these open up the way into his inner life as a man: the *Contes philosophiques*.

What is inside this shrewd, warm, meaty, well-organized, and distinctly opportunist novelist in his early thirties? Fundamentally, underlying the common sense, there is the outstanding characteristic of the whole Balzac family—monomania, a power that drives them all to the single consuming passion. It makes its appearance in the first long work he published and which lifted him out of promise into achievement: *La Peau de chagrin*.

BALZAC HAD WRITTEN a good deal of the topical book on marriage when in his late twenties he was being taken about by the Duchesse d'Abrantès, and the worldly voice in many pages of that book must have come, as I have said, from her. Now he went back obediently, embarrassed by his ties, to appease Mme de Berny. He was dodging his debts and choked with the journalism by which he had to live. He had agreed to write a monograph on Virtue and, being a good trencherman, a *Physiologie gastronomique*. Mme de Berny sadly appealed to him to take her on a holiday in Touraine and—we can surmise—though she admired his appetite for life, she may have warned him. He began to write his first memorable philosophical tale.

They traveled over the bad roads by diligence and arrived at a pretty little cottage outside Tours on the banks of the Loire, called La Grenadière, on the water's edge. With her, and back in the country of his boyhood, he always recovered the lost and buried life that reawakened his imagination. There is a touching account of the young man in his thirties rowing the woman in her fifties on the river: she is wearing a pretty gray dress and a cape with blue ribbons in it. She takes off her gloves and trails her hand in the water. They take a steamboat all the way to Nantes and another to Saint-Nazaire. The sea air blows the staleness of Paris out of him.

> If you only knew what Touraine is like! One forgets everything there. I don't mind that the people there are stupid; they are happy. Happy people generally are stupid. Glory, politics, the future, literature are just pellets for killing lost dogs. Virtue, happiness, life—it's 600 francs a year on the banks of the Loire. Put your foot in La Grenadière, my house at St. Cyr...

(He was thinking of his childhood and the house where his nurse, the gendarme's wife, had lived)

...beside a marvellous river, the banks covered with honeysuckle.... Touraine has the effect of *foie gras* on me and one is in it up to the chin: the wine is delicious. It does not make one drunk: it beatifies. I have gone down to the sea by river at three or four sous a league. I have felt my mind widen as the river widens. I have swum in the sea, breathed pure air and sunshine. How I understand pirates and adventurers and rebels! My dear friend, literature at the moment is nothing but a trade for prostitutes who sell themselves for 100 sous; it leads nowhere.... My idea is to drift, discover, risk my life—sink an English ship!

The artist is reawakened. As usual more than one book came into his head: once he had started *La Peau de chagrin*, the idea of writing a series of Rabelaisian tales in concocted medieval French came to him. He began on those as well. Behindhand with his journalism, he sent Mme de Berny up to Paris to deliver a third of an article he had written. She ran into the Revolution of 1830—the three violent days which put Louis Philippe on the throne. Balzac was indifferent to that. He ended a letter to a friend:

When at night one sees the beautiful skies here, one just wants to unbutton one's flies and piss on the heads of all the royal houses.

Later in the year he went to Mme de Berny again. She was now living with her children at La Bouleanière, a house she had taken on the Fontainebleau road near Nemours. There he finished *La Peau de chagrin*. It is one of Balzac's torrential pieces of writing. Appropriately for a book written in the nineteenth century, it is a book about the nature of power: it defines his life and is prophetic of his own fate. Like the work of all novelists, Balzac's novels are diffused autobiography; but, in certain books, Balzac draws on his youth directly again and again. In long portions of *Louis Lambert*, in *Le Lys dans la vallée*, in *Illusions perdues* he presents revised, transposed versions of the same experience. He is obsessed by the past, by projecting the sources of his inner life, by self-explanation. In *La Peau de chagrin* there is not only his literal experience as the poor young man of the rue Lesdiguières, but there is the impelling inner fantasy that will shape, sustain, and in the end destroy him.

THE STORY MIGHT COME out of the fantastic tales of Hoffmann or the *Arabian Nights*; also it has an amusing connection with Balzac's early follies as a reckless buyer of bric-à-brac. We see in Raphael, the poor student, the young Balzac dreaming of love and wealth, buying the magic skin in the notorious wooden galleries of the Palais Royal, torn between a humble love and the adolescent dream of a luxurious mistress, moving toward the scene where he will grasp the magic skin and have his first wild desire granted. He has been warned that desire burns us up and that the will to enact it destroys us.

The plot is too well known to need further description, but we see that the fantasy is a diagnosis. It is Balzac's first exposure of the cynical and ruthless individualism that is corrupting and will go on corrupting a materialist society that worships money and power. The nasty little crimes of the lawyer's office are now transposed into a romantic key: in glorifying the lust for gold, society is being denatured. Raphael's personal adventure shows the spiritual consequence of conforming to the spirit of the times. He desires the female idol of the city, Foedora, the woman who allures and maddens by the coldness of her heart and never satisfies. She plays with the intellect of the young man, for she knows that to listen to the fevered young intellectual is to enslave him. He hides in her bedroom to watch her going to bed, and he hears her groan, "Oh God," in apparent weariness with the sterile life she is leading. He is quite wrong.

> "Yes, I remember," says Foedora, "I was thinking of my broker when I said it. I had forgotten to ask him to convert my fives into threes, and during the day the threes have gone down in price."

The moral is that Raphael's intellect has made him a dreamer, the dream realized enslaves him, and he is never satisfied. He now desires great wealth, the skin shrinks; he shuts himself away but disaster follows. His hiding place is discovered by Pauline, the humble girl who loves him, and he dies in one last bout of sexual excess.

The allegory has its moments of melodrama: Balzac will always be prone to that, but it is, on the whole, absorbed by eloquence and invention. The tradition of Molière is powerful enough to allay the absurdities of the Hoffmann-like romance, and the construction has the skill of dance and counterdance. It is a brilliant coup of Balzac's irony—for he never quite surrenders to his own extreme ideas—that, in his bitter withdrawal from temptation, Raphael infects the cautious old antique seller from whom he bought the skin with a desire for the debauches he has so prudently avoided and so brings him to destruction.

WHEN THE BOOK was published in 1831, critics complained that the eloquence was commonplace. As Gautier, the aesthete, and other friends agreed, Balzac "appeared not to know his own language"; but it flowed, it had the spell of the voice of a talker who is carried away and who depends on the presence of his personality. Balzac is always felt as a sanguine presence in his writing, breathless with knowledge, fantasy, and things seen. He likes a strong outline. He admired Monnier, the cartoonist; and the coarse line of caricature is often used to carry him across the large, argued panorama he is drawing. But Gautier, who believed in Balzac's greatness, also said that no other great writer was so humble about his prose or struggled more to improve it. Naively he asked advice; his revisions and rewritings show the trouble he took with his awkward sentences.

With all its defects, even with the confusion about the content of the parable, *La Peau de chagrin* made him a famous and important figure in Paris. He was no longer an apprentice. Women tried to find out if he had ever known the icy and luxurious Foedora. About Raphael's love for her he wrote what was true of all his love affairs, even his love for Mme de Berny when he wrote his declaration to her: that, at the beginning, love was an idea in his head before it was in his heart or even his senses; that he was moved by the will to dominate and make himself loved; and then suddenly he lost control of himself and found that what had begun in the head turned into a love that enslaved.

As for Foedora, he said in a letter, "The total of the women who have had the impertinence to recognize themselves as Foedora now stands, to my knowledge, at 72." She is obviously a *belle dame sans merci*, an adolescent's dream. There is a rumor, all the same, that once Balzac hid in the bedroom of Olympe Pélissier, a courtesan of the time who was the mistress of Eugène Sue, the dandy and enormously successful writer, whom Balzac envied. Olympe could have made that remark about her investments, for she had been left a small fortune by an American lover and on it had risen from poverty to prudent wealth. But she was noted for warmheartedness.

Balzac, when accused by his Polish mistress at the end of his life of having been Olympe Pélissier's lover, gave a denial that is so elaborate as to be unbelievable. He claimed that he had been no more than her confidant during one of her quarrels with Sue; and it is a fact that Balzac and Sue were lifelong friends. But Mme de Berny was very jealous of her. "I shall not be able to come and see you today," she wrote in a note, "but I'm afraid you are not going to fulfil your promise to get rid of Olympe.... All this chasing after other women has left too many stains on our love...."

IN THE NEXT two or three years he turned many times from his realistic studies to other revealing philosophic tales: *L'Elixir de longue vie, Le Chef d'oeuvre inconnu*. But above all *La Recherche de l'absolu* contains the theme of a destiny that is the directing force in his imagination.

> Our passions, vices, our inborn extremism, our pleasures and our pains are torrents of the mind flowing through us. When a man concentrates on violent ideas at any given point, he is destroyed by them as if he had been pierced by a dagger.

In this sense, all Balzac's characters have a core of monomania: that is to say, from the Romantics he rejected he retained the notion that the driving force in life is something disconnected from social circumstance. Balthazar Claes will willingly burn all the furniture in his house in order to keep his furnace going—the furnace that is required by his obsession with the discovery of the quintessential metal or substance out of which matter and spirit are made.

In his own life Balzac was to burn himself out. He was about to pour out books like *Louis Lambert, Eugénie Grandet,* and *Le Père Goriot,* the stories of a secret society, *L'histoire des treize, Le Médecin de campagne,* and *Le Lys dans la vallée.* To say that he worked is inadequate: he seemed to have a ceaseless engine in his brain. At eight in the evening he would go to bed and be awakened at midnight by Auguste, his valet, and what he called his monastic life began. He put on the monk's robe of white cashmere, with its golden chain, and sat down by the light of his candles at the small table. He said of this table:

> It has seen all my wretchedness, knows all my plans, has overheard my thoughts. My arm almost committed violent assault upon it as my pen raced along the sheets.

The paper was in small sheets with a bluish tint so as not to irritate the eyes. He wrote hour after hour, and when he flagged and his head seemed to burst, he went to the coffee pot and brewed the strongest black coffee he could find made from the beans of Bourbon, Martinique, and Mocha. He was resorting to a slow course of coffee poisoning, and it has been estimated that in his life he drank 50,000 cups of it. When dawn came he stopped writing and, imitating Napoleon, lay for an hour in a hot bath. At nine, messengers brought him proofs from the printers and he began the enormous task of altering almost everything he had written, and in that handwriting that drove printers mad: the completed novel might run only to 200 pages, but in its successive stages the manuscript might run to 2,000. This was work for the morning. He broke off for a light lunch of an egg or a sandwich. Back to proofs and letters in the afternoon; at five he saw a few friends, and after dinner, by eight o'clock, he was in bed once more.

On Photography by Susan Sontag was originally published October 18, 1973.

SUSAN SONTAG

On Photography

WE LINGER UNREGENERATELY in Plato's cave, still reveling, our age-old habit, in mere images of the truth. But being educated by photographs isn't like being educated by older, more crafted images. For one thing, there are a great many more images around claiming our attention. Daguerre started the inventory, with faces, and since then just about everything has been photographed; or so it seems. This very insatiability of the photographing eye changes the terms of confinement in the cave, our world. In teaching us a new visual code, photographs alter and enlarge our notions of what is worth looking at and what we have a right to observe. The most grandiose result of the photographic enterprise is to give us the sense that we can hold the whole world in our heads—as an anthology of images.

Movies and television programs light up walls, flicker, and go out; but with still photographs the image is also an object, lightweight, cheap to produce, easy to carry about, accumulate, store. In Godard's *Les Carabiniers* (1963), two sluggish lumpenpeasants are lured into joining the King's army by the promise that they will be able to loot, rape, kill, or do whatever else they please to the enemy, and get rich. But the suitcase of booty that Michel Ange and Ulysse triumphantly bring home, years later, to their wives turns out to contain only picture postcards, hundreds of them, of monuments, department stores, mammals, wonders of nature, methods of transport, works of art, and other classified treasures from around the globe. Godard's gag vividly parodies the equivocal magic of the photographic image. Photographs are perhaps the most mysterious of all the objects that make up, and thicken, the environment we recognize as "modern." Photographs really are experience captured, and the camera is the ideal arm of consciousness in its acquisitive mood.

To photograph is to appropriate the thing photographed. It means putting oneself into a certain relation to the world that feels like knowledge—and, therefore, like power. A now notorious first fall into alienation, habituating people to abstract the world into printed words, is supposed to have engendered that surplus of Faustian energy and psychic damage needed to build modern, inorganic societies. But print seems a less treacherous form of leaching out the world, of turning it into a mental object, than photographic images, which provide most of the knowledge people have about the look of the past and the reach of the present. What can be read about the world is frankly an interpretation, as are older kinds of flat-surface visual statements, like paintings and drawings. Photographed images do not seem to be statements about the world so much as pieces of it: miniatures of reality that anyone can make or acquire.

Photographs, which fiddle with the scale of the world, themselves get reduced, blown up, cropped, retouched, doctored, tricked out. They age, plagued by the usual ills of other objects made of paper. They are lost, or become valuable, are bought and sold; they are reproduced. Photographs, which package the world, seem to invite packaging. They are stuck in albums, tacked on walls, printed in newspapers, collected in books. Cops alphabetize them; museums exhibit them.

PHOTOGRAPHS FURNISH EVIDENCE. Something we hear about but doubt seems "proven" when we're shown a photograph of it. In one version of its utility, the camera record incriminates. Starting with their use by the Paris police in the murderous round-up of Communards in June 1871, photographs become a useful tool of modern states in the surveillance and control of their increasingly mobile populations. In another version of its utility, the camera record passes for incontrovertible proof that a given thing happened. The picture may distort; but there is always a presumption that something exists, or did exist, which is "like" what's in the picture.

Whatever the limitations (through amateurism) or pretensions (through artistry) of the individual photographer, a photograph seems to have a more innocent, and therefore more accurate, relation to visible reality than do other mimetic objects. Virtuosi of the noble image like Paul Strand and Edward Steichen, composing mighty, unforgettable photographs decade after decade, still want, first of all, to show something "out there," just like the Polaroid owner for whom photographs are a handy, fast form of note-taking, or the shutterbug with a Brownie who takes snapshots as souvenirs of daily life.

Despite the presumption of veracity that gives all photographs authority, interest, seductiveness, the work that photographers do is also part of the usually shady commerce between art and truth. Even when photographers attempt to serve reality, they're still haunted by tacit imperatives of taste and conscience. The immensely gifted members of the Farm Security Administration photographic project of the late 1930s (among them Walker Evans, Dorothea Lange, Ben Shahn, Russell Lee) would take dozens of frontal pictures of one of their sharecropper subjects until satisfied that they had gotten just the right look on film—the precise expression on the subject's face that supported their own notions about poverty, despair, exploitation, dignity, light, texture, and space.

In deciding how a picture should look, in preferring one exposure to another, standards are always being imposed on the subject. Although there is a sense in which the camera does indeed capture reality, not just interpret it, photographs are as much an interpretation of the world as any other work of art. Those occasions when taking photographs is relatively undiscriminating, promiscuous, or self-effacing do not lessen the didacticism of the whole enterprise. This very passivity—and ubiquity—of the photographic record is photography's "message," its aggression.

Images which idealize (like most fashion and animal photography) are no less aggressive than work which makes a virtue of plainness (like class pictures, still lifes of the bleaker sort, and mug shots). There is an aggression implicit in every use of the camera. This is as evident in the 1840s, that brief period which Walter Benjamin considers photography's greatest, the mere ten years that preceded its "industrialization," as in all the succeeding decades, during which technology made possible an ever-increasing spread of that mentality which looks at the world as a set of potential photographs. Even for these masters of the first decade, David Octavius Hill and Julia Margaret Cameron, Hugo and Nadar, who used the camera as a means of getting painterly images, the point of taking photographs was a vast departure from the aims of painters. From its start, photography implied the capture of the largest possible number of subjects. Painting never had so imperial a scope. The subsequent "industrialization" of camera technology only continues a promise inherent in photography from its very beginning: to democratize all experiences by translating them into images.

The "industrialization" of photography that Benjamin deplores in his essay of 1931 is much further advanced now, forty years later, than even he could have imagined. That age when taking photographs required a cumbersome and expensive contraption—the toy of the clever, the wealthy, and the obsessed—seems remote indeed from the era of sleek pocket cameras which anyone can use. The first cameras, made in France and England in the late 1830s, had only inventors and buffs to operate them. Since there were then no professional photographers, there could not be amateurs either. In this first decade, taking photographs had no clear social use; it was a gratuitous, that is, an artistic activity, without yet being an art. Contrary to what Benjamin argues, it was only with "industrialization" that photography became an art. As "industrialization" provided social uses for the operations of the photographer, so the reaction against these uses inspired the self-consciousness and taste for stylistic experiments of photography-as-art.

RECENTLY PHOTOGRAPHY has become almost as widely practiced as sex and dancing—which means that, like every other mass art form, photography is not practiced by most people as an art. It is mainly a social rite, a defense against anxiety, and a tool of power. Memorializing the achievements of individuals considered as members of families (as well as of other groups) is the earliest popular use of photography. For at least a century, the wedding photograph has been as much a part of the ceremony as the prescribed verbal formulas. Cameras are part of family life. According to a sociological study made in France, most households have a camera, but a household with children is twice as likely to have at least one camera as a household in which there are no children. Not to take pictures of one's children, particularly when they are small, is a sign of parental indifference, just as not turning up for one's graduation picture is a gesture of adolescent rebellion.

Through photographs, each family constructs a portrait of itself—a kit of images that bears witness to its connectedness. It hardly matters what activities are photographed so long as photographs get taken and are cherished. Photography becomes a rite of family life just when, in the industrializing countries of Europe and America, the very institution of the family starts undergoing radical surgery. As that claustrophobic unit, the nuclear family, was being carved out of the much larger traditional family, photography came along to reinforce symbolically the imperiled family life. Those ghostly traces, photographs, supply the token presence of the dispersed relatives. A family's photograph album is generally "about" the extended family—and, often, is all that's left of it.

As photographs give people an imaginary sense of possession of a past that is unreal, they also help people to take possession of space in which they are insecure. Thus, photography is linked with one of the most influential of modern activities: tourism. It seems positively unnatural to travel for pleasure without taking a camera along. For the bemused and somewhat anxious vacationer, the photograph offers indisputable evidence that the trip was made, that fun was had. Photographs document consumption carried on outside the view of family, friends, neighbors. Dependence on the camera as the device that makes real what one is experiencing doesn't fade when people travel more. Taking photographs fills the same need for the sophisticates accumulating photograph-trophies of their boat trip up the Albert Nile or their fourteen days in China as it does for vacationers taking snapshots of the Eiffel Tower.

A way of certifying experience, taking photographs is also a way of re-fusing it—by converting experience into an image, a souvenir. Travel be-comes a strategy for accumulating photographs. The very activity of taking pictures is soothing. Most tourists feel compelled to put the camera be-tween themselves and whatever is remarkable that they encounter. Lacking other responses, they take a picture. This gives shape to experience: stop, take a photograph, and move on. The method especially appeals to people handicapped by a ruthless work ethic—Germans, Japanese, and Ameri-cans. They have something to do that is like a friendly imitation of work: they can take pictures.

People robbed of their past seem to be the most fervent picture takers, at home and abroad. Everyone who lives in an industrialized society has lost the past to some degree, but in certain countries, such as the United States and Japan, the break with the past has been particularly traumatic. Right now, the fabled American tourist of the Fifties and Sixties, rich with dollars and Babbittry, is being replaced by the Japanese tourist, newly released from his island prison by the miracle of overvalued yen, who is generally armed with two cameras, one on each hip.

IN A FULL-PAGE AD currently running in many European weeklies, a small group of people stand pressed together, peering out of the photograph, all but one looking stunned, excited, upset. The one who wears a different expression holds a camera to his eye; he seems self-possessed, almost smil-ing. While the others are passive, clearly alarmed spectators, having a camera has transformed one person into something active, a voyeur. Only he has mastered the situation.

What do these people see? We don't know. And it doesn't matter. It is an Event: something worth seeing—and therefore worth photograph-ing. The ad copy, white letters across the dark lower third of the photo-graph like news coming over a teletype machine, consists of just six words: "...Prague...Woodstock...Vietnam...Sapporo...Londonderry...LEICA."

Crushed hopes, youth antics, colonial wars, and winter sports are alike—are equalized by the camera.

Part of the horror of such recent coups of photojournalism as the pictures of bonzes reaching for the gasoline can, of a Pakistani prisoner on his back about to be impaled, comes from the awareness of how plausible it has become, in situations where the photographer has the choice between a photograph and a life, to choose the photograph. The person who intervenes cannot record; the person who is recording cannot intervene. The omnipresence of cameras persuasively suggests that time consists of interesting events, events worth photographing. This, in turn, makes it easy to feel that any event, once underway, and whatever its moral character, ought to be allowed to complete itself—so that something else can be brought into the world, the photograph. After the event has ended, the picture will still exist. Thus on the event is conferred a kind of immortality (and importance) it would never otherwise have enjoyed. While real people are out there killing themselves or other real people, the photographer stays behind his camera, creating a tiny element of another world: the image-world that bids to outlast us all.

While the camera is an observation station, the act of photographing is more than passive observing. Taking pictures, like sexual voyeurism, is a way of tacitly—often explicitly—encouraging whatever is going on to keep on happening. To take a picture is to have an interest in things as they are, in the status quo remaining unchanged (at least for as long as it takes to get a good picture), to be in complicity with whatever makes a subject interesting, worth photographing—including, when that's the interest, another person's pain or misfortune.

"I HAVE ALWAYS thought of photography as a naughty thing to do—that was one of my favorite things about it," Diane Arbus wrote, "and when I first did it I felt very perverse." Being a professional photographer can be thought of as naughty, to use Arbus's Pop word, if the photographer seeks out subjects considered to be naughty, taboo, marginal. But naughty subjects are harder to find these days. And what is the perverse part of taking pictures? Professional photographers must often have sexual fantasies when they are behind the camera. Perhaps the perversion lies in the fact that these fantasies are both plausible and inappropriate.

In *Blow-Up* (1967), Antonioni has the fashion photographer played by David Hemmings convulsively writhing above Veruschka's body with his camera clicking. Naughtiness, indeed. In fact, using a camera is not a very good way of pushing someone around sexually. Between photographer and subject there has to be distance. The camera doesn't rape, or even possess, though it may presume, intrude, trespass, distort, exploit, and, at the farthest reach of metaphor, assassinate—all activities that, unlike the sexual push and shove, can be conducted from a distance, and with some detachment.

There is a much odder sexual fantasy in Michael Powell's extraordinary movie *Peeping Tom* (1958), which is not about a peeping tom but about a homicidal photographer who kills women while photographing them, with a weapon concealed in his camera; he develops the films, and runs them off at night for his solitary pleasure. Not once does he touch his subjects. He doesn't desire their bodies; he wants their photographed images, particularly those showing them experiencing their own death. The film assumes connections between impotence and aggression, professionalized "looking" and cruelty, which point to the central fantasy connected with the camera. The camera as phallus is, at most, a flimsy variant of the inescapable metaphor that everyone unself-consciously employs. However hazy our awareness of this fantasy, it is named without subtlety whenever we talk about "loading" and "aiming" a camera, about "shooting" a film.

The old-fashioned camera was clumsier and harder to reload than a Brown Bess musket. The modern camera is trying to be a ray gun. One ad reads:

> The Yashica Electro-35 GT is the spaceage camera your family will love. Take beautiful pictures day or night. Automatically. Without any nonsense. Just aim, focus and shoot. The GT's computer brain and electronic shutter will do the rest.

Like a car, a camera is sold as a predatory weapon—one that's as automated as possible, ready to spring. Popular taste expects an easy, invisible technology. Manufacturers reassure their customers that taking pictures demands no skill, that the machine is all-knowing, and responds to the slightest pressure of the will. It's as simple as turning the ignition key or pulling the trigger.

Like guns and cars, cameras are fantasy machines whose use is addictive. However, contrary to the rhetoric of ordinary language and advertising, they are not as lethal as guns and cars. For cars being marketed like guns there is at least this much truth in the hyperbole: except in wartime, cars kill more people than guns do. The camera does not kill, so it seems to be all a bluff—like a man's fantasy of having a gun, knife, or tool between his legs. Still, there is something predatory in the act of taking a picture. To photograph people is to violate them, by seeing them as they never see themselves, by having knowledge of them they can never have. To photograph is to turn people into objects that can be symbolically possessed. To photograph someone is a sublimated murder, just as the camera is the sublimation of a gun. Taking pictures is a soft murder, appropriate to a sad, frightened time.

PERHAPS PEOPLE WILL LEARN to act out more aggressions with cameras and fewer with guns, with the price being an even more image-choked world. One situation where people are switching from bullets to film is the photographic safaris that are replacing gun safaris in East Africa. The hunters have Hasselblads instead of Winchesters; instead of looking through the telescopic sight to aim a rifle, they look through a viewfinder. In end-of-the-century London, Samuel Butler complained that "there is a photographer in every bush, going about like a roaring lion seeking whom he may devour." The photographer is now charging real beasts, beleaguered and getting too rare to kill.

Guns have metamorphosed into cameras in this unique comedy, the ecology safari, because nature has ceased to be what it always was—what people needed protection from. Now nature—discovered to be pathetic, endangered, mortal—needs to be protected from people. When we are afraid, we shoot. But when we are nostalgic, we take pictures.

It is a nostalgic time right now, and likely to remain so for a while. Photography is an elegiac art, a twilight art. There is no subject the photographer might attempt that could not be touched with pathos. All photographs are *memento mori*. To take a photograph is to participate in another person's (or thing's) mortality, vulnerability, mutability. Precisely by slicing out this moment and freezing it, all photographs testify to time's relentless melt.

Cameras begin duplicating the world at the time when the human landscape starts to undergo a vertiginous rate of change. Just when the greatest number of forms of life are being destroyed in the shortest space of time, a device is invented to record what is disappearing. The textured Paris of Atget and Brassaï is mostly gone. Like the dead relatives and friends preserved in the family album, whose presence in photographs exorcises some of the horror and guilt of their disappearance, so the photographs of neighborhoods now torn down, rural places disfigured and made barren, supply our pocket relation to the past.

A photograph is both a pseudo-presence and a token of absence. Like a wood fire in a room, photographs—especially those of people, of distant landscapes and faraway cities, of the vanished past—are incitements to reverie. The sense of the unattainable that can be set off by photographs feeds directly into the erotic feelings of those for whom desirability is enhanced by distance. The lover's photograph in a woman's wallet, the poster photograph of a rock star over an adolescent's bed, the snapshots of a cabdriver's children above his dashboard—all such talismanic uses of photographs express a feeling both sentimental and implicitly magical, attempts to contact another reality.

PHOTOGRAPHS CAN BE aids to desire in the most direct, utilitarian way—as when someone keeps photographs of anonymous archetypes of desire as an aid to masturbation. The situation is more complex when photographs are used to stimulate the moral impulse. Desire has no history. It is made up of archetypes and in that sense is abstract. But moral feelings are embedded in history, whose personae are always concrete, whose situations are always specific. Thus, almost opposite rules hold true for the use of the photograph to awaken desire and its use to awaken conscience. The images that mobilize conscience are always specific to a given historical situation. The more general they are, the less likely they are to be effective.

A photograph that brings news of some unsuspected zone of misery can't make a dent in public opinion unless there is an appropriate context of feeling and attitude. The photographs Matthew Brady took of the horrors of the battlefields did not make people any less keen to go on with the Civil War. The photographs of skeletal prisoners held at Andersonville inflamed Northern public opinion—against the South. (The effect of the Andersonville photographs must have been partly due to the very novelty, at that time, of seeing photographs.) The political understanding that many Americans came to in the 1960s would allow them, looking at the photographs Dorothea Lange took of Nisei on the West Coast being transported to internment camps in 1942, to recognize their subject for what it was—a crime committed by the government against a large group of American citizens. Few people who saw the photographs in the 1940s could have had so unequivocal a reaction; the ground for such a judgment barely existed then. Photographs cannot create a moral position, but they can reinforce one—and can help build a nascent one.

Photographs may be more memorable than moving images—because they are a neat slice of time. Television is a stream of underselected images, each of which cancels its predecessor. A still photograph is a "privileged moment," turned into a slim object that one can keep and look at again. Photographs like the one taken in 1971 and put on the front page of most newspapers in the world—a naked child running down a South Vietnamese highway toward the camera, having just been hit by American napalm, her arms open, screaming with pain—were of great importance in mobilizing antiwar sentiment in this country from 1967 on. And each one was certainly more memorable than a hundred hours of televised barbarities.

One would like to believe that the American public would not have been so unanimous in its acquiescence to the Korean War if it had been confronted with photographic evidence of the devastation of Korea, an ecocide and genocide in some respects even more thorough than the ones inflicted on the Vietnamese a decade later. But the supposition is trivial. The public did not see such photographs because there was, ideologically, no space for them. Americans did have access to photographs of the sufferings of the Vietnamese because journalists felt backed in their efforts to get those photographs, some people having redefined the event as a savage colonialist war. The Korean War was understood differently—as another struggle of the Free World against the Soviet Union and China—and, given that characterization, photographs of the cruelty of unlimited firepower would have been irrelevant. If an event is now defined as something worth photographing, it is still ideology (in the broadest sense) that tells us what constitutes an event. And it is never photographic evidence which can construct—more properly, invent—events. Without a politics, photographs of the slaughter-bench of history are not identifiable as such.

THE QUALITY OF FEELING, including moral outrage, that people can muster in response to photographs of the oppressed, the exploited, the starving, and the napalmed also depends on the degree of their familiarity with these images. The photographs of Biafrans starving in the 1960s had less impact for some people than Werner Bischof's photographs of Indian famine victims in the 1950s because those images had become banal, and the photographs appearing now in magazines of Tuareg families dying of starvation in the Southern Sahara may seem to many like an unbearable replay of a now familiar atrocity exhibition.

Photographs shock us in so far as they show us something novel. Unfortunately, the ante keeps getting raised—partly through the very proliferation of such images of horror. One's first encounter with the photographic inventory of ultimate horror is a kind of revelation, perhaps the only revelation people are granted now, a negative epiphany. For me, it was photographs of Bergen-Belsen and Dachau which I came across by chance in a bookstore in Santa Monica in July 1945. Nothing I have seen—in photographs or in real life—ever cut me as sharply, deeply, instantaneously. Ever since then, it has seemed plausible to me to think of my life as being divided into two parts: before I saw those photographs (I was twelve) and after. My life was changed by them, though not until several years later did I understand what they were about. What good was served by seeing them? They were only photographs—of an event I had scarcely heard of and could do nothing to affect, of suffering I could hardly imagine and could do nothing to relieve. When I looked at those photographs, something was broken. Some limit had been reached, and not only that of horror; I felt irrevocably grieved, wounded, but a part of my feelings started to tighten; something went dead; something is still crying.

To suffer is one thing; another thing is living with the photographed images of suffering, which does not necessarily strengthen conscience and the ability to be compassionate. It can also corrupt them. Once one has seen such images, one has started down the road of seeing more—and more. Images transfix. Images anesthetize. An event known through photographs certainly becomes more real than it would have been if one had never seen the photographs—think of the Vietnam War. But, after repeated exposure to images, it also becomes less real.

There is the same law for evil as for pornography. The shock of photographed atrocities wears off with repeated viewings, just as the surprise and bemusement one feels the first time one sees a pornographic movie wear off after seeing a few more. The sense of taboo that makes us indignant and sorrowful is not much sturdier than the sense of taboo that regulates our definition of what is obscene. And both have been sorely tried in recent years. The vast photographic catalog of misery and injustice throughout the world has given everyone a certain familiarity with atrocity, making the horrible seem more ordinary—making it appear familiar, remote ("It's only a photograph"), inevitable. At the time of the first photographs of the Nazi camps, there was nothing banal about these images. After almost thirty years, we may be reaching a saturation point. In these last decades, "concerned" photography has done at least as much to deaden conscience as to arouse it.

The ethical content of photographs is fragile. With the exception of certain photographs, like the camps and Vietnam, most photographs don't keep their emotional charge. A photograph of 1900 that was affecting then because of its subject would, today, be more likely to move us because it is a photograph taken in 1900. The particular qualities and intentions of photographs tend to be swallowed up in the generalized pathos of time past. Aesthetic distance seems built into the very experience of looking at photographs, if not right away, then with the passage of time. Time eventually positions most photographs, even the very amateurish, at the level of art.

THE "INDUSTRIALIZATION" of photography permitted its rapid absorption into rational—i.e., bureaucratic—ways of running society. No longer toy images, photographs became part of the furniture of the environment—a touchstone and confirmation of that reductive approach to reality which is called "realistic." Photographs were enrolled in the service of important institutions of control, notably the family and the police, as symbolic objects and pieces of information. Thus, in the bureaucratic cataloging of the world, many important documents are not valid unless they have affixed to them a photograph-token of the citizen's face.

The "realistic" view of the world compatible with bureaucracy redefines knowledge—as techniques and information. Photographs are valued because they give information. They tell one what there is: they make an inventory. In fact, except to cops, novelists, and historians, even their value as information is trivial. The information that photographs can give starts to seem more important than it really is at that moment in cultural history when everyone is thought to have a right to something called "news." Photographs were seen as a way of giving information to people who do not take easily to reading. The *Daily News* still calls itself "New York's Picture Newspaper," its bid for populist identity. At the opposite end of the scale, *Le Monde*, a newspaper designed for skilled, well-informed readers, runs no photographs at all. The presumption is that, for such readers, a photograph could only illustrate the analysis contained in an article.

A new sense of the notion of "information" has been constructed around the photographed image. The photograph is a thin slice of space as well as time. In a world ruled by photographic images, all borders ("framing") seem arbitrary. Anything can be separated from anything else. All that is necessary is to frame the subject differently. Through photographs, the world becomes a series of unrelated, free-standing particles; and history, past and present, a set of anecdotes and *faits divers*. It makes reality atomic, "manageable," and opaque. It is a view of the world which denies interconnectedness. The ultimate wisdom of the photographed image is to say: "There is the surface. Now, think—or, rather, feel, intuit—what is beyond it, what the reality must be like if it looks this way." Strictly speaking, there is never any understanding in a photograph, but only an invitation to fantasy and speculation.

PHOTOGRAPHY IMPLIES that we know about the world if we accept it as the camera records it. But this is the opposite of understanding, an approach which starts from not accepting the world as it looks. All possibility of understanding is rooted in the ability to say no. Strictly speaking, it is doubtful that a photograph can help us to understand anything. The simple fact of "rendering" a reality doesn't tell us much about that reality. A photograph of the Krupp factory, as Brecht points out, tells us little about this institution. The "reality" of the world is not in its images, but in its functions. Functioning takes place in time, and must be explained in time. Only that which narrates can make us understand.

The limit of photographic knowledge of the world is that, while it can arouse conscience, it can, finally, never be ethical or political knowledge. In itself, the knowledge gained through still photographs will always be some kind of sentimentalism—whether cynical or humanist. It will always be knowledge at bargain prices—a semblance of knowledge, a semblance of appropriation, a semblance of rape, a semblance of wisdom. Photographs have a great effect on our ethical sensibility, by making us feel that the world is more available than it really is. By furnishing this already crowded world with a duplicate world of images, photography subtly devalues the world and undermines the possibility of having fresh responses to it.

Being involved with photographs is an aesthetic consumerism to which we are all, understandably, addicted. We are image-junkies now. It is a glorious form of mental pollution. Poignant longings for beauty, for an end to probing below the surface, for a redemption and celebration of the body of the world—all these good feelings are expressed in the pleasures we take in photographs. But other, more doubtful longings get expressed as well.

Andrei D. Sakharov

How I Came to Dissent *by Andrei D. Sakharov was originally published March 21, 1974.*
From Sakharov Speaks *by Andrei D. Sakharov, copyright © 1974 by Alfred A. Knopf, Inc.*
Reprinted by permission of Alfred A. Knopf, Inc.

ANDREI D. SAKHAROV

How I Came to Dissent

IN GIVING AUTOBIOGRAPHICAL information, I hope to put an end to false rumors with respect to facts which have frequently been misrepresented in the press, because of ignorance or sensationalism.

I was born in 1921 in Moscow, into a cultured and close family. My father was a teacher of physics and the author of several widely known textbooks and popular-science books. From childhood I lived in an atmosphere of decency, mutual help and tact, a liking for work, and respect for the mastery of one's chosen profession. In 1938 I completed high school and entered Moscow State University, from which I was graduated in 1942. Between 1942 and 1945 I worked as an engineer at a war plant, where I developed several inventions having to do with methods of quality control.

Between 1945 and 1947 I did graduate work under the guidance of a well-known Soviet scientist, the theoretical physicist Igor Evgenevich Tamm. A few months after defending my dissertation in the spring of 1948, I was included in a research group working on the problem of a thermonuclear weapon. I had no doubts about the vital importance of creating a Soviet superweapon—for our country and for the balance of power throughout the world. Carried away by the immensity of the task, I worked very strenuously and became the author or coauthor of several key ideas. In the Western press I have often been called "the father of the hydrogen bomb." This description reflects very inaccurately the real (and complex) situation of collective invention—something I shall not discuss in detail.

IN THE SUMMER of 1950, almost simultaneously with the beginning of work on the thermonuclear weapon, I.E. Tamm and I began work on the problem of a controlled thermonuclear reaction; i.e., on the use of the nuclear energy of light elements for purposes of industrial energetics. In 1950 we formulated the idea of the magnetic thermo-isolation of high-temperature plasma, and completed estimates on the parameters for thermonuclear

141

synthesis installations. This research, which became known abroad from the paper read by I.V. Kurchatov at Harwell in 1956 and from the materials of the First Geneva Conference on the Peaceful Use of Atomic Energy, was recognized as pioneering. In 1961 I proposed, for the same purposes, heating deuterium with a beam from a pulse laser. I mention these things here by way of explaining that my contributions were not limited to military problems.

In 1950 our research group became part of a special institute. For the next eighteen years I found myself caught up in the rotation of a special world of military designers and inventors, special institutes, committees and learned councils, pilot plants and proving grounds. Every day I saw the huge material, intellectual, and nervous resources of thousands of people being poured into creating the means of total destruction, a force potentially capable of annihilating all human civilization. I noticed that the control levers were in the hands of people who, although talented in their own way, were cynical. Until the summer of 1953 the top boss of the atomic project was Beria, who ruled over millions of slave-prisoners. Almost all the construction was done with their labor. Beginning in the late Fifties, one got an increasingly clearer picture of the collective might of the military-industrial complex and of its vigorous, unprincipled leaders, blind to everything except their "job."

I was in a rather special position. As a theoretical scientist and inventor, relatively young and (moreover) not a Party member, I was not involved in administrative responsibility and was exempt from Party ideological discipline. My position enabled me to know and see a great deal. It compelled me to feel my own responsibility; and at the same time I could look upon this whole perverted system as something of an outsider. All this prompted me—especially in the ideological atmosphere which came into being after the death of Stalin and Twentieth Congress of the CPSU—to reflect in general terms on the problems of peace and mankind, and in particular on the problems of a thermonuclear war and its aftermath.

Beginning in 1957 (not without the influence of statements on this subject made throughout the world by such people as Albert Schweitzer, Linus Pauling, and others) I felt myself responsible for the problem of radioactive contamination from nuclear explosions. As is known, the absorption of the radioactive products of nuclear explosions by the billions of people inhabiting the earth leads to an increase in the incidence of several diseases and birth defects because of so-called subthreshold biological effects; for example, because of damage to DNA molecules—the bearers of heredity. When the radioactive products of an explosion get into the atmosphere, each megaton of the power of a nuclear explosion means thousands of unknown victims. And each series of tests of a nuclear weapon (whether they be conducted by the US, the USSR, Great Britain, China, or France) involves tens of megatons; i.e., tens of thousands of victims.

IN MY ATTEMPTS to explain this problem, I encountered great difficulties— and a reluctance to understand. I wrote memorandums (as a result of one of them I.V. Kurchatov made a trip to Yalta to meet with N.S. Khrushchev in an unsuccessful attempt to stop the 1958 tests), and I spoke at conferences. I remember that in the summer of 1961 there was a meeting between atomic scientists and the chairman of the Council of Ministers, Khrushchev. It turned out that we were to prepare for a series of tests which would bolster up the new policy of the USSR on the German question (the Berlin Wall). I wrote a note to Khrushchev, saying: "To resume tests after a three-year moratorium would undermine the talks on banning tests and on disarmament, and would lead to a new round in the armaments race— especially in the sphere of intercontinental missiles and anti-missile defense." I passed it up the line. Khrushchev put the note in his breast pocket and invited all present to dine.

At the dinner table he made an off-the-cuff speech which I remember for its frankness, and which did not reflect merely his personal position. He said more or less the following. Sakharov is a good scientist. But leave it to us, who are specialists in this tricky business, to make foreign policy. Only force—only the disorientation of the enemy. We can't say aloud that we are carrying out our policy from a position of strength, but that's the way it must be. I would be a slob, and not chairman of the Council of Ministers, if I listened to the likes of Sakharov. In 1960 we helped to elect Kennedy with our policy. But we don't give a damn about Kennedy if he is tied hand and foot—if he can be overthrown at any moment.

Another and no less dramatic episode occurred in 1962. The ministry, acting basically from bureaucratic interests, issued instructions to proceed with a routine test explosion which was actually useless from the technical point of view. The explosion was to be powerful, so that the number of anticipated victims was colossal. Realizing the unjustifiable, criminal nature of this plan, I made desperate efforts to stop it. This went on for several weeks—weeks which, for me, were full of tension. On the eve of the test I phoned the minister and threatened to resign. The minister replied: "We're not holding you by the throat." I was able to put a phone call through to Ashkhabad, where Khrushchev was stopping on that particular day, and begged him to intervene. The next day I had a talk with one of Khrushchev's close advisers. But by then the time for the test had already been moved up to an earlier hour, and the carrier aircraft had already transported its burden to the designated point for the explosion. The feeling of impotence and fright which seized me on that day has remained in my memory ever since, and it has worked much change in me as I moved toward my present attitude.

IN 1962, I VISITED the minister of the atomic industry, who at that point was in a suburban government sanatorium together with the deputy minister of foreign affairs, and presented an important idea that had been brought to my attention at that time by one of my friends. By then, talks on the banning of nuclear testing had already been going on for several years, the stumbling block being the difficulty of monitoring underground explosions. But radioactive contamination is caused only by explosions in the atmosphere, in space, and in the ocean. Therefore limiting the agreement to banning tests in these three environments would solve both problems (contamination and monitoring). It should be noted that a similar proposal had previously been made by President Eisenhower, but at the time it had not accorded with the thinking of the Soviet side. In 1963 the so-called Moscow Treaty, in which this idea was realized, was concluded on the initiative of Khrushchev and Kennedy. It is possible that my initiative was of help in this historic act.

In 1964 I spoke at a conference of the Academy of Sciences USSR (in connection with the election of one of Lysenko's companions-in-arms) and publicly touched on the "prohibited" subject of the situation in Soviet biology in which, for decades, modern genetics had been attacked as a "pseudo-science" and scientists working in that field had been subjected to harsh persecutions and repressions. Subsequently I developed these thoughts in greater detail in a letter to Khrushchev. Both the speech and the letter found a very broad response, and later helped to correct the situation to some extent. It was at this time that my name first appeared in the Soviet press—in an article by the president of the Academy of Agricultural Sciences which contained the most unpardonable attacks on me.

FOR ME, PERSONALLY, these events had great psychological significance. Also, they expanded the circle of persons with whom I associated. In particular, I became acquainted during the next few years with the Medvedev brothers, Zhores and Roy. A manuscript by the biologist Zhores Medvedev, which was passed from hand to hand, circumventing the censor, was the first *samizdat* work I had read. (*Samizdat* was a word which had come into use a few years before to denote a new social phenomenon.) In 1967 I also read the manuscript of a book by the historian Roy Medvedev on the crimes of Stalin. Both books, especially the latter, made a very strong impression on me. However our relations may have turned out, and whatever my subsequent disagreements with the Medvedevs on matters of principle, I cannot minimize their role in my own development.

In 1966 I was one of the signers of a collective letter on the "cult" of Stalin sent to the Twenty-third Congress of the CPSU. In that same year I sent a telegram to the Supreme Soviet USSR about a new law, then being drafted, which would facilitate large-scale persecutions for one's convictions. (Article 190–191 of the RSFSR Criminal Code). Thus for the first time my own fate became intertwined with the fate of that group of people—a group which was small but very weighty on the moral (and, I dare say, the historical) plane—who subsequently came to be called "dissenters" (*inakomyslyashchie*). (Personally I am fonder of the old Russian word for "freethinkers," *volnomyslyashchie*.) Very shortly thereafter I had occasion to write a letter to Brezhnev protesting the arrest of four of them: A. Ginzburg, Yu. Galanskov (who perished tragically in a camp in 1972), V. Lashkova, and Dobrovolsky. In connection with this letter and my previous actions, the minister heading up the department for which I worked said of me: "Sakharov is an outstanding scientist and we have rewarded him well, but he is stupid as a politician."

In 1967, for a publication which circulated among my colleagues, I wrote a "futurological" article on the future role of science in the life of society, and on the future of science itself. In that same year, for the *Literaturnaya gazeta*, the journalist E. Henry (Genri) and I wrote an article on the role of the intelligentsia and the danger of a thermonuclear war. The Central Committee of the CPSU did not authorize the publication of the article. But by means unknown to me it got into the *Political Diary*—a supposedly secret publication, something like *samizdat* for higher officials. A year later both of these articles, which remained little known, served as the basis for a work destined to play a central role in my activity for social causes.

EARLY IN 1968 I began work on a book which I called *Thoughts on Progress, Peaceful Coexistence, and Intellectual Freedom*. I wanted that book to reflect my thoughts on the most important problems facing mankind: thoughts on war and peace, on dictatorship, on the prohibited subject of Stalinist terror and freedom of thought, on demographic problems and the pollution of the environment, on the role that can be played by science and technological progress. The general tenor of the book was affected by the time of its writing—the height of the "Prague Spring." The basic ideas which I tried to develop in *Thoughts* were neither very new nor original. Essentially it was a compilation of liberal, humanistic, and "scientocratic" ideas based on information available to me and on personal experience. Today I regard this work as eclectic, pretentious in places, and imperfect ("raw") in terms of form. Nonetheless its basic ideas are dear to me. In it I clearly formulated the thesis (which strikes me as very important) that the rapprochement of the socialist and capitalist systems, accompanied by democratization, demilitarization, and social and technological progress, is the only alternative to the ruin of mankind.

Beginning in May and June of 1968, *Thoughts* was widely distributed in the USSR. This was the first work of mine which was taken up by *samizdat*. In July and August came the first foreign reports of my book. Subsequently *Thoughts* was repeatedly published abroad in large printings and provoked a great flow of responses in the press of many countries. In addition to the content of the work, an important role in all this was undoubtedly played by the fact that it was one of the first sociopolitical works to reach the West, and that moreover its author was a highly decorated representative of the "secret" and "dread" specialty of atomic physics. (Unfortunately, this sensationalism still envelops me, especially in the pages of the mass press in the West.)

The publication of *Thoughts* abroad immediately resulted in my being taken off secret projects (in August of 1968), and in the restructuring of my entire way of life. It was precisely at that time that I, acting under the influence of impulses I now consider unsound, transferred almost all my savings to a government fund (for the construction of a hospital for cancer patients), and to the Red Cross. At that time I had no personal contacts with people in need of help. Today, constantly seeing around me people who need not only protection but material help, I often regret my overly hasty gesture.

IN 1969 I WAS SENT to work at the Physics Institute of the Academy of Sciences USSR, where I had once done graduate work and then been a collaborator with Igor Evgenevich Tamm. Although this meant a substantial drop in salary and job status, I was still able to continue scientific work in that field of physics most interesting to me: the theory of elementary particles. Unfortunately, however, in recent years I have not been satisfied with my productivity in scientific work. Two things have played a decisive role in this. First, the fact that, as theoretical physicists go, I am well along in years. Second, the stressful—and recently very alarming—situation in which people close to me, my family, and I have found ourselves.

Meantime, events in society and an inner need to oppose injustice continued to urge me toward new actions. Early in 1970 another open letter to the leaders of the state was published by Valentin Turchin (the physicist and mathematician), Roy Medvedev, and myself. The subject of the letter was the interdependence of the problems of democratization and techno-economic progress. In June I took an active part in the campaign to free the other Medvedev brother—the biologist Zhores—from illegal confinement in a psychiatric hospital. About that same time I joined in a collective supervisory protest[1] to the Procurator's Office USSR on the case of General P.G. Grigorenko, who by decision of a Tashkent court had been sent for compulsory treatment to a special prison-type hospital of the MVD[2] USSR in the town of Chernyakhovsk.

The reason for this was the fact that Grigorenko had repeatedly made public appeals in defense of political prisoners and in defense of the rights of the Crimean Tatars, who in 1944 had been resettled from the Crimea with great cruelties under the Stalinist tyranny, and who today cannot return to their homeland. Our appeal, which pointed out the many patent violations of the law in the Grigorenko case, was never answered (which is also a crude violation of the law). Thus even more closely than in 1968, I was brought into contact with what is perhaps one of the most shameful aspects of present-day Soviet reality: illegality and the cynical persecution of persons coming out in defense of basic human rights. But at the same time I got to know several of these persons, and subsequently many others. One of those who joined in the collective protest on the Grigorenko case was Valery Chalidze, with whom I became very close.

I BECAME EVEN MORE FAMILIAR with the problems of defending human rights in October 1970, when I was allowed to attend a political trial. The

---

[1] I.e., a protest demanding that the procurator's office intervene (as it is entitled to do under Soviet law) to order a review of a case "by way of supervision" [translator's note].

[2] Ministry of Internal Affairs [translator's note].

mathematician Revolt Pimenov and the puppet-show actor Boris Vail had been charged with distributing *samizdat*—giving friends books and manuscripts to read. The items named in their case included an article by Djilas, the Czech manifesto "Two Thousand Words," Pimenov's personal commentaries on Khrushchev's speech at the Twentieth Congress, etc. I sat in a courtroom filled with "probationers" of the KGB, while the friends of the defendants remained in a hallway on the ground floor throughout the trial. This is one more feature of all political trials, without exception. Formally, they are open. But the courtroom is packed in advance with KGB agents specially designated for the purpose, while another group of agents stands around the court on all sides. They are always in civilian clothes, they call themselves *druzhinniki*,[3] and they are allegedly preserving public order. This is the way it was (with negligible variations) in all cases when I was allowed to enter the courtroom. As for the passes enabling me to attend, they were apparently issued in acknowledgment of my previous services.

Pimenov and Vail were sentenced to five years of exile each, despite the fact that Vail's lawyer, at the appellate hearing, had argued convincingly that he had taken no part at all in the incidents incriminating him. In his concluding remarks Boris Vail said that an unjust sentence has an effect not only on the convicted person but on the hearts of judges.

From the autumn of 1971 on I was outside the line formed by the *druzhinniki*. But nothing else had changed. At the trial of the well-known astrophysicist Kronid Lyubarsky (who was charged with the same thing: distributing *samizdat*), a very significant and tragic show was put on. We were not allowed in the courtroom. And when the session began, the "unknown persons in civilian clothes" used force to push us out from the vestibule of the court into the street. Then a big padlock was hung on the door leading into the people's court. One has to see all these senseless and cruel dramatics with one's own eyes to feel it to the fullest. But why all this? The only answer I can give is that the farce being performed inside the courthouse is even less intended for public disclosure than the farce outside the courthouse. The bureaucratic logic of legal proceedings looks grotesque in the light of public disclosure, even when there is formal observance of the law—which is by no means always the case.

The sentence received by Pimenov and Vail, so harsh and unjust from the viewpoint of natural human standards, is relatively lenient compared to

3 I.e., members of a *druzhina* or voluntary auxiliary police detachment [translator's note].

the decisions of Soviet courts in other cases of a similar nature, especially in recent years. Vladimir Bukovsky, known to the whole world for his protests in defense of people incarcerated in psychiatric hospitals for political reasons, was sentenced to twelve years: two years of prison, five years of camp, and five years of exile. K. Lyubarsky was sentenced to five years of imprisonment. The sentences passed outside of Moscow are even harsher. The young psychiatrist Semyon (Samuel) Gluzman was sentenced to seven years of imprisonment. I once happened to see Semyon for a few minutes at a railroad station, and I was astounded by the purity of his countenance—by a kind of effective goodness and directness. At the time I had no way of suspecting that such a fate was in store for him! It is generally supposed that the reason for the reprisal against Gluzman was the assumption that he was in the author of "Expert Examination *in Absentia* in the Grigorenko Case." But at the trial this charge was not brought. V. Morozov and Yu. Shukhevich, both authors of memoirs about their terms in camp, were sentenced by a Ukrainian court to fourteen and fifteen years, respectively, of imprisonment and exile. And the number of similar reprisals has grown rapidly.

BEFORE PROCEEDING FURTHER, I should like to say a few words about why I attach so much importance to the matter of defending political prisoners—defending the freedom of one's convictions. In the course of fifty-six years our country has undergone great shocks, sufferings, and humiliations, the physical annihilation of millions of the best people (best both morally and intellectually), decades of official hypocrisy and demagoguery, of internal and external time-serving. The era of terror, when tortures and special conferences[4] threatened everyone, when they seized the most devoted servants of the regime simply for the general count and to create an atmosphere of fright and submission—that era is now behind us.

But we are still living in the spiritual atmosphere created by that era. Against those few who do not go along with the prevalent practice of compromise, the government uses repression as before. Together with judicial repressions, the most important and decisive role in maintaining this atmosphere of internal and external submission is played by the power of the state, which manipulates all the levers of economic and social control. This, more than anything else, keeps the body and soul of the majority of people in a state of dependence.

---

[4] Special conferences (or boards) was the designation given, in the Stalin era, to secret drumhead courts [translator's note].

Another major influence on the psychological situation in the country is the fact that people are weary of endless promises of economic flowering in the very near future, and have ceased altogether to believe in fine words. The standard of living (food, clothing, housing, possibilities for leisure), social conditions (children's facilities, medical and educational institutions, pensions, labor protection, etc.)—all this lags far behind the level in advanced countries. An indifference to social problems—an attitude of consumerism and selfishness—is developing among the broad strata of the population. And among the majority, protest against the deadening official ideology has an unconscious, latent character. The religious and national movements are the broadest and most conscious. Among those who fill the camps or are subjected to other persecutions are many believers and representatives of national minorities.

One of the mass forms of protest is the desire to leave the country. Unfortunately, it must be noted that sometimes the striving toward a national revival takes on chauvinistic traits, and borders upon the traditional "everyday" hostility toward "aliens." Russian anti-Semitism is an example of this. Thus a part of the Russian opposition intelligentsia is beginning to manifest a paradoxical closeness to the secret Party-state doctrine of nationalism, which in fact is increasingly replacing the antinational and antireligious myth of Bolshevism. Among some people the same feeling of dissatisfaction and internal protest takes on other asocial forms (drunkenness, crime).

It is very important that the façade of prosperity and enthusiasm not conceal from the world this real picture of things. Our experience must not come to nothing. And it is equally important that our society gradually emerge from the dead end of unspirituality, which closes off the possibilities not only for the development of spiritual culture but for progress in the material sphere.

I AM CONVINCED that under the conditions obtaining in our country a position based on morality and law is the most correct one, as corresponding to the requirements and possibilities of society. What we need is the systematic defense of human rights and ideals and not a political struggle, which would inevitably incite people to violence, sectarianism, and frenzy. I am convinced that only in this way, provided there is the broadest possible public disclosure, will the West be able to recognize the nature of our society; and that then this struggle will become part of a worldwide movement for the salvation of all mankind. This constitutes a partial answer to the question of why I have (naturally) turned from worldwide problems to the defense of individual people.

The position of those who, beginning with the trials of Sinyavsky and Daniel, Ginzburg and Galanskov, have struggled for justice as they understand it can probably be compared with the position of the world-famous apolitical organization Amnesty International. In any democratic country the question of the legality of such activity could not even arise. In our country, unfortunately, such is not the case. Dozens of the most famous political trials, and dozens of prisoners in psychiatric hospitals of the prison type, provide a graphic demonstration of this.

In recent years I have learned a great deal about Soviet juridical practice by attending trials and receiving much information about the course of similar trials in other cities [besides Moscow]. I have also learned a great deal about conditions in places of confinement: about malnutrition, pitiless formalism, and repressions against prisoners. In several statements I called the attention of world public opinion to this problem, which is vitally important for the 1.7 million Soviet prisoners and indirectly has a deep influence on many important aspects of the moral and social life of the whole country. I have appealed, and I again appeal, to all international organizations concerned with this problem—and especially to the International Red Cross—to abandon their policy of nonintervention in the internal affairs of the socialist countries as regards defending human rights, and to manifest the utmost persistence.

I have also spoken out on the institution of "conditional release with obligatory assignment to labor," which in a political sense represents a vestige of the Stalinist system of mass forced labor, and which is very frightening in a social sense. It is difficult even to imagine the nightmare of the barracks for the "conditionally released persons," with almost general drunkenness, fistfights, and throat-slitting. This system has broken the lives of many people. The preservation of the camp system and forced labor is one of the reasons why extensive regions of the country are off-limits for foreigners. It would appear that the realization of any successful international cooperation in developing our very rich resources is impossible without the abolishment of this system.

Another problem which has claimed my attention in recent years is that of the psychiatric repressions used by organs of the KGB as an important auxiliary means of stifling and frightening dissenters. There is no doubt of the tremendous social danger of this phenomenon.

I feel that I owe a debt too great to be repaid to the brave and good people who are incarcerated in prisons, camps, and psychiatric hospitals because they struggled to defend human rights.

IN THE AUTUMN of 1970, V.N. Chalidze, A.N. Tverdokhlebov, and I joined in founding the "Human Rights Committee." This act on our part attracted great attention in the USSR and abroad. From the day of the committee's founding, A.S. Volpin took an active part in its work. This was the first time that such an association had made its appearance in our country; and its members did not have a very precise idea of what they should do and how they should do it. Yet the committee did a great deal of work on several problems, particularly in studying the question of compulsory confinement in psychiatric hospitals for political reasons. At the present time the work of the committee is being carried on by I.R. Shafarevich. G.S. Podyapolsky, and myself. As was true of the "Initiative Group" created somewhat earlier, the very existence of the committee as a free group of associates independent of the authorities has a unique and very great moral significance for our country.

The second article in my forthcoming collection[5] is a Memorandum, written in the first months of 1971 and sent to L.I. Brezhnev in March of that year. In form, the Memorandum is a kind of synopsis of an imaginary dialogue with the leadership of the country. I am not convinced that this form is literarily successful, but it is compact. As for the content, I endeavored to set forth my positive demands in the political, social, and economic spheres. Fifteen months later, not having received any reply, I published the Memorandum, adding an afterword which stands on its own.

In publishing the Memorandum I did not make any changes in the text. In particular, I did not change the treatment of the problem of Soviet-Chinese relations—something I now regret. I still do not idealize the Chinese variant of socialism. But I do not regard as correct that evaluation of the danger of Chinese aggression *vis-à-vis* the USSR which is given in the Memorandum. In any case, the Chinese threat cannot serve as a justification for the militarization of our country and the absence of democratic reforms in it.

I HAVE ALREADY said something about those documents in the collection which are associated with the defense of the rights of individual people.

5 This article appears as the foreword to a collection of Sakharov's recent writings, which was published in May 1974 by Knopf as *Sakharov Speaks*, edited by Harrison E. Salisbury [editor's note].

During those years I learned of an increasingly large number of tragic and heroic fates, some of which have been reflected in the pages of the collection. For the most part, the documents of this cycle require no commentary.

In April of 1972 I drew up the text of an appeal to the Supreme Soviet USSR to grant amnesty to political prisoners and abolish capital punishment. The documents were timed to coincide with the Fiftieth Anniversary of the USSR. I have already explained why I attribute such prime importance to the former of these questions. As for the latter, the abolishment of capital punishment is an extremely important act, both morally and socially, for any country. And in our country, with its very low level of legal consciousness and widespread animosity, this act would be especially important. I succeeded in gathering about fifty signatures for the appeals. Each of them represented a very thoughtful moral and social act on the part of the signer. I felt this with particular force while I was gathering the signatures. Many more people refused [than signed], and the explanations offered by some of them told me a good deal about the inner reasons for the thoughts and acts of our intelligentsia.

In September 1971, I sent a letter to the members of the Presidium of the Supreme Soviet USSR on freedom of emigration and unobstructed return. My letter to the US Congress in September of 1973 was another *démarche* on this same subject. In these documents I call attention to various aspects of this problem, including the important role that its solution would play in the democratization of our country, and in raising its standard of living to the level of the advanced countries. The correctness of this idea can be shown by the example of Poland and Hungary, where today freedom to leave the country and return to it is not so heavily encumbered as in our country.

In the summer of 1973 I was interviewed by Ulle Stenholm, correspondent for a Swedish radio station, who asked me questions of a general character. This interview had a broad response in the USSR and foreign countries. I received several dozen letters expressing indignation at the "slanderous" line I had taken. (It should be borne in mind that letters of the opposite kind usually do not reach me.) The Soviet *Literaturnaya gazeta* published an article about me entitled "A Supplier of Slander." Ulle Stenholm, who had interviewed me and published his text without distortions, was recently deprived of his entry visa and the possibility of continuing his work in the USSR. This was an outrageous violation of the rights of an honest and intelligent journalist, who had become a friend of my family. One cannot rule out the possibility that the latter circumstance played its own role in the illegality practiced upon him. The interview was verbal, and neither questions nor answers were discussed in advance. This must be taken into account in evaluating the document, which represents an unconstrained conversation, in a home setting, on very serious, basic problems.

In this interview, as in the Memorandum and the Afterword, I went beyond the limits of the subject of human rights and democratic freedoms, and touched on economic and social problems, which generally speaking require special—and perhaps even professional—training. But these problems are of such vital importance to every person that I am not sorry they came up for discussion. My opponents were especially irritated by my description of our country's system as state capitalism with a Party-state monopoly and the consequences, in all spheres of social life, which flow from such a system.

Important basic problems of the détente in international tensions in their connection with a proviso for democratizing and opening up Soviet society were reflected in the interview of August–September 1973.

IN RECENT YEARS I have carried on my activities under conditions of ever-increasing pressure on me, and especially on my family. In September of 1972 our close friend Yury Shikhanovich was arrested. In October of 1972 Tatyana, my wife's daughter, who was doing very well in her studies, was expelled from the university in her last year under a formal and far-fetched pretext. Throughout the year we were harassed by anonymous telephone calls, with threats and absurd accusations. In February of 1973 the *Literaturnaya gazeta* published an article by its editor-in-chief, Chakovsky, dealing with a book by Harrison Salisbury. In this article I was characterized as an extremely naive person who quoted the New Testament, "coquettishly waved an olive branch," "played the holy fool," and "willingly accepted the compliments of the Pentagon." All this was said in connection with my *Thoughts*, which thus after five years was mentioned in the Soviet press for the first time.

In March, likewise for the first time, I was summoned to the KGB for a talk (allegedly because my wife and I had jointly offered to give surety for our friend Yury Shikhanovich). In June Tatyana's husband was deprived of work in connection with having made application to go and study in the US, pursuant to an invitation. In July the above mentioned article, "A Supplier of Slander," appeared. Also in July my wife's son Aleksey was refused admission to the university, apparently on special orders from above. In August I was summoned by the deputy procurator of the USSR, Malyarov.

The basic content of the talk was threats. Then immediately after the interview of August 21, on the problems of détente, Soviet newspapers reprinted items from foreign Communist papers and a letter from forty academicians declaring I was an opponent of relaxation of international tensions. Next came a nationwide newspaper campaign in which I was condemned by representatives of all strata of our society.

In late September our apartment, thoroughly observed by the KGB, was visited by persons who called themselves members of the "Black September" organization. They threatened reprisals not only on me but on the members of my family. In November an investigator who was a colonel in the KGB summoned my wife for repeated interrogations which lasted many hours. My wife refused to participate in the investigation, but this did not immediately put an end to the summonses. Previously she had publicly stated that she had sent to the West the diary of Eduard Kuznetzsov, which had come into her hands. But she felt she was entitled not to tell what was done, or how it was done, by way of its distribution. The investigator warned her that her actions made her liable under Article 70 of the RSFSR Criminal Code, with a period of punishment of up to seven years. It seems to me this is quite enough for one family.

SOON AFTER THE *coup d'état* in Chile, the writers A. Galich and V. Maksimov joined with me in an appeal to the new government expressing fears for the life of the outstanding Chilean poet Pablo Neruda. Our letter was not political in nature and had no other aims than strictly humane ones. But in the Soviet press, and in the pro-Soviet foreign press, it provoked an explosion of feigned indignation as allegedly "defending the fascist junta." Moreover, the letter itself was quoted inaccurately, and two of its authors— Galich and Maksimov—were in general "forgotten." The aim of the organizers of this campaign—to compromise me at least in this way if it couldn't be done otherwise—was only too obvious.

But to digress from the subject of patently unscrupulous opponents and turn to opinions which more objectively reflect liberal social opinion in the West, it must be said that this whole story brought to light a typical misunderstanding which merits discussion. As a rule, liberal social opinion in the democratic countries takes an international position, protesting against injustice and violence not only in one's own country but throughout the world. It was not by accident that I said "as a rule." Unfortunately, it is very frequently the case that the defense of human rights in the socialist countries, by virtue of an opinion of the special progressiveness of their regimes, falls outside (or almost falls outside) the field of activity of foreign organizations. The greater part of my efforts has been aimed precisely at surmounting this situation, which has been one of the reasons for our tragedies.

BUT THAT IS not the point at issue here. Instead I should like to talk about that part of the Western liberal intelligentsia (still a small part) which extends its activities to the socialist countries as well. These people look to the Soviet dissenters for a reciprocal, analogous international position with respect to other countries. But there are several important circumstances they do not take into account: the lack of information; the fact that a Soviet dissenter is not only unable to go to other countries but is deprived, within his own country, of the majority of sources of information; that the historical experience of our country has weaned us away from excessive "leftism," so that we evaluate many facts differently from the "leftist" intelligentsia of the West; that we must avoid political pronouncements in the international arena, where we are so ignorant (after all, we do not engage in political activity in our own country); that we must avoid getting into the channel of Soviet propaganda, which so often deceives us.

We know that in the Western countries there are vigilant and influential forces which protest (better and more effectively than we do) against injustice and violence there. We do not justify injustice or violence, wherever they appear. We do not feel that there is necessarily more of both in our country than in other countries. But at the moment our strength cannot suffice for the whole world. We ask that all this be taken into account, and that we be forgiven the errors we sometimes make in the dust kicked up by polemics.

The general position reflected in the materials in my forthcoming collection is closer to that of *Thoughts* than might appear at first glance. [There are] differences in the treatment of political or politico-economic questions which are of course immediately apparent. But since I lay no claim to the role of discoverer or political adviser, this is less essential than the spirit of free debate and the concern for fundamental problems which, I should like to think, are found both in *Thoughts* and in the recent writings.

The majority of my writings are either addressed to the leaders of our state or have a specific foreign addressee. But inwardly I address them to all people on earth, and in particular to the people of my country, because they were dictated by concern and anxiety for my own country and its people.

I AM NOT a purely negative critic of our way of life: I recognize much that is good in our people and in our country, which I ardently love. But I have been compelled to fix attention on negative phenomena, since they are precisely what the official propaganda passes over in silence, and since they represent the greatest damage and danger. I am not an opponent of détente, trade, or disarmament. To the contrary, in several of my writings I have called for just these things. It is precisely in convergence that I see the only way to the salvation of mankind. But I consider it my duty to point out all the hidden dangers of a false détente, and to call for the use of the entire arsenal of means, of all efforts, to achieve real convergence, accompanied by democratization, demilitarization, and social progress. I hope that the publication of my writings will be of some use in that cause.

Moscow, December 31, 1973
—*translated by Guy Daniels*

Gustav Mahler

Mahler Now by Pierre Boulez was originally published October 28, 1976.
Published in the US in 1976 by Rizzoli International Publications Inc., New York.
Copyright © 1976 by Belser Verlag, Stuttgart.

PIERRE BOULEZ

Mahler Now

HOW LONG IT TOOK for Mahler to emerge, not from the shadows but from purgatory. A tenacious purgatory, which for a thousand reasons would not let go of him. He was too much of a conductor and not enough of a composer; moreover, even as a composer Mahler could not disengage himself from his role as conductor: he had too much dexterity and not enough mastery. What is more, he mixed it all up. While his work shows no direct traces of the operas he directed with such passion, he nonetheless abused the noble symphonic domain by casting on it bad theatrical seed: sentimentality, vulgarity, and an insolent and unbearable disorder intrude noisily and heavily into this well-guarded territory.

Nevertheless, a handful of devotees have kept watch during Mahler's posthumous exile and they can be easily divided into two camps: progressives and conservatives. The latter pride themselves on being the real defenders of Mahler's work, which, they believe, the progressives have betrayed.

Mahler had the misfortune to be a Jew in a period of intense nationalism. Totally silenced in his own country, this outcast faded from memory and almost disappeared. Further, there is the myth in which Mahler and Bruckner appear as the Castor and Pollux of the symphony. It was thought impossible, after Beethoven, to go beyond Nine: the symphonic dynasty would be cursed by destiny should it attempt to advance beyond that fateful number. (In the meantime, however, some less gifted composers have accomplished this feat.) What could possibly be left after all this?

What is left is the memory, for one thing, of a conductor who was both wonderful and difficult, exact and eccentric. Some of Mahler's scores—the shorter ones—which are easy to grasp and to accept. For a long time these had to suffice, while the traditional symphonic appetite was satisfied by other less complex and less demanding pieces. Since performances of Mahler's works were rare, it was almost impossible for them to create much of a following. Many went so far as to doubt not only the intrinsic value but even the sincerity of Mahler's project. For their part, the moderns felt they had gone beyond Mahler, and relegated him to an outmoded romanticism, altogether lacking in contemporary interest, which they viewed with a certain pity.

THE EXCESSIVE, ABUNDANT quality of this *fin de siècle* music went against the grain of modern composers who were more and more interested in economy. The reckless extension of time, the surplus of instruments, the supercharged feelings and gestures . . . form had to break down under these excesses! What could be the value of music in which the relation of idea to form is lost in the swamps of expressivity? We seem to confront the end of a world which sickens through its wealth, chokes on its abundance. Both the best and the worst that can befall it is infatuation, a sentimental apoplexy. Goodbye to this obese and degenerate romanticism!

Goodbye?

If the works insist on surviving, they cannot be banished. You dismiss them? Abruptly? They nevertheless remain.

Now that the period of cleansing is over we see that it has left some skeletons behind. After a period of inattention that which is authentic emerges once more, forces us to reconsider our views, and insistently questions our negligence. Were we guilty or were we superficial? Can we justify ourselves? This work was preserved by pious but fanatically greedy hands (I mean hands without the generosity that paves the way to the future by means of the past), monopolized by fidelity (at what point does loyalty become treason?). Presented in this manner, Mahler's work could inspire great distrust, a distrust that even made us suspect that the composers of the Vienna school had succumbed to a sentimental, provincial attachment in admiring Mahler. At first glance the link between them and Mahler was not obvious while the antinomies were flagrantly clear.

But the moderns turned from asceticism to exuberance. Armed with this new perspective, they began to explore the past. They were informed by their recent experience which made them vigilant and careful. Tired of crude sensations, one-dimensional meanings, they dreamed of ambiguities—of a world where the categories were not so simple.

Order? Who needs this constraining notion?

All right. Let's forget about all such restrictive ideas as order, the homogeneousness of ideas and style, and the clarity of musical structures. But is it so simple? Certainly not. Especially if one does not want to be influenced by external circumstances. How difficult it is, in the case of Mahler, to steer free of the legend which stubbornly mingles his life and his work—the melodrama and the agony. Let us give the enthusiastic exegesis of his work its due and go on to confront directly the uneven monuments he left behind.

MAHLER'S WORK makes us uneasy, in part because it seems to waver between sentimentality and irony, nostalgia and criticism. There is no real contradiction here: it is rather like the swing of a pendulum, a sudden change of light in which certain musical ideas that might otherwise be considered banal and superfluous become, under this exacting prism, indispensable revelations. Does Mahler still seem so banal (a view which was carried to the point of seeing his work as lacking in imagination) or is this banality not based on a sense of Mahler's popular appeal? At first Mahler's music would seem to depend on comfortable clichés, mawkish repetitions, and an entire landscape and a past that are remembered in vignettes. Some are delighted by this, while others find it irritating, but neither group can get beyond their first impression of Mahler's work. This is merely an antechamber...

Yes, this "banal" material exists in Mahler's work. Sometimes it may seem limited and excessively predictable: the source hardly changes from one work to the next. Once we have cited the march and all the military or funereal music that derives from it, the dances in 3/4 time (Ländler, waltzes, or minuets), the whole provincial repertory of folklore, we have just about covered all of Mahler's "borrowed" and easily identified thematic sources. From his first work to his last, there is one constant: the clichés Mahler inherited from either "elevated" or "low brow" musical history.

In contrast to this reservoir of clichés, we find an array of grand theatrical gestures—a heroic and sublime music of the spheres and of infinity. The worst that can be said of this element of Mahler's work is that some of its intensity has faded. But how can one account for the fact that gestures which seem dead in the work of other composers retain their power to move us in Mahler's work? Could it be that, despite their triumphal appearance, these gestures cover an enormous insecurity? How far we are, when we listen to Mahler, from self-assured romanticism—proud and heroic. And how far we are from the naiveté of romanticism's first approaches to folklore. No one can fail to hear the nostalgia in the world of Mahler; but in his music, for better or worse, nostalgia is modified by criticism, even sarcasm. Sarcasm? Isn't that the ultimate example of an unmusical characteristic? We know that music likes undisguised meanings and lends itself badly to the interplay of irony and sincerity. One can never tell: Is this true, is that a caricature? If there is a libretto, one can orient oneself without too much difficulty. But what about pieces of "pure" music?

AMBIGUITY OR BANTER can only really be understood against the background of a text based on well-recognized conventions. Mahler often needs to do little else than distort these conventions (through exaggerated or misplaced emphases, condensed or stretched-out tempos, or unusual, prismatic, or fragmented instrumentation) to play his game of seesaw. The aggressive humor of such music envelops everything in an unreal, ghostly color, as if the subject had been X-rayed and now appeared to us as a sooty jumble of boughs and branches which both alarms and defeats us: a world of fleshless, rattling bones, realistically evoked by the bizarre, even grotesque combinations of sounds; a world born of a nightmare and ready at any time to return to it; a world of shadows—colorless, without substance, of ashes. How sharply and rigorously this world is captured, this spectral universe where the memory falls apart.

Are we drawn to Mahler's music only because he knew how to convey accurately certain sentimental, bizarre reflections on a damned world? Would that be enough to retain and enthrall us? The reason for the current fascination with Mahler surely lies in the hypnotic force of a vision which passionately embraced the end of an age—an age that had to die so that another could arise from its ashes. Mahler's music describes the myth of the Phoenix almost too literally.

But, beyond this vision of dusk, a more surprising upheaval in symphonic music is brought about by Mahler's work. With determination, sometimes even with savagery, he attacked the hierarchy of forms which had been fluid before his time but which were now congealed in rigid and decorative conventions. Was it the theater that drove him toward this dramatic destruction of constricting forms? Just as Wagner overthrew the artificial form of the opera in order to create a drama of demiurgical proportions, so too Mahler revolutionized the symphony, devastated that all too orderly terrain, and imbued that most logical of forms with his demons. Isn't one in fact reminded of Beethoven—the barbarian who in his time sowed disorder and chaos, and who, for the first time, pushed the musical forms in which he was trained beyond their "reasonable" possibilities.

CAN WE SPEAK of an extra-musical dimension to Mahler's work? Some have done so and here the "programs" Mahler wrote for his music—and which he later repudiated—have led to much misunderstanding about the descriptive intentions of his work. For such intentions would have been neither an innovation of Mahler's nor something peculiar to him. On the contrary they were typical of an era which (following Berlioz and Liszt) hoped to excite the musical imagination through images which were mainly borrowed from literature but were also derived from the visual arts, from an unequal competition with painting.

Mahler's extra-musical dimension abandoned these borderline pursuits and affected the very substance of music, its organization, its structure, and its power. His vision and his technique possess the epic dimension of narrative, and Mahler is like a novelist in his methods and his use of material. He still called his pieces symphonies; he retained the nomenclature of the movements (scherzo, slow movement, finale) though their number and order vary from work to work. The occasional intrusion of vocal elements at various points in the symphony, the use of such theatrical effects as placing instruments off-stage, were two of Mahler's innovations which ate away at the notion of distinct musical genres. Only the novelist works in a form elastic enough to permit him to play such games with his material. Released from the visual theater (his professional obsession), Mahler surrendered himself almost frenetically to this freedom to mix the genres. He refused to distinguish between materials of differing quality and mixed all the basic material at his disposal in a carefully controlled construction that was nonetheless detached from irrelevant formal limitations. Homogeneity, hierarchy—absurd notions in his case—are disregarded; he transmits his vision to us with all the elements of nobility, triviality, tension, and relaxation that it entails. He makes no choices, for to choose would be treason: he would betray his fundamental plan.

To listen to Mahler is to perceive the musical flow differently. A first hearing gives the impression that the purely musical forms in Mahler's work are unable to support the vast accumulation of facts, and that the narration—I insist that it is a musical narration—pointlessly meanders; the weight of the elements destroys the structure, the form dissolves in a multiplicity of layers, the direction of the piece gets lost under the welter of episodes, and these overflowing movements buckle beneath the superabundance of the material and of its rhetorical excesses.

A purely "musical" hearing of Mahler's work would tend to support these arguments. But then how is one supposed to listen to his work? How is one supposed to perceive it? Should one be borne along by the narration alone and let oneself drift along with its psychological fluctuations? Is one only meant to pay attention to the music's epic dimension and the élan it confers on the imagination, and refrain from considering the details of the pieces? One can listen to Mahler that way. His music is powerful enough to accommodate a passive listener; but is that the most enriching way to listen to Mahler? Ideally, one would be able to follow exactly the density of the narrative.

WHAT *HASN'T* BEEN said about the length of Mahler's pieces? When referring to Schubert we speak of "heavenly lengths," but how can one describe the formidable periods of time of certain movements of Mahler's symphonies? Nothing could be more exhausting and tedious than to hear a bad performance of these extended movements (and if this is a problem for the listener, it is an even greater one for a conductor: the only difference is the degree of intensity and preparation). A comparison to classical architecture with its familiar reference points is futile; one has to accept the density of musical events in Mahler's work—the density of musical time which, according to the dramatic situation, is either relaxed or tense. The elasticity of musical time is the basis of all music, although normally it is not the most impressive phenomenon we perceive when we hear music. But in Mahler there is always a tendency for it to be the most important element; it frequently controls all the other parts, it guides us and helps us to distinguish what we can listen to without much effort from what must be approached with almost analytical acuteness. The elasticity of musical time in Mahler allows us to perceive his narrative scheme and immediately helps us set in order proliferating sounds.

We have to adapt our hearing to the internal organization of the movements, especially the huge epic movements; but each of the movements within the symphony itself demands a different kind of listening because the aesthetic point of view of each movement is different and because the value, or rather the density, of each movement does not by any means carry the same weight in the symphony's overall organization. Mahler's musical universe is not a homogeneous one; it takes the risk of using incongruous elements like citations and parody, and finds their use legitimate. Mahler's music teaches us to listen in ways that are more varied, ambiguous, richer.

Mahler's work is one of curious extremes: his excessively short lieder are followed by his excessively long symphonies. There are no works of average length. It is astonishing... One might even prefer the immediately gripping perfection—without problems—and the clearly transcribed texts that characterize his short songs. One might argue that Mahler's essential ideas are expressed in his lieder and that there is hence no reason to stretch, lengthen, and enlarge the pieces beyond all expectation. But however perfect the songs are, Mahler's real strength lies in his immoderately long movements which often present problems; his difficult struggle with pieces of epic dimensions is a more fascinating undertaking than his successes with a form whose boundaries are clearly established.

MAHLER PROBABLY WOULD be less attractive if he were free of his occasional difficulties. His "hyper-dimensional" approach has very little in common with those bombastic, egomaniacal musical tendencies of the *fin de siècle* composers who seem to represent the satisfactions of abundance in its moment of paroxysm. In Mahler's work one senses a profound anxiety as if he had agonized over the decision to stir up a world grown beyond all rational control. Mahler took upon himself the dizzying task of creating a body of work in which agreement and contradiction appear in equal measure. Dissatisfied with the known dimensions of the musical experience, Mahler sought an order that was less clearly arranged than is customary and would be enjoyed less complacently. An ideal work would defy the established categories, indeed would reject them as such while participating in all of them. When viewed as the intersection of the theater, the novel, and the poem, the symphony becomes an ideal meeting ground. Musical expression lays claim to everything that is usually denied it, and stands ready to assume all the possibilities of existence. It truly becomes philosophy while escaping the restrictions of purely verbal communication.

But is the ambitiousness of such a project compatible with an economy of means? Would such a conception leave room for what might be called an ascetic use of sound? We know, of course, that discipline and a restricted use of the available material have often yielded wonderful results. As the spirit delves further into the depths of creation, it often needs fewer of the external appurtenances at its disposal. The inventive spirit eschews apparent riches in order to achieve the deepest creation. At that time, the method of transmitting the work is of little importance. Perfectly mastered sounds are not merely consigned to a humble station, but also are endowed with the most unusual attribute of all: absence. This is true of music used during meditation: it is a song of oneself communicated beyond the reality of sound. It is certainly true of Bach, and is almost true of Beethoven, who couldn't stand the violin. Even as Wagner rejoiced in creating a profusion of sounds and in using innumerable instruments, his work also contains this economy of means—this asceticism—which is the subliminal essence of his work. One must not forget the example of Wagner. Within musical thinking, he represents a fusion, an amalgam, of the concept and the means.

But is there too much emphasis on the means and not enough on the concept in Mahler's work? If indeed this is so, then one might say that Mahler misused his ability and that his work is little more than a seductive but fruitless exercise of virtuosity or eccentricity; while no one doubted his dexterity and skill, Mahler's contemporaries accused him of covering up a lack of content, of trying to distract the attention of the listener with tricks, and of trying to turn musical perception toward superficial and wholly unnecessary procedures. Didn't Mahler, who was after all a conductor, have that defect which all interpreters are said to share: a lack of conceptual originality or, at best, uncertainty about such conceptions? Didn't Mahler try to cover up this inadequacy through the kinds of manipulation in which he was well versed because of his profession? Many people have a grudge against the hybrid race of composer-conductors whom they frequently accuse of cheating, of treachery, or, at best, of knowing how to maneuver too well.

INDEED, THERE IS virtuosity in Mahler's work; it is obvious though not showy. When Mahler is conventional, he still usually knows how to be brilliantly inventive with sound. His virtuosity can be located in a well-defined historical perspective and does not, strictly speaking, explore any really unknown territory. It accepts—even if only to transgress—those romantic forms of instrumentation which, little by little, became conventions, norms of nineteenth-century music. Mahler's preference for the horn would alone confirm this if there weren't many other indications that clearly show the connection. His facility in using the different instruments is so great one might be tempted to call it nonchalance, were it not for Mahler's painstakingly exact scores which are complete to the last detail.

Not without reason, Mahler was obsessed with the accuracy of his scores. As a conductor, he had ample occasion to observe how "freely" notations were read and rendered by instrumentalists and how frequently—whether from laziness or from not paying attention—they were ignored. In his notation, Mahler struggles as best he can both against inertia and against the acquired habits (mechanically "natural" reactions) which he so distrusted. As if he knew—and he must have known—that his musical material was sometimes ambiguous and moved uncertainly between irony and sentimentality, his scores abound with warnings and calls to order.

One cannot miss Mahler's irrepressibly personal voice in the many positive as well as negative instructions; he exhorts and restrains, urges on and applies the brakes, impels and rouses the critical sense. What one must do, first of all, is to know what to do—the expected quality is achieved primarily by avoiding mistakes. Actually, Mahler went further than any composer before him in providing an explicit interpretative structure for his work. He incorporated the requirements of the interpreter into the very fabric of his invention, not because he was tyrannized by them, but because Mahler had such a masterful grasp of interpretation that he could not be satisfied with what existed and anticipated what might be possible by extension and extrapolation. That, and not some empty virtuosity, is the mark of the professional interpreter—a man who was in daily contact both with the masterworks of a stirring vocation and also with the precise tasks and obligations of a constraining technique.

But it would be wrong to infer from this that the demands of a score must lead to a rigid interpretation of all the markings, that living authority becomes posthumous constraint, that exactitude and correctness suffice to do justice to a mind like Mahler's which was nothing if not mobile, that objective observance of the instructions could supplant a great subjective re-creation. This unimaginative and servile view is not the way to interpret Mahler. While he warned his interpreters about certain things, he did not mean to inhibit them; from all we know about him, he was no supporter of inhibited interpretations. But Mahler knew better than to mistake sloppiness for "interpretation." He knew that the most demanding kind of freedom actually requires the strictest discipline; otherwise it becomes a caricature and an approximation—a travesty, often a gross one, of an otherwise profound and honorable truth. For the more one succumbs to the frenzies of the moment, the more the original intention is betrayed. Such tendencies destroy the essential ambiguity of Mahler's music and, in doing so, trivialize it and empty it of profound content. Moreover, such license destroys the subliminal structure which balances the various developments in the work and creates instead an unbalanced, chaotic interpretation. Mahler's magnetic fields are infinitely subtler than a crude experiment with iron filings.

WHAT MAKES UNDERSTANDING Mahler difficult is undoubtedly the split between gesture and material; the gesture tends to become ever more "grandiose," while the material risks become more and more "vulgar." Mahler's incoherence derives both from this fundamental contradiction as well as from the impossibility of joining together the multiple aspects of his state of mind in the composition itself. As a result, Mahler's musical ideas seem grouped around several essential polarities. The more deeply one examines Mahler's work, the denser it becomes. The work acquires this density not by getting thicker but by a multiplicity of lines: polyphony develops through constant and continuous crisscrossing during which the elements attach themselves more and more to a determined theme. It is no easy task to reconcile a meticulous attention to detail with the broad scope of the project itself, but it is precisely this accomplishment that restored an unstable balance to the forces that Mahler needed for his work. The difficulty in getting a firm hold on these contradictory dimensions of composition and of making them congruent posed the same problems for Mahler as it does for us when we listen to his work—problems which reveal the deepest and most personal aspect of his creation.

It does not seem unjust now that Mahler's work needed some time before it became convincing to listeners. Our era is more attracted by the exuberance and lushness rejected by previous generations as superfluous and impure. But this idea of a simple reaction does not, by itself, explain the increasing attraction of a work that was once rejected as too ambiguous, and now is esteemed precisely for its ambiguity. To link Mahler's work with a progressive movement, which quickly and easily leads us to the Vienna school, would be to violate the facts as we know them. There is too much nostalgia at work in his music, too much rewriting of the past, to permit us in good faith to construct a revolutionary Mahler who unleashed an irreversible process of radical innovation.

Mahler's first followers were guilty of a kind of nostalgic thinking: they saw the sentimental and rejected the critical aspect of his work which made them uneasy. On the other hand there has been a stubborn effort to circumvent the categories of the past, to force them to say things which originally lay outside their province. These limits have been so stretched out as to make it impossible to claim that Mahler is the last representative of a particular tradition. In a very special way he is also part of the future. This is clearer now than it once was since many of the stylistic ideas of Mahler's own time have been reconsidered and purified, and since we are now prepared to imagine a more "constructed" language, a more complex expressiveness, and a more open synthesis.

The sources of Mahler's inspiration—even the geography of those sources—may still seem limited to us, may seem to be too connected to a world which was incapable of renewing itself and which was obsessively concerned with certain forms of expression that reflected a disappearing social order. But since, for all practical purposes, these sources no longer exist we can view them more serenely, as valuable testimonies about things we cannot know directly. In consequence, this material assumes the value of a document—a source—which we should not reject but rather look at as the first step of future inventions. In this way, we can give most of our attention to its transformation and transmutation. Throughout Mahler's entire work we may perceive the evolution of expression from certain identical basic elements which then become our essential points of reference. The breadth and complexity of Mahler's gestures as well as the variety and intensity of the steps in his invention—these are what bring Mahler close to us; they make him essential for today's thinking about the future of music.

Pablo Picasso

Your Show of Shows by John Richardson was originally published July 17, 1980, as a review of Picasso: Oeuvres reçues en paiement des droits de succession, *catalog of an exhibition at the Grand Palais, Paris, October 11, 1979 to January 7, 1980, Editions de la Réunion des Musées Nationaux; "Pablo Picasso: A Retrospective," an exhibition at The Museum of Modern Art, May 22 to September 16, 1980;* Pablo Picasso: A Retrospective, *edited by William Rubin, The Museum of Modern Art/New York Graphic Society;* Picasso: The Cubist Years 1907–1916, *A Catalogue Raisonné of the Paintings and Related Works, text by Pierre Daix, New York Graphic Society/Little, Brown.*

JOHN RICHARDSON

Your Show of Shows

IN THE MID-1950S, Picasso had the contents of his Paris studio shipped to the villa he had recently bought at Cannes. Among the treasures, household goods, and accumulated rubbish—the artist was a compulsive hoarder—were seventy portfolios. The day Picasso decided to go through these, I happened to be present. Few had been opened since 1939, some not since 1914. Although Picasso was vague about what was in the portfolios, there was reason to believe that they contained most of the works on paper that he had kept for himself, because they were too precious, personal, exploratory, or else too scabrous to exhibit, let alone put on the market. And here we should bear in mind that, as he grew older, Picasso retained much of his best work, drawings especially. So it was with the trepidation felt by Howard Carter when the first pickaxe probed Tutankhamen's burial chamber that we watched Picasso fiddle tantalizingly with the knots.

Picture our dismay when the artist threw open a bulging portfolio and gleefully showed us sheet after sheet of paper, some of it to be sure emanating from eighteenth-century Italy or nineteenth-century Japan, but all uniformly blank. "Far too good to use"—the artist knew he could count on our emphatic denials. Was Picasso up to one of his celebrated teases? Was he perhaps reenacting the *Chef-d'oeuvre inconnu*? No, the next portfolio contained Ingresque portrait drawings, many of them unpublished, of family and friends; another disgorged *papiers collés*, some not even glued together, and so forth. Sometimes there would be a disappointment—reams of identical posters, old newspapers—more often surprises: one of Rimbaud's exercise books, numerous lithographs by that rare printmaker Rodolphe Bresdin, quantities of Picasso's poems (why haven't more of these been published?), and some puzzling watercolors of large heads. Early Marie Laurencins? Wrong, they were the amateurish oeuvre, what little remained of it, of Picasso's first *maîtresse en titre*, Fernande Olivier. "No worse than any other woman painter," Picasso said.

As Picasso scanned his own drawings, I could not help being struck by his total concentration, at the same time scary detachment about himself. It was as if he were examining work he had never seen before by an artist quite unknown to him. "*Je est un autre*": Rimbaud's disturbing line came forcibly to mind. "Not bad," he could comment, but more in the spirit of a teacher going over a student's work than in pride of execution or ownership. "Wouldn't the Museum of Modern Art like to get their hands on all this for their up-and-coming show?" (this was in 1956) Picasso grinned malevolently. "This is what *I* call a retrospective," and all of a sudden he made a great to-do about locking everything away.

TWENTY-THREE YEARS would pass before Picasso had *his* retrospective—at the Grand Palais in Paris in 1979. It consisted of all the paintings and sculpture and the best of the drawings and prints (roughly a quarter of the artist's estate) which the French government had accepted in lieu of taxes, and was a most moving exhibition. This was partly because Dominique Bozo (first curator-in-chief of the newly founded Picasso museum) had exercised his right to first choice of the artist's holdings with such skill that he had skimmed much of the cream off Picasso's Picassos. But it was also refreshing because the composition of the show was dictated by the wayward, even aleatory pattern of the artist's collecting rather than the all too predictable preferences of art historians.

Before honoring the late artist's promise to make major loans to the retrospective that would take over the entire Museum of Modern Art in New York, Bozo was obliged to exhibit the best of this bequest in Paris. And it was perhaps inevitable, in view of the haste with which the exhibition was organized and the haphazard nature of the material at Bozo's disposal, that the installation was slapdash, and the representation of the artist's development spotty. But these defects were a virtue to the extent that they helped to evoke the prodigality and disorder of the artist's various studios and conveyed the feeling that somewhere in the vicinity work was still in progress. The display of these private treasures brought Picasso back in spirit. It was as if he were still around.

More to the point, there was not the least whiff of the restorer's lab or the bank vault, or of produce which had gone stale on gallery or institutional walls. True, many of the works at the Grand Palais had been published or exhibited, but even those who thought they knew Picasso's private collection by heart were stunned by revelation after revelation.

New avenues of research were opened up by the early sketchbooks and drawings of 1906–1908—Cubism in the making. As for the huge hoard of sculpture, some familiar, some unfamiliar, this proved yet again that Picasso is by far the most protean and inventive sculptor of this or any other century.

In its freshness and unfamiliarity, Bozo's show had the virtue of enabling us to see Picasso anew. Not only did it effectively quell any doubts that may have arisen regarding Picasso's stature, but it reinforced faith in his powers. For, in the opinion of many, the last paintings had tarnished the artist's reputation; so inevitably had death.

THE GREAT EXHIBITION that fills the entire exhibition space of The Museum of Modern Art is a far, far grander affair—a retrospective to end all retrospectives. It is of course big, but not that much bigger than the Paris show in 1966–1967. The difference is that it is much more discriminatingly chosen and much more handsomely installed. For once full justice has been done to the variety of genres, styles, media, and techniques that makes Picasso the most prodigious and versatile artist of all time. Instead of splitting things up into "periods," the organizers, William Rubin and Dominique Bozo, have emphasized the continuity of Picasso's development. If this gives a spurious logic to the oeuvre, no matter. It makes for coherence and enables the artist's energy to manifest itself in one vast wave instead of a succession of spurts.

Let us also record our gratitude—since nobody else seems to be doing so—to Alfred Barr, whose Picasso shows at MOMA in 1939, 1946, 1957, and 1962, exemplary catalogs, and perceptive acquisition policy where Picasso was concerned paved the way for the present exhibition. The fact that Barr has been struck down by illness is no reason for MOMA to forget him. How he haunts the place!

If there are gaps in the MOMA show, it is not the fault of the organizers, who are said to have left no string unpulled in their efforts to obtain key loans. So far as the US goes, the most conspicuous absentee is the National Gallery's huge circus painting, *Family of Saltimbanques* (1905), but at least it is readily accessible in Washington. Far more disastrous is the nonarrival of the Russian loans: twelve irreplaceable works that chart the early course of Cubism. Our condolences to Rubin, but he might have spared us the comment (*New York Times*, May 18) that these paintings will "be missed only by art historians." This smacks of elitism.

Let us, however, concentrate on the overwhelming quantity of works that *have* been obtained, starting with the wealth of juvenilia. Much of this is unfamiliar, since it emanates from the artist's estate, or from Picasso's sister's collection, now in the Museo Picasso, Barcelona. The early drawings reveal that Picasso was not so much a child prodigy as an enormously assiduous student at great pains to perfect his technique. So determined was he to live down the ineptitude of his art-teacher father that, by the age of fifteen, he had developed into a draughtsman of phenomenal authority. Likewise the brushwork of his earliest paintings has an energy and sensibility that are astonishingly mature, and at odds with their juvenile sentiment of subject.

Later in life, Picasso used to say that his innate facility had been more of a curse than a blessing, that he had always had a hard time making things difficult for himself; and in this respect Cézanne was to be envied for his initial lack of technical accomplishment. It would have been simple to fall back on slick bravura effects like the other Barcelona artists. Instead Picasso forced himself to look at whatever was in front of him as if it had never been looked at by him or anyone else before. And it is this that gives the early work its edge.

It is instructive to follow Picasso's early search for a style as well as an identity through the works of his Barcelona period, especially in the precocious self-portraits that reveal the artist trying out a succession of masks and roles: eighteenth-century aristocrat, *fin-de-siècle* visionary, down-at-heel bohemian, top-hatted dandy, and many more. Interesting that the man who was to become the greatest manipulator in the history of art started his manipulative games on himself.

Meanwhile Picasso had the good fortune to spend his formative years in a city that was one of the most progressive in Europe. Thanks largely to Gaudí, Barcelona had become a hotbed of art nouveau, and the young artists and poets who befriended Picasso kept in touch with the latest developments in Paris, London, and Vienna. Passionate admirers of Nietzsche, they subscribed—some of them at least—to a semiserious belief that the century about to dawn would see the emergence of a glorious new art and the coming of a Messianic artist: a Nietzschean superman with a Dionysiac style. A self-portrait of this period (now lost), which the artist inscribed three times over with the words "*Yo el Rey,*" suggests that Picasso implicitly believed in his divine right as an artist and also saw himself fulfilling this regal role—*stupor mundi*! And two other prophetic drawings which *are* in the show, both entitled *Pierrot Celebrating the New Year*, and which, it is significant, are dated January 1, 1900, hint that the "King" might on occasion double as a clown.

IT WAS NOT until Picasso left Barcelona for Paris that his stylistic oscillations were to assume a fixed pattern in the *triste* mannerisms of the so-called Blue period. But for all its bittersweet charm, this style depended too much on academic virtuosity to satisfy the artist for long; and his tubercular models are depicted in terms that are too picturesque, too full of self-pity to carry much conviction. No wonder Picasso later dismissed the etiolated subjects of this phase as "nothing but sentiment." Here exception must be made for certain portraits and *La Vie* (1903), the haunting allegory of impotence inspired by the suicide of the artist's friend, Casagemas, two years earlier. Otherwise, I find the Blue period more interesting iconographically for the first intimations of certain obsessive themes—for instance, the sleeper watched and the confrontation of two women with or without a mirror—and certain prototypes—those alienated, blank-faced waifs and melancholy outcasts—that recur again and again in the artist's work.

Despite all that has been written about Picasso's early iconography, its origins are still unclear. Much research remains to be done, above all in the files of art magazines that Picasso might have seen on his father's bookshelves, to judge by the very close resemblance between the *Youth on Horseback*, a study for *The Watering Place* of 1906 (Warrington Collection, Cincinnati), and a drawing (a study for *Rienzi*) by William Holman Hunt, published in *The Magazine of Art*, No. 1, 1891.[1] This important unpublished discovery by Robert Isaacson opens up the possibility of other similar links.

A very different contribution to our understanding, or misunderstanding, of the Blue period was made by the late Edgar Wind, who maintained that the sentimental images of the artist's early years represent the true Picasso. Subsequent changes of style, Wind claimed, are simply a succession of freakish masks contrived by the artist to conceal an innate banality of vision. This theory with which Wind sought to impugn most of Picasso's oeuvre on the grounds of speciousness is in itself specious, but it is not entirely without insight or value. For it challenges us to look at certain works

---

[1] As an illustration to Hunt's article, "The Proper Mode and Study of Drawing Addressed to Students."

in a new light; the *Demoiselles d'Avignon*, for instance. Virtually everyone from Alfred Barr ("the sheer expressionist violence") to Pierre Daix ("[Picasso] loaded his picture with tension and violence") emphasizes the violence of the *Demoiselles*. But isn't this violence—for example, the famous "African" (simian?) striations on the two right-hand faces—at odds with the Symbolist overtones of Picasso's allegorical brothel scene? Weren't Picasso's demonic masks in danger of changing, obscuring, or negating any meaning the allegory ever had? Hadn't style and content drifted too far apart for even Picasso to straddle? Why else is the *Demoiselles* unfinished and unresolved?

BUT BACK TO the exhibition: if, thanks to the Russians, the period following the *Demoiselles* is not as well represented as we or the organizers would like, this is more than made up for by the glorious section devoted to the great years of Cubism—a section that constitutes a magnificent exhibition in itself. Rubin's incomparable selection of masterpieces and supporting works reveals more fully than ever before how, with Cézanne's help, Picasso so swiftly scaled the heights of great art and remained there, side by side with Braque, for six extraordinarily productive years (1908–1914). Far from being content with their discoveries, the two founders of Cubism pushed inexorably ahead and came up with a new notation of form and space, thanks to which reality could be perceived in a more "tactile" way. The main point of these noble paintings is that, for all their metaphysical overtones, they brought the subject, be it fruit dish or mountain, within reach, thus allowing the beholder, in Braque's words, "to take full possession of things."

Such a dazzling display of Picassos makes us forget that Cubism was essentially a combined operation, carried out by "two mountaineers roped together," as Braque, co-founder of the movement, later said. It is, therefore, only fair to recall that Braque, the absent partner, made equally sublime contributions to Cubism. In the words of Uhde, the German collector (whose prissy portrait is one of the joys of the MOMA show): where Braque was "*clair, mesuré, bourgeois,*" Picasso was "*sombre, excessif, révolutionnaire.*" "In the spiritual marriage which they entered into," Uhde concluded, "one contributed a great sensibility, the other a great plastic awareness."

At the same time this section of the show emphasizes the fact that MOMA's own collection of Cubist works is more comprehensive than any other. One reservation, however: too many paintings belonging to this and other US institutions have had their surfaces marred by well-meaning, if misguided, restorers. True, pollution necessitates a protective coating for vulnerable surfaces, but need this be so noticeable? To subject these delicate grounds to wax-relining and, worse, a shine, is as much of a solecism as frying a peach.

Too few restorers realize how adamant Picasso and Braque were that Cubist paintings must be matte, *never* varnished. If a shiny surface were required, the artist could always add varnish to his pigment or employ glossy house-paint like ripolin. As Braque insisted, any form of gloss falsifies the rapports between color, tone, and texture on which the delicate harmony of Cubist compositions depends. You will see what I mean if you compare the awful sheen on the important *Nude Woman* (1910), in the National Gallery in Washington, with the fresco-like surface of the Prague pictures or the two great compositions that recently came to light in Picasso's private collection. In this respect it is ironical that the paintings which were collected by Gertrude Stein and removed from Alice Toklas's custody on the grounds that they were not well enough cared for should have suffered more at the hands of restorers than they ever did from Gertrude's pets or Alice's benign neglect.

However, what else can one expect when publishers of art books—the late Albert Skira was the original culprit—have accustomed the public to ultra-glossy reproductions? Thanks to this trend, eyes accustomed to the wet look that varnish gives are apt to find the real thing a letdown. Can one blame restorers for giving the public what it has grown accustomed to?

ALL OF WHICH brings me to the *catalogue raisonné* of Picasso's Cubist oeuvre by Pierre Daix and Joan Rosselet. The color plates, alas, are glossy, but in most other respects this volume will satisfy the very high expectations which these authors' indispensable catalog of the Blue and Pink periods encouraged us to entertain. Picasso students who are weary of battling with the chaotic organization and chronological inaccuracies of Zervos's thirty-three volumes are now assured of a reliably accurate work of reference. And accuracy is essential, if the successive stylistic changes that revolutionized the course of twentieth-century art, some of them in a matter of weeks, are to be properly charted. In a volume of this magnitude (893 illustrated entries) there are bound to be blemishes but these are few. All in all, the authors are to be congratulated on the brilliant way they have marshaled a vast amount of information. Let us hope that they devote a companion volume to Braque's Cubist work, for as Daix generously admits, "It is absurd to try and separate the team."

Daix is also to be congratulated on the accuracy and thoroughness of his text—a laudably detailed and in many ways perceptive analysis of Picasso's Cubist achievements. If Daix occasionally comes across less lucidly than some of his predecessors in the field—John Golding and Douglas Cooper, Robert Rosenblum and Edward Fry—it is because he has adapted "to the problems of cubism . . . Claude Lévi-Strauss's methods for the study of anthropology and myths." When Daix borrows Lévi-Strauss's theory of *bricolage* or sees Cubist developments in terms of "signs," "which can only be identified and decoded when [they] can be recognized in [their] different uses and [their] career[s] followed up," he clouds rather than clarifies the understanding of a process whose beauty lies in the fact that it was intuitive and free of theory. And when Daix uses Lévi-Strauss's claim that "light is shed on every work or version of a work by what it transforms, distorts, opposes, denies or affirms" to inflate simple confrontations into "duels" and "primitive onslaughts," darkness descends and art history suffers.

The rhetoric of structuralism is often a stumbling block. For instance, Daix sees the *Demoiselles* as evidence of Picasso "lashing out uncompromisingly at" or "flaunting the window of a Mediterranean brothel at" or even "cocking a snook" at—what? Matisse's *Joy of Living* (sic). Overkill. Apropos the rapports, or lack of them, between the two artists, Daix might have considered the significance of the Matisse painting—the highly simplified, heavily outlined portrait of the artist's daughter, Marguerite—that Picasso chose when the artists exchanged works in 1907. At the time Picasso was accused of having picked a bad painting out of malice, but, as he confirmed many years later, he chose it because he was fascinated by its daring simplifications. According to Picasso, the key influence at this turning point in Matisse's career was not Byzantine mosaics (as Barr has suggested) but the fact that two of the artist's children, Pierre and Jean, had just begun to draw; the crude outlines and flat washes of their childish daubs suggested to their father how to condense and simplify. When Picasso chose this painting, he knew exactly what he could learn from it, as the spareness of his work of late 1908 reveals.

UNLIKE DAIX, RUBIN does not try to update Barr's historical analysis which made MOMA's earlier Picasso catalogs so indispensable. Instead he has tried in his catalog to present what he calls a "kind of art history without words" —that is to say a meaningful layout in the place of a text—and has reproduced "every painting, sculpture, work on paper, and ceramic in the exhibition—over two hundred of them in color."

Rubin's juxtapositions and confrontations are undeniably eloquent; my only complaint is that, despite all the care his staff has taken, the color plates, even of the museum's own paintings, are as catastrophic as the ones that disfigured MOMA's otherwise excellent Cézanne catalog. If the printers can't control the red separations, the museum should stick to black and white.

In place of exegesis, Rubin's catalog includes a detailed and copiously illustrated chronology, compiled under "extreme pressure" by Jane Fluegel. Despite a few inaccuracies in the later sections (by no stretch of the imagination can *The Charnel House* be said to "constitute a pendant to *Guernica*"; Picasso's 1949 visit to Italy is omitted; the first meeting with Jacqueline did not take place in Perpignan but in Cannes), this chronology—early sections especially—is a most useful feature. But it would have been more useful still if events in the artist's life had been pegged to stylistic developments; if, for instance, instead of merely suggesting that the paraphrases of Delacroix's *Femmes d'Alger* were "perhaps a tribute to Matisse," Miss Fluegel had told us that these works were inspired by Picasso's discovery of Jacqueline's resemblance to the right-hand figure in Delacroix's Algerian scene; she might also have mentioned that Jacqueline had spent many years in Africa. These facts would have helped to explain the orientalist references in Picasso's work of this period.

For the facts of his life have more bearing on Picasso's art than is the case with any other great artist, except perhaps van Gogh. The more we know about his day-to-day existence and particularly his domestic arrangements, the easier it is to unravel the mysteries and metamorphoses of Picasso's development. This is especially true after 1918, when abrupt changes in style imply that one wife or mistress has been substituted for another. Thus the pattern of stylistic infidelity can be said to follow the pattern of amorous infidelity. So long as the artist was alive, a biographer—especially one as loyal as Roland Penrose—was unable to delve deeply enough into Picasso's private affairs to be able to perceive the ramifications of this pattern with any clarity. Now, however, that the artist is dead, every crumb of information should be gathered while there is time. In no other great life are the minutiae of gossip so potentially significant.

DORA MAAR, probably the most perceptive of the artist's companions, once told me that at any given period of the artist's post-Cubist life there were five factors that determined his way of life and likewise his style: the woman with whom he was in love; the poet, or poets, who served as a catalyst; the place where he lived; the circle of friends who provided the admiration and understanding of which he never had enough; and the dog who was his inseparable companion and sometimes figured in the iconography of his work. On occasion these factors overlapped: Jaime Sabartés, Picasso's secretary, survived four different regimes. But as a rule, when the wife or mistress changed, virtually everything else changed.

Max Jacob is of course the poet whom we associate with Picasso's early years in Paris and Apollinaire with Cubism. Later, if we are to go along with Dora Maar's theory, we should see Cocteau as a catalyst for the neoclassic period presided over by the artist's first wife, Olga; Breton and the Surrealists for the "Metamorphic" period presided over by Marie-Thérèse; Eluard for *l'époque Dora* (1936–1947); Eluard and Aragon for *l'époque Françoise* (1945–1953); and, despite Picasso's malicious comments about his war record, Cocteau again from the mid-Fifties until his death for *l'époque Jacqueline*.

For such a lightweight, Cocteau had a tremendous impact on Picasso, his influence persisting from 1916 into the Twenties. Thanks to Cocteau, Picasso embarked on an association with Diaghilev (beginning with his décor for the ballet *Parade*) and met his first wife, the ravishing Russian dancer, Olga. Thanks largely to Cocteau, he moved to a smart apartment and took to frequenting the Proustian world of "*le tout Paris.*" But above all the poet confirmed the artist in his budding taste for neoclassicism. This phenomenon, whose glacial embrace so many Parisian artists, musicians, and writers were to experience, should be seen in part at least as a reaction against the disorder of the First World War. One of its attractions for Picasso was that it represented the very antithesis of synthetic Cubism. For a time the two-dimensional cutouts of synthetic Cubism exist side by side with the gigantic bathers, pneumatic ballerinas, and galumphing nymphs of neoclassicism, but after 1920 the latter gradually take over, as Rubin's lavish display of this period demonstrates.

However, besides reflecting the modish dictates of Cocteau's manifesto, *Le Rappel à l'Ordre*, Picasso's adoption of this new style reflects the *embourgeoisement* brought about by marriage to a woman who, besides being silly and irredeemably square, was infatuated and jealous to the point of insanity. The reaction against a life of first nights followed by nice little dinners followed by hysterical scenes was not long in coming. Just as Picasso's love for his wife paralleled his adoption of neoclassicism, so did his subsequent hatred of her parallel his rejection of it. Not that this was by any means the last time Picasso expressed his feelings about women in neoclassic terms.

THE FAILURE OF Picasso's marriage and the demise of the backward-looking style that it engendered are proclaimed by the cacophony, the metamorphic contortions of *La Danse* (1925). Part Dionysiac Charleston, part *in memoriam*, this is the most forward-looking of Picasso's post-Cubist works and in the artist's opinion (as he told Roland Penrose) "a finer work than *Guernica*"—partly I suspect by virtue of its not being an official commission, which was something the artist had always been at pains to avoid. That *La Danse* stands in relation to the second half of the artist's development much as the *Demoiselles d'Avignon* does to the first half is too often overlooked, though not by John Golding, who has reminded us that both these paintings were featured in the same number of *La Révolution surréaliste* (1925).

Besides *La Danse*, a chance meeting with a seventeen-year-old blonde, Marie-Thérèse Walter, outside the Galeries Lafayette (January 1927) opened the way for the next set of stylistic developments. Within a few months of this pickup, Picasso's work betrayed the otherwise well-kept secret that he had a new companion. Not that he did portraits of Marie-Thérèse; what gave the show away was the frenzied sexuality and voluptuous forms of the new paintings and, a bit later, monumental sculptures that the artist took to doing. The fact that Marie-Thérèse was a sleepy, easy-going girl who loved swimming and was often to be found in the company of a sister, on the beach or at Picasso's new house (Château de Boisgeloup)—all this can be deduced from paintings of mammoth women, asleep or reading, by the sea or in a garden. Monsters of sex appeal! Once again a new style had evolved under the influence of the mistress's persona, or rather Picasso's perception of it.

The extent to which Marie-Thérèse's sexuality pervades Picasso's work of the early Thirties can be appreciated as never before in the spectacular group of paintings and sculptures of the late 1920s and early 1930s, which Rubin has arranged to such telling effect. Has sheer physical passion ever been made so palpable in paint or bronze? And yet for all their raunchiness, these Marie-Thérèses have a tenderness and warmth that make Matisse's girls of the same period seem cold and contrived and, in the same way, the mountainous Jacquelines of Picasso's old age look frustrated and menacing.

The switch from voluptuousness to violence in the mid-Thirties has its roots in an unhappy combination of events: more out of thwarted love than greed, Picasso's estranged wife tried to appropriate half his property (including the studio contents); at the same time Marie-Thérèse became pregnant. In the face of these worries, Picasso virtually abandoned painting for poetry (February 1935). Further problems lay ahead: not long after Marie-Thérèse gave birth, Picasso fell for a beautiful young photographer and painter, Dora Maar, whom he had met through Eluard. Meanwhile civil war was boiling up in Spain.

The fallow period—almost a year—paid off. When Picasso resumed painting, his work was heavily influenced by Surrealist poetry. Melancholy allegories feature mortally wounded Picassos in the form of bulls, bull-fighters, and Minotaurs confronted by Marie-Thérèses in the form of gored horses or classical nymphs crowned with wreaths; there is even a lot of the blue that self-pity brings out. And then all of a sudden, thanks partly to the advent of Dora, Picasso is back at his Dionysiac best. The series of women's heads—all to some extent portraits—which continue for the next eight years constitute the artist's most sustained achievement since Cubism.

BUT FIRST CAME *Guernica*. This huge polemical panel in which Picasso pits himself against Goya (specifically *The Third of May, 1808*, soon to be *Guernica*'s neighbor in the Prado) is permeated by Dora's presence. She not only photographed it at different stages of completion, but she actually painted bits of it, and the figure holding a lamp is unquestionably a likeness of Dora.[2] Moreover, she was an important link with Surrealists like Eluard, who supported the Popular Front against Franco and whose ideas may well have played a part in the gestation of *Guernica*.

Dora was a formidable muse. Even in the earliest portraits of her one senses that a struggle to the death has broken out between this highly strung intellectual beauty and her demonic lover. Once again Picasso's manipulation of his mistress's life parallels his manipulation and redistribution of her features. Thus for Dora he contrived a supple new style that could express a range of emotions from rapture through tenderness and grief to loathing in contortions that are sometimes lyrical but more often monstrous. Meanwhile Picasso continued to paint Marie-Thérèse. Sometimes he would portray both women on the same day in the same pose but each

---

[2] So far as I know, nobody has published the fact that Dora Maar worked on *Guernica*. Many of the vertical strokes on the horse's body were painted by her.

in a different morphology (Dora angular; Marie-Thérèse all curves). Sometimes he would paint one mistress in ways that recalled the other; or he would do a painting in which the blonde Marie-Thérèse could see tell-tale traces of the flamboyantly smart Dora—dark hair in a snood, heavily made-up eyes—cropping up in what was otherwise a likeness of her. Was Marie-Thérèse being supplanted? Yes. "These facts betray themselves in my work," Picasso once said. "It must be painful for a girl to see in a painting that she is on the way out." How heartless and brutal! And yet Picasso was also capable of the utmost tenderness toward the women in his life, as well as much kindness and generosity toward his friends. To dismiss him as a fiend is as misguided as promoting him as a saint.

While consummating his passions in paint, Picasso likewise consummated feelings of guilt and hatred in diabolical portraits of his vengeful wife. One of these is in the MOMA show, although it is not identified as such (*Lady in a Straw Hat*, catalog, page 331). The contrast between this obscene yenta, crowned by a grotesquely dainty hat, and the ideal beauty which the artist portrayed so affectionately in the early years of marriage is a chastening one.

Do not, however, imagine that the number of people present in these distorted "portraits" is limited to one or two. On his summer visits to Mougins in 1937 and 1938 the artist was accompanied not only by Dora Maar but by Paul Eluard, and his wife, Nusch. He also saw a lot of Lee Miller (Penrose), the American photographer, and of Ines (subsequently his housekeeper) and her two sisters. Picasso did separate portraits of all these women; he likewise did composite portraits, ones in which the features of three or even four people blend into a single image. In other works of the period Picasso arbitrarily manipulates the sex of one of his friends: Eluard gets a coif and is transformed into an *Arlésienne*, also into a Provençal peasant woman suckling a kitten.

One more bizarre element must be taken into account, if we want fully to understand these paintings. Picasso had recently acquired an Afghan dog, Kazbek, and he often grafted the elongated muzzle and floppy ears of this animal onto the face of Dora—a comment, he claimed, on "the animal nature of women" (e.g., page 346).

STAYING ON IN PARIS after it was occupied, Picasso made no overt references to the war in his work, but he painted some of the grimness of it into his portraits of Dora, particularly the agonized, skull-like heads he executed in 1943. These paintings can have left Dora in no doubt that love had soured into rage. "She always frightened me," Picasso said much later of the highly strung woman cooped up with him by the Occupation. Poor Dora! When Picasso left her, she suffered a nervous collapse and had to be entrusted to Dr. Jacques Lacan's care; she subsequently became a recluse. But by that time paintings of a fresh young face free of angst reveal that Picasso had taken a new mistress: Françoise Gilot.

Once again everything changed. Picasso and Françoise set up house on the French Riviera; he fathered two children, took a more active part in politics, acquired a new dog, and adopted a simple new style—spare, serene, optimistic—in keeping with this idyllic new relationship. He also experimented to brilliant effect with a new medium (lithography) and a new craft (pottery). All went well until Françoise made it clear that, unlike her predecessors, she resented being manipulated. As she has recorded in her book, *Life with Picasso*, she was exasperated by Picasso's view that women were "either goddesses or doormats." And so, after eight years, she left the artist, but not before the tensions between them had manifested themselves in some grim paintings of domestic life. The MOMA show includes the exquisite *Femme Fleur* portrait of Françoise (1946) and a few others, but on the whole it does scant justice to *l'époque Françoise*. None of the Matisse-like portraits (1948–1949) is included, nor any of the *Antipolis* compositions.

Françoise's departure (1953) was followed by an uneasy interim period. Once again Picasso expressed his sorrows in allegory; the so-called *Verve* series of drawings that bear witness to the dilemma of an old man confronted by desirable young models. At the same time, contrary to his usual custom, Picasso devoted some forty paintings and drawings to a beautiful girl, Sylvette David, who was not his mistress. The absence of emotional involvement is immediately apparent in the lack of tension and expressiveness— presumably why this corny series has been excluded from the present show. Meanwhile Picasso continued to pay court to three different women in three different parts of France, until, in the summer of 1954, his choice finally settled on a young divorcée, Jacqueline Roque (subsequently his wife), who had come to Cannes to work for the Ramiés—Picasso's potters.

Picasso lost no time in reverting to his old habit and soon contrived a new style with which to express the allure of his new mistress. But how inappropriate the first portraits of Jacqueline seemed! It was difficult to equate such a demure girl with such a dramatic, such an intense air; and a long neck (see page 414) was not her most conspicuous feature. But once again Picasso's insight was born out by events; within a few months his mistress came to resemble the portraits in personality and even looks—Dorian Gray in reverse!

The old manipulator always prided himself on the premonitory powers of his portraits, often in the way they foretold unfortunate developments in the life or character of his female companion. Especially eerie are some of Picasso's later portraits of Jacqueline, which predict the pathetic widow who would emerge in all her misery after the artist's death. Yet other portraits include presentiments of a different kind. In the early years of the affair Jacqueline's health was poor—"Women's ills are always their fault," Picasso used to say—and the artist swore that some of his more anguished portraits anticipated Jacqueline's bouts of sickness by a few days. More to do with her response to psychosomatic suggestion than with the painter's prophetic powers, I always felt.

"I WOULD LIKE people to have almost a sense of vertigo, to leave this exhibition reeling," Rubin has announced. I don't know about vertigo, but by the end of the show, I was certainly reeling, not least because the last twenty years of the artist's life are charted in a rather erratic manner. Many critics, I know, hold the view that the artist's old age represents a decided decline in his powers. This is not true. If the same discrimination and space that have been lavished on earlier sections were in evidence in the last galleries, the show could have ended with a bang.

It tails off largely because the organizers, who elsewhere have done such an exemplary job of installation, have relegated some of the artist's finest late works—his versions of Velásquez, Delacroix, and Manet—to a grab-bag section of all periods, entitled "Paraphrases." These would make much more sense hung in their chronological place. Far from being mere stylistic exercises, these hybrids are crucial to our understanding of the artist's penultimate style. For they demonstrate how Picasso, canniest of art historians, vainly pursued immortality by painting himself into the company of the immortals. As Picasso said to Hélène Parmelin, "I have a feeling that Delacroix, Giotto, Tintoretto, El Greco and the rest, as well as all the modern painters, the good and the bad, the abstract and the non-abstract, are all standing behind me watching me at work."

This obsession with art and artists of the past is most evident in the fantastic series of 347 prints that Picasso executed in 1968. In these playful allegories a figure, who may or may not be Picasso, often in the company of another figure, who may or may not be Jacqueline, rubs shoulders with artists out of the past and their mistresses, characters out of French and

Spanish literature, and people out of the artist's personal mythology. Rapists in plumed hats, lecherous old masters, stuffy gentlemen from the court of Philip II, girls with their legs in the air perform a variety of sexual antics, but these are more knockabout than erotic. Whether they represent circus or seraglio, brothel or battlefield, these scenes are really about the studio—the center of the artist's world, the setting for his fantasies—where Picasso had immured himself.

What I find particularly poignant about Picasso's late works is the mixture of self-mockery and megalomania in the artist's conception. In the teeth of death—the archenemy that Picasso could neither exorcise nor face —he set about constructing his own peculiar pantheon with himself sardonically ensconced at the heart of things. By remaking the past in the present, he seemed to think he could stretch time and outwit mortality. After all, art had enabled Proust to manipulate the laws of time and Joyce to cram the whole of history into one man's day. By the same token, Picasso—most Faustian of artists—was determined to turn yesterdays into tomorrows.

AS PICASSO ENTERED his ninth decade, his energy hardly flagged. With time running out, he jettisoned more and more—virtually all considerations of color, structure, *facture*, finish, and style—in his race to summarize, in shorthand if need be, the black thoughts and jokes and sexual pangs that still preyed on his mind. Consequently many of the late paintings, less so the drawings, are helter-skelter to the point of sloppiness — speed painting. Time and again the artist would adumbrate an ambitious composition, then optimistically conclude it with a signature, before any valid pictorial solution was in sight. And yet the best of these monstrous figures, all gaping eyes and banana fingers, pack a fierce punch. Like it or not, a painting like *The Young Bather with Sand Shovel* (1971) has the impact of a Mack truck. Up to the day of Picasso's death in 1973 the power was never switched off.

All the same, a sad end. Of course it would have been more dignified if the great man could have died in the odor of artistic sanctity, like Titian or Rembrandt or Cézanne. But, let us face it, by his eighties, let alone nineties, fear of death overshadowed everything else in life and made inward looks unthinkable. To believe Picasso, he had no faith of any kind; to believe Jacqueline, he was capable of being *"plus catholique que le pape."* Either way, he was addicted to superstitions of the blackest sort. As his daughter said, it was all very Spanish. And so for this other Faust there could be no peace of mind, no *Saintes-Victoires*.

Ernst Jünger

An Aesthete at War *by Bruce Chatwin was originally published March 5, 1981, as a review of Ernst Jünger's Diaries:* Jardins et Routes, Diaries, Vol I: 1939–1940; Premier Journal Parisien, Diaries, Vol. II: 1941–1943; Second Journal Parisien, Diaries, Vol. III: 1943–1945. *Christian Bourgois, Paris. Copyright © 1981 by Bruce Chatwin. Reprinted with permission of Wylie, Aitken & Stone, Inc.*

BRUCE CHATWIN

An Aesthete at War

I

ON JUNE 18, 1940, Mr. Churchill ended his speech to the Commons with the words "This was their finest hour!" and, that evening, a very different character, in the gray officer's uniform of the Wehrmacht, sat in the Duchesse de la Rochefoucauld's study at the Château de Montmirail. Her uninvited guest was a short, athletic man of forty-five, with a mouth set in an expression of self-esteem and eyes a particularly arctic shade of blue. He leafed through her books with the assured touch of the bibliomane and noted that many bore the dedications of famous writers. A letter slipped from one and fell to the floor—a delightful letter written by a boy called François who wanted to be a pilot. He wondered if the boy was now a pilot. Finally, after dark, he settled down to write his diary. It was a long entry—almost two thousand words—for his day, too, had been eventful.

In the morning, he had discussed the risks of getting burned alive with a tank driver in oil-soaked denims: "I had the impression that Vulcan and his 'ethic of work' was incarnate in such martial figures." After luncheon, he had stood in the school playground and watched a column of ten thousand French and Belgian prisoners file past: "...an image of the dark wave of Destiny herself,...an interesting and instructive spectacle" in which one sensed the "mechanical, irresistible allure peculiar to catastrophes." He had chucked them cans of beef and biscuits and watched their struggles from behind an iron grille: the sight of their hands was especially disturbing.

Next, he had spotted a group of officers with decorations from the Great War, and invited them to dine. They were on the verge of collapse, but a good dinner seemed like a reversal of their fortunes. Could he explain, they asked, the reasons for their defeat? "I said I considered it the Triumph of the Worker, but I do not think they understood the sense of my reply. What could they know of the years we have passed through since 1918? Of the lessons we have learned as if in a blast furnace?"

THE ABSENT DUCHESS had reason to thank the man who nosed in her private affairs. Captain Ernst Jünger was, at that moment, the most celebrated German writer in uniform. No catastrophe could surprise him since for twenty years his work had harped on the philosophical need to accept death and total warfare as the everyday experience of the twentieth century. Yet he tempered his assent to destruction with an antiquarian's reverence for bricks and mortar, and had saved the château.

Indeed, he had saved a lot of things in the blitzkrieg. A week earlier, he had saved the Cathedral of Laon from looters. He had saved the city's library with its manuscripts of the Carolingian kings. And he had employed an out-of-work wine waiter to inspect some private cellars and save some good bottles for himself. Bombs, it was true, had fallen in the La Rochefoucaulds' park. A pavillion had burned out, leaving in one window a fragment of glass that "reproduced exactly the head of Queen Victoria." Otherwise, after a bit of tidying up, the place was just as its owners had left it. Moreover, Captain Jünger had other reasons for feeling pleased with himself.

> The Maxims [of La Rochefoucauld] have long been my favorite bedside reading. It was an act of spiritual gratitude to save what could be saved. For properties of such value, the essential is to protect them during the critical days.

Easier said than done! "The route of the invasion is strewn with bottles, champagne, claret, burgundy. I counted at least one for every step, to say nothing of the camps where one could say it had rained bottles. Such orgies are in the true tradition of our campaigns in France. Every invasion by a German army is accompanied by drinking bouts like those of the gods in the *Edda*."

A junior officer remarked how strange it was that the looting soldiers destroyed musical instruments first: "It showed me in a symbolic fashion how Mars is contrary to the Muses . . . and then I recalled the large painting by Rubens illustrating the same theme. . . ." How strange, too, that they left the mirrors intact! The officer thought this was because the men wanted to shave—but Jünger thought there might be other reasons.

THESE DIARIES—three volumes of them—have recently reappeared in France, where the translation of Jünger's work is a minor literary industry.

To English-speaking readers, however, he is known by two books—*Storm of Steel* (1920), a relentless glorification of modern warfare, and *On the Marble Cliffs*, his allegorical, anti-Nazi capriccio of 1939 that describes an assassination attempt on a tyrant and appears, in retrospect, to be a prophecy of the von Stauffenberg bomb plot of 1944.

Yet Jünger's partisans—more French perhaps than German—claim for him the status of "great writer," a thinker of Goethean wisdom, whose political leanings toward the extreme right have robbed him of the recognition he deserves. Certainly, the scale of his erudition is titanic: his singularity of purpose is unswerving, and even at eighty-five he continues to elaborate on the themes that have held his attention for over sixty years. He is—or has been—soldier, aesthete, novelist, essayist, the ideologue of an authoritarian political party, and a trained taxonomic botanist. His lifelong hobby has been the study of entomology: indeed, what the butterfly was to Nabokov, the beetle is to Jünger—especially the armor-plated beetle. He is also the connoisseur of hallucinogens who took a number of "trips" with his friend Albert Hofmann, the discoverer of lysergic acid.[1]

He writes a hard, lucid prose. Much of it leaves the reader with an impression of the author's imperturbable self-regard, of dandyism, of cold-bloodedness, and, finally, of banality. Yet the least promising passages will suddenly light up with flashes of aphoristic brilliance, and the most harrowing descriptions are alleviated by a yearning for human values in a dehumanized world. The diary is the perfect form for a man who combines such acute powers of observation with an anaesthetized sensibility.[2]

HE WAS BORN IN 1895, the son of a pharmacist from Hanover. By 1911, bored by the conventional world of his parents, he joined the Wandervogel Movement and so became acquainted with the values of Open Air, Nature, Blood, Soil, and Fatherland: already he was the expert beetle-hunter

---

[1] For a description of Jünger's "tripping," see Albert Hofmann, *LSD—My Problem Child* (McGraw-Hill, 1980), chapter 7, "Radiance from Ernst Jünger."

[2] Other works by Ernst Jünger: *The Storm of Steel* (*In Stahlgewittern*), translated by B. Creighton, 1929, reprinted by Howard Fertig, 1975. *Sur les Falaises de Marbre* (*Auf den Marmorklippen*), Gallimard, Paris, 1942. The English translation of *On the Marble Cliffs* was published by John Lehmann in 1947, and again as a Penguin Modern Classic, with an introduction by George Steiner, in 1970. German-speaking readers are referred to Jünger's complete *Werke*, Klett Verlag, Stuttgart. To my knowledge, the only full-length study of Jünger in English is *Ernst Jünger: A Writer of Our Time* by J.P. Stern (Yale University Press, 1953).

who spent many happy hours with his killing bottle. Two years later, he ran away to the Sahara and joined the Foreign Legion, only to be brought back by his father. In 1914, on the first day of war, he enlisted in the 73rd Hanoverian Fusiliers and emerged in 1918 "punctured in twenty places," with the highest military decoration, the *Croix pour le Mérite*, an enlarged sense of personal grandeur, and in possession of a meticulous diary that recorded the horrific beauty of trench warfare and the reckless gaiety of men under fire. The Fall of Germany was thus the making of Jünger.

Storm of Steel made him the hero of a generation of young officers who had given all and ended up, if lucky, with the Iron Cross. Gide praised it as the finest piece of writing to come out of the war. Certainly, it is quite unlike anything of its time—none of the pastoral musings of Siegfried Sassoon or Edmund Blunden, no whiffs of cowardice as in Hemingway, none of the masochism of T. E. Lawrence, or the compassion of Remarque. Instead, Jünger parades his belief in Man's "elementary" instinct to kill other men—a game which, if played correctly, must conform to a chivalric set of rules. (In a later essay, "Battle as Inner Experience," he sets forth his views on the innate gratifications of hand-to-hand fighting.) Finally, you end up with a picture of the war as a grim, but gentlemanly, shooting party. "What a bag!" he exclaims when they capture 150 prisoners. Or: "Caught between two fires, the English tried to escape across the open and were gunned down like game at a *battue*." And how strange it was to gaze into the eyes of the young Englishman you'd shot down five minutes before!

Even in his early twenties, Jünger presents himself as an aesthete at the center of a tornado, quoting Stendhal that the art of civilization consists in "combining the most delicate pleasures... with the frequent presence of danger." At Combles, for example, he finds an untenanted house "where a lover of beautiful things must have lived"; and though half the house gets blown to bits, he goes on reading in an armchair until interrupted by a violent blow on his calf: "There was a ragged hole in my puttees from which blood streamed to the floor. On the other side was the circular swelling of a piece of shrapnel under the skin." No one but a man of Jünger's composure could describe the appearance of a bullet hole through his chest as if he were describing his nipple.

After the war, he took up botany, entomology, and marine biology, first at Leipzig, then in Naples. Like so many others of his generation, he was saturated by the garbled form of Darwinism as doctored for nationalist purposes. Yet he was too intelligent to fall for the cruder versions of the theory that led members of the German scientific establishment to condone the slaughter of Gypsies and Jews—recognizing, as he did, that any theory is also the autobiography of the theorist and can but reflect an "infinitesimal part of the whole." His pleasures in biology tended toward the Linnaean classification of species—aesthetic pleasures that offered him a glimpse of the Primordial Paradise as yet untainted by Man. Moreover, the insect world, where instincts govern behavior as a key fits a lock, had an irresistible attraction to a man of his utopian vision.

By 1927, he was back in Berlin where his friends were a mixed bag that included Kubin, Dr. Goebbels, Bertolt Brecht, and Ernst Toller. He became a founding member of the National Bolshevist Caucus—a zealous, extremist political party that flourished for a while in late Weimar, negligible in its effect on history, though not without interesting theoretical implications. These so-called "Prussian Communists" hated capitalism, hated the bourgeois West, and hoped to graft the methods of Bolshevism onto the chivalric ideals of the Junkers. Their leader, Ernst Niekisch, visualized an alliance of workers and soldier-aristocrats who would abolish the middle classes. Jünger himself was the ideologue of the movement and, in 1932, published a book that was to have been its manifesto.

The Worker (*Der Arbeiter*) is a vaguely formulated machine-age utopia whose citizens are required to commit themselves to a "total mobilization" (the origin of the term is Jünger's) in the undefined interests of the State. The Worker, as Jünger understands him, is a technocrat. His business, ultimately, is war. His freedom—or rather, his sense of inner freedom—is supposed to correspond to the scale of his productivity. The aim is world government—by force.

Not surprisingly, the movement petered out. Niekisch was later arrested by the Gestapo and was murdered, in 1945, in jail. As for Jünger, his war record gave him a certain immunity from the Nazis and he retreated into a private, almost eremitic, life of scientific contemplation and *belles lettres*. Though he deplored Hitler as a vulgar technician who had misunderstood the metaphysics of power, he did nothing to try to stop him, believing anyway that democracy was dead and the destiny of machine-age man was essentially tragic: "The history of civilization is the gradual replacement of men by things." Yet, again and again, he insists that the wars of the twentieth century are popular wars—wars, that is, of the People, of the *canaille*, and not of the professional soldier. From his viewpoint, albeit an oblique one, National Socialism was a phenomenon of the left.

THROUGHOUT THE MIDDLE THIRTIES, Jünger wrote essays, traveled to the tropics, and kept a cold eye on the Fatherland. By 1938, at the time of the Generals' Plot, he seems to have flirted with resistance to Hitler, and one night at his house at Ueberlingen, near Lake Constance, he met a young, patriotic aristocrat, Heinrich von Trott zu Solz (whose elder brother, Adam, was the ex-Rhodes scholar and friend of England who would be hanged for his part in the von Stauffenberg plot of July 1944). What passed between them, Jünger does not relate. What is certain is that the visit gave him the idea for a story.[3]

On the Marble Cliffs is an allegorical tale, written in a frozen, humorless, yet brilliantly colored style that owes something to the nineteenth-century Decadents and something to the Scandinavian sagas. The result is a prose equivalent of an art nouveau object in glass, and the plot is much less silly than it sounds in précis:

Two men—the narrator and Brother Otho (not to be distinguished from Jünger himself and his own brother, the poet Friedrich Georg) are aesthetes, scientists, and soldiers who have retired from war to a remote cliffside hermitage, where they work on a Linnaean classification of the region's flora, and harbor a lot of pet snakes. Far below lies the Grand Marina, a limpid lake surrounded by the farms, the vineyards, and cities of a venerable civilization. To the north there stretches an expanse of steppe-land where pastoral nomads drive their herds. Beyond that are the black forests of Mauretania, the sinister realm of the Chief Ranger (*Oberförster*) with his pack of bloodhounds and gang of disciplined freebooters in whose ranks the brothers once served.

The *Oberförster* is planning to destroy the Grand Marina:

> He was one of those figures whom the Mauretanians respect as great lords and yet find somewhat ridiculous—rather as an old colonel is received in the regiment on occasional visits from his estates. He left an imprint on one's mind if only because his green coat with its gold-embroidered ilexes drew all eyes to him.... (His own eyes), like those of hardened drinkers, were touched with a red flame, but expressed both cunning and unshakeable power—yes, at times, even majesty. Then we took pleasure in his company and lived in arrogance at the table of the great....

As evil spreads over the land "like mushroom-spawn over rotten wood," the two brothers plunge deeper and deeper into the mystery of

---

3 For a biography of Adam von Trott zu Solz, see Christopher Sykes, *Troubled Loyalty* (London, 1968).

flowers. But on a botanical expedition to the Mauretanian forest in search of a rare red orchid, they stumble on the *Oberförster's* charnel house, Köppels-Bleek, where a dwarf sings gaily as he scrapes at a flaying bench:

> Over the dark door on the gable end a skull was nailed fast, showing its teeth and seeming to invite entry with its grin. Like a jewel in its chain, it was the central link of a narrow gable frieze which appeared to be formed of brown spiders. Suddenly we guessed that it was fashioned of human hands....

The brothers' discovery of the orchid gives them a "strange feeling of in-vulnerability" and the strength to continue their studies. But one day, just before the *Oberförster* launches his attack on the Marina, they are visited by one of his henchmen, Braquemart, and the young Prince of Sunmyra.

Braquemart is a "small, dark, haggard fellow, whom we found some-what coarse-grained but, like all Mauretanians, not without wit." The Prince, on the other hand, is "remote and absent-minded" with an "air of deep suffering" and the "stamp of decadence." This pair, of course, is plan-ning a *coup d'état*, which fails when the *Oberförster* unleashes his blood-hounds. The leader of the pack is called Chiffon Rouge, i.e., Red Flag, and, in a scene of appalling ferocity, everyone gets mangled and killed except for the two brothers, who are saved by the miraculous intervention of their own pet lance-head vipers. Later, at Köppels-Bleek, they find the heads of the two conspirators on poles, Braquemart having killed himself first "with the capsule of poison that all Mauretanians carry." But on the "pale mask of the Prince from which the scalped flesh hung in ribbons... there played the shadow of a smile intensely sweet and joyful, and I knew then that the weaknesses had fallen from this noble man with each step of his martyr-dom...."—which description can be compared to the photo of Adam von Trott, as he heard the death sentence, in the People's Court, five years after Jünger wrote his book.[4]

On The Marble Cliffs sold 35,000 copies before it was suppressed early in 1940. How it slipped through the censor machine of Dr. Goebbels is less of a mystery when one realizes that Braquemart was modeled on Dr. Goebbels himself, who was flattered and amused by it, and later alarmed by its popularity among the officer caste. Jünger himself claimed then—as now—that the fable is not specifically anti-Nazi, but "above all that." And I

---

4 Sykes, *Troubled Loyalty*, p. 447: "Yet the expression on his face showed an extra-ordinary serenity, and there is almost the suspicion of a smile. His loyalty was no longer troubled."

don't doubt that he conceived it as a contemptuous, sweeping, Spenglerian statement on the destruction of the old Mediterranean-based civilization of Europe: the *Oberförster* could, at a pinch, stand for Stalin as well as Hitler.

At a meeting of the Nazi Party, Reichsleiter Boulher is supposed to have said: "Mein Führer, this time Jünger has gone too far!" but Hitler calmed him down and said: "Let Jünger be!" All the same, the writer's friends advised him to get into uniform; and so by the fall of 1939 he found himself with the rank of captain, posted to the Siegfried Line, convinced, by now, that the private journal was the only practical medium for literary expression in a totalitarian state.

IN HIS INTRODUCTION to his diaries, Jünger invokes the story of seven sailors who agreed to study astronomy on the Arctic island of St. Maurice during the winter of 1633, and whose journal was found beside their bodies when the whaling ships returned the following summer. The fate of Jünger's journal is to be that of Poe's "Ms. Found in a Bottle"—a record thrown into an uncertain future by a man who may die tomorrow, yet who cherishes his writing as a man "cherishes those of his children who have no chance of surviving."

Their German title, *Strahlungen*, means "Reflections"—in the sense that the writer collects particles of light and reflects them onto the reader. In this case the light is lurid—yet once read, these books are never forgotten. They are surely the strangest literary production to come out of the Second World War, stranger by far than anything by Céline or Malaparte. Jünger reduces his war to a sequence of hallucinatory prose poems in which things appear to breathe and people perform like automata or, at best, like insects. So when he focuses on occupied Paris the result is like a diorama in the entomological department of a natural history museum.

II

THE OPENING PAGES find Jünger in April 1939 at a new house in Kirchhorst near Hanover, putting the final touches to *On the Marble Cliffs* and having bad dreams about Hitler, whom he calls by the pseudonym of Kniébolo. By wintertime, he is exchanging desultory fire with the French batteries across the Rhine. He saves the life of a gunner, and gets another Iron Cross. Among his reading: the Bible, Melville's *Bartleby the Scrivener*, and Boethius's *Consolation of Philosophy*. He sleeps in a reed hut, in a sleeping bag lined with rose-colored silk, and on his forty-fifth birthday a young officer brings him a bottle of wine with a bunch of violets tied round the neck.

After the invasion of France, there is a gap until April 1941 when he surfaces in Paris as "Officer with Special Mission attached to the Military Command"—his job: to censor mail and sound out the intellectual and social life of the city. And he remains in Paris, with interruptions, until the Americans are at the gates.

He presents himself as the zealous Francophile who believes that France and Germany have everything to offer each other. Indeed, everything does point to collaboration. Pétain's armistice is still popular; anti-Semitism flourishing; and Anglophobia given an enormous boost by the sinking of the French fleet at Mers-el-Kebir. There is even talk of avenging Waterloo and, when Stalin enters the war, "*Les Anglo-Saxons travaillent pour Oncle Jo.*" Besides, Jünger's French friends are determined the war shall cramp their style as little as possible. And how well-mannered the newcomers are! What a relief after all those years of Americans in Paris!

IN THE FIRST WEEKS, Captain Jünger is a tourist in the city of every German soldier's dream. He lives at the Hotel Raphäel, and goes on long walks alone. He inspects the gargoyles of Notre-Dame, the "Hellenistic" architecture of La Madeleine ("A church if you please!"), and notes that the obelisk in the Place de la Concorde is the color of a champagne sorbet. With his friend General Speidel, he goes to the Marché aux Puces; idles the hours away in antiquarian bookshops, and, sometimes, goes to watch a revue of naked girls: many are the daughters of White Russian émigrés, and with one small, melancholic girl he discusses Pushkin and Aksakov's *Memoirs of Childhood*.

Paris is full of strange encounters. On Bastille Day, a street player sets aside his violin to shake his hand. He rounds up drunken soldiers from a *hôtel de passe* and talks to a gay, eighteen-year-old whore. On May 1 he offers lilies-of-the-valley to a young *vendeuse*: "Paris offers all manner of such meetings. You hardly have to look for them. No wonder: for she is built on an Altar of Venus." He takes another girl to a milliner's, buys her a green-feathered hat "the size of a hummingbird's nest," and watches her "expand and glow like a soldier who has just been decorated." Meanwhile, his wife reports from Kirchhorst the contents of her very intellectual dreams.

Then the restaurants. He gets taken to Maxim's but takes himself to Prunier—"the little dining room on the first floor, fresh and smart, the color of pale aquamarine." "We lived off lobster and oysters in those days," he told me—though by 1942 the average Parisian was next to starving. One night he dines at the Tour d'Argent: "One had the impression that the people sitting up there on high, consuming their soles and the famous duck, were looking with diabolical satisfaction, like gargoyles, over the sea of gray roofs which sheltered the hungry. In such times, to eat, and to eat well, gives one a sensation of power." Another evening, when the Allies bomb the Renault factory, killing five hundred workers, "the event, viewed from our *quartier*, had rather the appearance of the play of light in a shadow theater."

His entry into the higher circles of collaboration begins with a lunch on the Avenue Foch, given for Speidel by Ferdinand de Brinon, Vichy's unofficial ambassador to the Occupant. There is a vase of startling white orchids "enameled, no doubt, in the virgin forest to attract the eyes of insects." There is Madame de Brinon, Jewish herself but sneering at the *youpins* (Jews). There is Arletty, whose latest film is showing in the cinemas. (After the Liberation, accused of a German lover, she will turn those eyes on the judge and murmur "*Que je suis une femme . . .*" and get off.) But the star of the party is the playwright Sacha Guitry, who entertains them with anecdotes: of Octave Mirbeau, dying in his arms and saying: "*Ne collaborez, jamais!*"—meaning: "Never write a play with someone else!"

At a lunch in Guitry's apartment, Jünger admires the original manuscript of *L'Education sentimentale* and Sarah Bernhardt's golden salad bowl. Later, he meets Cocteau and Jean Marais, "a plebeian Antinous," and Cocteau tells how Proust would receive visitors in bed, wearing yellow kid gloves to stop him from biting his nails, and how the dust lay, "like chinchillas," on the commodes. He meets Paul Morand, whose book on London describes the city as a colossal house: "If the English were to build the

Pyramid, they should put this book in the chamber with the mummy." Madame Morand is a Romanian aristocrat and keeps a gray stone Aztec goddess in her drawing room: they wonder how many victims have fallen at its feet. When Jünger sends her a copy of *The Worker*, she sends a note to his hotel: "For me the art of living is the art of making other people work and keeping pleasure for myself."

Thursday is the *salon* of Marie-Louise Bousquet, the Paris correspondent of *Harper's Bazaar*, who introduces her German guest to his French "collaborationist" colleagues—Montherlant, Jouhandeau, Léautaud, and Drieu la Rochelle, the editor of the *Nouvelle Revue Française*, whose own war book, *La Comédie de Charleroi*, is a tamer counterpart to *Storm of Steel*—Drieu who will kill himself after several attempts, in 1945, leaving a note for his maid: "Celeste, let me sleep this time." On one of these Thursdays, Jünger brings an officer friend and his hostess says: "With a regiment of young men like that, the Germans could have walked over France without firing a shot."

Then there is Abel Bonnard, a travel writer and Vichy minister of education, who loved German soldiers and of whom Pétain said: "It's scandalous to entrust the young to that *tapette*." They talk of sea voyages and paintings of shipwrecks—and Jünger, who sees in the shipwreck an image of the end of the world in miniature, is delighted when Bonnard tells of a marine artist called Gudin, who would smash ship models in his studio to get the right effect.

He visits Picasso in his studio in the rue des Grands Augustins. The master shows a series of asymmetrical heads which Jünger finds rather monstrous. He tries to lure him into a general discussion of aesthetics but Picasso refuses to be drawn: "There are chemists who spend their whole lives trying to find out what's in a lump of sugar. I want to know one thing. What is color?"

BUT PARIS IS NOT all holiday. Shortly after his arrival, Captain Jünger is ordered to the Bois de Bologne to supervise the execution of a German deserter, who has been sheltered by a Frenchwoman for nine months. He has trafficked on the black market. He has made his mistress jealous, even beaten her, and she has reported him to the police. At first, Jünger thinks he will feign illness, but then thinks better of it: "I have to confess it was the spirit of higher curiosity that induced me to accept." He has seen many people die, but never one who knew it in advance. How does it affect one?

There follows one of the nastiest passages in the literature of war—a firing squad painted in the manner of early Monet: the clearing in the wood, the spring foliage glistening after rain, the trunk of the ash tree riddled with the bullet holes of earlier executions. There are two groups of holes, one for the head and one for the heart, and inside the holes a few black meat flies are sleeping. Then the arrival—two military vehicles, the victim, guards, grave diggers, medical officer and pastor, also a cheap white wood coffin. The face is agreeable, attractive to women; the eyes wide, fixed, avid "as if his whole body were suspended from them"; and in his expression something flourishing and childlike. He wears expensive gray trousers and a gray silk shirt. A fly crawls over his left cheek, then sits on his ear. Does he want an eye band? Yes. A crucifix? Yes. The medical officer pins a red card over his heart, the size of a playing card. The soldiers stand in line; the salvo; five small black holes appear on the card like drops of rain; the twitching; the pallor; the guard who wipes the handcuffs with a chiffon handkerchief. And what about the fly that danced in a shaft of sunlight?

The effectiveness of Jünger's technique intensifies as the war proceeds. The atmosphere in which he clothes the Military Command reminds one of a Racine tragedy, in which the central characters are either threatened or doomed, and all numbed into elegant paralysis by the howling tyrant offstage. Yet, though the clock ticks on toward catastrophe, they are still allowed to hope for the reprieve of a negotiated peace with the Allies.

Earlier in 1942, German officers can still raise a toast: "Us—after the Deluge!" By the end of the year, it is apparent that the Deluge is also for them. After lunching with Paul Morand at Maxim's, Jünger sees three Jewish girls arm in arm on the rue Royale with yellow stars pinned to their dresses, and, in a wave of revulsion, feels ashamed to be seen in public. Later, on a mission to the Caucasus in December, he hears a General Müller spell out the details of the gas ovens. All the old codes of honor and decency have broken down, leaving only the foul techniques of German militarism. All the things he has loved—the weapons, the decorations, the uniforms—now, suddenly, fill him with disgust. He feels remorse but not much pity, and dreads the nemesis to come. By the time he gets back to Paris, the Final Solution is in full swing, the trains are running to Auschwitz, and a Commander Ravenstein says: "One day my daughter will pay for all this in a brothel for niggers."

LETTERS FROM HOME tell of nights of phosphorous and cities in flames. Cologne Cathedral is hit by bombs, and a man from Hamburg reports seeing "a woman carrying in each of her arms the corpse of a carbonized infant." After a terrible raid on Hanover, Jünger asks the art dealer Etienne Bignou to bring up from his safe Douanier Rousseau's canvas *La Guerre, ou la Chevauchée de la Discorde.* "This picture is one of the greatest visions of our times.... [It has] an infantine candour...a kind of purity in its terror that reminds me of Emily Brontë."

He checks his address book and crosses out the names of the dead and missing. He reads the Book of Job. He visits Braque. He has his copy of *Catalogus Coleopterorum* rebound, and works on an "Appeal to the Youth of Europe," to be called *The Peace.* A hermaphrodite butterfly gives him the idea for a treatise on symmetry and, in one brilliant aside, he writes that the genius of Hitler was to realize that the twentieth century is the century of cults—which was why men of rational intelligence were unable to understand or to stop him.

Meanwhile, with hopes of an Allied invasion, Paris recovers her perennial toughness. The Salon d'Automne of 1943 is particularly brilliant. "Artists," he observes, "continue to create in catastrophe like ants in a half-destroyed anthill." Women's hats have taken on the shape of the Tower of Babel. Frank Jay Gould, an American trapped in France, reads *On the Marble Cliffs* and says: "This guy goes from dreams to reality."

Suddenly, in February 1944, Jünger has to dash to Berlin to rescue his son Ernstel who, in a moment of enthusiasm, has blurted out: "The Führer should be shot!" He succeeds in getting Dönitz to reduce the sentence, but from now on he is under suspicion from the Gestapo. Back in Paris, he gets a whiff of the plot to assassinate Hitler and, one evening in May, he dines with Karl-Heinrich von Stülpnagel, the commander-in-chief. The general is tremendously erudite and plunges into a discussion of Byzantine history, of Plato, Plotinus, and the Gnostics. He is "Hitler's biggest enemy" but he is also tired and tends to repeat himself. "In certain circumstances," he says, "a superior man must be prepared to renounce life." They talk into the night. Both men are botanists and they talk of the nightshade family—nicandra, belladonna, datura—the plants of perpetual sleep.

After the Normandy landings, his friend Speidel—the man who will "forget" the order to V-bomb Paris—tells of his visit to Hitler, now sunk in demented vegetarianism, yelling of "new weapons of destruction." When the July Plot fails, Von Stülpnagel tries to blow his brains out, but blinds himself only, and is strangled in a Berlin prison. Jünger, who had a date to dine with him that evening, comments thus on the futility of the enterprise: "It will change little and settle nothing. I have already alluded to this in describing the Prince of Sunmyra in *On the Marble Cliffs*."

Panic at the Hotel Raphäel. The Americans are near, and the *salon* hostesses gearing for a change. At a last luncheon for her German friends, Florence Jay Gould comes back from the telephone, smiling: "*La Bourse reprend.*" It's time for goodbyes. A last Thursday with Marie-Louise Bousquet, who says: "Now the Tea-Time boys are coming." A last conversation with the Princesse de Sixte-Bourbon. A last bottle of Chambertin 1904 with its art nouveau label. And here is his last entry for Paris:

14 August, en route
Sudden departure at dusk. In the afternoon, last farewells. I left the room in order and put a bouquet on the table. I left *pourboires*. Unfortunately I left in a drawer some irreplaceable letters.

The rest of Captain Jünger's war is not a happy story. Relieved of his functions, he goes home to Kirchhorst where he sorts out his papers, reads tales of shipwrecks, reads Huysmans's *A Rebours*, and waits for the rumble of American tanks. When a telegram comes with news of Ernstel's death on the Italian front, he loses the will to be clever and reveals the stricken horror of a parent who has lost what he loves the most. A photo of Ernstel hangs next to that of his protector General Speidel in his library.

JÜNGER REFUSED TO APPEAR before a "de-Nazification" tribunal on the grounds that he had never been a Nazi. But the whole course of his career put him outside the pale for the postwar German literary establishment. If his ideal was "the desert" then he was condemned, until recently, to stay in it. Since 1950 he has lived in the beautiful rolling country of Upper Swabia, at Wilflingen, in a house that lies opposite a castle of the Barons von Stauffenberg, where, by coincidence, Pierre Laval was interned after his escape from France in 1944. (Siegmaringen, Marshall Pétain's residence and the scene of Céline's *D'un Château l'autre* is only a few miles down the road.)

My own visit to Jünger five years ago was an odd experience. At eighty, he had snow-white hair but the bounce of a very active schoolboy. He had a light cackling laugh and tended to drift off if he was not the center of attention. He had recently published a book describing his experiments with drugs, from his first sniff of ether to lysergic acid, and was about to publish an enormous novel called *Eumeswil*. The ground floor of the house was furnished in the Biedermeier style, with net curtains and white faience stoves, and was inhabited by his second wife, a professional archivist and textual critic of Goethe. Jünger's own quarters upstairs had the leathery look of a soldier's bunker, with cabinets for beetles on the landing and a sea of memorabilia—fossils, shells, helmets from both wars, skeletons of animals, and a collection of sandglasses. (In 1954 he wrote *A Treatise on the Sandglass*— a philosophical meditation on the passage of time.)

If I had hoped for more memories of Paris under the Occupation, I was disappointed. In answer to questions, he simply recited an excerpt from the diary, though occasionally he would rush to the filing cabinet and come back with some *pièce justificative*. One of these was a letter from his friend Henri de Montherlant, quoting a remark of Tolstoy: "There is no point in visiting a great writer because he is incarnate in his works." Since I had an interest in Montherlant, I was able to draw Jünger out a little further, and he returned again from the filing cabinet, this time flourishing a rather blotchy sheet of Xerox paper on which was written:

> *Le suicide fait partie du capitale de l'humanité.*
> — *Ernst Jünger*
> *8 juin 1972.*

This aphorism of Jünger's dates from the Thirties, and the story goes that Alfred Rosenberg once said: "It's a pity Herr Jünger doesn't make use of his capital." But the scene you have to imagine is this:

Montherlant, dying of cancer, is sitting in his apartment on the Quai Voltaire, surrounded by his collection of Greek and Roman marbles. On his desk are a bottle of champagne, a revolver, a pen, and a sheet of paper. He writes:

> "*Le suicide fait partie....*"

Bang!
The blotches were photocopies of blood.

Nadezhda Mandelstam

Nadezhda Mandelstam (1899–1980) by Joseph Brodsky was originally published March 5, 1981. It appeared as "Nadezhda Mandelstam (1899–1980): An Obituary" in Less Than One *by Joseph Brodsky. Copyright © 1981, 1986 by Joseph Brodsky. Reprinted by permission of Farrar, Straus & Giroux, Inc.*

Nadezhda Mandelstam

(1899–1980)

OF THE EIGHTY-ONE YEARS of her life, Nadezhda Mandelstam spent nineteen as the wife of Russia's greatest poet in this century, Osip Mandelstam, and forty-two as his widow. The rest was childhood and youth. In educated circles, especially among the literati, being the widow of a great man is enough to provide an identity. This is especially so in Russia, where in the Thirties and in the Forties the regime was producing writers' widows with such efficiency that in the middle of the Sixties there were enough of them around to organize a trade union.

"Nadya is the luckiest widow," Anna Akhmatova used to say, having in mind the universal recognition coming to Osip Mandelstam at about that time. The focus of this remark was, understandably, on her fellow poet, and right though she was this was the view from the outside. By the time this recognition began to arrive, Mrs. Mandelstam was already in her sixties, her health extremely precarious and her means meager. Besides, for all the universality of that recognition, it did not include the fabled "one sixth of the entire planet," i.e., Russia itself. Behind her were already two decades of widowhood, utter deprivation, the Great (obliterating any personal loss) War, and the daily fear of being grabbed by the agents of state security as a wife of an enemy of the people. Short of death, anything that followed could only mean respite.

I met her for the first time precisely then, in the winter of 1962, in the city of Pskov, where together with a couple of friends I went to take a look at the local churches (the finest, in my view, in the empire). Having learned about our intentions to travel to that city, Anna Akhmatova suggested we visit Nadezhda Mandelstam, who was teaching English at the local pedagogical institute, and gave us several books for her. That was the first time I heard her name: I didn't know that she existed.

She was living in a small communal apartment consisting of two rooms. The first room was occupied by a woman whose name, ironically enough, was Nietsvetaeva (literally: Non-Tsvetaeva), the second was Mrs. Mandelstam's. It was eight square meters large, the size of an average American bathroom. Most of the space was taken up by a cast-iron twin-sized bed; there were also two wicker chairs, a wardrobe chest with a small mirror, and an all-purpose bedside table, on which sat plates with the leftovers of her supper and, next to the plates, an open paperback copy of *The Hedgehog and the Fox*, by Isaiah Berlin. The presence of this red-covered book in this tiny cell, and the fact that she didn't hide it under the pillow at the sound of the doorbell, meant precisely this: the beginning of respite.

The book, as it turned out, was sent to her by Akhmatova, who for nearly half the century remained the closest friend of the Mandelstams: first of both of them, later of Nadezhda alone. Twice a widow herself (her first husband, the poet Nikolai Gumilev, was shot in 1921 by the Cheka—the maiden name of the KGB; the second, the art historian Nikolai Punin, died in a concentration camp belonging to the same establishment), Akhmatova helped Nadezhda Mandelstam in every way possible, and during the war years literally saved her life by smuggling Nadezhda into Tashkent, where some of the writers had been evacuated, and by sharing with her the daily rations. Even with her two husbands killed by the regime, with her son languishing in the camps (for about sixteen years, if I am not mistaken), Akhmatova was somewhat better off than Nadezhda Mandelstam, if only because she was recognized, however reluctantly, as a writer, and was allowed to live in Leningrad and Moscow. For the wife of an enemy of the people big cities were simply off limits.

For decades this woman was on the run, darting through the back waters and provincial towns of the big empire, settling down in a new place only to take off at the first sign of danger. The status of nonperson gradually became her second nature. She was a small woman, of slim build, and with the passage of years she shriveled more and more, as though trying to turn herself into something weightless, something easily pocketed in the moment of flight. Similarly, she had virtually no possessions; no furniture, no art objects, no library. The books, even foreign books, never stayed in her hands for long: after being read or glanced through they would be passed on to someone else—the way it ought to be with books. In the years of her utmost affluence, at the end of the Sixties and the beginning of the Seventies, the most expensive item in her one-room apartment in the outskirts of Moscow was a cuckoo clock on the kitchen wall. A thief would be disillusioned here; so would be those with an order for search.

IN THOSE "AFFLUENT" YEARS following the publication in the West of her two volumes of memoirs* that kitchen became the place of veritable pilgrimages. Nearly every other night the best of what survived or came to life in the post-Stalin era in Russia gathered around the long wooden table which was ten times bigger than the bedstead in Pskov. It almost seemed that she was about to make up for decades of being a pariah. I doubt, though, that she did, and somehow I remember her better in that small room in Pskov, or sitting on the edge of a couch in Akhmatova's apartment in Leningrad, where she would come from time to time illegally from Pskov, or emerging from the depth of the corridor in Shklovsky's apartment in Moscow, where she perched before she got the place of her own. Perhaps I remember that more clearly because there she was more in her element as an outcast, a fugitive, "the beggar-friend," as Osip Mandelstam calls her in one of his poems, and that is what she remained for the rest of her life.

There is something quite breathtaking in the realization that she wrote those two volumes of hers at the age of sixty-five. In the Mandelstam family Osip was the writer, she wasn't. If she wrote anything before those volumes, it was letters to her friends or appeals to the Supreme Court. Nor is hers the case of someone reviewing a long and eventful life in the tranquillity of retirement. Because her sixty-five years were not exactly normal. It's not for nothing that in the Soviet penal system there is a paragraph specifying that in certain camps a year of serving counts for three. By this token, the lives of many Russians in this century came to approximate in length those of Biblical patriarchs. With whom she had one more thing in common: devotion to justice.

Yet it wasn't this devotion to justice alone that made her sit down at the age of sixty-five and use her time of respite for writing these books. What brought them into existence was a recapitulation, on the scale of one, of the same process that once before had taken place in the history of Russian literature. I have in mind the emergence of great Russian prose in the second half of the nineteenth century. That prose, which appears as though out of nowhere, as an effect without traceable cause, was in fact simply a spinoff of the nineteenth century's Russian poetry. It set the tone for all

* Translated as *Hope Against Hope* and *Hope Abandoned* (both published by Atheneum, in 1970 and 1973, and translated by Max Hayward).

subsequent writing in Russian, and the best work of Russian fiction can be regarded as a distant echo and meticulous elaboration of the psychological and lexical subtlety displayed by the Russian poetry of the first quarter of that century. "Most of Dostoevsky's characters," Anna Akhmatova used to say, "are aged Pushkin heroes, Onegins and so forth."

POETRY ALWAYS PRECEDES PROSE, and so it did in the life of Nadezhda Mandelstam, and in more ways than one. As a writer, as well as a person, she is a creation of two poets with whom her life was linked inexorably: Osip Mandelstam and Anna Akhmatova. And not only because the first was her husband and the second her lifelong friend. After all, forty years of widowhood could dim the happiest memories (and in the case of this marriage they were few and far between, if only because this marriage coincided with the economic devastation of the country, caused by revolution, civil war, and the first five-year plans). Similarly, there were years when she wouldn't see Akhmatova at all, and a letter would be the last thing to confide to. Paper, in general, was dangerous. What strengthened the bond of that marriage as well as of that friendship was a technicality: the necessity to commit to memory what could not be committed to paper, i.e., the poems of both authors.

In doing so in that "pre-Gutenberg epoch," in Akhmatova's words, Nadezhda Mandelstam certainly wasn't alone. However, repeating day and night the words of her dead husband was undoubtedly connected not only with comprehending them more and more but also with resurrecting his very voice, the intonations peculiar only to him, with a however fleeting sensation of his presence, with the realization that he kept his part of that "for better or for worse" deal, especially its second half. The same went for the poems of the physically often absent Akhmatova, for once set in motion this mechanism of memorization won't come to a halt. The same went for other authors, for certain ideas, for ethical principles—for everything that couldn't survive otherwise.

And gradually those things grew on her. If there is any substitute for love, it's memory. To memorize, then, is to restore intimacy. Gradually the lines of those poets became her mentality, became her identity. They supplied her not only with the plane of regard or angle of vision; more important, they became her linguistic norm. So when she set out to write her books, she was bound to gauge—by that time already unwittingly, instinctively—her sentences against theirs. The clarity and remorselessness of her pages, while reflecting the character of her mind, are also inevitable stylistic consequences of the poetry that had shaped that mind. Both in their content and style, her books are but a postscript to the supreme version of language which poetry essentially is and which became her flesh through learning her husband's lines by heart.

TO BORROW W. H. AUDEN'S PHRASE, great poetry "hurt" her into prose. It really did, because those two poets' heritage could be developed or elaborated upon only by prose. In poetry they could be followed only by epigones. Which has happened. In other words, Nadezhda Mandelstam's prose was the only available medium for the language itself to avoid stagnation. Similarly, it was the only medium available for the psyche formed by that poets' use of language. Her books, thus, were not so much memoirs and guides to the lives of two great poets, however superbly they performed these functions; these books elucidated the consciousness of the nation. Of the part of it, at least, that could get a copy.

Small wonder, then, that this elucidation results in an indictment of the system. These two volumes by Mrs. Mandelstam indeed amount to a Day of Judgment on earth for her age and for its literature—a judgment administered all the more rightfully since it was this age that had undertaken the construction of earthly paradise. A lesser wonder, too, that these memoirs, the second volume especially, were not liked on either side of the Kremlin Wall. The authorities, I must say, were more honest in their reaction than the intelligentsia: they simply made possession of these books an offense punishable by law. As for the intelligentsia, especially in Moscow, it went into actual turmoil over Nadezhda Mandelstam's charges against many of its illustrious and not so illustrious members of virtual complicity with the regime, and the human flood in her kitchen significantly ebbed.

There were open and semi-open letters, indignant resolutions not to shake hands, friendships and marriages collapsing over whether she was right or wrong to consider this or that person an informer. A prominent dissident declared, shaking his beard: "She shat over our entire generation"; others would rush to their dachas and lock themselves up there, to tap out antimemoirs. This was already the beginning of the Seventies, and some six years later these same people would become equally split over Solzhenitsyn's attitudes toward the Jews.

There is something in the consciousness of literati that cannot stand the notion of someone's moral authority. They resign themselves to the existence of a First Party Secretary, or of a Führer, as to a necessary evil, but they would eagerly question a prophet. This is so, presumably, because being told that you are a slave is less disheartening news than being told that morally you are a zero. After all, a fallen dog shouldn't be kicked. However, a prophet kicks the fallen dog not to finish it off but to get it back on its feet. The resistance to those kicks, the questioning of a writer's assertions and charges, comes not from the desire for truth but from the intellectual smugness of slavery. All the worse, then, for the literati when the authority is not only moral but also cultural—as it was in Nadezhda Mandelstam's case.

I'D LIKE TO VENTURE here one step further. By itself reality per se isn't worth a damn. It's perception that promotes reality to meaning. And there is a hierarchy among perceptions (and, correspondingly, among meanings), with the ones acquired through the most refined and sensitive prisms sitting at the top. Refinement and sensitivity are imparted to such a prism by the only source of their supply: by culture, by civilization, whose main tool is language. The evaluation of reality made through such a prism—the acquisition of which is one goal of the species—is therefore the most accurate, perhaps even the most just. (Cries of "Unfair!" and "Elitist!" that may follow the aforesaid from, of all places, the local campuses must be left unheeded, for culture is "elitist" by definition, and the application of democratic principles in the sphere of knowledge leads to equating wisdom with idiocy.)

It's the possession of this prism supplied to her by the best Russian poetry of the twentieth century, and not the uniqueness of the size of her grief, that makes Nadezhda Mandelstam's statement about her piece of reality unchallengeable. It's an abominable fallacy that suffering makes for greater art. Suffering blinds, deafens, ruins, and often kills. Osip Mandelstam was a great poet *before* the Revolution. So was Anna Akhmatova, so was Marina Tsvetaeva. They would have become what they became even if none of the historical events that befell Russia in this century had taken place: because they were *gifted*. Basically, talent doesn't need history.

WOULD NADEZHDA MANDELSTAM have become what she became had it not been for the Revolution and all the rest that followed? Probably not, for she met her future husband in 1919. But the question itself is immaterial; it leads us into the murky domains of the law of probability and of historical determinism. After all, she became what she became not because of what took place in Russia in this century but rather in spite of it. A casuist's finger will surely point out that from the point of view of historical determin-

ism "in spite of" is synonymous with "because." So much then for historical determinism, if it gets so mindful about the semantics of some human
"in spite of."

For a good reason, though. For a frail woman of sixty-five turns out to
be capable of slowing down, if not averting in the long run, the cultural
disintegration of a whole nation. Her memoirs are something more than a
testimony of her times; it's the view of history in the light of conscience
and culture. In that light history winces, and an individual realizes his
choice: between seeking that light's source and committing an anthropo-
logical crime against himself.

She didn't mean to be so grand, nor did she simply try to get even with
the system. For her it was a private matter, a matter of her temperament, of
her identity and what had shaped that identity. As it were, her identity had
been shaped by culture, by its best products: her husband's poems. It's
them, not his memory, that she was trying to keep alive. It's to them, and
not to him, in the course of forty-two years that she became a widow. Of
course she loved him, but love itself is the most elitist of passions. It acquires its stereoscopic substance and perspective only in the context of culture, for its takes up more place in the mind than it does in the bed. Outside of that setting it falls flat into one-dimensional friction. She was a
widow to culture, and I think she loved her husband more at the end than
on the day they got married. That is probably why readers of her books
find them so haunting. Because of that, and because the status of the modern world vis-à-vis civilization also can be defined as widowhood.

If she lacked anything, it was humility. In that respect she was quite unlike her two poets. But then they had their art, and the quality of their
achievements provided them with enough contentment to be, or to pretend to be, humble. She was terribly opinionated, categorical, cranky, disagreeable, idiosyncratic; many of her ideas were half-baked or developed on
the basis of hearsay. In short, there was a great deal of one-upwomanship
in her, which is not surprising given the size of the figures she was reckoning with in reality and later in imagination. In the end, her intolerance
drove a lot of people away, but that was quite all right with her, because she
was getting tired of adulation, of being liked by Robert McNamara and
Willy Fisher (the real name of Colonel Rudolph Abel). All she wanted
was to die in her bed, and, in a way, she looked forward to dying, because
"up there I'll be again with Osip." "No," replied Akhmatova, upon hearing
this. "You've got it all wrong. Up there it's now me who is going to be with
Osip."

HER WISH CAME TRUE, and she died in her bed. Not a small thing for a Russian of her generation. There undoubtedly will surface those who will cry that she misunderstood her epoch, that she lagged behind the train of history running into the future. Well, like nearly every other Russian of her generation, she learned only too well that that train running into the future stops at the concentration camp or at the gas chamber. She was lucky that she missed it, and we are lucky that she told us about its route. I saw her last on May 30, 1972, in that kitchen of hers, in Moscow. It was late afternoon, and she sat, smoking, in the corner, in the deep shadow cast by the tall cupboard onto the wall. The shadow was so deep that the only things one could make out were the faint flicker of her cigarette and the two piercing eyes. The rest—her smallish shrunken body under the shawl, her hands, the oval of her ashen face, her gray, ashlike hair—all were consumed by the dark. She looked like a remnant of a huge fire, like a small ember that burns if you touch it.

Andy Warhol

The Rise of Andy Warhol by Robert Hughes was originally published February 18, 1982, as a review of Andy Warhol: Das Graphische Werk, 1962–1980, *catalog by Hermann Wünsche, distributed by Castelli Graphics (New York) and* Andy Warhol: A Print Retrospective, *an exhibition at Castelli Graphics, November 20 to December 22, 1981.*

ROBERT HUGHES

The Rise of Andy Warhol

TO SAY THAT Andy Warhol is a famous artist is to utter the merest commonplace. But what kind of fame does he enjoy? If the most famous artist in America is Andrew Wyeth, and the second most famous is LeRoy Neiman (Hugh Hefner's court painter, inventor of the Playboy femlin, and drawer of football stars for CBS), then Warhol is the third. Wyeth, because his work suggests a frugal, bare-bones rectitude, glazed by nostalgia but incarnated in real objects, which millions of people look back upon as the lost marrow of American history. Neiman, because millions of people watch sports programs, read *Playboy*, and will take any amount of glib abstract-expressionist slather as long as it adorns a recognizable and pert pair of jugs. But Warhol? What size of public likes his work, or even knows it at first hand? Not as big as Wyeth's or Neiman's.

To most of the people who have heard of him, he is a name handed down from a distant museum-culture, stuck to a memorable face: a cashiered Latin teacher in a pale fiber wig, the guy who paints soup cans and knows all the movie stars. To a smaller but international public, he is the last of the truly successful social portraitists, climbing from face to face in a silent delirium of snobbery, a man so interested in elites that he has his own society magazine. But Warhol has never been a *popular* artist in the sense that Andrew Wyeth is or Sir Edwin Landseer was. That kind of popularity entails being seen as a normal (and hence, exemplary) person from whom extraordinary things emerge.

Warhol's public character for the last twenty years has been the opposite: an abnormal figure (silent, withdrawn, eminently visible but opaque, and a bit malevolent) who praises banality. He fulfills Stuart Davis's definition of the new American artist, "a cool Spectator-Reporter at an Arena of Hot Events." But no mass public has ever felt at ease with Warhol's work.

Surely, people feel, there must be something empty about a man who expresses no strong leanings, who greets everything with the same "uh, gee, great." Art's other Andy, the Wyeth, would not do that. Nor would the midcult heroes of *The Agony and the Ecstasy* and *Lust for Life*. They would discriminate between experiences, which is what artists are meant to do for us.

WARHOL HAS LONG seemed to hanker after the immediate visibility and popularity that "real" stars like Liz Taylor have, and sometimes he is induced to behave as though he really had it. When he did ads endorsing Puerto Rican rum or Pioneer radios, the art world groaned with secret envy: what artist would not like to be in a position to be offered big money for endorsements, if only for the higher pleasure of refusing it? But his image sold little rum and few radios. After two decades as voyeur-in-chief to the marginal and then the rich, Warhol was still unloved by the world at large; all people saw was that weird, remote guy in the wig. Meanwhile, the gesture of actually being in an ad contradicted the base of Warhol's fame within the art world. To the extent that his work was subversive at all (and in the Sixties it was, slightly), it became so through its harsh, cold parody of ad-mass appeal—the repetition of brand images like Campbell's soup or Brillo or Marilyn Monroe (a star being a human brand image) to the point where a void is seen to yawn beneath the discourse of promotion.

The tension this set up depended on the assumption, still in force in the Sixties, that there was a qualitative difference between the perceptions of high art and the million daily instructions issued by popular culture. Since then, Warhol has probably done more than any other living artist to wear that distinction down; but while doing so, he has worn away the edge of his work. At the same time, he has difficulty moving it toward that empyrean of absolute popularity, where LeRoy Neiman sits, robed in sky-blue polyester. To do that, he must make himself accessible. But to be accessible is to lose magic.

The depth of this quandary, or perhaps its lack of relative shallowness, may be gauged from a peculiar exhibition mounted last November by the Los Angeles Institute of Contemporary Art: a show of portraits of sports stars, half by Neiman and half by Warhol, underwritten by Playboy Enterprises. It was a promotional stunt (LAICA needs money, and exhibitions of West Coast conceptualists do not make the turnstiles rattle) but to give it a veneer of respectability the Institute felt obliged to present it as a critique of art-world pecking orders. Look, it said in effect: Neiman is an arbitrarily rejected artist, whose work has much to recommend it to the serious eye (though *what*, exactly, was left vague); we will show he is up there with Warhol.

This effort backfired, raising the unintended possibility that Warhol was down there with Neiman. The Warhol of yore would not have let himself in for a fiasco like the LAICA show. But then he was not so ostentatiously interested in being liked by a mass public. This may be why his output for the last decade or so has floundered—he had no real subjects left; why *Interview*, his magazine, is less a periodical than a public relations sheet; and why books like *Exposures* and *POPism* get written.[1]

Between them *POPism: The Warhol Sixties* and *Exposures* give a fairly good picture of Warhol's concerns before and after 1968, the year he was shot. Neither book has any literary merit, and the writing is chatty with occasional flecks of diminuendo irony—just what the package promises. *POPism* is mostly surface chat, *Exposures* entirely so. For a man whose life is subtended by gossip, Warhol comes across as peculiarly impervious to character. "I never knew what to think of Eric," he says of one of his circle in the Sixties, a scatterbrained lad with blond ringlets whose body, a post-script tells us, was found in the middle of Hudson Street, unceremoniously dumped there, according to "rumors," after he overdosed on heroin. "He could come out with comments that were so insightful and creative, and then the next thing out of his mouth would be something *so* dumb. A lot of the kids were that way, but Eric was the most fascinating to me because he was the most extreme case—you absolutely couldn't tell if he was a genius or a retard."

Of course, poor Eric Emerson—like nearly everyone else around the Factory, as Warhol's studio came to be known—was neither. They were all cultural space-debris, drifting fragments from a variety of Sixties subcultures (transvestite, drug, s&m, rock, Poor Little Rich, criminal, street, and all the permutations) orbiting in smeary ellipses around their unmoved mover. Real talent was thin and scattered in this tiny universe. It surfaced in music, with figures like Lou Reed and John Cale; various punk groups in the Seventies were, wittingly or not, the offspring of Warhol's Velvet Underground. But people who wanted to get on with their own work avoided the Factory, while the freaks and groupies and curiosity-seekers who filled it left nothing behind them.

---

[1] Andy Warhol, *Andy Warhol's Exposures* (Grosset and Dunlap, 1979); Andy Warhol and Pat Hackett, *POPism: The Warhol Sixties* (Harcourt Brace Jovanovich, 1980).

Its silver-papered walls were a toy theater in which one aspect of the Sixties in America, the infantile hope of imposing oneself on the world by terminal self-revelation, was played out. It had a nasty edge, which forced the paranoia of marginal souls into some semblance of style; a reminiscence of art. If Warhol's "Superstars," as he called them, had possessed talent, discipline, or stamina, they would not have needed him. But then, he would not have needed them. They gave him his ghostly aura of power. If he withdrew his gaze, his carefully allotted permissions and recognitions, they would cease to exist; the poor ones would melt back into the sludgy undifferentiated chaos of the street, the rich ones end up in McLean's. Valerie Solanas, who shot him, said Warhol had too much control over her life.

Those whose parents accused them of being out of their tree, who had unfulfilled desires and undesirable ambitions, and who felt guilty about it all, therefore gravitated to Warhol. He offered them absolution, the gaze of the blank mirror that refuses all judgment. In this, the camera (when he made his films) deputized for him, collecting hour upon hour of tantrum, misery, sexual spasm, campery, and nose-picking trivia. It too was an instrument of power—not over the audience, for which Warhol's films were usually boring and alienating, but over the actors. In this way the Factory resembled a sect, a parody of Catholicism enacted (not accidentally) by people who were or had been Catholic, from Warhol and Gerard Malanga on down. In it, the rituals of dandyism could speed up to gibberish and show what they had become—a hunger for approval and forgiveness. These came in a familiar form, perhaps the only form American capitalism knows how to offer: publicity.

WARHOL WAS THE first American artist to whose career publicity was truly intrinsic. Publicity had not been an issue with artists in the Forties and Fifties. It might come as a bolt from the philistine blue, as when *Life* made Jackson Pollock famous; but such events were rare enough to be freakish, not merely unusual. By today's standards, the art world was virginally naive about the mass media and what they could do. Television and the press, in return, were indifferent to what could still be called the avant-garde. "Publicity" meant a notice in *The New York Times*, a paragraph or two long, followed eventually by an article in *Art News* which perhaps five thousand people would read. Anything else was regarded as extrinsic to the work—something to view with suspicion, at best an accident, at worst a gratuitous distraction. One might woo a critic, but not a fashion correspondent, a TV producer, or the editor of *Vogue*. To be one's own PR outfit was, in the eyes of the New York artists of the Forties or Fifties, nearly unthinkable—hence the contempt they felt for Salvador Dali. But in the 1960s all that began to change, as the art world gradually shed its idealist premises and its sense of outsidership and began to turn into the Art Business.

Warhol became the emblem and thus, to no small extent, the instrument of this change. Inspired by the example of Truman Capote, he went after publicity with the voracious single-mindedness of a feeding bluefish. And he got it in abundance, because the Sixties in New York reshuffled and stacked the social deck: the press and television, in their pervasiveness, constructed a kind of parallel universe in which the hierarchical orders of American society—vestiges, it was thought, but strong ones, and based on inherited wealth—were replaced by the new tyranny of the "interesting." Its rule had to do with the rapid shift of style and image, the assumption that all civilized life was discontinuous and worth only a short attention span: better to be Baby Jane Holzer than the Duchesse de Guermantes.

To enter this turbulence, one might only need to be born—a fact noted by Warhol in his one lasting quip, "In the future, *everyone* will be famous for fifteen minutes." But to remain in it, to stay drenched in the glittering spray of promotional culture, one needed other qualities. One was an air of detachment; the dandy must not look into the lens. Another was an acute sense of nuance, an eye for the eddies and trends of fashion, which would regulate the other senses and appetites and so give detachment its point.

DILIGENT AND FRIGID, Warhol had both to a striking degree. He was not a "hot" artist, a man mastered by a particular vision and anxious to impose it on the world. Jackson Pollock had declared that he wanted to be Nature. Warhol, by contrast, wished to be Culture and Culture only: "I want to be a machine." Many of the American artists who rose to fame after abstract expressionism, beginning with Jasper Johns and Robert Rauschenberg, had worked in commercial art to stay alive, and other pop artists besides Warhol, of course, drew freely on the vast reservoir of American ad-mass imagery. But Warhol was the only one who embodied a culture of promotion as such. He had enjoyed a striking success as a commercial artist, doing everything from shoe ads to recipe illustrations in a blotted, perky line derived from Saul Steinberg. He understood the tough little world, not yet an "aristocracy" but trying to become one, where the machinery of fashion, gossip, image-bending, and narcissistic chic tapped out its agile pizzicato. He knew packaging, and could teach it to others.

Warhol's social visibility thus bloomed in an art world which, during the Sixties, became more and more concerned with the desire for and pursuit of publicity. Not surprisingly, many of its figures in those days—crass social climbers like the Sculls, popinjays like Henry Geldzahler, and the legion of insubstantial careerists who leave nothing but press cuttings to mark their passage—tended to get their strategies from Warhol's example.

Above all, the working-class kid who had spent so many thousands of hours gazing into the blue, anesthetizing glare of the TV screen, like Narcissus into his pool, realized that the cultural moment of the mid-Sixties favored a walking void. Television was producing an affectless culture. Warhol set out to become one of its affectless heroes. It was no longer necessary for an artist to act crazy, like Salvador Dali. Other people could act crazy for you: that was what Warhol's Factory was all about. By the end of the Sixties craziness was becoming normal, and half of America seemed to be immersed in some tedious and noisy form of self-expression. Craziness no longer suggested uniqueness. Warhol's bland translucency, as of frosted glass, was much more intriguing.

Like Chauncey Gardiner, the hero of Jerzy Kosinski's *Being There*, he came to be credited with sibylline wisdom because he was an absence, conspicuous by its presence—intangible, like a TV set whose switch nobody could find. Disjointed public images—the Campbell's soup cans, the Elvises and Lizzes and Marilyns, the electric chairs and car crashes and the jerky, shapeless pornography of his movies—would stutter across this screen; would pour from it in a gratuitous flood.

BUT THE CIRCUITRY behind it, the works, remained mysterious. (Had he made a point of going to the shrink, like other New York artists, he would have seemed rather less interesting to his public.) "If you want to know all about Andy Warhol," he told an interviewer in those days, "just look at the surface of my paintings and films and me, and there I am. There's nothing behind it." This kind of coyness looked, at the time, faintly threatening. For without doubt, there was something strange about so firm an adherence to the surface. It went against the grain of high art as such. What had become of the belief, dear to modernism, that the power and cathartic necessity of art flowed from the unconscious, through the knotwork of dream, memory, and desire, into the realized image? No trace of it; the paintings were all superficies, no symbol. Their blankness seemed eerie.

They did not share the reforming hopes of modernism. Neither Dada's caustic anxiety, nor the utopian dreams of the Constructivists; no politics, no transcendentalism. Occasionally there would be a slender, learned spoof, as when Warhol did black-and-white paintings of dance-step diagrams in parody of Mondrian's black-and-white *Fox Trot*, 1930. But in general, his only subject was detachment: the condition of being a spectator, dealing hands-off with the world through the filter of photography.

Thus his paintings, roughly silkscreened, full of slips, mimicked the dissociation of gaze and empathy induced by the mass media: the banal punch of tabloid newsprint, the visual jabber and bright sleazy color of TV, the sense of glut and anesthesia caused by both. Three dozen Elvises are better than one; and one Marilyn, patched like a gaudy stamp on a ground of gold leaf (the favorite color of Byzantium, but of drag queens too) could become a sly and grotesque parody of the Madonna-fixations of Warhol's own Catholic childhood, of the pretentious enlargement of media stars by a secular culture, and of the similarities between both. The rapid negligence of Warhol's images parodied the way mass media replace the act of reading with that of scanning, a state of affairs anticipated by Ronald Firbank's line in *The Flower Beneath the Foot*: "She reads at such a pace . . . and when I asked her *where* she had learnt to read so quickly she replied, 'On the screens of Cinemas.'"

Certainly, Warhol had one piercing insight about mass media. He would not have had it without his background in commercial art and his obsession with the stylish. But it was not an *aperçu* that could be developed: lacking the prehensile relationship to experience of Claes Oldenburg (let alone Picasso), Warhol was left without much material. It is as though, after his near death in 1968, Warhol's lines of feeling were finally cut; he could not appropriate the world in such a way that the results meant much as art, although they became a focus of ever-increasing gossip, speculation, and promotional hoo-ha. However, his shooting reflected back on his earlier paintings—the prole death in the car crashes, the electric chair with the sign enjoining SILENCE on the nearby door, the taxidermic portraits of the dead Marilyn—lending them a fictive glamour as emblems of fate. Much breathless prose was therefore expended on Andy, the Silver Angel of Death, and similar conceits. (That all these images were suggested by friends, rather than chosen by Warhol himself, was not stressed.)

PARTLY BECAUSE OF this gratuitous aura, the idea that Warhol was a major interpreter of the American scene dies hard—at least in some quarters of the art world. "Has there ever been an artist," asked Peter Schjeldahl at the end of a panegyric on Warhol's fatuous show of society portraits at the

Whitney two years ago, "who so coolly and faithfully, with such awful intimacy and candor, registered important changes in a society?" (Well, maybe a couple, starting with Goya.) Critics bring forth such borborygms when they are hypnotized by old radical credentials. Barbara Rose once compared his portraits, quite favorably, to Goya's. John Coplans, the former editor of *Artforum*, wrote that his work "almost by choice of imagery, it seems, forces us to squarely face the existential edge of our existence."

In 1971 an American Marxist named Peter Gidal, later to make films as numbing as Warhol's own, declared that "unlike Chagall, Picasso, Rauschenberg, Hamilton, Stella, most of the Cubists, Impressionists, Expressionists, Warhol never gets negatively boring"—only, it was implied, positively so, and in a morally bracing way. If the idea that Warhol could be the most interesting artist in modern history, as Gidal seemed to be saying, now looks a trifle *voulu*, it has regularly been echoed on the left—especially in Germany, where, by one of those exquisite contortions of social logic in which the Bundesrepublik seems to specialize, Warhol's status as a blue chip was largely underwritten by Marxists praising his "radical" and "subversive" credentials.

Thus the critic Rainer Crone, in 1970, claimed that Warhol was "the first to create something more than traditional 'fine art' for the edification of a few." By mass producing his images of mass production, to the point where the question of who actually made most of his output in the Sixties has had to be diplomatically skirted by dealers ever since (probably half of it was run off by assistants and merely signed by Warhol), the pallid maestro had entered a permanent state of "anaesthetic revolutionary practice"— delicious phrase! In this way the "elitist" forms of middle-class idealism, so obstructive to art experience yet so necessary to the art market, had been short-circuited. Here, apparently, was something akin to the "art of five kopeks" Lunacharsky had called on the Russian avant-garde to produce after 1917. Not only that: the People could immediately see and grasp what Warhol was painting. They were used to soup cans, movie stars, and Coke bottles. To make such bottles in a factory in the South and sell them in Abu Dhabi was a capitalist evil; to paint them in a factory in New York and sell them in Dusseldorf, an act of cultural criticism.

THESE EFFORTS TO assimilate Warhol to a "revolutionary" aesthetic now have a musty air. The question is no longer whether such utterances were true or false—Warhol's later career made them absurd anyway. The real question is: How could otherwise informed people in the Sixties and Seventies imagine that the man who would end up running a gossip magazine and cranking out portraits of Sao Schlumberger for a living was really a cultural subversive? The answer probably lies in the change that was coming over their own milieu, the art world itself.

Warhol did his best work at a time (1962–1968) when the avant-garde, as an idea and a cultural reality, still seemed to be alive, if not well. In fact it was collapsing from within, undermined by the encroaching art market and by the total conversion of the middle-class audience; but few people could see this at the time. The ideal of a radical, "outsider" art of wide social effect had not yet been acknowledged as fantasy. The death of the avant-garde has since become such a commonplace that the very word has an embarrassing aura. In the late Seventies, only dealers used it; today, not even they do, except in Soho. But in the late Sixties and early Seventies, avant-garde status was still thought to be a necessary part of a new work's credentials. And given the political atmosphere of the time, it was mandatory to claim some degree of "radical" political power for any nominally avant-garde work.

Thus Warhol's silence became a Rorschach blot onto which critics who admired the idea of political art—but would not have been seen dead within a hundred paces of a realist painting—could project their expectations. As the work of someone like Agam is abstract art for those who hate abstraction, so Warhol became realist art for those who loathed representation as "retrograde." If the artist, blinking and candid, denied that he was in any way a "revolutionary" artist, his admirers knew better; the white mole of Union Square was just dissimulating. If he declared that he was only interested in getting rich and famous, like everyone else, he could not be telling the truth; instead, he was parodying America's obsession with celebrity, the better to deflate it. From the recesses of this exegetical knot, anything Warhol did could be taken seriously. In a review of *Exposures*, the critic Carter Ratcliff solemnly asserted that "he is secretly the vehicle of artistic intentions so complex that he would probably cease to function if he didn't dilute them with nightly doses of the inane." But for the safety valve of Studio 54, he would presumably blow off like the plant at Three Mile Island, scattering the culture with unimagined radiations.

One wonders what these "artistic intentions" may be, since Warhol's output for the last decade has been concerned more with the smooth development of product than with any discernible insights. As Harold Rosenberg remarked, "In demonstrating that art today is a commodity of the art market, comparable to the commodities of other specialized markets, Warhol has liquidated the century-old tension between the serious artist and the majority culture." It scarcely matters what Warhol paints; for his clientele, only the signature is fully visible. The factory runs, its stream of products is not interrupted, the market dictates its logic. What the clients want is *a* Warhol, a recognizable product bearing his stamp. Hence any marked deviation from the norm, such as an imaginative connection with the world might produce, would in fact seem freakish and unpleasant: a renunciation of earlier products. Warhol's sales pitch is to soothe the client by repetition while preserving the fiction of uniqueness. Style, considered as the authentic residue of experience, becomes its commercial-art cousin, styling.

Warhol has never deceived himself about this: "It's so boring painting the same picture over and over," he complained in the late Sixties. So he must introduce small variations into the package, to render the last product a little obsolete (and to limit its proliferation, thus assuring its rarity), for if all Warhols were exactly the same there would be no market for new ones. Such is his parody of invention, which now looks normal in a market-dominated art world. Its industrial nature requires an equally industrial kind of *facture*: this consists of making silk-screens from photos, usually Polaroids, bleeding out a good deal of the information from the image by reducing it to monochrome, and then printing it over a fudgy background of decorative color, applied with a wide loaded brush to give the impression of verve. Only rarely is there even the least formal relationship between the image and its background.

This formula gave Warhol several advantages, particularly as a portraitist. He could always flatter the client by selecting the nicest photo. The lady in Texas or Paris would not be subjected to the fatigue of long scrutiny; in fact she would feel rather like a *Vogue* model, whether she looked like one or not, while Andy did his stuff with the Polaroid. As social amenity, it was an adroit solution; and it still left room for people who should know better, like the art historian Robert Rosenblum in his catalog essay to Warhol's portrait show at the Whitney in 1979, to embrace it: "If it is instantly clear that Warhol has revived the visual crackle, glitter, and chic of older traditions of society portraiture, it may be less obvious that despite his legendary indifference to human facts, he has also captured an incredible range of psychological insights among his sitters." Legendary, incredible, glitter, insight: stuffing to match the turkey.

THE PERFUNCTORY AND INDUSTRIAL nature of Warhol's peculiar talent and the robotic character of the praise awarded it appears most baldly of all around his prints, which were recently given a retrospective at Castelli Graphics in New York and a *catalogue raisonnée* by Hermann Wünsche. "More than any other artist of our age," one of its texts declares, "Andy Warhol is intensively preoccupied with concepts of time"; quite the little Proust, in fact. "His prints above all reveal Andy Warhol as a universal artist whose works show him to be thoroughly aware of the great European traditions and who is a particular admirer of the glorious French Dixneuvième, which inspired him to experience and to apply the immanent qualities of 'pure' peinture." No doubt something was lost in translation, but it is difficult to believe that Hans Gerd Tuchel, the author, has looked at the prints he speaks of. Nothing could be flatter or more perfunctory, or have less to do with those "immanent qualities of pure peinture," than Warhol's recent prints. Their most discernible quality is their transparent cynicism and their Franklin Mint approach to subject matter. What other "serious" artist, for instance, would contemplate doing a series called "Ten Portraits of Jews of the Twentieth Century,"[2] featuring Kafka, Buber, Einstein, Gertrude Stein, and Sarah Bernhardt? But then, in the moral climate of today's art world, why not treat Jews as a special-interest subject like any other? There is a big market for bird prints, dog prints, racing prints, hunting prints, yachting prints; why not Jew prints?

Yet whatever merits these mementos may lack, nobody could rebuke their author for inconsistency. The Jew as Celebrity: it is of a piece with the ruling passion of Warhol's career, the object of his fixated attention—the state of being well known for well-knownness. This is all *Exposures* was about—a photograph album of film stars, rock idols, politicians' wives, cocottes, catamites, and assorted bits of International White Trash baring their teeth to the socially emulgent glare of the flashbulb: I am flashed, therefore I am. It is also the sole subject of Warhol's house organ, *Interview*.

INTERVIEW BEGAN AS a poor relative of *Photoplay*, subtitled "Andy Warhol's Movie Magazine." But by the mid-Seventies it had purged itself of the residue of the "old" Factory and become a punkish *feuilleton* aimed largely at the fashion trade—a natural step, considering Warhol's background. With the opening of Studio 54 in 1977, the magazine found its

<hr />

[2] The Jewish Museum, September 17, 1981, to January 4, 1982.

"new" Factory, its spiritual home. It then became a kind of marionette theater in print: the same figures, month after month, would cavort in its tiny proscenium, do a few twirls, suck or snort something, and tittup off again—Marisa, Bianca, Margaret Trudeau, and the rest of the fictive stars who replaced the discarded Superstars of the Factory days.

Because the magazine is primarily a social-climbing device for its owner and staff, its actual gossip content is quite bland. Many stones lie unturned but no breech is left unkissed. As a rule the interviews, taped and transcribed, sound as though a valet were asking the questions, especially when the subject is a regular advertiser in the magazine. Sometimes the level of gush exceeds the wildest inventions of S. J. Perelman. "I have felt since I first met you," one interviewer exclaims to Diane von Furstenberg, "that there was something extraordinary about you, that you have the mystic sense and quality of a pagan soul. And here you are about to introduce a new perfume, calling it by an instinctive, but perfect name." And later:

> Q. I have always known of your wonderful relationship with your children. By this, I think you symbolize a kind of fidelity. Why did you bring back these geese from Bali?
> A. I don't know.
> Q. You did it instinctively.
> A. Yes, it just seemed right. One thing after the other.... It's wild.
> Q. There's something about you that reminds me of Aphrodite.
> A. Well, she had a good time.

Later, Aphrodite declares that "I don't want to be pretentious," but that "I was just in Java and it has about 350 active volcanoes. I'll end up throwing myself into one. I think that would be very glamorous."

In politics, *Interview* has one main object of veneration: the Reagans, around whose elderly flame the magazine flutters like a moth, waggling its little thorax at Jerry Zipkin, hoping for invitations to White House dinners or, even better, an official portrait commission for Warhol. Moving toward that day, it is careful to run flattering exchanges with White House functionaries like Muffie Brandon. It even went so far as to appoint Doria Reagan, the daughter-in-law, as a "contributing editor." To its editor, Reagan is *Caesar Augustus Americanus* and Nancy a blend of Evita and the Virgin Mary, though in red. Warhol seems to share this view, though he did not always do so. For most of the Seventies he was in some nominal way a liberal Democrat, like the rest of the art world—doing campaign posters for McGovern, trying to get near Teddy Kennedy. Nixon, who thought culture was for Jews, would never have let him near the White House. When

Warhol declared that Gerald Ford's son Jack was the only Republican he knew, he was telling some kind of truth. However, two things changed this in the Seventies: the Shah, and the Carter administration.

ONE OF THE ODDER ASPECTS of the late Shah's regime was its wish to buy modern Western art, so as to seem "liberal" and "advanced." Seurat in the parlor, SAVAK in the basement. The former Shahbanou, Farah Diba, spent millions of dollars exercising this fantasy. Nothing pulls the art world into line faster than the sight of an imperial checkbook, and the conversion of the remnants of the American avant-garde into ardent fans of the Pahlavis was one of the richer social absurdities of the period. Dealers started learning Farsi, Iranian fine-arts exchange students acquired a sudden cachet as research assistants, and invitations to the Iranian embassy—not the hottest tickets in town before 1972—were now much coveted.

The main beneficiary of this was Warhol, who became the semi-official portraitist to the Peacock Throne. When the *Interview* crowd were not at the tub of caviar in the consulate like pigeons around a birdbath, they were on an Air Iran jet somewhere between Kennedy Airport and Tehran. All power is delightful, as Kenneth Tynan once observed, and absolute power is absolutely delightful. The fall of the Shah left a hole in *Interview*'s world: to whom could it toady now? Certainly the Carter administration was no substitute. Those southern Baptists in polycotton suits lacked the finesse to know when they were being flattered. They had the social grace of car salesmen, drinking Amaretto and making coarse jests about pyramids. They gave dull parties and talked about human rights. The landslide election of Reagan was therefore providential. The familiar combination of private opulence and public squalor was back in the saddle; there would be no end of parties and patrons and portraits. The Wounded Horseman might allot $90 million for brass bands while slashing the cultural endowments of the nation to ribbons and threads; who cared? Not Warhol, certainly, whose work never ceases to prove its merits in the only place where merit really shows, the market.

Great leaders, it is said, bring forth the praise of great artists. How can one doubt that Warhol was delivered by Fate to be the Rubens of this administration, to play Bernini to Reagan's Urban VIII? On the one hand, the shrewd old movie actor, void of ideas but expert at manipulation, projected into high office by the insuperable power of mass imagery and secondhand perception. On the other, the shallow painter who understood more about the mechanisms of celebrity than any of his colleagues, whose entire sense of reality was shaped, like Reagan's sense of power, by the television tube. Each, in his way, coming on like Huck Finn; both obsessed with serving the interests of privilege. Together, they signify a new moment: the age of supply-side aesthetics.

In El Salvador by Joan Didion was originally published November 4, 1982.
Copyright © 1982 Joan Didion. Reprinted by permission of the author.

JOAN DIDION

In El Salvador

I

THE THREE-YEAR-OLD El Salvador International Airport is glassy and white and splendidly isolated, conceived during the waning of the Molina "National Transformation" as convenient less to the capital (San Salvador is forty miles away, until recently a drive of several hours) than to a central hallucination of the Molina and Romero regimes, the projected beach resorts, the Hyatt, the Pacific Paradise, tennis, golf, water-skiing, condos, Costa del Sol; the visionary invention of a tourist industry in yet another republic where the leading natural cause of death is gastrointestinal infection. In the general absence of tourists these hotels have since been abandoned, ghost resorts on the empty Pacific beaches, and to land at this airport built to service them is to plunge directly into a state in which no ground is solid, no depth of field reliable, no perception so definite that it might not dissolve into its reverse.

The only logic is that of acquiescence. Immigration is negotiated in a thicket of automatic weapons, but by whose authority the weapons are brandished (army or national guard or national police or customs police or treasury police or one of a continuing proliferation of other shadowy and overlapping forces) is a blurred point. Eye contact is avoided. Documents are scrutinized upside-down. Once clear of the airport, on the new highway that slices through green hills rendered phosphorescent by the cloud cover of the tropical rainy season, one sees mainly underfed cattle and mongrel dogs and armored vehicles, vans, and trucks and Cherokee Chiefs fitted with reinforced steel and bulletproof Plexiglas an inch thick.

Such vehicles are a fixed feature of local life, and are popularly associated with disappearance and death. There was the Cherokee Chief seen following the Dutch television crew killed in Chalatenango province in March. There was the red Toyota three-quarter-ton pickup sighted near the van driven by the four American Maryknoll workers on the night they were killed in December 1980. There are the three Toyota panel trucks, one yellow, one blue, and one green, none bearing plates, reported present at each of the summer mass detentions (a "detention" is another fixed feature of local life and often precedes a "disappearance") in the Amatepec district of San Salvador. These are the details—the models and colors of armored vehicles, the makes and calibers of weapons, the particular methods of dismemberment and decapitation used in particular instances—on which the visitor to Salvador learns immediately to concentrate, to the exclusion of past or future concerns, as in a prolonged amnesiac fugue.

TERROR IS THE GIVEN of the place. Black-and-white police cars cruise in pairs, each with the barrel of a rifle extruding from an open window. Roadblocks materialize at random, soldiers fanning out from trucks and taking positions, fingers always on triggers, safetys clicking on and off. Aim is taken as if to pass the time. Every morning *El Diario de hoy* and *La Prensa Gráfica* carry cautionary stories. "*Una madre y sus dos hijos fueron asesinados con arma cortante (corvo) por ocho sujetos desconocidos el lunes en la noche*": a mother and her two sons hacked to death in their beds by eight *desconocidos*, unknown men. The same morning's paper: the unidentified body of a young man, strangled, found on the shoulder of a road. Same morning, different story: the unidentified bodies of three young men, found on another road, their faces partially destroyed by bayonets, one face carved to represent a cross.

It is largely from these reports in the newspapers that the United States embassy compiles its body counts, which are transmitted to Washington in a weekly dispatch referred to by embassy people as "the grim-gram." These counts are presented in a kind of tortured code that fails to obscure what is taken for granted in El Salvador, that government forces do most of the killing. In a January 15 memo to Washington, for example, the embassy issued a "guarded" breakdown on its count of 6,909 "reported" political murders between September 16, 1980, and September 15, 1981. Of these 6,909, 922 were "believed committed by security forces," 952 "believed committed by leftist terrorists," 136 "believed committed by rightist terrorists," and 4,889 "committed by unknown assailants," the famous *desconocidos* favored by those San Salvador newspapers still publishing. (By whom the remaining ten were committed is unclear.) The memo continued:

The uncertainty involved here can be seen in the fact that responsibility cannot be fixed in the majority of cases. We note, however, that it is generally believed in El Salvador that a large number of the unexplained killings are carried out by the security forces, officially or unofficially. The Embassy is aware of dramatic claims that have been made by one interest group or another in which the security forces figure as the primary agents of murder here. El Salvador's tangled web of attack and vengeance, traditional criminal violence and political mayhem make this an impossible charge to sustain. In saying this, however, we make no attempt to lighten the responsibility for the deaths of many hundreds, and perhaps thousands, which can be attributed to the security forces. . . .

THE BODY COUNT kept by what is generally referred to in San Salvador as "the Human Rights Commission" is higher than the embassy's, and documented periodically by a photographer who goes out looking for bodies. The bodies he photographs are often broken into unnatural positions, and the faces to which the bodies are attached (when they are attached) are equally unnatural, sometimes unrecognizable as human faces, obliterated by acid or beaten to a mash of misplaced ears and teeth or slashed ear to ear and invaded by insects. "*Encontrado en Antiguo Cuscatlán el día 25 de marzo 1982: camison de dormir celeste,*" the typed caption reads on one photograph: found in Antiguo Cuscatlán March 25, 1982, wearing a sky-blue night shirt. The captions are laconic. Found in Soyapango May 21, 1982. Found in Mejicanos June 11, 1982. Found at El Playón May 30, 1982, white shirt, purple pants, black shoes.

The photograph accompanying that last caption shows a body with no eyes, because the vultures got to it before the photographer did. There is a special kind of practical information that the visitor to El Salvador acquires immediately, the way visitors to other places acquire information about the currency rates, the hours for the museums. In El Salvador one learns that vultures go first for the soft tissue, for the eyes, the exposed genitalia, the open mouth. One learns that an open mouth can be used to make a specific point, can be stuffed with something emblematic; stuffed, say, with a penis, or, if the point has to do with land title, stuffed with some of the dirt in question. One learns that hair deteriorates less rapidly than flesh, and that a skull surrounded by a perfect corona of hair is not an uncommon sight in the body dumps.

All forensic photographs induce in the viewer a certain protective numbness, but dissociation is more difficult here. The disfigurement is too routine. The locations are too near, the dates too recent. There is the presence of the relatives of the disappeared: the women who sit every day in this cramped office on the grounds of the archdiocese, waiting to look at the spiral-bound photo albums in which the photographs are kept. These albums have plastic covers bearing soft-focus color photographs of young Americans in dating situations (strolling through autumn foliage on one album, recumbent in a field of daisies on another), and the women, looking for the bodies of their husbands and brothers and sisters and children, pass them from hand to hand without comment or expression.

> One of the more shadowy elements of the violent scene here [is] the death squad. Existence of these groups has long been disputed, but not by many Salvadorans.... Who constitutes the death squads is yet another difficult question. We do not believe that these squads exist as permanent formations but rather as ad hoc vigilante groups that coalesce according to perceived need. Membership is also uncertain, but in addition to civilians we believe that both on- and off-duty members of the security forces are participants. This was unofficially confirmed by right-wing spokesman Maj. Roberto D'Aubuisson who stated in an interview in early 1981 that security force members utilize the guise of the death squad when a potentially embarrassing or odious task needs to be performed.
>
> —*from the confidential but later declassified January 15, 1982, memo previously cited, drafted for the State Department by the political section at the embassy in San Salvador*

The dead and pieces of the dead turn up in El Salvador everywhere, every day, as taken for granted as in a nightmare, or a horror movie. Vultures of course suggest the presence of a body. A knot of children on the street suggests the presence of a body. Bodies turn up in the brush of vacant lots, in the garbage thrown down ravines in the richest districts, in public rest rooms, in bus stations. Some are dropped in Lake Ilopango, a few miles east of the city, and wash up near the lakeside cottages and clubs frequented by what remains in San Salvador of the sporting bourgeoisie. Some still turn up at El Playón, the lunar lava field of rotting human flesh visible at one time or another on every television screen in America but characterized as recently as June in the *El Salvador News Gazette*, an English language weekly edited by an American named Mario Rosenthal, as an "uncorroborated story... dredged up from the files of leftist propaganda." Others turn up at Puerta del Diablo, above Parque Balboa, a national *Turicentro* still described, in the April–July 1982 issue of *Aboard TACA*, the magazine provided passengers on the national airline of El Salvador, as "offering excellent subjects for color photography."

I DROVE UP to Puerta del Diablo one morning last summer, past the Casa Presidencial and the camouflaged watchtowers and heavy concentrations of troops and arms south of town, on up a narrow road narrowed further by landslides and deep crevices in the roadbed, a drive so insistently premonitory that after a while I began to hope that I would pass Puerta del Diablo without knowing it, just miss it, write it off, turn around and go back. There was however no way of missing it. Puerta del Diablo is a "view site" in an older and distinctly literary tradition, nature as lesson, an immense cleft rock through which half of El Salvador seems framed, a site so romantic and "mystical," so theatrically sacrificial in aspect, that it might be a cosmic parody of nineteenth-century landscape painting. The place presents itself as pathetic fallacy: the sky "broods," the stones "weep," a constant seepage of water weighting the ferns and moss. The foliage is thick and slick with moisture. The only sound is a steady buzz, I believe of cicadas.

Body dumps are seen in El Salvador as a kind of visitors' must-do, difficult but worth the detour. "Of course you have seen El Playón," an aide to President Alvaro Magaña said to me one day, and proceeded to discuss the site geologically, as evidence of the country's geothermal resources. He made no mention of the bodies. I was unsure if he was sounding me out or simply found the geothermal aspect of overriding interest. One difference between El Playón and Puerta del Diablo is that most bodies at El Playón appear to have been killed somewhere else, and then dumped; at Puerta del Diablo the executions are believed to occur in place, at the top, and the bodies thrown over. Sometimes reporters will speak of wanting to spend the night at Puerta del Diablo, in order to document an actual execution, but at the time I was in Salvador no one had.

The aftermath, the daylight aspect, is well documented. "Nothing fresh today, I hear," an embassy officer said when I mentioned that I had visited Puerta del Diablo. "Were there any on top?" someone else asked. "There were supposed to have been three on top yesterday." The point about whether or not there had been any on top was that usually it was necessary to go down to see bodies. The way down is hard. Slabs of stone, slippery with moss, are set into the vertiginous cliff, and it is down this cliff that one begins the descent to the bodies, or what is left of the bodies, pecked and maggoty masses of flesh, bone, hair. On some days there have been helicopters circling, tracking those making the descent. Other days there have been militia at the top, in the clearing where the road seems to run out, but on the morning I was there the only people on top were a man and a woman and three small children, who played in the wet grass while the woman started and stopped a Toyota pickup. She appeared to be learning how to drive. She drove forward and then back toward the edge, apparently following the man's signals over and over again.

We did not speak, and it was only later, down the mountain and back in the land of the provisionally living, that it occurred to me that there was a definite question about why a man and a woman might choose a well-known body dump for a driving lesson. This was one of a number of occasions, during the two weeks my husband and I spent in El Salvador, on which I came to understand, in a way I had not understood before, the exact mechanism of terror.

WHENEVER I HAD nothing better to do in San Salvador I would walk up in the leafy stillness of the San Benito and Escalón districts, where the hush at midday is broken only by the occasional crackle of a walkie-talkie, the click of metal moving on a weapon. I recall a day in San Benito when I opened my bag to check an address, and heard the clicking of metal on metal all up and down the street. On the whole no one walks up here, and pools of blossoms lie undisturbed on the sidewalks. Most of the houses in San Benito are more recent than those in Escalón, less idiosyncratic and probably smarter, but the most striking architectural features in both districts are not the houses but their walls, walls built upon walls, walls stripped of the usual copa de oro and bougainvillea, walls that reflect successive generations of violence: the original stone, the additional five or six or ten feet of brick, and finally the barbed wire, sometimes concertina, sometimes electrified; walls with watchtowers, gun ports, closed-circuit television cameras, walls now reaching twenty and thirty feet.

San Benito and Escalón appear on the embassy security maps as districts of relatively few "incidents," but they remain districts in which a certain oppressive uneasiness prevails. In the first place there are always "incidents"—detentions and deaths and disappearances—in the barrancas, the ravines lined with shanties that fall down behind the houses with the walls and the guards and the walkie-talkies; one day in Escalón I was introduced to a woman who kept the lean-to that served as a grocery store in a barranca just above the Hotel Sheraton. She was sticking prices on bars of Camay and Johnson's baby soap, stopping occasionally to sell a plastic bag or two filled with crushed ice and Coca-Cola, and all the while she talked in a low voice about her fear, about her eighteen-year-old son, about the boys who had been taken out and shot on successive nights recently in a neighboring barranca.

IN THE SECOND PLACE there is, in Escalón, the presence of the Sheraton it-self, a hotel that has figured rather too prominently in certain local stories involving the disappearance and death of Americans. The Sheraton always seems brighter and more mildly festive than either the Camino Real or the Presidente, with children in the pool and flowers and pretty women in pas-tel dresses, but there are usually several bulletproofed Cherokee Chiefs in the parking area, and the men drinking in the lobby often carry the little zippered purses that in San Salvador suggest not passports or credit cards but Browning 9-mm. pistols.

It was at the Sheraton that one of the few American *desaparecidos*, a young free-lance writer named John Sullivan, was last seen, in December of 1980. It was also at the Sheraton, after eleven on the evening of January 3, 1981, that the two American advisers on agrarian reform, Michael Hammer and Mark Pearlman, were killed, along with the Salvadoran director of the Institute for Agrarian Transformation, José Rodolfo Viera. The three were drinking coffee in a dining room off the lobby, and whoever killed them used an Ingram MAC-10, without sound suppressor, and then walked out through the lobby, unapprehended. The Sheraton has even turned up in the investigation into the December 1980 deaths of the four American Maryknoll workers. In *Justice in El Salvador: A Case Study*, prepared and re-leased this summer in New York by the Lawyers Committee for Interna-tional Human Rights, there appears this note:

> On December 19, 1980, the [Duarte government's] Special Investigative Commission reported that "a red Toyota 3/4-ton pick-up was seen leaving (the crime scene) at about 11:00 PM on December 2" and that "a red splotch on the burned van" of the churchwomen was being checked to determine whether the paint splotch "could be the result of a collision be-tween that van and the red Toyota pick-up." By February 1981, the Mary-knoll Sisters' Office of Social Concerns, which has been actively monitor-ing the investigation, received word from a source which it considered reli-able that the FBI had matched the red splotch on the burned van with a red Toyota pick-up belonging to the Sheraton hotel in San Salvador....
> Subsequent to the FBI's alleged matching of the paint splotch and a Sheraton truck, the State Department has claimed, in a communication with the families of the church women, that "the FBI could not determine the source of the paint scraping."

There is also mention in this study of a young Salvadoran businessman named Hans Christ (his father was a German who arrived in El Salvador at the end of World War II), a part-owner of the Sheraton. Hans Christ lives now in Miami, and that his name should have even come up in the Maryknoll investigation made many people uneasy, because it was Hans Christ, along with his brother-in-law, Ricardo Sol Meza, who, in April of 1981, were first charged with the murders of Michael Hammer and Mark Pearlman and José Rodolfo Viera at the Sheraton. These charges were later dropped, and were followed by a series of other charges, arrests, releases, expressions of "dismay" and "incredulity" from the US Embassy, and even, recently, confessions to the killings from two former National Guard corporals, who testified that Hans Christ had led them through the lobby and pointed out the victims. Christ and Ricardo Sol Meza have said that the dropped case against them was a government frame-up, and that they were only having drinks at the Sheraton the night of the killings, with a National Guard intelligence officer. It was logical for Hans Christ and Ricardo Sol Meza to have drinks at the Sheraton because they both had interests in the hotel, and Ricardo Sol Meza had just opened a roller disco, since closed, off the lobby into which the killers walked that night. The killers were described by witnesses as well dressed, their faces covered. The room from which they walked is no longer a restaurant, but the marks left by the bullets are still visible, on the wall facing the door.

Whenever I had occasion to visit the Sheraton I was apprehensive, and this apprehension came to color the entire Escalón district for me, even its lower reaches, where there were people and movies and restaurants. I recall being struck by it on the canopied porch of a restaurant near the Mexican embassy, on an evening when rain or sabotage or habit had blacked out the city and I became abruptly aware, in the light cast by a passing car, of two human shadows, silhouettes illuminated by the headlights and then invisible again. One shadow sat behind the smoked-glass windows of a Cherokee Chief parked at the curb in front of the restaurant; the other crouched between the pumps at the Esso station next door, carrying a rifle. It seemed to me unencouraging that my husband and I were the only people seated on the porch. In the absence of the headlights the candle on our table provided the only light, and I fought the impulse to blow it out. We continued talking, carefully. Nothing came of this, but I did not forget the sensation of having been in a single instant demoralized, undone, humiliated by fear, which is what I meant when I said that I came to understand in El Salvador the mechanism of terror.

II

3/3/81: Roberto D'Aubuisson, a former Salvadoran army intelligence officer, holds a press conference and says that before the US presidential election he had been in touch with a number of Reagan advisers and those
contacts have continued. The armed forces should ask the junta to resign,
D'Aubuisson says. He refuses to name a date for the action, but says,
"March is, I think, a very interesting month." He also calls for the aban-
donment of the economic reforms. D'Aubuisson had been accused of plot-
ting to overthrow the government on two previous occasions. Observers
speculate that since D'Aubuisson is able to hold the news conference and
pass freely between Salvador and Guatemala, he must enjoy considerable
support among some sections of the army.... 3/4/81: In San Salvador, the
US Embassy is fired upon; no one is injured. Charge d'Affaires Frederic
Chapin says, "This incident has all the hallmarks of a D'Aubuisson operation. Let me state to you that we oppose coups and we have no intention
of being intimidated."

> *—from the "Chronology of Events Related to Salvadoran Situa-
> tion" prepared periodically by the United States embassy in San
> Salvador*

Since the Exodus from Egypt, historians have written of those who sacrificed and struggled for freedom: the stand at Thermopylae, the revolt of
Spartacus, the storming of the Bastille, the Warsaw uprising in World War
II. More recently we have seen evidence of this same human impulse in
one of the developing nations in Central America. For months and
months the world news media covered the fighting in El Salvador. Day
after day, we were treated to stories and film slanted toward the brave freedom fighters battling oppressive government forces in behalf of the silent,
suffering people of that tortured country. Then one day those silent suffering people were offered a chance to vote to choose the kind of government
they wanted. Suddenly the freedom fighters in the hills were exposed for
what they really are: Cuban-backed guerrillas.... On election day the people of El Salvador, an unprecedented [1.5 million] of them, braved ambush
and gunfire, trudging miles to vote for freedom.

> *—President Reagan, in his June 8, 1982, speech before both
> houses of the British Parliament, referring to the March 28 elec-
> tion which resulted in the ascension of Roberto D'Aubuisson to
> the presidency of the Constituent Assembly*

From whence he shall come to judge the quick and the dead. I happened to
read President Reagan's speech one evening in San Salvador when President
Reagan was in fact on television, with Doris Day, in *The Winning Team*, a

1952 Warner Brothers picture about the baseball pitcher Grover Cleveland Alexander. I reached the stand at Thermopylae about the time that *el salvador del Salvador* began stringing cranberries and singing "Old St. Nicholas" with Miss Day. "*Muy bonita*," he said when she tried out a rocking chair in her wedding dress. "*Feliz Navidad*," they cried, and, in accented English, "*Play ball!*"

As it happened, "play ball" was a phrase I had come to associate in El Salvador with Roberto D'Aubuisson and his followers in the Nationalist Republican Alliance, or ARENA. "It's a process of letting certain people know they're going to have to play ball," embassy people would say, and: "You take a guy who's young, and everything 'young' implies, you send him signals, he plays ball, then we play ball." American diction in this situation tends toward the studied casual, the can-do, as if sheer cool and Bailey bridges could shape the place up. Elliott Abrams told *The New York Times* in July that punishment within the Salvadoran military could be "a very important sign that you can't do this stuff any more," meaning kill the citizens. "If you clean up your act, all things are possible," is the way Jeremiah O'Leary, a special assistant to US national security adviser William Clark, described the American diplomatic effort in an interview given the *Los Angeles Times* just after the March 28 election. He was speculating on how Ambassador Deane Hinton might be dealing with D'Aubuisson. "I kind of picture him saying, 'Goddamnit Bobbie, you've got a problem and . . . if you're what everyone said you are, you're going to make it hard for everybody.'"

ROBERTO D'AUBUISSON is a chain smoker, as were many of the people I met in El Salvador, perhaps because it is a country in which achieving a death related to smoking remains remote. I never met Major D'Aubuisson, but I was always interested in the adjectives used to describe him. "Pathological" was the adjective, modifying "killer," used by former Ambassador Robert E. White (it was White who refused D'Aubuisson a visa, after which, according to the embassy's "Chronology of Events" for June 30, 1980, "D'Aubuisson manages to enter the US illegally and spends two days in Washington holding press conferences and attending luncheons before turning himself in to immigration authorities"), but "pathological" is not a word one hears in-country, where meaning tends to be transmitted in code.

In-country one hears "young" (the "and everything 'young' implies" part is usually left tacit), even "immature"; "impetuous," "impulsive," "impatient," "nervous," "volatile," "highstrung," "kind of coiled-up," and, most frequently, "intense," or just "tense." Offhand it struck me that Roberto D'Aubuisson had some reason to be tense, in that General José Guillermo García, who has remained a main player through several changes of government, might logically perceive him as the wild card who could queer everybody's ability to refer to his election as a vote for freedom. As I write this I realize that I have fallen into the Salvadoran mind-set, which turns on plot, and, since half the players at any given point in the game are in exile, on the phrase "in touch with."

"I've known D'Aubuisson a long time," I was told by Alvaro Magaña, the banker the Army made, over D'Aubuisson's rather frenzied objections ("We stopped that one on the one-yard line," Deane Hinton told me about D'Aubuisson's play to block Magaña), provisional president of El Salvador. We were sitting in his office upstairs at the Casa Presidencial, an airy and spacious building in the tropical colonial style, and he was drinking cup after Limoges cup of black coffee, smoking one cigarette with each, carefully, an unwilling actor who intended to survive the accident of being cast in this production. "Since Molina was president. I used to come here to see Molina, D'Aubuisson would be here, he was a young man in military intelligence, I'd see him here." He gazed toward the corridor that opened onto the interior courtyard, with cannas, oleander, a fountain not in operation. "When we're alone now I try to talk to him. I do talk to him, he's coming for lunch today. He never calls me Alvaro, it's always *usted, Señor, Doctor*. I call him Roberto. I say, 'Roberto, don't do this, don't do that,' you know."

Magaña studied in the United States, at Chicago, and his four oldest children are now in the United States, one son at Vanderbilt, a son and a daughter at Santa Clara, and another daughter near Santa Clara, at Notre Dame in Belmont. He is connected by money, education, and temperament to oligarchal families. All the players here are densely connected: Magaña's sister, who lives in California, is the best friend of Nora Ungo, the wife of Guillermo Ungo, and Ungo spoke to Magaña's sister in August when he was in California raising money for the FMLN-FDR, which is what the opposition to the Salvadoran government was called this year. The membership and even the initials of this opposition tend to be fluid, but the broad strokes are these: the FMLN-FDR is the coalition of the Revolutionary Democratic Front (FDR) and the five guerrilla groups in the Farabundo Martí National Liberation Front (FMLN). These five groups are the Salvadoran Communist Party (PCS), the Popular Forces of Liberation (FPL), the Revolutionary Party of Central American Workers (PRTC), the

Peoples' Revolutionary Army (ERP), and the Armed Forces of National Resistance (FARN). Within each of these groups, there are further factions and sometimes even further initials, as in the PRS and LP-28 of the ERP.

During the time that D'Aubuisson was trying to stop Magaña's appointment as provisional president, members of ARENA, which is supported heavily by other oligarchal elements, passed out leaflets referring to Magaña, predictably, as a Communist, and, more interestingly, as "the little Jew." The manipulation of anti-Semitism is an undercurrent in Salvadoran life that is not much discussed and probably worth some study, since it refers to a tension between those families who solidified their holdings in the mid-nineteenth century and those later families, some of them Jewish, who arrived in El Salvador and entrenched themselves around 1900. I recall asking a well-off Salvadoran about the numbers of his acquaintances within the oligarchy who have removed themselves and their money to Miami. "Mostly the Jews," he said.

> *In San Salvador*
> *in the year 1965*
> *the best sellers*
> *of the three most important*
> *book stores*
> *were:*
> *The Protocols of the Elders of Zion;*
> *a few books by*
> *diarrhetic Somerset Maugham;*
> *a book of disagreeably*
> *obvious poems*
> *by a lady with a European name*
> *who nonetheless writes in Spanish about our*
> *country*
> *and a collection of*
> *Reader's Digest condensed novels.*

—"San Salvador" by Roque Dalton García,
translated by Edward Baker*

The late Roque Dalton García was born into the Salvadoran bourgeoisie in 1935, spent some years in Havana, came home in 1973 to join the ERP, and, in 1975, was executed, on charges that he was a CIA agent, by his own comrades. The actual executioner was said to be Joaquín Villalobos, who is now about thirty years old, commander of the ERP, and a key figure

---

* *El Salvador: The Face of Revolution*, by Robert Armstrong and Janet Shenk (South End Press, 1982), p. 11.

in the FMLN, which, as the Mexican writer Gabriel Zaid pointed out last winter in *Dissent*, has as one of its support groups the Roque Dalton Cultural Brigade. The Dalton execution is frequently cited by people who want to stress that "the other side kills people too, you know," an argument common mainly among those like the State Department with a stake in whatever government is current in El Salvador, since, if it is taken for granted in Salvador that the government kills, it is also taken for granted that the other side kills; that everyone has killed, everyone kills now, and, if the history of the place suggests any pattern, everyone will continue to kill.

"Don't say I said this, but there are no issues here," I was told this summer by a high-placed Salvadoran. "There are only ambitions." He meant of course not that there were no ideas in conflict, but that the conflicting ideas were held exclusively by people he knew; that, whatever the outcome of any fighting or negotiation or coup or countercoup, the Casa Presidencial would ultimately be occupied not by *campesinos* and Maryknolls but by the already entitled, by Guillermo Ungo or Joaquín Villalobos or even by Roque Dalton's son, Juan José Dalton, or by Juan José Dalton's comrade in the FPL, José Antonio Morales Carbonell, the guerrilla son of José Antonio Morales Ehrlich, a former member of the Duarte junta, who had himself been in exile during the Romero regime. In an open letter written shortly before his arrest in San Salvador in June of 1980, José Antonio Morales Carbonell had charged his father with an insufficient appreciation of "Yankee imperialism." José Antonio Morales Carbonell and Juan José Dalton tried together to enter the United States last summer, for a speaking engagement in San Francisco, but were refused visas by the embassy in Mexico City.

Whatever the issues were that had divided Morales Carbonell and his father and Roque Dalton and Joaquín Villalobos, the prominent Salvadoran to whom I was talking seemed to be saying, they were issues that fell somewhere outside the lines normally drawn to indicate "left" and "right." That this man saw *la situación* as only one more realignment of power among the entitled, a conflict of "ambitions" rather than "issues," was, I recognized, what many people would call a conventional bourgeois view of civil conflict, and offered no solutions, but the people with solutions to offer were mainly somewhere else, in Mexico or Panama or Washington.

THE PLACE BRINGS everything into question. One afternoon when I had run out of the Halazone tablets I dropped every night in a pitcher of tap water (a demented *gringa* gesture, I knew even then, in a country where anyone who had not been born there was at least mildly ill, including the nurse at the American embassy), I walked across the street from the Camino Real to the Metrocenter, which is referred to locally as "Central America's Largest Shopping Mall." I found no Halazone at the Metrocenter but became absorbed in making notes about the mall itself, about the Muzak playing "I Left My Heart in San Francisco" and "American Pie" ("... *singing, This will be the day that I die...*") although the record store featured a cassette called *Classics of Paraguay*, about the pâté de foie gras for sale in the supermarket, about the guard who did the weapons-check on everyone who entered the supermarket, about the young matrons in tight Sergio Valente jeans, trailing maids and babies behind them and buying towels, big beach towels printed with maps of Manhattan that featured Bloomingdale's; about the number of things for sale that seemed to suggest a fashion for "smart drinking," to evoke modish cocktail hours. There were bottles of Stolichnaya vodka packaged with glasses and mixer, there were ice buckets, there were bar carts of every conceivable design, displayed with sample bottles.

This was a shopping center that embodied the future for which El Salvador was presumably being saved, and I wrote it down dutifully, this being the kind of "color" I knew how to interpret, the kind of inductive irony, the detail that was supposed to illuminate the story. As I wrote it down I realized that I was no longer much interested in this kind of irony, that this was a story that would not be illuminated by such details, that this was a story that would perhaps not be illuminated at all, that this was perhaps even less a "story" than a true *noche obscura*. As I waited to cross back over the Boulevard de los Heroes to the Camino Real I noticed soldiers herding a young civilian into a van, their guns at the boy's back, and I walked straight ahead, not wanting to see anything at all.

—*November 4, 1982*

James Joyce

Joyce at 100 by Richard Ellmann was originally published November 18, 1982.

RICHARD ELLMANN

Joyce at 100

JAMES JOYCE THOUGHT about his centenary long before it occurred to his readers to do so. He scrawled in a notebook on Bloomsday, the day of *Ulysses*, in 1924, "Today 16 of June twenty years after. Will anybody remember this date." His Stephen Dedalus in *Ulysses* asks the same question as he jots down lines for a new poem, "Who ever anywhere will read these written words?" Stephen also recalls, with a twinge, how before leaving for Paris he gave instructions that in the event of his death his epiphanies should be deposited in all the major libraries of the world, *including Alexandria*: "Someone was to read them there after a few thousand years...." The library at Alexandria having been burned centuries before, chances were slim that anyone would be reading his epiphanies there at any time.

Still, if Joyce mocked such immortal longings it was because he had immortal longings to mock. His brother Stanislaus, who drew a sharp line between fiction and fact, remembered that James had given him similar instructions for the disposal of his poems and epiphanies before leaving for Paris in 1902. No one will object to brave youths displaying youthful bravado. Flushed with talent, or its semblance, they have all claimed with Shakespeare,

> *Not marble, nor the gilded monuments*
> *Of princes, shall outlive this powerful rime.*

Sometimes they've been right.

Joyce was convinced that a great future lay in store for him, and on the promise of it he allowed people to help him secure it. In 1904 he thought briefly that the moment had arrived; an Irish-American millionaire named Kelly seemed about to lend him money to start up a weekly magazine which was to be called *The Goblin*. Joyce said to his friend Francis Sheehy Skeffington, who was to be the coeditor, "I think I'm coming into my kingdom." Unfortunately, millionaire Kelly withdrew. Eight years later the same phrase occurs in a letter from Joyce to his wife: "I hope that the day may come when I shall be able to give you the fame of being beside me when I have entered into my Kingdom."

That he was still borrowing "left right and centre" did not dishearten him. In 1907 his second child was born in a pauper ward, but in that atmosphere Joyce confided to his brother, "My mind is of a type superior to and more civilized than any I have met up to the present." An empty wallet did not impede his conviction of spiritual affluence. His confidence persisted as he grew older, and his putative kingdom continued to include the posterity for whom he thought his books would be required texts. When a friend asked him why he was writing *Finnegans Wake* in the way he was, Joyce replied, with a brag intended to provoke a smile, "To keep the critics busy for three hundred years."

THE FIRST HUNDRED of these three hundred years Joyce appears to have weathered quite well. His books are indeed studied all over the world, and have their effect even on those who do not read them. Anthony Burgess says over and over again that Joyce has had no influence whatever on English fiction; he then contradicts the statement with novel after novel. If nothing else, writers in England as elsewhere have to choose when they start a novel whether to be traditional, when in the pre-Joycean past they could be traditional without scruple. Joyce does not lack for admirers. He does not lack for detractors either.

His detractors are repelled by the Joyce fans who obsessively follow Leopold Bloom's trail around Dublin, or climb the stairs of the Martello tower at Sandycove, or drink at the much refurbished bar in Davy Byrne's. Still, such activities are not more pernicious, or cultic, than climbing Wordsworth's Helvellyn, or visiting Hawthorne's House of the Seven Gables in Salem or Proust's aunt's house in Illiers. If Joyce particularly inspires such pilgrimages, it is perhaps because we long to be on closer terms with this *scriptor absconditus*, this indrawn writer, in the hope of achieving an intimacy with him which he does not readily extend.

Another reason for seeing the places described in his books is that Joyce, although he transformed them into words, did not invent them. He said, "He is a very bold man who dares to alter in the presentment, still more to deform, whatever he has seen and heard." This was in connection with the book *Dubliners*. He was always trying to verify details in the city which was almost a thousand miles from the table at which he was writing about it. How many feet down was the area in front of the house at 7 Eccles Street? What kind of trees were there on Leahy's Terrace?

Some of Joyce's flavor comes as a reward for this zeal. For example, in *A Portrait of the Artist as a Young Man*, Stephen Dedalus, after protesting to the rector that he has been unjustly pandied, leaves the rector's room and walks down the long corridor. At the end of it he bumps his elbow against the door. I am told that generations of Clongowes pupils have bumped their elbows against this same door.

Joyce attended so carefully to such minute particulars that he claimed that if Dublin were destroyed, the city could be reconstructed from his books. Its immortality would be assured through his. Other novelists are, however, much more likely to present a city in reconstructable form. Joyce offers no architectural information, only places to bump elbows or to lean them, to see out of the corner of an eye, to recognize by a familiar smell. The city rises in bits, not in masses. Anything else would be travelogue.

HE WAS AT ONCE dependent upon the real, and superior to it. His attitude may be elicited from a story he once told his French Academician friend, Louis Clillet. It was about an old Blasket Islander who had lived on his island from birth, and knew nothing about the mainland or its ways. But on one occasion he did venture over, and in a bazaar found a small mirror, something he had never seen in his life. He bought it, fondled it, gazed at it, and as he rowed back to the Blaskets he took it out of his pocket, stared at it some more, and murmured, "Oh Papa! Papa!" He jealously guarded the precious object from his wife's eye, but she observed that he was hiding something and became suspicious. One hot day, when both were at work in the fields, he hung his jacket on a hedge. She saw her chance, rushed to it, and extracted from a pocket the object her husband had kept so secret. But when she looked at the mirror, she cried, "Ach, it's nothing but an old woman!" and angrily threw it down so that it broke against a stone.

For Joyce the story had many implications, such as that man was filial and woman was vain. But the main one was that a mirror held up to nature will reflect the holder's consciousness as much as what is reflected. He could quote with approval Pater's remark "Art is life seen through a temperament."

When Joyce was young so many subjects pressed urgently upon him that he had only to choose among them. As he grew older he needed more hints. He sometimes thought he must alter his quiet life so as to secure them. Of course he could say defensively, to Djuna Barnes, "[Johann Sebastian] Bach led a very uneventful life." But when he was with Ernest Hemingway he discussed the possibility of going to Africa. Mrs. Joyce encouraged him: "Jim can do with a spot of that lion hunting," she said. "The thing we must face," said Joyce, whose sight was bad, "is that I couldn't see the lion." His wife was not to be silenced: "Hemingway'd describe him to you and afterwards you could go up and touch him and smell of him. That's all you'd need."

BUT THE MATERIAL he needed lay closer to home. For the main theme of *Ulysses* and of his play *Exiles* Joyce could rely on an incident that did not happen but that he briefly thought had happened. A one-time friend claimed in 1909 that Nora Barnacle, in the days when Joyce was courting her, had shared her favors with himself. But when Joyce was actually writing his novel and play nine years later, he had trouble reactivating the jealousy he had once felt so intensely. His wife complained to their friend Frank Budgen, "Jim wants me to go with other men so that he will have something to write about." She seems to have failed him in this wifely duty. She did however oblige him to the extent of beginning a letter to him with the words "Dear Cuckold," with the helpful aim of sharpening his pen for *Ulysses*.

Joyce for his part made comparable sacrifices for his art. In 1917 and 1918 he was beginning to write the "Nausicaa" episode of *Ulysses*, in which Bloom ogles a girl named Gerty MacDowell on the beach. Joyce seems to have felt that he must do something similar. He made overtures to two women, perhaps with his book ulteriorly in mind. The first occurred in Locarno, where he went for a time to enjoy a milder climate than Zurich. I learned about it through a coincidence. James Atherton, the Joyce scholar, gave a lecture in Manchester, and a woman in the audience came up to him afterward and said she had a friend in Germany who had known Joyce in Locarno in 1918. He sent me the address and I eventually got in communication with the German friend, who proved to be a woman doctor—one of the first woman doctors in Germany—named Gertrude Kaempffer.

In 1917 Dr. Kaempffer was staying above Locarno, in Orselina, recovering from tuberculosis after having nearly died of the disease. Joyce, afflicted with serious eye trouble, was living at the Pension Daheim. One evening Gertrude Kaempffer came down by funicular railway to visit some friends of hers in the same pension. They introduced her to Joyce, who because of his three published books and his obvious intellectual distinction had a certain local celebrity. He took an immediate interest in the young doctor, and after some talk offered to see her to the funicular. But her friends whispered to her that Mrs. Joyce would be jealous, so Dr. Kaempffer declined.

They happened to meet next day, however, in front of the spa hotel near the casino. After some conversation he walked part of the way home with her. When she offered her hand in parting, he held it in his hands for a moment, stroked it, and told her how fond he was of such delicate skin, of such fine, slender hands. (She considered her hands only to be thin and sickly.) Gerty MacDowell—the object of Bloom's prurient scrutiny—has a similar "waxen pallor" and, as we are told, "her hands were of finely veined alabaster with tapering fingers and as white as lemon juice and queen of ointments could make them though it was not true that she used to wear kid gloves in bed or take a milk footbath either." Joyce lent Gertrude Kaempffer *A Portrait of the Artist as a Young Man*. She was interested, and asked his help with certain words which she did not understand.

Joyce probably assumed that as a doctor she had much knowledge of the world, but in fact during her medical course her fellow students and professors had cosseted her as one of the first women students, and at the end of it she fell ill; so she was inexperienced and rather startled by the sexual overtures which Joyce soon made. She was fascinated by his mind, he indifferent as she felt to hers. When she would not agree, he asked her to correspond with him, and to use for the purpose the poste restante in Zurich. (Bloom also uses the poste restante in his clandestine correspondence with Martha Clifford.) Dr. Kaempffer reluctantly said no; she was put off by the idea of exchanging letters in secret.

Still, he occupied her thoughts, and she opened with interest the two letters he sent to her. Molly Bloom recalls how Bloom "wrote me that letter with all those words in it," and in *A Portrait of the Artist* Joyce depicts Stephen Dedalus's act of writing obscene letters and leaving them about in the hope that some girl will find them. With Gertrude Kaempffer Joyce indulged a kindred proclivity. Their correspondence seemed like Stephen's to be, though it was not, outside space and time. He said he loved her, and made clear that his love was physical. He hoped she had the same feelings. He said he wished to be entirely straightforward, and to leave to her the decision about intimacy.

THEN, PERHAPS TO EXCITE her as well as himself, he described in his fastidious handwriting his first sexual experience. It had occurred when he was fourteen. He was walking with the family nanny near some woods when she asked him to look the other way. He did so, and heard the sound of liquid splashing on the ground. Joyce used the word "piss," with which the young doctor was unfamiliar. The sound aroused him. "I jiggled furiously," he wrote. She did not understand this phrase either, but on later inquiry was told by someone that it was a kind of Scottish dance.

In *Finnegans Wake* the principal character, Earwicker, is accused of having performed the same act opposite two micturating girls:

> Slander, let it lie its flattest, has never been able to convict our good and great and no ordinary...Earwicker, that homogenius man, as a pious author called him, of any graver impropriety than that...of having behaved with ongentilmensky immodus opposite a pair of dainty maidservants in the swoolth of the rushy hollow whither...dame nature in all innocence and spontaneously and about the same hour of the eventide sent them both....

Joyce evidently recognized a farcical shamefulness in his own behavior. He confided in one of his letters to Gertrude Kaempffer another frailty: he found it particularly provocative when lying with a woman, he said, to be afraid of being discovered.

Gertrude Kaempffer did not regard these sentiments as fetching, and perhaps they were written more to indulge his own fantasy than in the hope of sharing it with her. She tore up the letters, in case anyone should read them, and did not reply. They would not meet again until a year later when, on her way to visit friends in Zurich, she caught sight in a public place of an unhappy-looking, emaciated man, and moved closer to see if it could be Joyce. He suddenly turned around, recognized her and greeted her warmly, and invited her to a cafe. She could not go, having an appointment. Might she not come to the hotel later for a drink? Foreseeing embarrassment, she refused again. Joyce looked pained, shook hands, and said goodbye.

All that survived of this abortive idyll was a recollection of having been aroused by a woman named Gertrude. At least he could draw one thing from it—the name of the young woman over whom Bloom excites himself in the "Nausicaa" episode—Gerty. As he said in *Giacomo Joyce*, "Write it, damn you, write it! What else are you good for?"

HE NEEDED MORE hints for the episode than the aloof Dr. Kaempffer provided, and the second of his forays occurred some months after the first, this time in Zurich. We have known something of this affair ever since Professor Heinrich Straumann of the University of Zurich obtained, just after the Second World War, the love letters Joyce wrote during it. More recently some details have come to light that make the context clearer. One day in 1918 Joyce looked out of a window in his flat and happened to see, in a flat in the next building, a young woman pulling a toilet chain. It was a scene that, as we have observed, had distinct erotic implications for him. He contrived to speak to this young woman, whose name was Marthe Fleischmann, on the street. She had a limp, and he would give the same limp to Gerty MacDowell in the "Nausicaa" episode. He stared at her with amazement as if they had met before, and was later to tell her that she looked exactly like a young woman he had seen many years before on the Dublin strand. Marthe Fleischmann seems to have coyly declined this gambit.

How far his feelings derived from the needs of his novel, and how far the novel from his amorous needs, were questions he did not have to answer. As he had written his brother thirteen years before, "There cannot be any substitute for the individual passion as the motive power of every-thing—art and philosophy included." Joyce kept watching for Marthe Fleischmann, and she, far from ignoring his attentions, closed the shutters of her windows. He wrote her an ardent letter in French, in a disguised handwriting, marked especially by his use of Greek *e*'s. He would have Mrs. Yelverton Barry in *Ulysses* complain that Bloom wrote to her "an anony-mous letter" in prentice backhand full of indecent proposals and would have Bloom use Greek *e*'s in corresponding with another Martha. Joyce begged Marthe to tell him her name. She will not mind if he suggests she is Jewish, for after all Jesus lay in the womb of a Jewish mother. As for him-self, he is a writer, and at a pivotal moment in his life. His age is the same as Dante's when he began the *Divine Comedy* and as Shakespeare's when he fell in love with the Dark Lady of the *Sonnets* (a date we don't know). He is supremely unhappy; he must see her.

Marthe yielded to these importunities and agreed to meet him. Whether she was Jewish or not, Joyce did not spend much time on reli-gion; rather he turned the conversation to the congenial subject of women's drawers, always a titillating topic for him, and one which figures promi-nently in the "Nausicaa" episode. It was not easy for Marthe to meet him because, as she archly confided, she had a "guardian" named Rudolf Hilt-pold. Hiltpold was really her lover, the man who paid her rent. He was vig-ilant and she had to be circumspect. Joyce inscribed a copy of *Chamber Music* to her and left it in her letterbox. It was an appropriate gift for Martha, especially since he has Bloom in *Ulysses* reflect jokingly about the relation of chamber music to chamber pots.

Evidently Marthe was impressed. Gerty MacDowell in "Nausicaa" would also be interested in poetry, though of an even more hopeless kind.

Joyce now prepared a curious ceremony. On February 2, 1919, his thirty-seventh birthday, he arranged for her to have tea at the studio of his friend Frank Budgen. A note he sent to her that morning is headed "Marias Lichtmesse," or Candlemas, which also takes place on February 2, the feast commemorating the Purification of the Virgin Mary. He evidently wished to infuse a touch of Mariolatry in his sexual approach, and in *Ulysses* he parallels Bloom's secular adoration of Gerty MacDowell with a men's retreat at a church dedicated to the Virgin. For the occasion Joyce borrowed a handsome Jewish candlestick, such as is lighted during the festival of Chanukah, and brought it to Frank Budgen's studio. He explained that Marthe would be arriving a little later.

Budgen had scruples about assisting his friend in this infidelity and said so. Joyce replied severely, "If I permitted myself any restraint in this matter it would be spiritual death to me." Rather than feel guilty of spiritual murder, Budgen gave in. There were further preparations. Budgen's paintings would do well enough as decor, except that there were no nudes among them. The painter had therefore to whip up a charcoal drawing of a voluptuous nude on the spot. Joyce said that in spite of his unwillingness to use given names, on this one occasion he and Budgen must call each other not Joyce and Budgen, but Jim and Frank, and use the intimate form "*du*," because he had spoken so often of Budgen to Marthe that she would find strange any more formal style of address.

Marthe arrived for Candlemas and Chanukah. When candles are lighted on Candlemas the priest speaks of them as symbolizing the light that shall enlighten the Gentiles and also the glory of the people of Israel. This text seemed to give warrant to Joyce's syncretism. He lit the Jewish candlestick ostensibly so she could see the paintings better, actually to lend a Judeo-Christian glimmer to the erotic rendezvous. He toured the paintings with her, and, as Budgen recalled, won a reproachful smirk from Marthe when he called to her attention the fat nude. Eventually Joyce took her home. He met Budgen later that evening and confided, "I have explored the coldest and hottest parts of a woman's body." Gerty MacDowell reproaches Bloom, "You saw all the secrets of my bottom drawer."

Such scientific lechery would be mocked in the "Circe" episode of *Ulysses*. Presumably it remained exploratory, or so Budgen, knowing his friend's latent inhibitions, surmised. As for Marthe, she always referred to her acquaintance with Joyce as "*eine Platonische Liebe.*" A day or two later Joyce was asked by another friend why he had borrowed the candlestick, and replied, "For a black mass." Bloom, ruminating about Gerty, and at the same time remembering the words "Next year in Jerusalem" from still another Jewish festival, that of Passover, conflates the two in the "Nausicaa" episode by thinking how she "showed me her next year in drawers."

Further meetings with Marthe Fleischmann now became out of the question. The redoubtable "guardian" Rudolf Hiltpold got wind of the matter and wrote a threatening letter to Joyce. Joyce went at once to see him, assured him that nothing had happened, and gave him all of Marthe's letters. Hiltpold was mollified. Still, Marthe's haughty, naughty beguilements helped Joyce to compose the "Nausicaa" episode, a point he confirmed by sending her a postcard with greetings to Nausicaa from Odysseus. Her limp, her coyness, her prattling about Platonic love, her responsiveness to his interest in drawers all went to furnish out Gerty MacDowell, whose first name and pallid hands had come to him from his earlier attraction to Gertrude Kaempffer. The assignation on the Virgin Mary's Candlemas, with Chanukah and Passover trimmings, would have its uses. His would-be infidelities had served his book, if not his peculiar life.

THESE TWO INCIDENTS give a sense of Joyce's seeking cues for *Ulysses* and, no doubt, for himself, by listening to songs of Sirens. Still, closeness to life was not enough. I want now, a little more reverently, to inquire what manner of writer he thought he was. Granted that he believed himself from earliest youth to be an artist, it was as an Irish artist that he wished to become known. To that extent he was and always would be a part of the national literary revival. Although he spoke of *Finnegans Wake* as a universal history, the universe is given a distinct Irish coloration, and in a way the whole book is an arabesque on the Irish ballad of the title.

Similarly, his first work, now lost, written when he was nine, was on the most Irish of subjects—the death of Charles Stewart Parnell. In his youth perhaps his most passionate literary enthusiasm was for James Clarence Mangan, whom he complimented as "the national poet of Ireland," and as one who (he said) "had the whole past of the country at the back of his head," an ideal he marked out for himself as well. "An Irish safety pin is more important to me than an English epic," he remarked. Yet it was not Ireland as it had been that attracted him, but Ireland as it might be. Joyce was affected by the talk of renaissance that was in the air, and in the earliest as well as in the final version of *A Portrait of the Artist*, that is, from 1904 to 1914, he ended by summoning in his imagination a new Irish nation.

The Irishness of his books was a distinguishing mark. *Dubliners*, he told his brother, was "a moral history of the life I knew," and to his publisher Grant Richards he wrote, "My intention was to write a chapter of the moral history of my country." Joyce is often considered amoral; he regarded himself as a moralist. Stephen Dedalus concludes *A Portrait* with the words, "I go to encounter for the millionth time the reality of experience and to forge in the smithy of my soul the uncreated conscience of my race." Irony-hunters, who abound in Joyce studies, have been reluctant to take this expressed ambition of Stephen's seriously. Joyce did so, however; in an earnest letter to his wife in 1912 he said, "I am one of the writers of this generation who are perhaps creating at last a conscience in the soul of this wretched race." His books move obliquely, even urbanely, toward this goal. In nine articles he wrote for a Triestine newspaper he presented his country's plight in more downright fashion. He offered these in 1914 to a publisher in Rome. They were not accepted: a pity, since they would have confirmed Joyce's "political awareness," a quality he valued in Turgenev.

If he was not a nationalist of anyone else's school he was his own nationalist. His brother records a conversation they had in April 1907; Stanislaus argued against a free Ireland on the grounds that freedom would make it intolerable. "What the devil are your politics?" asked James. "Do you not think Ireland has a right to govern itself and is capable of doing so?" As an Irish writer, Joyce in 1912 went to Arthur Griffith, the head of the newspaper *Sinn Fein*, to secure his help in having *Dubliners* issued by an Irish firm. Griffith, later to be Ireland's first president, was powerless to help but received him with respect.

As Irish artist, Joyce could be contemptuous toward his literary compatriots, whom he derided as serving lesser gods than his own. He was nevertheless modest before his own art. He had many of the self-doubts that are often attributed only to lesser writers. Though his first book was verse, he did not pride himself greatly on it, and even denied to Padraic Colum in 1909 that he was a poet. Of course he did not like it when others agreed with his estimate; Ezra Pound was one of those who deeply offended him in the late 1920s by urging him to file his new poems in the family Bible. Joyce published them anyway, but he hedged his claim for them by giving them the title of *Pomes Penyeach*. He considered lyricism to be a vital part of his revelation of himself in his art, yet he played down his lyrics like a man unwilling to risk all on that throw. He was sufficiently affected by the criticism of early parts of *Finnegans Wake* to consider turning the book over to James Stephens for completion. As for *Ulysses*, he said of it to Samuel

Beckett, "I may have oversystematized *Ulysses*," though in fact Joyce had a Dantean skill in making what was systematic appear entirely improvisatory.

WHILE HE WAS WRITING his first book, Joyce owned up to uncertainties about the works with which he hoped to make his name. Of *Dubliners* he said to his brother, "The stories seem to be indisputably well done, but, after all, perhaps many people could do them as well." His autobiographical novel awakened even more misgivings. He had composed about twenty chapters of it under the title *Stephen Hero* when he abruptly announced to Stanislaus that he was changing the book's scope and redoing the early parts because they were not well written. When he had revised them, he was still dissatisfied. He decided to change the novel completely; instead of having sixty-three chapters, as once planned, it would have only five. He would omit all its first part, in which he dealt with Stephen before he started his schooling. Instead he would begin at school. The name of his hero, Dedalus, would be changed to Daly. Stanislaus roundly objected to all these changes. "Tell me, " said his brother, "is the novel to be your puke or mine?" An even less savory metaphor of the literary art comes in *Finnegans Wake* when Shem is accused, this time by his brother, of forming an encaustic ink out of his own urine and excrement, and writing on the only foolscap available, his own body.

The decision to make the book into five chapters was to stand. Otherwise, the new version pleased him little better. On December 15, 1907, he complained to Stanislaus, in effect, "The book begins at a railway station like most college stories; there are three companions in it, and a sister who dies by way of pathos. It is the old bag of tricks and a good critic would probably show that I am still struggling even in my stories with the stock figures discarded in Europe half a century ago." Stanislaus labored to reassure him. After all, there were not three companions, he said, but five. Sister Isabel died in the book because their brother Georgie had died in actual fact. Joyce conceded, "I didn't consciously use stock figures, but I fear that my mind, when I begin to write, runs in the groove of what I've read." This statement, recorded by Stanislaus in the third person, is the best hint we have that Joyce was determined to ungroove himself, to stand literature on its head. He did just that, and evidently he intended it from the start.

These remarks intimate what revisions he now made in *A Portrait of the Artist as a Young Man*. He eliminated sister Isabel from the book. No pathos, then. The opening scene at the railway station, evidently one in which Stephen arrives at Clongowes Wood College, is also left out. Joyce did not expunge Stephen's preschool days entirely, but he condensed them into three or four pages. The picture of infant consciousness, with shapes and touches and smells all distinct if not yet understood, and with words beginning to reverberate, was so astonishing as to provide William Faulkner with the technique for the equally admirable portrait of an idiot's mind in *The Sound and the Fury*.

After this overture we might expect Joyce to take up the narrative in a sequential way, but there are telltale marks that he is not doing so. We gradually realize that Stephen has a fever, and that what we have been reading is not a history but a deliberate hodgepodge of memories of his earlier schooldays and holidays at home, rendered with the discontinuity and intensity appropriate to fever. Not until two thirds of the way through the first chapter does Joyce change the tense, and when he does so he is signaling not only Stephen's recovery from fever, but also Stephen's apprehension of his own distinctness as a recording consciousness. In *Ulysses* Joyce employs a somewhat comparable method by having Stephen recall the last two years of his life in a kind of fit, not of fever this time but of remorse.

RECENT RESEARCHES at Clongowes by Bruce Bradley have disclosed something more about Joyce's method in this first chapter of *A Portrait*. Although his own life provided him with much material, he ruthlessly departed from it where he needed. The first chapter culminates when Stephen, unjustly pandied by Father Dolan, protests to the rector. We know from Joyce's autobiographical recollections to Herbert Gorman that this incident was based upon fact. What we have not known until now is that this was by no means the only punishment Joyce received at Clongowes. The Punishment Book from that time is incomplete, but its surviving pages disclose no fewer than three other transgressions by Joyce in February and March 1889, at which time he was only seven years old. He was given two pandies in February for not bringing a book to class, six in March for muddy boots, and four the same month for "vulgar language," an offense he would repeat with growing frequency for the rest of his life. Since these three punishments were presumably meted out with just cause, Joyce ignored them and dealt only with the great injustice inflicted by Father Dolan. So Stephen became a victim, and a heroic one whose protests against unjust pandying at a Jesuit school could be a prelude to his larger protests in youth against church and state.

During the year 1907 Joyce hesitated about keeping the name of

Dedalus for his hero. If he had changed him to Daly, he could write the book on the same realistic level as his epiphanies and stories of Dublin life. Call him Dedalus, and he would have to justify the oddity of this name for an Irishman; he would be able to do so only by connecting the contemporary character with the mythical artificer of wings and labyrinth. Some years later Joyce would speak of his art as "extravagant excursions into forbidden territory," and in choosing Dedalus over Daly he made such an excursion. The result was that in the last two chapters, instead of describing only Stephen's movement outward from Ireland, Joyce represents also another movement, downward into myth. On a superficial level Stephen is dissociating himself from, on a basic level he is achieving an association with, Greek Daedalus; he is becoming himself a creature of myth. This decision led Joyce on to *Ulysses*. When asked why he had used the *Odyssey* so prominently in that book, Joyce replied, "It is my method of working." The method was established in 1907, when he threw Stephen Daly out and invited Stephen Dedalus in.

AFTER HE COMPLETED *A Portrait of the Artist as a Young Man*, Joyce had pretty well exhausted the possibilities of the artist hero. For his next book he needed a new impulse. He was beginning to find it long before he used it, in 1907 also. In that year his remarks to his brother indicate that he was situating himself in relation to Ibsen, a figure he had idolized in his youth. "Auld Aibsen always wrote like a gentleman," he said, and added that he himself would not write so. On May 16, 1907, he commented, "Life is not so simple as Ibsen represents it. Mrs. Alving, for instance, is Motherhood and so on.... It's all very fine and large, of course. If it had been written at the time of Moses, we'd now think it wonderful. But it has no importance at this age of the world. It is a remnant of heroics, too."

Joyce was very much opposed to heroics. "For me," he went on, "youth and motherhood are these two beside us." He pointed to a drunken boy of about twenty, a laborer, who had brought his mother into the trattoria where Joyce and Stanislaus were talking, while the mother was leading him home. He was hardly able to speak but was expressing his contempt for someone as well as he could. "I would like to put on paper the thousand complexities in his mind...." Joyce was obviously imagining the dense consciousness that he would give to his characters in *Ulysses*. He went on, "Absolute realism is impossible, of course. That we all know. But it's quite enough that Ibsen has omitted *all* question of finance from his thirteen dramas." Stanislaus took it upon himself to object, "Maybe there are some people who are not so preoccupied about money as you are." "Maybe so, by God," said his brother, "but I'd like to take twenty-five lessons from one of those chaps."

Given a writer so convinced that old ways would not do for him, *Ulysses* was from the start designed to break with precedents. "The task I set myself technically in writing a book from eighteen different points of view and in as many styles, all apparently unknown or undiscovered by my fellow tradesmen, that and the nature of the legend chosen would be enough to upset anyone's mental balance," Joyce (whose mental balance was not upset) confided to Harriet Weaver. In this book he set himself as many difficulties as he could, knowing that his genius would be equal to them. There is the title itself, so abrupt in its insistence on a mythical background, which, however, is never mentioned as it was in *A Portrait of the Artist*. The author's silence about it is intimidating, yet the relation to the *Odyssey* is problematic, and its intensity varies from chapter to chapter, or even from page to page. Joyce felt at liberty to deal with Homer as highhandedly as Virgil had done, keeping the basic typology but varying and omitting and adding as his own book required.

In the first episodes he realized his ambition of rendering the thousand complexities in the mind, and for the first time in literature we have all the lapses and bursts of attention, hesitations, half-recollections, distractions, sudden accesses or flaggings of sexual interest, feelings of hunger or nausea, somnolence, sneezing, thoughts about money, responses to the clouds and sunlight, along with the complications of social behavior and work.

Joyce's power is shown not only in the density of sensations, but also in the poetry and humor that infuse the principal characters and in the spirited irony of the narrator. Yet to mention these characteristics is to be put in mind of others. There is an extraordinary counterpoint between the first three chapters dealing with Stephen Dedalus and the next three dealing with Bloom. It is not only the implicit parallel of their responses at the same hours of the day, but the inner nature of the incidents that are described. So at the start of the first chapter, Buck Mulligan, holding a shaving bowl as if it was a chalice, claims to be transubstantiating the lather in it into the body and blood of Christ. Bloom makes an unspoken derisive commentary on this miracle when, at the end of the fourth chapter, he has a bowel movement and so in effect transubstantiates food into feces. Stephen ponders the way that states and churches alike have engaged in persecutions and sadistic wars, while Bloom thinks about the masochism that attracts devotees to confess and ask for punishment. A recognition of sadomasochism seems to bind the characters together, though they have not yet met. Then Stephen, as he walks along the strand and sees the debris heaped up by the waves, thinks darkly of the process of life as one from birth to decay to death. In the parallel passage in Bloom's morning, Bloom attends a funeral, and is put in mind of the process from death through decay to new birth. What we thought were two parallel lines proves to be a circle.

AS THE BOOK proceeds, the circle is itself questioned and sometimes mocked. And the reign of order gives way to the reign of chaos. The physical universe, so glancingly built up in all its multiplicity in the early episodes, begins to lose its plausibility. Space and time, once so distinct, are shaken almost out of recognition. The reader, like the narrative, is caught up in the agitations and images of the unconscious mind. Our daytime selves are almost overwhelmed by this night. Yet in all the disorder Joyce keeps as firm a hand as he had when all was order in the early chapters. At the end he gives us back our world, somewhat the worse for wear, based no longer upon primal certitude but upon affirmation in the face of doubt, as the universe hangs upon the void. And while he prided himself on his novel's physicality, and ended with a supposedly fleshly monologue, what we recognize in reading Molly Bloom's soliloquy is that she is no more fleshly than Hamlet, and that for her too the mind affects everything. The tenor of her thoughts is to acknowledge grudgingly that her husband, who recognizes her wit and musical talent and inner nature, is a better man than her lover Blazes Boylan.

She pays Bloom the ultimate compliment, one rarely heard by men from women: "I saw he understood or felt what a woman is." Penelope recognizes Ulysses not by his scar but by his imagination. Although Joyce said jocularly of her that she is the flesh that always affirms, she is not to be identified with unconsciousness, or Mother Nature, or fertility. Her amorous career has been limited. She has copulated a little, she has ruminated a great deal. Bodies do not exist without minds. Molly may not be capable of impersonal thought, as Bloom is, but she has a good sharp practical intelligence. She is in fact cerebral too—a great and unexpected tribute from a writer who in life said many unpleasant things about women.

JOYCE THOUGHT of his books as way stations on a psychic journey. His last book, *Finnegans Wake*, was an even more "extravagant excursion into forbidden territory," since it invaded the region of language itself, a region which other novelists had left inviolate. Dante obliged Italian literature to use the vernacular instead of Latin. Joyce's invention of Finnegans-Wake-ese was not intended to change literature so fundamentally, though it has had its imitators. Rather he wished to find an adequate medium to describe the world of night, the world of dream, the world of the unconscious, the world of madness. In such an atmosphere neither shapes, events, nor words could be intact. As he wrote in a letter, "One great part of every human existence is passed in a state which cannot be rendered sensible by the use of wideawake language, cutanddry grammar and goahead plot." Every person experiences this other state, but Joyce also envisaged a "universal history" in which he would represent the night world of humanity. This night world had always been associated with dark fantasies, but no one had described its work.

The principal work of the night shift of humanity—meaning its involuntary, accidental, half-conscious stages, is the perpetual de-creation and re-creation of language. The tongue slips, no one knows why. We go to sleep speaking Latin and wake up speaking French. Words break up, combine with words mysteriously imported from other languages, play tricks upon their own components. In the twinkling of a closed eye a red rose becomes a red nose, a phoenix becomes a finish, a funeral becomes a funforall.

Joyce insisted that he was working strictly in accordance with the laws of phonetics, the only difference being that he accomplished in one fictional night what might take hundreds of years to occur through gradual linguistic change. He commented to a friend, Jacques Mercanton, "I reconstruct the life of the night the way the Demiurge goes about his creation, on the basis of a mental scenario that never varies. The only difference is that I obey laws I have not chosen. And he?" (He did not continue.) When people complained that the puns he was obliged by his scenario to use were trivial he made the famous retort, "Yes, some of my means are trivial, and some are quadrivial." When they said his puns were childish, he accepted the supposed blame with alacrity. He prided himself on not having grown up. His voice, he said, had never changed in adolescence. "It's because I've not developed. If I had matured, I wouldn't be so committed to the *folie* of writing *Work in Progress*." Keeping the child in the man gave him access to the universe that adults repressed.

IN THESE WAYS Joyce radicalized literature, so that it would never recover. He reconstituted narrative, both external and internal; he changed our conception of daytime consciousness and of nighttime unconsciousness.

He made us reconsider language as a product and prompter of unconscious imaginings. These did not come to him as experiments or as innovations; he did not regard himself as an experimenter. Rather they were solutions to the literary and intellectual problems he set himself.

Yet though his determination to change the way we think about ourselves and others as well as the way we read required the most elaborate methods, Joyce always insisted—to use a Dantean pun—that his means were one thing, his meaning another. Complication was not in itself a good. "Can you not see the simplicity which is at the back of all my disguises?" he asked his wife before they eloped together. He objected to slavishness and ignobility; he thought they were fostered by conventional notions of heroism, which turned people into effigies rather than men and women. He wished them to know themselves as they really were, not as they were taught by church and state to consider themselves to be. He gave dignity to the common life that we all share.

As he wrote to his brother, "Anyway, my opinion is that if I put down a bucket into my own soul's well, sexual department, I draw up Griffith's and Ibsen's and Skeffington's and Bernard Vaughan's and St. Aloysius' and Shelley's and Renan's water along with my own. And I am going to do that in my novel (inter alia) and plank the bucket down before the shades and substances above mentioned to see how they like it: and if they don't like it I can't help them." Yet he was not impervious to those other qualities also held in common, moments of exaltation and lyricism as important as they were infrequent.

He made no personal claims. "A man of small virtue, inclined to extravagance and alcoholism" was how he described himself to the psychologist Jung. He disclaimed genius, disclaimed imagination, only asserted that when he was writing his mind was as nearly normal as possible. He wished to give his contemporaries, especially his Irish ones, a good look at themselves in his polished looking glass—as he said—but not to destroy them. They must know themselves to become freer and more alive. Shear away adhesion to conventions and shibboleths, and what have we left? More, I think, than Lear's forked animal. We have the language-making and -using capacity, we have affections and disaffections, we have also humor, through which we tumble to our likeness with others. That likeness lies in sad as well as joyful moments. The province of literature, as Joyce and his hero Stephen Dedalus both define it with unaccustomed fervor, is the external affirmation of the spirit of man, suffering and rollicking. We can shed what he called "laughtears" as his writings confront us with this spectacle.

Karl R. Popper

The 'Truth' of Karl Popper *by Jonathan Lieberson was originally published on* November 18 *and* December 2, 1982, *as a two-part review of* Postcript to the Logic of Scientific Discovery *by Karl R. Popper, edited by W.W. Bartley, III, Rowman and Littlefield;* Karl Popper *by Anthony O'Hear, Routledge and Kegan Paul;* In Pursuit of Truth: Essays on the Philosophy of Karl Popper on the Occasion of his Eightieth Birthday, *edited by Paul Levinson, Humanities. The second article was entitled* The Romantic Rationalist.

JONATHAN LIEBERSON

The 'Truth' of
Karl Popper

I

KARL POPPER IS the author of a striking treatise on scientific method, *The Logic of Scientific Discovery*, as well as the celebrated wartime tract against totalitarianism notorious for its irreverent denunciations of Plato and Hegel, *The Open Society and Its Enemies*. He is an independent, versatile, lucid, and eloquent philosopher, among the most distinguished of contemporary thinkers who have undertaken the task—once a commonplace aspiration among philosophers but currently regarded by most of them as unduly ambitious—of constructing a rational critical system that would illuminate the entire range of human experience—science, art, morality, politics.

Though he has been much honored, his reputation has always been uncertain. Some—and not only philosophers, but scientists, politicians, artists—have professed to find unsurpassable wisdom in his works, while others, no less acute, regard the work as too blunt, oversimplified, audacious, disfigured by blunders and ungenerous presentations of opponents' positions and by poor scholarship. For many, Popper's work is the last expression of the neo-Kantian critical rationalism which flourished over a century ago, before skeptical intellects rendered it obsolete.

As Anthony O'Hear explains clearly, Popper has been for many years engaged to show through argument and illustration that a pervasive way of thinking about human knowledge should be replaced by what he regards as a more rational and coherent one. What in fact goes on when we come to know a mathematical proof or the chemical composition of a substance or the name of a neighbor? What procedures do we follow, if any? And what, after all, is human knowledge? These questions have led Popper, like so many other philosophers, to the somewhat abstract concerns of the "theory of knowledge" and particularly to the analysis of the methods and aims of science and scientific knowledge, the most successful and reliable knowledge we possess.

A PROMINENT TRADITION in modern philosophy has held that all of human knowledge is founded or "based" on "experience." As Popper describes one version of this view, the mind at birth is like an empty box. The box has windows or openings—the senses—through which information passes in the form of "ideas," "atomic data," "molecular experiences." These items are pure, and "directly" perceived by us; they form the building blocks or "foundations" of all our knowledge. They "associate" with one another, giving rise to concepts ("swan," "whiteness") and to expectations ("All swans are white"), which are strengthened by repetition of conforming instances; even the most complex, abstract theories of modern physics could be shown by a patient genetic analysis to be "built up" from these humble beginnings.

It is no longer widely held that we arrive at hypotheses like "All swans are white" by "abstracting" them from elementary experiences, but nearly every modern philosophy of science has agreed with the box theory that repetition of certain instances somehow supports or confirms our hypotheses and raises the degree of rational confidence we may have for claiming them to be true.

This entire view of science, according to Popper, is misconceived. To him it suggests that scientists are engaged in an impossible "quest for certainty." For one thing, it relies on a primitive psychology that supposes that there could be an infallible foundation in experience for human knowledge. Like the pragmatist John Dewey and his own teacher, the psychologist and educational theorist Karl Bühler, Popper believes that in our quest for knowledge there are simply no "secure" starting points that do not have presuppositions; such starting points can be found neither in a priori dogma nor in sense experience: we are, he says, never in a situation prior to all theorizing. Whenever we see or smell or listen, or indeed think at all, we are in a determinate situation comprising prior interests, theories, needs, aims, expectations; the "pure" elementary data of the box theory are figments plucked out of thin air.

Secondly, Popper thinks that induction is mythical. No one has encountered or inspected all possible polar bears, but judging from the sample we have come across, can't we rationally claim that most polar bears are white? And can't this claim—while of course it cannot ever amount to a proof—be strengthened by seeing more white polar bears? Do we not know generalizations (such as "Most polar bears are white") based on observed instances that are extrapolated to cover unobserved instances in the past and future? And is it not perverse to deny that we rely constantly, in science and in daily life, upon propositions for which the available evidence is not logically conclusive? And perverse to deny that such nondemonstrative evidence can be graded for its probative force? Indeed, don't men's lives depend upon such discrimination in the law?

We have already seen that Popper denies that we generalize from "sensations" or pure "elementary experiences" to the truth of hypotheses like "All swans are white." If by "induction" he meant merely this, most contemporary philosophers would agree with him; for there are no "pure" sensations, and even if there were, they couldn't entail the truth or falsity of a hypothesis. But Popper rejects "induction" in a second sense as well: he denies that we can rationally generalize from any number of *statements* such as "This is a white swan" to claims about the truth or probability of hypotheses such as "All swans are white." Like David Hume, Popper argues that induction (in this latter sense) is not a logically reputable inference: a hundred or a million observed white polar bears provide no decisive reasons for thinking that all polar bears are white; good reasons could only be found by inspecting all polar bears that have existed, exist, or will exist and concluding that each of them is white. There is no "justification" of induction, for all attempted ones end up in an infinite regress or in some a priori dogma. We cannot be sure the future will resemble the past. No matter how many times you have witnessed the rising of the sun, you are not entitled to assume rationally that it will, or even probably will, rise tomorrow; it might explode tonight, or melt, or, for that matter, burst into song. This much can be found in Hume; but unlike Hume, Popper does not claim that induction must therefore be a nonrational habit or custom. He argues the startling and provocative position that induction does not exist and has never been used. We do follow something like a "method" in acquiring knowledge, he says, but it is quite different from induction.

POPPER IS ESPECIALLY concerned to point out the flaws of the box theory and the belief in induction in the case of science. No scientific theory, he claims, not even the greatest of them, Newton's universal mechanics, has ever been "established" or "verified": after all, if Newton's theory was certain or "inductively proved," how could it have been overthrown and superseded by Einstein's theory of relativity? The simple fact, says Popper, is that we cannot "justify" a claim to the truth of *any* empirical hypothesis. Even trite statements like "This is a glass of water" or "This is a polar bear" are unverifiable; indeed, according to Popper, *no positive reasons* can be given for their truth.

Why is this so? The reason is that the words that appear in them, such as "glass" or "water," are in Popper's view "universals"—they depend on definitions that apply to all glasses and all water—and "cannot be correlated with any specific sense-experience. (An 'immediate experience' is *only once* 'immediately given'; it is unique)."[1] Moreover, these universal terms denote "lawlike behavior" on the part of the objects they describe, and so "transcend experience": to call something a bear, for example, implies many things that go far beyond what we actually observe, e.g., that it will die, that it will not grow wings, that it was created through sexual reproduction. For this reason, ordinary "observation" statements like "This is a bear" are "soaked in theory" and possess no privileged status as "final" or "ultimate" or as "more certain" than other statements.

Indeed, according to Popper, their epistemic status is no different from that of universal statements like "All polar bears are white," although they are logically simpler. Nevertheless, even though the problem of showing *one* single object to be a polar bear is logically as difficult as showing that all are, Popper asserts that the simpler statements of observation are "easier to test" and might be more likely to be agreed on than other statements. But this is not because experience proves them; as he frankly acknowledges, experience can cause, or "motivate," us to "accept" or "reject" such statements, but this "acceptance" or "rejection" is logically a "free decision" or "convention." Nothing in life or logic compels us to accept it. So, in effect, according to Popper's view, *all* empirical hypotheses—whether that copper conducts electricity or that this is a pencil—are "conjectural" in the radical sense that we shall never be able to have rational confidence that they are true, let alone "know" them for certain or with probability. Whatever knowledge we have is *permanently* "fallible" and "conjectural," although most of us would agree to accept some conjectures as more credible than others.

But if this is so, how can we go about trying to secure human knowledge? Popper thinks he has a more rational and coherent answer than "inductivism." We cannot justify a claim that a hypothesis is true, but we can

---

[1] Karl Popper, *The Logic of Scientific Discovery* (Basic Books, 1959), p. 95.

retain both rationality and the empiricist's demand that our knowledge be supported by observation. For while no number of white polar bears could establish or verify the claims that all are white, nevertheless a single polar bear that is *not* white can *falsify* the hypothesis. This inference, he says, is rational (unlike induction) and, moreover, is "based" upon observation—for people might come to "agree" that a particular black polar bear exists.

POPPER'S DESCRIPTION of the "logic" of the natural and social sciences rests upon this logical insight. We need not be disturbed by the loss of induction and the foundations of the box theory, he says: if we wish to seek the truth, then the only rational way of doing so is to do it indirectly. We cannot give any positive reasons for holding our theories to be true or probable. But we can replace justification—the practice of producing valid reasons in favor of the truth of our theories—by rational criticism—the practice of producing valid reasons against them. In science, instead of trying to show how right we are, we should forget about starting points and try to *improve* our current stock of hypotheses, whatever its source. First of all, we should make our ideas logically falsifiable or capable of being criticized. This is something like an intellectual duty of the scientist—a duty, Popper claims, that was not fulfilled by those thinkers like Freud and some followers of Marx who claimed to be "scientific" and yet failed to lay down in advance the conditions under which they would give up such theories as that all dreams are "wish-fulfillments" or that the collapse of capitalism will occur. Secondly, we should systematically *search for errors* in our theories. We should jump to bold conclusions and then ruthlessly try to overthrow them by tests; this is the rational way by which we might, with luck, learn from our mistakes and draw nearer to the truth.

We will, of course, never be able to be sure we have found the truth. All that we will be able to do is to claim that our theories have *so far* not been falsified by severe tests, that they have withstood our efforts to overthrow them. In other words, the best we can hope for is that we find not positive but critical reasons for thinking that our ideas are not true but "preferable" to other theories in the *search* for truth. Popper believes that it is on the basis of such critical reasons that we are convinced, for example, that the Copernican model of the solar system has more truth to it than, say, Aristotle's: our reasons for this conviction, he writes,

> consist in *the story of the critical discussion*, including the critical evaluation of observations, of all the theories of the solar system since Anaximander, not overlooking Heraclitus' hypothesis that a new sun was born every day,

or the cosmologies of Democritus, Plato, Aristotle, Aristarchus, and Ptolemy. It was not so much the accumulation of observations by Tycho as the critical rejection of many conjectures by Kepler, Descartes, and others, culminating in Newton's mechanics and its subsequent critical examination, which ultimately persuaded everybody that a great step had been made towards the truth. This persuasion, this belief, this preference, is reasonable because it is based upon the result of the present state of critical discussion; and a preference for a theory may be called "reasonable" if it is arguable, and if it withstands *searching critical argument*—ingenious attempts to show it is not true, or not nearer to the truth than its competitors. [2]

THIS PICTURE OF SCIENCE as a matter of conjectures and refutations has not been without critics of its own. Falsification as a logical technique among others in science was known to some medieval writers and was stressed at the beginning of our century by the American pragmatist C. S. Peirce. But critics complain that Popper not only places too stringent demands on scientists in making their hypotheses falsifiable, but vastly exaggerates the role of falsification in scientific inquiry. He requires that scientists formulate their ideas so that potentially refuting instances be specified *in advance* of testing them; and further, that should the theory be contradicted by results of tests, it should not be rescued by ad hoc hypotheses that do nothing more than account for discrepancies and make no new predictions.

But critics of Popper, such as O'Hear and T.S. Kuhn, have suggested that many great theories in science, such as Newton's theory of universal gravitation, were not falsifiable in this sense. For one thing, the interpreters of these theories frequently referred to such "ideal" or "limiting" conceptions as "frictionless surfaces," and "perfectly rigid bodies," which are only joined to the materials of actual experiments through long chains of reasoning and subsidiary hypotheses, so that the status of experimental evidence as confirming or refuting such theories is inherently vague. The adverse outcome of tests need not be taken as falsifying them, but rather as clarifying their scope of application.

Secondly, most important scientific theories are flexible systems of assumptions compatible with a variety of specific formulations: Newton's theory, for example, does not predict observational results unless it is joined with a large number of other assumptions, themselves modifiable; we cannot therefore regard a false prediction as decisively overthrowing the *theory*—as opposed to one of these auxiliary assumptions. If the planet

[2] *Realism and the Aim of Science*, p. 59.

Jupiter were tomorrow to assume a square orbit, we most likely would not condemn Newtonian theory before postulating that some unusual interfering force created the deviation from Jupiter's predicted orbit.

Finally, critics say that the historical behavior of scientists has rarely conformed to Popper's prescribed method; when theories have gotten into trouble—as Newton's "celestial mechanics" did on more than one occasion—scientists have often invoked ad hoc hypotheses to rescue them. As O'Hear notes, the physicist Pauli "postulated the existence of the neutrino simply to preserve energy conservation in the theory of radioactive nuclear disintegration long before any test was envisaged or there was any theoretical basis for it."

WAS IT NECESSARILY "wrong" or "irrational" for scientists to behave this way? Such thinkers as Kuhn and Popper's close colleague, the late Imre Lakatos, have claimed it was not: in their view, Popper incorrectly focuses upon the testing of individual theories, whereas in fact what is critical in science is the development of some fundamental insight or "paradigm"— that all things are composed of atoms, that light is a wave phenomenon. The improved expression of such an insight in a *series* of theories is what constitutes most scientific research. Such theories are rarely thought by scientists to be the whole truth in any case—they are called "promising" or "worthy of attention"—so that to try to refute them may be gratuitous.[3]

What testing accomplishes, these writers claim, is to assist us in locating the shortcomings of our ideas and to help us to improve them, so that it may be perfectly "rational" for scientists occasionally to dogmatically set aside apparent falsifications as "anomalies." If they did not, the merits of their ideas might never be discovered. Popper's exclusive stress on negative arguments, "counterexamples," and destructive criticism would eliminate, in practice, both the leniency and the useful dogmatism that characterize science. Popper's most ferocious critics, such as his one-time disciple Paul K. Feyerabend, go much further. They not only argue that most celebrated scientific theories have never been "falsifiable" or "falsified" in the sense Popper prescribes. They also insist that his "criterion" of falsifiability demarcating science from nonscience is just a logical toy, one more instance of the depressing attempt on the part of so-called philosophers of science to

---

3 See, for example, the papers of Kuhn and Lakatos in *Criticism and the Growth of Knowledge*, edited by Imre Lakatos and Alan Musgrave (Cambridge University Press, 1970).

squeeze and warp the teeming variety of scientific attitudes and inquiries—for example, the manner in which they appraise evidence—into severe logical calculi and formal "rules."[4]

What is Popper's response to these criticisms? As we shall see in a second article, he has altered few of the philosophical tenets he first formulated in his twenties and thirties, and has instead vigorously redefended his position and prodigiously extended and generalized his views in a metaphysical world picture unexpected from a philosopher widely thought to confine himself to the narrow ambit of epistemology and the logic of science.

4 Paul K. Feyerabend, *Against Method* (New Left Books/Schocken, 1978).

II

APART FROM HIS celebrated writings on the "open society" and its enemies, Karl Popper is chiefly known as a logician of science who has denied that science employs induction, and who has claimed that what demarcates science from nonscience, in particular metaphysics, is that scientists seek the truth by vigorously trying to falsify their theories. This has become one of the most celebrated and controversial views of science to have been put forward during this century. Earlier I noted that vigorous objections have been raised to Popper's view, most recently in the book under review by Anthony O'Hear, and, as we shall see, there are strong reasons for questioning Popper's thesis.

First, however, a common misunderstanding of Popper's work should be clarified. His preoccupation with the logic of scientific method and his early association with some members of the Vienna Circle have frequently led readers to link him with logical positivism and a contempt for metaphysics. What is less well known, and perhaps surprising, however, is that Popper has devoted a number of years to outlining a metaphysics of his own, one drawing on evolutionary theory, that depicts the continuity of method between men and other organisms and more generally articulating the place of man and his intellectual products in nature. This vision, he reminds us, is not a scientific theory itself: it is not falsifiable. Popper regards his own "metaphysical" theory and his evolutionary epistemology as "conjectural" in character: while such conjectures are not empirically testable, he claims, they may, like other nontestable and nondemonstrable theories, such as realism and idealism, be helpful to us. Furthermore, they might be arguable.

WHAT IS THIS "vision"? Popper conjectures that "what is true in logic is true in psychology." Induction is logically invalid, does not "exist" in logic and so no one (and no animal) has ever performed one. All organisms, according to Popper's phrase, "from the amoeba to Einstein," are problem solvers who use the method of trial and error. In nature, as Darwin taught, the plural forms of life evolve from a small number of simple forms by virtue of the mechanisms of heredity, variation through mutation, and natural selection. Of course, the lower organisms lack language and cannot formulate their hypotheses and guesses, but even they do something similar to what we do: they carry out "trial" solutions to problems of adaptation and adjustment, and the "errors" in these trials are eliminated by natural selection. As we solve problems of bridge building or scientific explanation, then, so spiders "solve" problems of where to build their webs and bacteria "solve" problems of overcoming antibiotics. Most organisms other than man *incorporate* the "solutions" to the problems confronted by their predecessors in their very anatomical design; they die off when these solutions are no longer successful.

With man, according to Popper's "metaphysical" conjecture, things are different. Our invention and use of language creates a new "world," an "ontologically distinct" realm, which he calls "World 3" or the "third world." He thinks that it exists alongside the "first" world of material objects like glasses and polar bears—objects for whose existence, as we have seen, he cannot advance any decisive *empirical* reasons, only a "metaphysical" faith—and the "second" world of purely mental states, feelings, emotions, dispositions to act. The third world is the world of our intellectual products, the world of documented theories, problems, errors, standards, rules, values, the world of "objective knowledge"—knowledge that is an *object*, not (as the old "subjectivist" theory held) something that is "in" you or me, an expression of some mental state like certainty or "justified true belief."

This third world is composed of abstract entities—the discoveries of William Harvey, of Hilbert and Planck and Carnot, the imaginative worlds created by Pope and Swift and Flaubert; it contains the things we argue *about* when we discuss the truth of a prediction about money markets or the future of a political party. It contains the *content*, for example, of the passage in John 6 that Luther and Zwingli argued over, a content that was not identical with either the spoken or the written words used by these men or with their subjective states, a content that is not "subjective knowledge" but a public object. The third world is historical, for the ideas of men have arisen in time; it is also to a considerable degree autonomous, for it contains not only the ideas that men have proposed, but also their inter-relationships and unintended consequences. For example, the existence of prime numbers was surely not intended by whoever invented the natural numbers. Indeed, the third world even contains logical truths *about* these unintended products, truths, as Popper says, we can do nothing about, such as the nonexistence of a greatest prime number.

The third world is deeply implicated in the themes of Popper's mature philosophy: for example, he uses it to show that violence is not necessary. Unlike animals, we need not die if our theories are refuted, for theories are in the third world, not in our organisms or genetic system. In the democratic and pluralistic "open society" Popper cherishes, criticism of policies and institutions (which are World 3 objects) must therefore be protected and encouraged, and governments can be revised or replaced through critical discussion and without bloodshed, rather as hypotheses are replaced in science. This political system—as contrasted with systems that rely upon uncritical "nonfalsifiable," utopian, revolutionary, "total" blueprints for maintenance or change of the political order—is for Popper the embodiment of critical reason in human affairs.

THE THIRD WORLD is even invoked in Popper's philosophy of art. Just as we must give up the "subjectivist" view that human knowledge is an expression of some interior state, we must resist the theory that art is "self-expression," an overflowing of the contents of the mind onto a medium, paper or canvas or marble, and the language of aesthetic criticism—of "authenticity," "integrity," "sincerity"—that goes with it. All great art, Popper says, is anchored in the third world, in inherited problems and stylistic traditions. "Subjective" artists like Beethoven or Wagner did not regard their art as a means of self-transcendence but as the expression of something "inner" or "private": the attitude of "objective" artists like Bach, on the other hand, conforms to the principle that "the best work in science or in the arts or humanities is done when we forget about ourselves, and concentrate on World 3 issues as much as we possibly can."[1]

But more than this, the third world is connected with Popper's view of the self and human freedom: he believes that our very minds and selves have come into existence in the evolutionary process because of the inven-

---

[1] Pons Elders, editor, *Reflexive Water: The Basic Concerns of Mankind* (London, 1974), pp. 103–104 (debate between Sir Karl Popper and Sir John Eccles).

tion of language: we are self-conscious because we have learned language, and our minds are the evolutionary products or vehicles which enable us to grasp the abstract World 3. The recently published *Postscript to The Logic of Scientific Discovery* contains Popper's most ambitious statement of a metaphysics of the universe.[2] Like his theory of the three worlds, which it deepens and refines, this cosmological work defends metaphysical realism against idealism and subjectivism. One long volume of it argues against the intrusion of subjectivism in quantum mechanics. Many paradoxes in the theory of quantum mechanics derive, according to Popper, from the so-called "Copenhagen" interpretation of it promoted by Niels Bohr and his followers. This view holds that Heisenberg's celebrated "uncertainty relations," which follow from the theory, actually set "limits" to our knowledge in the realm of atomic physics because they imply that measurements of an elementary particle (such as an electron) "disturb" it, or "interfere" with it, thus making the measurement "dependent" on the "observer," and rendering objective knowledge of matter impossible.

Popper rejects this view as a species of "subjectivism" and argues that it is based not only on an arrogant suggestion that quantum theory is the last word in atomic theory, but also on a misunderstanding of the essentially statistical character of the theory. According to him, quantum theory is just like any other statistical (but objective) theory in physics: the "uncertainty relations" have nothing more to do with "uncertainty" or "limits of our knowledge" than any other statistical predictions. They show, if anything, the limitations of a probabilistic theory like quantum theory.

But Popper does not contest the "Copenhagen" view of quantum theory as implying that nature is "indeterministic." Indeed, he criticizes several forms of "scientific" determinism—the idea that if we know the present state of the world, all physical events, whether in the past or in the future, can be predicted (or retrodicted) with any desired degree of precision, including all the movements of human beings. He advances an array of logical arguments, some of them rather crude but others ingenious, against this famous principle. But his most passionately argued attack on it is based on considerations of human creativity and freedom. It is absurd, he writes, to suppose that "billions of years ago, the elementary particles of World 1 contained the poetry of Homer, the philosophy of Plato, and the

---

[2] The *Postscript* was largely written some twenty-five years ago as a sequel to *The Logic of Scientific Discovery*, but has only just been published.

symphonies of Beethoven as a seed contains a plant," or that a physicist, by studying the bodies of Mozart and Brahms with meticulous care, could write scores which were not actually written by them, but which they could have written if, say, their diet had been different.

ON POPPER'S OWN METAPHYSICAL VIEW the universe is "open": it has "pockets" of causality—ranges of events that are fully determined—but also realms that are unpredictable. One important reason for this conclusion, he says, is that human beings have introduced, via World 3, completely novel ideas into the universe, ideas which through human action have made a genuine difference to the course of events. He asks us, however, to distinguish carefully: it is one thing to say that determinism in one or another version is false; it is another to ensure the possibility of human freedom. The denial of determinism is not sufficient to make room for human freedom or creativity, he says, for what "we want to understand is not only how we may act *unpredictably and in a chancelike fashion*, but how can we act *deliberately and rationally*," how things like plans, purposes, arguments, and decisions can actually bring about modifications in the world. To do so, he continues, we need the extra notion that the world of particles and other material objects is *incomplete*, that it can be influenced by Worlds 2 and 3 and interact with them.

Popper's reflections on quantum theory and indeterminism are woven together in a remarkable "Metaphysical Epilogue," which adumbrates what he calls a "new and promising way of looking at the physical cosmos," a piece of "speculative physics" which, like other research programs in the history of science—like atomism or the unified field theory—is not itself empirically testable, but which might assist scientists in coming up with fruitful ideas. As he explains his "dream program," it is intended to preserve elements of the two views that created a schism in twentieth-century physics: the indeterminism of quantum theory on the one hand, and on the other the aspiration of Einstein and the rest to construct a "unified field theory" in which the opposition between matter and "field" (say, of force or energy) could be superseded and particles explained as "produced" by properties of fields or interactions between them.

In one interpretation of Einstein's view, matter was a "form" of electrical energy. Popper also seeks a unified field theory, but of a more ambitious variety. For him, the properties of matter—as well as its creation or destruction—might be explained as arising from fields of what he calls "propensities." But whereas earlier theories sought to explain no more than the disposition or propensity of particles to *behave* this way or that, Popper thinks that *all* physical properties of the world are propensities. Particles are just propensities to "realize" this or that behavior. But at the same time they are the result, or "actualization," of *other* propensities that make up the physical world. These propensities or possibilities, moreover, are real, as real as the gravitational forces that lock the planets of the solar system in their orbits, although some of them are unpredictable, "open." Popper only sketches his program, but he claims, or hopes, that if taken up by others, it will help resolve many problems: the metaphysical problems of matter and change and space and causation, but also the major difficulties that have been bedeviling quantum mechanics since its inception.

IF NOTHING ELSE, the *Postscript* will remind readers that Popper differs radically from those logical positivists with whom he is still sometimes identified, who held that nontestable cosmological speculation of this kind is a form of superstition or chicanery, if not simply nonsensical. The emphasis placed in these books on human creativity and the constant interaction of the three worlds should also highlight the oddity of O'Hear's criticism, suitably accompanied by quotations from Lukács, that Popper's third world is an untenable "reification" of language and criticism and has an "alienating quality," encouraging in us the idea that human institutions and human knowledge are governed by "inhuman laws."[3]

O'Hear fails adequately to convey the generosity and sweep of Popper's ideas—ideas which must have appealed powerfully to the young English philosophers he encountered when, returning to Europe from New Zealand (where he spent the war years), he first taught at the London

3 It should lead us to reexamine the related criticisms, found in the dark pages of the Frankfurt school, in Adorno and Habermas among others, that Popper is a "positivist," not perhaps a logical positivist, but someone who is hostile to theory and speculation, who believes in the "cognitive monopoly" of science and its supreme authority in matters of fact, or that rationality and knowledge are to be identified with scientific rationality and scientific knowledge, that all cognitively respectable investigations, whether in the social or the natural realm, should follow a specific "scientific methodology," and that technological control is the key to scientific success. In fact, Popper is committed to none of these views. On the question of the authority, exactitude, and reliability of science, compare Popper's remarks in his *Realism and the Aim of Science*: "I see science very differently. As to its authority, or confirmation, or probability, I believe that it is nil; it is all guesswork." Or: "I hold that science has no certainty, no rational reliability, no validity, no authority. "

School of Economics students who had been starved on a diet of logical analysis and problems of sense perception. O'Hear's book is a dry catalog of the errors in Popper and does not communicate the heat of the vision that turned a good number of these students into disciples and evangelists, into members of a "Popperian" school, bound to their master by undeviating loyalty (and subject to expulsion if remiss in this respect), convinced that he had struck a serious alternative to certain fundamental beliefs (like induction) woven into the texture of human thought.

Still, O'Hear largely succeeds in reinforcing the widespread impression that something is deeply amiss in Popper's philosophy of science. According to him, what is wrong is that Popper fails to appreciate how firmly entrenched induction is in our ways of thinking and acting; scientists "need" induction in order to perform actions—such as choosing between competing scientific theories—that arise in ordinary scientific research. And in any case, he continues, Popper himself cannot do without induction. For if we take him at his word, he is left with no resources for establishing reasons for rational choices between theories in science, or for supposing his method is in fact a means toward the goal of science, indeed with no good reasons for our "embarking on the scientific adventure" as he defines it. Such reasons, O'Hear assumes, could only arise from the admission of some determinate link between failed refutations, or "corroboration," on the one hand and truth on the other. When the full implications of Popper's rejection of induction are digested, we see that he is in fact committed to a vicious skepticism—a skepticism, says O'Hear, that Popper tries again and again to escape, sometimes by coming perilously close to admitting to the existence of induction after all.

THIS IS TRUE as far as it goes, but it does not go far enough. It does not really take Popper seriously enough. He is, as he writes, not interested in doing justice to "inductive intuitions"; he states again and again that induction is a myth; he is trying to *replace* our "inductive intuitions" with a different view of human knowledge and scientific method that dispenses with induction entirely. The problem is not just that Popper's alternative may offend common sense and the requirements of action, and that his argument would be better off if an element of induction were admitted into it. It is that he has not offered a coherent alternative at all. For as he describes science, it is self-defeating to engage in it: if you adopt his description of the aim of science as the truth, it is pointless to pursue his method of conjectures and refutations, for he denies they can arrive at any rational claim to the truth; on the other hand, if you endorse his method, the aim of science, astonishingly enough, has no legitimate connection with scientific research. This is not, perhaps, a logical inconsistency in his thought, but it amounts to something like a "practical" one.

One way of illustrating this difficulty focuses upon the role of testing in Popper's scientific method. For him, arriving at hypotheses—whether about the symptoms of a disease or voting patterns or astronomy—is a matter that is not susceptible to logical analysis; hypotheses are "free creations," and indeed it does not matter much where they come from. What matters is the "severe" critical controls that are applied to them in the stage of testing. It is these sober efforts that make science rational and distinguish it from pure speculation. They explain, for example, why we in some sense "know" that iron is heavier than water or that air has pressure, and why, on the other hand, we no longer take seriously the views that music has magnetic effects or that disease is a function of a person's "humoral economy." Scientists want to contribute to the "growth of knowledge," by which Popper means not just an aimless proliferation of hypotheses, but the critically controlled transformation of what we currently hold or take for granted—what he calls "background knowledge"—into a new body of conjectures which we hope might be nearer to the truth. Choice on the part of scientists in selecting theories to add to, or subtract from, "background knowledge" is therefore at the heart of Popper's concerns; presumably, these choices can be rational because they are informed by the results of testing and criticism. As he has written, "It is the *growth* of our knowledge, our way of choosing between theories, in a certain problem situation, which makes science rational."[4]

BUT WHAT EXACTLY do the critical controls amount to, according to Popper's noninductive view? If we acknowledge, as he insists we should, that there is no *proof* that we will find the truth, how can they even assist us in searching for the truth? The answer is that they could not amount to very much, since Popper has, in effect, pulled the rug from under our feet. Our tests, he says, can provide no positive reasons for the truth of any of our empirical hypotheses. But neither can they give us worthwhile negative or "critical" reasons: they are simply a report of failed attempts to falsify our ideas and make no reference to how these theories might fare in the future. In nei-

4 Karl Popper, *Conjectures and Refutations: The Growth of Scientific Knowledge* (Harper and Row, 1963), p. 248.

ther case can testing—the "rational" element in science—bear upon considerations pertaining to our aim of truth or even something like the truth.

Why, then, should scientists bother to test their hypotheses at all? Why should they, if such tests could never *in principle* provide them with any good reasons for thinking their hypotheses true? Would it not in fact follow that any hypothesis would be *as conjectural after any amount of testing is over* as it was before testing began? And if this is so, what critical controls could govern the so-called "growth of knowledge"—the alteration of the existing or "background" knowledge we currently accept in the search for truth? What considerations could possibly control this alteration? Since background knowledge is "taken for granted" and used to direct and guide future scientific inquiry, how could we ever find good reasons for introducing new hypotheses into background knowledge, and then taking them "for granted"? And if there is no answer to this question, what significant reasons could there possibly be for ever assuming that we have altered background knowledge in a manner favorable to the search for truth? At least Popper is consistent when he remarks that in his own view the success he happens to believe science has enjoyed in the past is "miraculously improbable, and therefore inexplicable."[5]

It might be said, however, that Popper does provide something like critical checks in science insofar as our tests, while they cannot help us in detecting the truth, might yet knock out or falsify many of our hypotheses. After all, finding a black polar bear *does* refute "All polar bears are white."

But even this modest claim is undermined by Popper's own view, for the same difficulty about testing we just examined breaks out when we consider the statements that falsify theories. It is formally correct to say that the statement "This is a black polar bear" falsifies "All polar bears are white." But then the latter statement also falsifies the former; logically, all we know is that the two clash. The issue turns on the claim that we have *found* a black polar bear. After seeing such a bear, most of us would no doubt say that our experiences have given us some reason for making such a claim.

BUT AS I EXPLAINED earlier, Popper does not hold this view. For him, "This is a black polar bear" is impossible to justify; it implies a vast number of testable consequences that "transcend" all observational experience. The

---

[5] Karl Popper, *Objective Knowledge: An Evolutionary Approach* (Oxford University Press, 1972), p. 28.

word "bear" is a construction intended to apply to all bears; it is not derived from direct experience. While the "acceptance" of its use might be caused or "motivated" by experience, it cannot be justified by it—"no more than by thumping the table."[6] According to Popper, all we can do with any such statement is to "decide" whether to "agree" to accept it: "from a logical point of view, the testing of a theory depends upon basic statements whose acceptance or rejection, in its turn, depends upon our *decisions*. Thus it is *decisions* which settle the fate of theories."[7] And these decisions are "free," ungrounded, and ungroundable in any decisive positive or negative reasons. "The acceptance of a refutation is nearly as risky as the tentative adoption of a hypothesis: it is the acceptance of a conjecture."[8]

But we are once more in a bind: if what Popper says is true, if even banal elementary statements of observation like "This is a glass" are unjustifiable, so that experience provides *no good reasons* for claiming them to be true, why should scientists make observations at all? Especially if they are interested in the *truths* that falsify hypotheses? How *could* rejection of theories as "falsified" be critically controlled on the basis of these "free decisions"?

It would seem, then, that the rational element in science—its critical controls and "our way of choosing between theories"—is for Popper entirely detached from the aim of finding the truth about the universe. This is the result of a conflict of doctrines within Popper's own view. If you seek the truth, the ban on induction prevents testing from making any determinate impact on your decisions to alter your "background knowledge" in the search for truth. From the point of view of seeking truth, you might as well just make guesses and not bother to test these guesses, since testing can in principle give you no good reasons for thinking you are making progress. On the other hand, if you adopt the *method* prescribed by Popper, you might as well give up the search for truth. If you adopt both Popper's aim and his method, then in practice not only are the "trials" or hypotheses in science "free creations" but so also are the guesses that "weed out errors"— so that all of science consists in "trials." But if this is so, then what of the "critical discussion" of science from Heraclitus to Einstein that Popper claims persuaded people that a "great step had been taken toward the truth"? Is this critical discussion distinguishable from a pointless multiplication or proliferation of guesses, a self-defeating enterprise checked only

---

6 *The Logic of Scientific Discovery*, p. 105.
7 *The Logic of Scientific Discovery*, p. 108.
8 Karl Popper, *Unended Quest: An Intellectual Autobiography* (Open Court, 1976), p. 99.

by the one thing we can be sure of, the inspection of logical relationships between statements?

WHILE POPPER CAN be admired for his stress on the critical nature of tests in science, and for his rejection of crude empiricist psychologies and the search for secure foundations of human knowledge, he has not succeeded in returning satisfactory answers to these simple questions.[9] Insofar as he has addressed them at all,[10] his response is this: testing is an important critical control on our search for truth because while it is true that failed refutation, or "corroboration," is not a measure or indicator of truth it does indicate how the truth *appears* to us in light of the present discussion; moreover, corroboration —whether of a theory like Newton's or of a statement like "This is a glass of water"—does provide good reasons not for the truth of these hypotheses, but for a *preference* for one of them in the *search* for truth. It provides "logically inconclusive reasons," that is to say, "for *conjecturing* that it is the most truthlike of the hypotheses competing at the time."[11] And this "conjecture" or "preference" is a "guess" of a higher order or level, a "metaconjecture" that the hypothesis is truthlike or that "further tests will not lead to any deviating results."[12]

But this solves precisely nothing. To say that we "prefer" "All polar bears are white" in the search for truth to "Some polar bears are white and some are black" in light of the present discussion just repeats what we already know, that we have not yet "decided" that we have found any black polar bears, and, contrary to Popper, does not provide any good reasons even for guessing that it is "the most truthlike of the hypotheses competing" at the present time.

9 Nor has his most scrupulous and diligent foot soldier. *In Pursuit of Truth*, a collection of essays in honor of Popper's eightieth birthday, contains, together with many sugary and obsequious expressions of praise from far-flung sources (including Isaac Asimov and Helmut Schmidt), a contribution by David Miller which purports to "refute" the major "falsifications of falsificationism." But, as he admits, the essay contains little that is not found in Popper. For the most part, it masterfully disposes (as does Popper) of relatively unimportant objections to falsificationism, and sidesteps the fundamental issues of why, on Popper's paradoxical view of science and its aims, we should bother to start, or stop, testing our hypotheses. Miller triumphantly ends his essay with the standard Popperian "challenge" to critics who do not "see" what he is trying to do, or "understand" him, to try to be more careful and to formulate their criticisms more clearly.

10 *Objective Knowledge*, Appendix 2.

11 *Objective Knowledge*, p. 84.

12 P. A. Schilpp, editor, *The Philosophy of Karl Popper* (Open Court, 1974), p. 1,114.

But more disturbing than this, if induction really does not exist—if we cannot rationally rely on inconclusive evidence for our beliefs—*how could* the results of testing provide any good reasons for a "higher-order conjecture"? How could testing provide good reasons for the conjecture that *testing* the proposition "All polar bears are white" will not lead to its falsification in the future? The truth or falsity of this conjecture is given no rational warrant by any of the tests we have performed so far, so why couldn't we have simply made this higher-order guess prior to testing? Why should we test a guess just in order to advance it as a guess all over again? Popper suggests, moreover, that it is rational to act on a well-tested hypothesis or conjecture—to use it—not because there are good reasons for thinking it true but because there are no reasons for supposing it is not true. But this is a desperate move. There are, on Popper's skeptical premises, all kinds of reasons for doubting any hypothesis. Why should we accept the higher-order conjecture? Why should we not test it in turn?

Popper, in short, claims that there are no good reasons for thinking a theory is true, but that there are nevertheless good "critical" reasons for conjecturing it to be true; but these critical reasons are of no account unless we have some reason for believing that we are thereby getting closer to the truth, and Popper fails to supply us with a good reason for doing so. His "preference" theory covers up with a cloud of words the problem of how testing serves any determinate and rational purpose in his scientific method. The problem is unaffected. That it remains so hints at difficulties relevant not only to his philosophy of science but more generally to his theory of knowledge as a whole, and even to some of his justifications of the open society as a social order designed to promote unfettered criticism, criticism that will encourage in its turn the growth of knowledge and better, more informed decisions concerning the "piecemeal social engineering" that is intended to improve the lot of the citizenry. Why should there be unlimited criticism of this kind if the results are as pointless as we have suggested? At the very least, it is impossible to accept Popper's grotesquely immodest claim to have completed the solution of the philosophical problem "whose more fundamental half was already solved by Hume," a problem he describes "with a little generosity" as "the problem of human knowledge."[13]

POPPER'S PHILOSOPHY OF SCIENCE is profoundly ambiguous: it is, he says, "empirical," but it is left unclear why scientists should consult experience.

---

[13] Schilpp, *The Philosophy of Karl Popper*, p. 1,014.

It is called "fallibilism," in which we "learn from our mistakes," but it is really an ill-concealed form of skepticism. It claims to surrender the quest for certainty, but it is precisely the standards of this quest—that if one is not *certain* of a proposition, one can never be rationally justified in claiming it to be true—that underlie Popper's rejection of induction (and the numerous doctrines that stem from this rejection). He asks scientists to search for new facts, new theories, new truths—but then adds that no matter how hard they search, all they will ever be able to know will be as risky when they are finished investigating it as it was when they began, and that the only things that can be other than "daring" guesses[14] are empty logical truths. This is not abandoning the straitjacket of the quest for certainty but turning it inside out.

By a queer transition, Popper calls his skeptical view "critical rationalism" and "objectivism." But it is small wonder that the most consistent of "Popperians" have been precisely those lapsed disciples of his, "anarchists" and "subjectivists" like Paul K. Feyerabend, who have persuaded themselves that psychological compulsions, habits, and whims are the actual, if well-nigh universally unacknowledged, motors of scientific change—an irrationalism similar to that which Popper deplored in Hume—and that science neither follows bodiless formulae nor yields genuine knowledge. *Les extrêmes se touchent*: as so often in the history of ideas, a formal "arch-objectivist" view offering precious little guidance to actual activities but trumpeting abstract formal principles leads through superficially persuasive steps of reasoning to a doctrine of "anything goes."

Popper is led to these difficulties by a combination of doctrines implausible in themselves and even less plausible in combination. He wrote his first book in reaction to the view that the empirical sciences are "reducible" to our sense experiences, and rightly held that this view hardly did justice to objective science. But he jumped to the other extreme, and adopted a largely formal approach to the theory of scientific knowledge. From this approach he developed his main views about the priority of logic over psychology, the rejection of induction on logical grounds, and the discovery of the method of conjectures and refutations as the best, because most "rational," scientific method.

But this unempirical approach, nourished by the horror of all "subjectivism," yields a conception of science and its guiding methods which is utterly inappropriate to its subject matter. As Popper recognizes, science (like

[14] Schilpp, *The Philosophy of Karl Popper*, p. 1,047.

the law) is a human activity, involving a problem-solving intellectual community governed by critical habits and principles. But these principles have themselves developed by trial and error and may develop further. None of these principles is "intrinsically" or "essentially" rational: their rationality lies in their success in promoting the ends of inquirers and resolving the problems of scientists. This is clearly seen in the case of induction: even if there are no formal rules codifying this practice, it hardly follows that it is "arbitrary" or "subjective" (let alone that it does not exist), simply on the grounds that it does not conform to the standards of rationality antecedently laid down by Popper.

INSTEAD OF ESPOUSING A VIEW as riddled with internal flaws as Popper's, we can reasonably continue to believe that there really are inductive practices, that people do discriminate differences of probative weight in evidence and do rely on logically inconclusive evidence for many beliefs they hold, and further that such evidence can, under certain circumstances, genuinely provide *rational* support for our claims to know a great variety of empirical statements. Popper's fear of "subjectivist" views has led him to exclude from the analysis of science not only those judgments correctly described as infected with bias or subjective distortions, but also what is *typical* in science: decisions and cases of deliberation which are not strictly dictated by universal and exceptionless rules, but which require personal judgment; consequently, he leaves outside the scope of critical guidance the practices that most need it.

Popper is indeed a rationalist of sorts — a Romantic rationalist. Throughout his work we find the image of scientists trying to impose their theories on nature and then awaiting the voice of nature in response; an emphasis on fierce competition between theories; a stress on risks, bold conjectures, and imaginative criticism; a hatred of the view that science is nothing more than technological control; an image of science as a never-ending struggle whose mainspring is contradiction, in which we deliberately seek contradictions in our hard-won syntheses and solutions to avoid stagnation and erect fresh hurdles and challenges; an idea of science as a process that pursues an aim that is elusive, perhaps unreachable, a process that counts as much as, if not more than, attaining the goal itself, a journey in which we heroically, impossibly, try to narrow the discrepancy between our finite grasp and our infinite aim. This picture has not enjoyed so distinguished (if not more convincing) an adherent since the days when it was applied to the moral realm, and sometimes to the whole of human existence, by such German Romantic writers as Fichte. Surely it is a powerful reason for Popper's appeal, probably more so than the arguments that have made him the scarecrow of "inductivists." The image Popper offers of our efforts to acquire the truth about the world may be momentarily intoxicating, and set up unusual and stimulating trains of thought, but, contemplated in a cool hour, it describes a wild-goose chase.

The Bull on the Mountain by Oliver Sacks was originally published June 28, 1984. Copyright © 1984 by Oliver Sacks. Reprinted by permission of Summit Books, a division of Simon & Schuster, Inc.

OLIVER SACKS

The Bull on the Mountain

SATURDAY THE 24TH of August started overcast and sullen in the Norwegian village where I was staying a few years ago, but there was promise of fine weather later in the day. I could start my climb early, through the low-lying orchards and woods, and by noon, I reckoned, reach the top of the mountain. By then, perhaps, the weather would have cleared, and there would be a magnificent view from the summit—the lower mountains all around me, sweeping down into Hardanger Fiord, and the great fiord itself visible in its entirety. "Climb" suggests scaling rocks, and ropes. But it was not that sort of climb, simply a steep mountain path. I foresaw no particular problems or difficulties. I was as strong as a bull, in the prime, the pride, the high noon of life. I looked forward to the walk with assurance and pleasure.

I soon got into my stride—a supple swinging stride, which covers ground fast. I had started before dawn, and by half past seven had ascended, perhaps, to two thousand feet. Already the early mists were beginning to clear. Now came a dark and piney wood, where the going was slower, partly because of knotted roots in the path and partly because I was enchanted by the world of tiny vegetation which sheltered in the wood, and was often stopping to examine a new fern, a moss, a lichen. Even so, I was through the woods by a little after nine, and had come to the great cone that formed the mountain proper and towered above the fiord to six thousand feet. To my surprise there was a fence and a gate at this point, and the gate bore a still more surprising notice: BEWARE OF THE BULL! in Norwegian, and for those who might not be able to read the words, a rather droll picture of a man being tossed.

I STOPPED, AND SCRUTINIZED the picture and scratched my head. A *bull?* *Up here?* What would a bull be doing up here? I had not seen even sheep in the pastures and farms down below. Perhaps it was some sort of joke, tacked there by the villagers, or by some previous hiker with an odd sense of humor. Or perhaps there *was* a bull, summering amid a vast mountain pasture, subsisting on the spare grass and scrubby vegetation. Well, enough of speculation! Onward to the top!

The terrain had changed again. It was now very stony, with enormous boulders here and there; but there was also a light topsoil, muddy in places because it had rained in the night, but with plenty of grass and a few scanty shrubs—fodder enough for an animal that had the whole mountain to graze.

The path was much steeper and fairly well marked, though, I felt, not much used. It was not exactly a populous part of the world. I had seen no visitors apart from myself, and the villagers, I imagined, were too busy with farming and fishing, and other activities, to go jaunting up the local mountains. All the better. I had the mountain to myself. Onward, upward— though I could not see the top, but I had already ascended, I judged, three thousand feet, and if the path ahead was simply steep, but not tricky, I could make the top by noon, as I had planned.

And so I forged ahead, keeping up a brisk pace despite the gradient, blessing my energy and stamina, and especially my strong legs, trained by years of hard exercise and hard lifting in the gym. Strong quadriceps muscles in the thighs, strong body, good wind, good stamina—I was grateful to Nature for endowing me well. And if I drove myself to feats of strength, and long swims, and long climbs, it was a way of saying "Thank you" to Nature and using to the full the good body she had given me.

Around eleven o'clock, when the shifting mists allowed, I had my first glimpses of the mountain top—not so far above me. I *would* make it by noon. There was still a light mist clinging here and there, sometimes shrouding the boulders so that they were difficult to make out. Occasionally a boulder, half seen through the mist, looked almost like a vast crouching animal, and would reveal its true nature only when I came closer. There were ambiguous moments when I would stop in uncertainty, while I descried the shrouded shapes before me.... But when it happened, it was not at all ambiguous!

THE REAL REALITY was not such a moment, not touched in the least by ambiguity or illusion. I had, indeed, just emerged from the mist, and was walking around a boulder big as a house, the path curving around it so that I could not see ahead, and it was this inability to see ahead that permitted the meeting. I practically trod on what lay before me—an enormous animal sitting in the path, and indeed wholly occupying the path, whose presence had been hidden by the rounded bulk of the rock. It had a huge horned head, a stupendous white body, and an enormous, mild, milk-white face. It sat unmoved by my appearance, exceedingly calm, except that it turned its vast white face up toward me. And in that moment it changed before my eyes, becoming transformed from magnificent to utterly monstrous. The huge white face seemed to swell and swell, and the great bulbous eyes became radiant with malignance. The face grew huger and huger all the time, until I thought it would blot out the universe. The bull became hideous—hideous beyond belief, hideous in strength, malevolence, and cunning. It seemed now to be stamped with the infernal in every feature. It became first a monster, and now the Devil.

I retained my composure, or a semblance of composure, for a minute in which, perfectly "naturally," as if turning about at the end of a stroll, I swung in mid-stride through 180 degrees, and deftly, daintily, began my descent. But then—oh horrible!—my nerve suddenly broke, dread overwhelmed me, and I ran for dear life—ran madly, blindly, down the steep, muddy, slippery path, lost here and there in patches of mist. Blind, mad panic!—there is nothing worse in the world, nothing worse—and nothing more dangerous.

I cannot say exactly what happened. In my plunging flight down the treacherous path I must have misstepped—stepped on to a loose rock, or into midair. It is as if there is a moment missing from my memory—there is "before" and "after," but no "in-between." One moment I was running like a madman, conscious of heavy panting and heavy thudding footsteps, unsure whether they came from the bull or from me, and the next I was lying at the bottom of a short sharp cliff of rock, with my left leg twisted grotesquely beneath me and in my knee such a pain as I had never, ever known before. To be full of strength and vigor one moment and virtually helpless the next, in the pink and pride of health one moment and a cripple the next, with all one's powers and faculties one moment and without them the next—such a change, such suddenness, is difficult to comprehend, and the mind casts about for explanations.

I had encountered this phenomenon in others—in my patients who had been suddenly stricken or injured, and now I was to encounter it in myself. My first thought was this: that there had been an accident, and that someone I knew had been seriously injured. Later, it dawned on me that the victim was myself; but with this came the feeling that it was not really serious. To show that it was not serious, I got to my feet, or rather I *tried* to, but I collapsed in the process, because the left leg was completely limp and floppy, and gave way beneath me like a piece of spaghetti. It could not support any weight at all, but just buckled beneath me, buckled backward at the knee, making me yell with pain. But it was much less the pain that so horribly frightened me than the flimsy, toneless giving-way of the knee and my absolute impotence to prevent or control it—and the apparent paralysis of the leg. And then, the horror, so overwhelming for a moment, disappeared in face of a "professional attitude."

"OK, Doctor," I said to myself. "Would you kindly examine the leg?"

VERY PROFESSIONALLY, and impersonally, and not at all tenderly, as if I were a surgeon examining "a case," I took the leg and examined it—feeling it, moving it this way and that. I murmured my findings aloud as I did so, as if for a class of students: "No movement at the knee, gentlemen, no movement at the hip.... You will observe that the entire quadriceps has been torn from the patella. But though it has torn loose, it has not retracted—it is wholly toneless, which might suggest nerve injury as well. The patella has lost its major attachment, and can be flipped around—so!—like a ball-bearing. It is readily dislocated—there is nothing to hold it.

"As for the knee itself"—and here I illustrated each point as I made it— "we find abnormal motility, a quite pathological range of motion. It can be flexed without any resistance at all"—here I manually flexed the heel to the buttock—"and can also be hyperextended, with apparent dislocation." Both movements, which I illustrated, caused me to scream. "Yes, gentlemen," I concluded, summarizing my findings, "a fascinating case! A complete rupture of the quadriceps tendon. Muscle paralyzed and atonic— probably nerve injury. Unstable knee joint—seems to dislocate backward. Probably ripped out the cruciate ligaments. Can't really tell about bone injury—but there could easily be one or more fractures. Considerable swelling, probably tissue and joint fluid, but tearing of blood vessels can't be excluded."

I TURNED with a pleased smile to my invisible audience, as if awaiting a round of applause. And then, suddenly, the "professional" attitude and persona broke down, and I realized that this "fascinating case" was *me—me myself*, fearfully disabled, and quite likely to die. The leg was utterly useless—far more so than if it had been broken. I was entirely alone, near the top of a mountain, in a desolate and sparsely populated part of the world. My whereabouts were known to nobody. This frightened me more than anything else. I could die where I lay, and nobody would know it.

Never had I felt so alone, so lost, so forlorn, so utterly beyond the pale of help. It hadn't occurred to me until then how terrifying and seriously alone I was. I had not felt "alone" when I was romping up the mountain (I never do when I am enjoying myself). I had not felt alone when I was examining my injury (I saw now what a comfort the imagined "class" was). But now, all of a sudden, the fearful sense of my aloneness rushed in upon me. I remembered that someone had told me, a few days before, of "a fool of an Englishman" who had climbed this very mountain, alone, two years before, and had been found a week later dead from exposure, having broken both his legs. It was at an altitude, and latitude, where the temperature sinks well below freezing at night, even in August. I had to be found by nightfall or I should never survive. I had to get lower, if I possibly could, because then at least there was a chance of my being seen. I even entertained hopes, now I came to consider things, that I might be able to descend the entire mountain, with a bum leg, by myself; and it was not until much later that I realized how this, above all, was a comforting delusion. Yet if I pulled myself together, did what I could, there was a sporting chance that I would make it yet.

I suddenly found myself very calm. First of all, I had to address myself to the leg. I had discovered that while any movement at the knee was agonizing, and indeed, literally, physiologically shocking, I was fairly comfortable when the leg lay flat and supported on the ground. But having no bone or "inner structure" to hold it, it had no protection against helpless passive movements at the knee, as might be caused by any unevenness in the ground. So, clearly, it needed an outer structure, or splint.

And here one of my idiosyncrasies came to my aid. Habit, more than anything else, made me carry an umbrella under practically all conditions, and it seemed natural enough, or purely automatic, that when I went for a walk in bad weather (even up a mountain more than a mile), I should take my stout and trusty umbrella with me. Besides, it had been useful as a walking stick on the way up. And now it found its finest moment—in splinting my leg. Without such a splint I could scarcely have moved. I snapped off the handle and tore my anorak in two. The length of the umbrella was just right—the heavy shaft almost matched the length of my leg—and I lashed it in place with strong strips of anorak, sufficiently firmly to prevent a helpless flailing of the knee, but not so tightly as to impede circulation.

By now about twenty minutes had elapsed since my injury, or possibly less. Could all this have occurred in so short a time? I looked at my watch to see if it had stopped, but the second hand was going around with perfect regularity. *Its* time, abstract, impersonal, chronological, had no relation to my time—*my* time which consisted solely of personal moments, life moments, crucial moments. As I looked at the dial, I matched, in imagination, the movement of the hands, going steadily round and round—the relentless regularity of the sun in the heavens—with my own uncertain descent of the mountain. I could not think of hurrying—that would exhaust me. I could not think of dawdling—that would be worse. I had to find the right pace, and steadily keep it up.

I found myself now gratefully taking note of my assets and resources, where before I could only take note of the injury. Mercifully, then, I had not torn an artery, or major vessel, internally, for there was only a little swelling around the knee and no real coolness or discoloration of the leg. The quadriceps was apparently paralyzed, it was true—but I made no further neurological examination. I had not fractured my spine or my skull in my fall. And—God be praised!—I had three good limbs, and the energy and strength to put up a good fight. And, by God, I would! This would be the fight of my life —the fight of one's life which is the fight *for* life.

I COULD NOT HURRY—I could only hope. But my hopes would be extinguished if I were not found by nightfall. Again I looked at my watch, as I was to do many anxious times again in the hours that followed. At these latitudes it would be a rather lengthy evening and dusk, starting around 6 and gradually getting darker and cooler. By 7:30 it would be quite cool, and difficult to see. I had to be found by about 8, at the latest. By 8:30 it would be pitch-black—impossible to see and impossible to proceed. And though by strenuous exercise I might, just conceivably, last through the night, the chances were distinctly, indeed heavily, against it. I thought, for a moment, of Tolstoy's "Master and Man"—but there were not two of us to keep each other warm. If only I had a companion with me! The thought suddenly came to me once again, in the words from the Bible not read since childhood, and not consciously recollected, or brought to mind, at all: "Two are better than one... for if they fall, the one will lift up his fellow; but woe to him that is alone when he falleth, for he hath not another to help him up." And, following immediately upon this, came a sudden memory, eidetically clear, of a small animal I had seen in the road, with a broken back, hoisting its paralyzed hind legs along. Now I felt exactly like that creature. The sense of my humanity as something apart, something above animality and morality—this too disappeared at that moment, and again the words of Ecclesiastes came to my mind: "For that which befalleth the sons of men befalleth beasts; as the one dieth, so dieth the other...so that a man hath no preeminence above a beast."

While splinting my leg, and keeping myself busy, I had again "forgotten" that death lay in wait. Now, once again, it took the Preacher to remind me. "But," I cried inside myself, "the instinct of life is strong within me. I want to live—and, with luck, I may still do so. I don't think it is yet my time to die." Again the Preacher answered, neutral, noncommittal: "To everything there is a season, and a time to every purpose under the heaven. A time to be born, and a time to die; a time...." This strange, deep, emotionless clarity, neither cold nor warm, neither severe nor indulgent, but utterly truthful, I had encountered in others, especially in patients who were facing death and did not conceal the truth from themselves; I had marveled, though in a way uncomprehendingly, at the simple ending of *Hadji Murad*—how, when Murad has been fatally shot, "images without feelings" stream through his mind; but now, for the first time, I encountered this—in myself.

These images, and words, and passionless feelings did not, as they say, go through my head "in a flash." They took their time—several minutes at least—the time they would have taken in reality, not in a dream; they were meditations, which did not hurry at all—but neither did they distract me in the least from my tasks. Nobody looking on (so to speak) would have seen me "musing," would have seen any pause. On the contrary, they would have been impressed by my brisk and workmanlike appearance and behavior, by the quick and efficient way in which I splintered my leg, made a brief check of everything, and set off downhill.

And so I proceeded, using a mode of travel I had never used before—roughly speaking, gluteal and tripedal. That is to say, I slid down on my backside, heaving or rowing myself with my arms and using my good leg for steering and, when needed, for braking, with the splintered leg hanging nervelessly before me. I did not have to think out this unusual, unprecedented, and—one might think—unnatural way of moving. I did it without thinking, and very soon got accustomed to it. And anyone seeing me rowing swiftly and powerfully down the slopes would have said, "Ah, he's an old hand at it. It's second nature to him."

THE LEGLESS don't need to be *taught* to use crutches: it comes "unthinkingly" and "naturally," as if the person had been practicing it, in secret, all his life. The organism, the nervous system, has an immense repertoire of "trick movements" and "backups" of every kind—completely automatic strategies, which are held "in reserve." We would have no idea of the resources that exist *in potentia* if we did not see them called forth as needed.

So it happened with me. It was a reasonably efficient mode of progress, as long as the path descended continually, and evenly, and not too steeply. If it was not even, the left leg would tend to catch on irregularities of all sorts—it seemed curiously inept at avoiding these—and I cursed it several times for being "stupid" or "senseless." I found, indeed, that whenever the terrain became difficult, I had to keep an eye on this not only powerless but stupid leg. Most frightening of all were those sections of the path which were too slippery or too steep, because it was difficult not to slide down almost uncontrollably, ending with a lurch or a crash which agonizingly buckled the knee and exposed the limitations of my improvised splint.

It occurred to me at one point, after a particularly sickening crash, to cry for help, and I did so, lustily, with Gargantuan yells, which seemed to echo and resound from one peak to another. The sudden sound in the silence startled and scared me; and then I had a sudden fear that it might startle the bull, which I had completely forgotten. I had a frightened vision of the animal, now furiously rearoused, charging down the path to toss or crush me. Trembling with terror, and with immense effort and pain, I managed to heave myself off the path until I was hidden behind a boulder. Here I remained for about ten minutes, until the continuing silence reassured me and I was able to crawl out and continue my descent.

I could not decide whether it had been foolish and provocative to yell, or whether my folly lay rather in fearing to yell. I decided, in any event, not to yell again; and whenever the impulse seized me I held my tongue, remembering that I was still in the bull's domain, where perhaps he maintained a sharp-eared dominion; and I would further say to myself, for good measure, "Why shout? Save your breath. You're the only human being in hundreds of square miles." And so I descended in absolute silence, not even daring to whistle aloud, for everywhere now I felt the bull listening. I even tried to mute the sound of my breathing. And so the hours passed, silently, slithering....

AT ABOUT 1:30—I had been traveling two hours—I came again to the swollen stream with stepping-stones that I had hesitated to cross even when climbing up, with both legs. Clearly, I could not "row" myself through this. I had therefore to turn over and "walk" on rigidly outstretched arms—and even so my head was only just out of the water. The water was fast-flowing, turbulent, and glacially cold, and my left leg, dropping downward, unsupported, out of control, was violently jarred by stones on the bottom, and sometimes blown like a flag sideways at a right angle to my trunk. My hip seemed almost as loose as my knee, but it caused me no pain—unlike my knee, which, excruciatingly, was buckled and dislocated as I crossed the stream. Several times I felt my consciousness ebbing and feared I would faint and drown in the stream; and I ordered myself to hold on, with strong language and threats.

"Hold on, you fool! Hold on for dear life! I'll *kill* you if you let go—and don't you forget it!"

I half collapsed when finally I made the other side, shuddering with cold, and pain, and shock. I felt exhausted, prostrated, at the end of my strength, and I lay stunned, motionless, for a couple of minutes. Then, somehow my exhaustion became a sort of tiredness, an extraordinarily comfortable, delicious languor.

"How nice it is here," I thought to myself. "Why not a little rest—a nap maybe?"

The apparent sound of this soft, insinuating, inner voice suddenly woke me, sobered me, and filled me with alarm. It was not "a nice place" to rest and nap. The suggestion was lethal and filled me with horror, but I was lulled by its soft, seductive tones.

"No," I said fiercely to myself. "This is Death speaking—and in its sweetest, deadliest Siren-voice. Don't listen to it now! Don't listen to it ever! You've got to go on whether you like it or not. You can't rest here—you can't rest anywhere. You must find a pace you can keep up, and go on steadily."

This good voice, this "Life" voice, braced and resolved me. My trembling stopped and my faltering too. I got going once more, and didn't falter again.

There came to my aid now melody, rhythm, and music (what Kant calls the "quickening" art). Before crossing the stream, I had *muscled* myself along—moving by main force, with my very strong arms. Now, so to speak, I was *musicked* along. I did not contrive this. It happened to me. I fell into a rhythm, guided by a sort of marching or rowing song, sometimes the Volga Boatmen's Song, sometimes a monotonous chant of my own, accompanied by the words *"Ohne Hast, ohne Rast! Ohne Hast, ohne Rast!"* ("Without haste, without rest"), with a strong heave on every *Hast* and *Rast*. Never had Goethe's words been put to better use! Now I no longer had to think about going too fast or too slow. I got into the music, got into

297

the swing, and this ensured that my tempo was right. I found myself perfectly coordinated by the rhythm—or perhaps subordinated would be a better term: the musical beat was generated within me, and all my muscles responded obediently—all save those in my left leg, which seemed silent—or mute? Does not Nietzsche say that when listening to music, we "listen with our muscles"? I was reminded of my rowing days in college, how the eight of us would respond as one man to the beat, a sort of muscle orchestra conducted by the cox.

Somehow, with this "music," it felt much less like a grim anxious struggle. There was even a certain primitive exuberance, such as Pavlov called "muscular gladness." And now, further, to gladden me more, the sun burst from behind the clouds, massaged me with warmth and soon dried me off. And with all this, and perhaps other things, I found my internal weather was most happily changed.

It was only after chanting the song in a resonant and resounding bass for some time that I suddenly realized that I had forgotten the bull. Or, more accurately, I had forgotten my fear—partly seeing that it was no longer appropriate, partly that it had been absurd in the first place. I had no room now for this fear, or for any other fear, because I was filled to the brim with music. And even when it was not literally (audibly) music, there was the music of my muscle orchestra playing—"the silent music of the body," in Harvey's lovely phrase. With this playing, the musicality of my motion, I myself became the music—"You are the music, while the music lasts." A creature of muscle, motion, and music, all inseparable and in unison with one another—except for that unstrung part of me, that poor broken instrument which could not join in and lay motionless and mute without tone or tune.

I had once, as a child, had a violin which got brutally smashed in an accident. I felt for my leg, now, as I felt long ago for that poor broken fiddle. Mixed with my happiness and renewal of spirit, with the quickening music I felt in myself, was a new and sharper and most poignant sense of loss for that broken musical instrument that had once been my leg. When will it recover, I thought to myself? When will it sound its own tune again? When will it rejoin the joyous music of the body?

BY TWO O'CLOCK the clouds had cleared sufficiently for me to get a magnificent view of the fiord beneath me, and of the tiny village I had left nine hours before. I could see the old church, where I had heard Mozart's great Mass in C minor the previous evening. I could almost see—no, I *could* see—

individual figures in the street. Was the air abnormally, uncannily, clear? Or was there some abnormal clarity in my perceptions?

I thought of a dream related by Leibniz, in which he found himself at a great height overlooking the world—with provinces, towns, lakes, fields, villages, hamlets, all spread beneath him. If he wished to see a single person—a peasant tilling, an old woman washing clothes—he had only to direct and concentrate his gaze: "I needed no telescope except my attention." And so it was with me: an anguish of yearning sharpened my eyes, a violent need to see my fellow men and, even more, to be seen by them. Never had they seemed dearer, or more remote. I felt so close, watching them as through a powerful telescope, and yet utterly removed, not part of their world. If only I had a flag or a flare—a rifle, a carrier pigeon, a radio transmitter! If only I could give a truly Gargantuan yell—one that would be heard ten miles away! For how could they know that here was a fellow creature, a crippled human being, fighting for his life five thousand feet above them? I was within sight of my rescuers, and yet I would probably die. There was something impersonal, or universal, in my feeling. I would not have cried, "Save *me*, Oliver Sacks!" but "Save this hurt living creature! Save *Life!*" the mute plea I know so well from my patients—the plea of *all* life facing the abyss, if it be strongly, vividly, rightly alive.

An hour passed, and another and another, under a glorious cloudless sky, the sun blazing pale-golden with a pure Arctic light. It was an afternoon of peculiar splendor, earth and air conspiring in beauty, radiant, suffused in serenity. As the blue and golden hours passed, I continued steadily on my downward trek, which had become so smooth, so void of difficulties, that my mind could move free of the ties of the present. My mood changed again, although I was to realize this only later. Long-forgotten memories, all happy, came unbidden to my mind: memories, first, of summer afternoons, tinged with a sunniness that was also happiness and blessedness—sun-warmed afternoons with my family and friends, summer afternoons going back and back into earliest childhood. Hundreds of memories would pass through my mind, in the space between one boulder and the next, and yet each was rich, simple, ample, and conveyed no sense of being hurried through.

Nor was it a flitting of faces and voices. Entire scenes were relived, entire conversations replayed, without the least abbreviation. The very earliest memories were all of our garden—our big old garden in London, as it used to be before the war. I cried with joy and tears as I saw it—our garden with its dear old iron railings intact, the lawn vast and smooth, just cut and rolled (the huge old roller there in a corner); the orange-striped hammock with cushions bigger than myself, in which I loved to roll and swing for hours; and—joy of my heart—the enormous sunflowers, whose vast inflorescence fascinated me endlessly and showed me at five the Pythagorean mystery of the world. (For it was then, in the summer of 1938, that I discovered that the whorled florets were multiples of prime numbers, and I had such a vision of the order and beauty of the world as was to be a prototype of every scientific wonder and joy I was later to experience.) All of these thoughts and images, involuntarily summoned and streaming through my mind, were essentially happy, and essentially grateful. And it was only later that I said to myself, "What is this mood?" and realized that it was a preparation for death. "Let your last thinks be all thanks," as Auden says.

At about six, rather suddenly, I noticed that the shadows were longer, and that the sun was lower in the heavens. Some part of me, Joshua-like, had thought to hold the sun in mid-course, to prolong to eternity the gold and azure afternoon. Now, abruptly, I saw that it was evening, and that in an hour, more or less, the sun would set.

NOT LONG AFTER THIS I came to a long transverse ridge commanding an unobstructed view of the village and fiord. I had attained this ridge at about ten in the morning: it had been about halfway between the gate and the point where I fell. Thus what had taken me little more than an hour to climb, had taken me, crippled, nearly seven hours to descend. I saw how grossly, how optimistically, I had miscalculated everything—comparing my "rowing" to striding, when it was, I could now see, six times as slow. How could I have imagined that one was half as fast as the other, and that the ascent from the relatively warm and populous low-lying farmland, which had taken four hours or so, could be retraced in just twice that time, bringing me within range of the highest farmhouse by dusk or nightfall. I had hugged to myself, like a warm comforter, in the long hours of my journey—interspersed with my exalted but not cozy thoughts—a warm, sweet vision of the waiting farmhouse, glowing softly like a Dutch interior, with a dumpy, motherly farmwife who would feed me and revive me with love and warm milk, while her husband, a dour giant, went to the village for help. I had been secretly sustained by this vision throughout the interminable hours of my descent, and now it vanished, suddenly, like a candle blown out, on the chill clarity of that high transverse ridge.

I could see now, what had been shrouded in mists on the way up in the morning, how far away, unattainably far, the village still was. And yet, though hope had just expired and died, I took comfort from seeing the village, and especially the church, gilded, or rather crimsoned now, in the long evening light. I could see straggling worshipers on their way to evening service and had the strangest persuasion that the service was for me. It came to me once more, and overwhelmingly, how I had sat in that church only the evening before, and heard the C-minor Mass, and so powerful was the memory that I could actually hear it in my ears—hear it with such vividness that I wondered, for a long second, whether it was again being sung below, and wafted up to me, miraculously, by some trick of the air. As I listened, profoundly moved, with tears on my face, I suddenly realized that it was not the Mass that I was hearing—no, not the Mass, but the Requiem instead. My mind, my unconscious, had switched one for the other. Or was it—again that uncanny acoustic illusion—was it that they *were* singing the Requiem, down there for me?

Shortly after seven the sun disappeared, seeming to draw, as it did so, all color and warmth from the world. There were none of the lingering effulgences of a more temperate sunset—this was a simpler, sterner, more Arctic phenomenon. The air was suddenly grayer, and colder, and the grayness and coldness seemed to penetrate right to my marrow.

The silence had become intense. I could no longer hear any sounds about me. *I could no longer hear myself.* Everything seemed embedded in silence. There were odd periods when I thought I was dead, when the immense calm became the calm of death. Things had ceased to happen. There was no happening any more. This must be the beginning of the end.

SUDDENLY, INCREDIBLY, I heard a shout, a long yodeling call which seemed very close to me. I turned, and saw a man and a boy standing on a rock, a little above me, and not ten yards from the path, their figures silhouetted against the darkening dusk. I never even saw my rescuers before they saw me. I think, in those last dark minutes, that my eyes had been fixed on the dim path before me, or had perhaps been staring unseeing into space—they had ceased to be on the lookout, constantly roving and scanning, as they had been at all times in the course of the day. I think, indeed, that I had become almost completely unaware of the environment, having, at some level, given up all thoughts of rescue and life, so that rescue, when it came, came from nowhere, a miracle, a grace, at the very last moment.

In another few minutes it would have been too dark to see. The man who yodeled was just lowering a gun, and the youth by his side was similarly armed. They ran down toward me. I needed no words to explain my condition. I hugged them both, I kissed them—these bearers of life. I stammered out, in broken Norwegian, what had happened on the heights, and what I could not put into words I drew in the dust.

The two of them laughed at my picture of the bull. They were full of humor, these two, and as they laughed I laughed too—and suddenly, with the laughter, the tragic tension exploded, and I felt vividly, so to speak, comically alive once again. I thought I had had every emotion on the heights, but—it now occurred to me—I hadn't laughed once. Now I couldn't stop laughing—the laughter of relief, and the laughter of love, that deep-down laughter that comes from the center of one's being. The silence was exploded, the quite deathly silence that had seized me, as in a spell, those last minutes.

The men were reindeer hunters, father and son, who had pitched camp nearby. Hearing a noise outside, a movement in the undergrowth, they had come out cautiously with their rifles at the ready, their minds on the game they might bag, and when they peered over the rock they saw that their game was me.

The huntsman gave me some aquavit from a flask—the burning fluid was indeed the "water of life." "Don't worry," he said, "I will go down to the village. I will be back within two hours. My son will stay with you. You're safe and sound—and the bull won't come here!"

From the moment of my rescue my memories become less vivid, less charged. I was in others' hands now and had no more responsibility to act, or feel. I said very little to the boy, but though we hardly spoke I found great comfort in his presence. Occasionally he would light me a cigarette—or pass me the aquavit his father had left. I had the deepest sense of security and warmth. I fell asleep.

It was less than two hours before a posse of stout villagers arrived carrying a litter—onto which they loaded me, with considerable difficulty. The flailing leg, which had lain silent and unnoticed for so long, objected loudly, but they carried me gently, rhythmically, down the steep mountain trail. At the gate—the gate, whose warning sign I had ignored!—I was transferred onto a sort of mountain tractor. As it jogged slowly downhill—first through woods, and then through orchards and farms—the men sang softly among themselves, and passed the aquavit around. One of them gave me a pipe to smoke. I was back—God be praised!—in the good world of men.

Marlene Dietrich

Girl from Berlin by Gabriele Annan was originally published February 14, 1985, as a review of Marlene Dietrich's ABC, *Ungar;* Marlène D. *by Marlene Dietrich, Grasset (Paris);* Sublime Marlene *by Thierry de Navacelle, St. Martin's;* Marlene Dietrich: Portraits 1926–1960, *introduction by Klaus-Jürgen Sembach and epilogue by Josef von Sternberg, Schirmer/Mosel, Grove;* Marlene, *a film directed by Maximilian Schell, produced by Karel Dirka; and* Dietrich *by Alexander Walker, Harper and Row.*

Girl from Berlin

MARLENE DIETRICH is generally agreed to have been eighty-four last December, old enough to be fond of old jokes. One of her favorites is a macabre conceit of her own called the deathbed Oscar. It is for old movie actors who have never won an award. If they suddenly find one being presented to them, they should conclude that death is not far off. A whiff of deathbed Oscar hangs around the recent spate of books about Dietrich herself. A biography by Dietrich's daughter Maria Riva is said to be ready for publication as soon as her mother dies. Naturally, it is expected to be full of revelations about a private life almost as carefully protected as Garbo's.

Marlene Dietrich's ABC first appeared in 1961. It is a collection of banal, worldly-wise aphorisms interspersed with sturdy recipes for beef tea and goulash. The autobiography *Marlène D.* is something of a mystery, but only a publishing one. It is described as "*traduit de l'américain par Boris Mattews*" (sic). There has never been an American edition, but there was a German one in 1979 called *Nehmt nur mein Leben*. The text is a confused affair, omitting some periods of Dietrich's life altogether, and establishing the sanctioned but obfuscating version of her origins and early life.

Navacelle's text in *Sublime Marlene* is what one expects a film star biography to be. The photographs are the thing; they come from John Kobal's collection and are mostly Hollywood stills. In *Portraits 1926–1960*, on the other hand, the photographs are all studio portraits. Most of the chosen photographers are—or were—specialists in glamour (Cecil Beaton, Don English, Hoyningen-Huene, Parkinson, Richee, Steichen, and so on); so glamour is the aspect of Dietrich they emphasize. But each also gets across some of her over- and undertones: her loucheness, irony, sexual ambiguity, camaraderie, detachment, and even her quality of being a sur-vivor par excellence, which has made her an icon to fans of nostalgia, "a thorn," in Benny Green's words, "in the side of time." Kenneth Tynan said she makes you feel that "whatever hell you inhabit, she has been there before and survived." Only Cecil Beaton in 1935 missed Dietrich's point altogether and snapped a pretty hat on a mindless, chic gazelle.

PORTRAITS HAS an introduction by Klaus-Jürgen Sembach, the director for the Zentrum für Industriekultur in Nuremberg. With German eagerness for making intellectual connections he links the Sternberg/Dietrich movies with the "International Style" of the 1930s, "a style of high precision, rationality, and, for all of that, sensuous effects.... The severe and at the same time voluptuous shimmer of Josef von Sternberg's films demonstrated a great affinity with this movement." You see at once what he means: gleaming Dietrich, the goddess of the chromium curve, Our Lady of the Hispano Suiza. Sembach continues: "At the same time, these films also revealed the risk inherent in this style of becoming too hermetic and remote. This outspoken aesthetic possessed immensely narcissistic traits." More than twenty years ago, Susan Sontag in her famous "Notes on Camp" cited as an example of what she meant by the term "the outrageous aestheticism of Sternberg's six American movies with Dietrich."

Everyone, including Dietrich herself, agrees that her Sternberg period was her greatest. In his films her toughness and sexual provocation were not so much veiled as enhanced and counterpointed by something protective, caressing, resigned, and even sad in her gestures and intonations, something dreamy and mysterious in her appearance (the result of virtuoso camera work). This is true even in *The Blue Angel* where she plays a cheap and callous little tart.

STERNBERG WAS BORN in Austria, grew up poor in America, and had worked for several years in Hollywood when UFA brought him to Berlin in 1929 to direct *The Blue Angel* in two simultaneous versions, English and German. He discovered Dietrich when he was looking for a girl to play opposite the star, Emil Jannings. In *Marlène D.* the chapter on Sternberg is called "Toi Svengali—Moi Trilby." Sternberg's chapter on Dietrich from his sardonic autobiography *Fun in a Chinese Laundry* is reprinted in *Portraits*. His account of how he found her, or rather of what he found, differs somewhat from hers. Her story is blurry but implies that she was a slip of a beginner, straight out of Max Reinhardt's prestigious drama school (which she probably never attended). His version is likely to be nearer the truth: Far from being a debutante, she was in her late twenties, with a husband and child, and had made nine films and a number of records, as well as appearing in reviews, musicals, and straight plays.

The records show her in full command of the husky, suggestive, inter-
sexual style of the Berlin nightclubs in the Twenties, with its mockingly
syncopated inflections and teasingly drawn-out bi- and trisyllabic vowels.
She was not the first or only growler, but she was surely one of the best.
Sternberg did not discover her sound, which to many of her fans means
more than her overexposed legs. They know by heart every sexy sigh in
"Johnny" and "Peter." Hemingway said "she could break hearts simply
with her voice." In fact she maintains that Sternberg made her raise her reg-
ister to a common squeak for the character of Lola-Lola. What he discovered was her personality, and even that, he admitted, she already had: he
merely taught her what to do with it.

He spotted her in a highbrow musical: "There was an impressive poise
about her (not natural, as it turned out, for she was an exuberant bubbler
when not restrained) that made me certain that she would lend a classic
stature to the turmoil the woman of my film would have to create. Here
was not only a model...designed by Rops, but Toulouse-Lautrec would
have turned a couple of handsprings had he laid eyes on her." Sternberg
summoned Dietrich for a test. Her attitude, when she turned up, was take
me or leave me; she had not even bothered to bring the music for the song
she was supposed to sing. Nevertheless, he took her. Had he managed to
guess how inconceivably obedient, hard-working, and patient she would
turn out to be in the studio? Whatever their relationship (and no one seems
to know exactly what that was) it was intense. Alexander Walker quotes
Sternberg saying to Peter Bogdanovich: "*I* am Miss Dietrich—Miss Dietrich is *me.*" And she agreed it was true. Anyway, she was perfect for the per-
fectionist tyrant.

WALKER'S BOOK CONTAINS a large number of photographs of Dietrich before Sternberg set eyes on her, and they make one respect those eyes even
more. She looks sexy—but also dumpy, with no neck, no waist, a pudgy
face, and mousy hair. Walker's photographs are extremely well chosen. He
has worked hard to establish facts, and his text is perceptive and decently
written. His special insight—and he makes it the theme of his book—is
that Dietrich's personality and career are rooted in being a Prussian officer's
daughter brought up to obey, endure, and never show her feelings. This is
an idea she too promotes about herself.

It is true that her father, Louis Dietrich, fought in the Franco-Prussian
War as an officer in a crack regiment. But by the time his daughter was
born thirty years later he was an officer in the police—quite a way down

the social ladder. Walker suggests Major Dietrich had to resign his commission because he married into trade—his wife was the daughter of a well-established Berlin jeweler. But it seems just as likely that he was never a professional soldier at all, but only a reservist. He died when Dietrich was ten. Her mother then married Eduard von Losch, who certainly was an officer and whose name sounds aristocratic. He died in 1917. His stepdaughter can't have seen much of him; in her autobiography she describes quite vividly the completely female environment in which she grew up because all the men were at the front. She also harps on the Prussian discipline imposed by her mother (whom she adored) and claims that it prepared her for being docile and long-suffering on the set.

Walker rides his hobbyhorse hard, reading "military undertones" into all the characters she created with Sternberg, beginning with Amy Jolly in *Morocco*, who follows her Foreign Legionnaire into the desert and "has to 'join up,' become one of the 'legion of lost women'.... She answers the regiment's call, passing up the life of civilian leisure and comfort...." One hopes that Walker noticed the London *Times*'s list of birthdays for December 27 where (wrongly dated 1904) Dietrich appears flanked by Air Vice Marshall Sir Derek Hodgkinson and Brigadier Dame Mary Tyrwhitt.

Still, what distinguishes Dietrich from other sex symbols is her comradely, if not necessarily soldierly, rapport with men. She is not simply their opposite, whether endearingly like Monroe or dangerously like Bardot or Raquel Welch; she is both their opposite and one of them, one of the boys, whether in the officers' mess (*Dishonored*) or the back room. No wonder she attaches great importance to her entertainment tours behind the battle fronts in World War II. She was one of the boys then, and a colonel to boot.

The German song "Lili Marlene" with its fortuitous echo of her name became her biggest number. It's a song about a girl, sung by a man—a dead soldier. When she sings it—and when she sings "Where Have All the Flowers Gone?"—her sense of the waste of war seems to be a man's. She is not a mother/sweetheart figure, but one of those about to die or already dead. Strange though this may seem, it is not unique; in Germany Lale Andersen made her name with *"Drei rote Rosen gabe sie mir"* ("she gave me three red roses"), sung by a soldier on his way to die at the front.

The mocking lesbian overtones in Dietrich's performances are something else again. She said she copied her famous top hat and tails from the English music hall star Vesta Tilley, whose heyday was between the last years of the nineteenth century and the First World War. Still, one can't imagine Tilley fondling a chorus girl as she runs on stage, or kissing a lady hard on the lips, as Dietrich does in *Morocco*.

EVERY ONE of the books under review is an attempt in one way or another to get at the truth behind the Dietrich legend—a carelessly thrown together document with missing pages and others doubtfully authentic. By far the most original undertaking is the disturbing documentary film *Marlene* (not yet released in the US) made by the Austrian-Swiss actor-director Maximilian Schell. He thought he could get Dietrich to reveal the truth, but all he got in answer to a direct question was: The truth about me—long pause—is that everything you read about me is untrue.

Schell was originally chosen by the producer Karel Dirka to do the interview with Dietrich that was to be the core of the film. It was to be conducted half in English and half in German. Schell is bilingual and Dietrich had admired his performance in *Judgment at Nuremberg* (1961), the film in which she played her last important role. The director chosen by Dirka was Peter Bogdanovich. Dietrich turned him down because she did not consider him sufficiently famous, and she bullied the reluctant Schell into directing as well as interviewing her. So there was tension from the start.

Like Truffaut's *Day for Night*, Schell's film is about making—or in his case, not making—the film he set out to make. Dietrich refused to appear in it and she never does—except in clips from old movies, newsreels, and tapes of her concerts. All you get is her voice on the sound track. Almost the first thing it says is *Quatsch*—nonsense. She repeats the word many times during the ninety-minute run, and almost as often she says *Kitsch*. Also *Dreck*. To call her uncooperative would be an understatement. She is dismissive—not only of Schell and the idea of making a film about her, but of almost anything else that comes up in their conversation: method acting, Proust, God ("If there's a power above He must be *meschugge*"), psychoanalysis, life after death, feminism, women ("I call them females"), Emil Jannings, and sex ("*Es geht auch ohne*"—one can manage without). Her disaffected *mutter* reduces the world to a gray stretch of ruins, like the aerial shots Schell cuts in of Berlin at the end of the war. Only a few indestructible people and values stick up from the rubble: Sternberg, Orson Welles ("You should cross yourself when you say his name"), Burt Bacharach, Remarque, Hemingway, Goethe, Rilke, professionalism, self-discipline, generosity with money, not being sentimental.

DIETRICH ABHORRED the idea of being filmed as an old woman, and possibly she means it more than many stars do when she says her private life is nobody's concern, not even her own: "*Ich gehe mich einen Dreck an*"—an idiosyncratic construction which could be loosely translated "I'm none of my own shitty business." Her contract, she repeats in answer to Schell's pleading, was to be interviewed, not photographed: "I've been photographed to death." She won't even let them film her flat in the Avenue Montaigne, and she won't discuss her films. Schell objects that in that case *his* film won't be very exciting. "I'm not contracted to be exciting," she barks.

Schell interviewed her for twelve hours spread over several days. He had a chance to memorize her apartment and then had it reconstructed in the studio. You see the set being assembled, you watch the lighting and camera crews at work. It is a beautiful film, visually poetic and glamorous, a fitting homage to Sternberg. The bogus apartment is shot through a half-open door against light streaming through muslin-curtained French windows. There are mirrors and console tables and busts. Members of the crew flit by, dark silhouettes with eyelashes showing up romantically *à contrejour*. Three ravishing young Dietrich look-alikes in tails and top hats lounge and twirl just out of focus. The Schell-Dietrich dialogue and the short-tempered exchanges among the production team are dreamily backed by "*Nimm Dich in acht vor blonden Fraun*" and "*Ich bin von Kopf bis Fuss auf Liebe eingestellt.*"

We move to the editing room where clips from Dietrich's films are run through to comments by Schell and his assistants. With them sits a small old German-Jewish lady, bewildered and bewildering, her presence as unexplained as that of the dark lady glimpsed in Andrei Tarkovsky's film *Mirror* (who is, in fact, the poet Marina Tsvetaeva, a friend of Tarkovsky's parents). But who is Schell's dark lady? The name Anni Albers appears on the cast list (which has only one column, of course, because everyone plays—or is—himself). Can she be the widow of the irresistible Hans Albers, a German cross between Gérard Depardieu and Maurice Chevalier, the raffish darling of the Berlin public before the war? In *The Blue Angel* it is Albers who displaces Emil Jannings in Dietrich's affections. But this old lady is a different Anni Albers: the widow of the abstract painter Josef Albers, and herself a distinguished textile designer and member of the Bauhaus. What is she doing in the cutting room? Perhaps she just happened to be there; she is a friend of Schell's. But her haunting look of displacement tempts one to see her as a symbol of the last years of the Weimar Republic, when Dietrich was in her prime.

As for the dialogue between Dietrich and Schell, it is a duel—a duel in the sun with Dietrich as the bull. It begins with her in the ascendant, ridiculing, teasing, taunting, refusing, denigrating. He has to coax, persuade, argue, threaten. Gradually her nihilism gets under his skin, though he remains silky, the emollient Austrian baritone contrasting with her Prussian snarl. Like an experienced bullfighter he shows off her ferocity until the moment of putting in the first barb. Then he asks her where in Berlin she was born. She can't remember. But she must remember the name of the street where she lived with her parents. *Quatsch*, of course not; and anyway, who cares? At this point the screen shows a selection of possible residences in prewar Berlin. It begins with dreary proletarian tenements and gradually works up the social scale, but not very far. The camera lingers at the last frame, a turn-of-the-century apartment block with sunless balconies like cave dwellings framed in baroque whorls of gray concrete. This may be where Dietrich lived immediately after her marriage in 1924 to the young assistant director Rudolf Sieber (their open marriage lasted until he died); or it may just as well be where her parents lived.

BY DWELLING ON HER IMPLAUSIBLE AMNESIA about her childhood Schell makes the first crack in Dietrich's official self-portrait (he has obviously worked up *Marlène D.*), which represents a young girl from a rich aristocratic family who trained with Reinhardt only because she had to give up studying the violin because of a wrist injury. Reminded of her nine films before *The Blue Angel*, Dietrich gets cross and brushes them aside— *Quatsch*, those were just bit parts (not true: some were leads).

Schell moves on to the famous audition with Sternberg. Eroticism is something I've never understood, she says tetchily. It wasn't what Sternberg chose me for. He chose me because he liked my cool—turning up there without my music. He chose me because I was *schnodderig*. *Schnodderigkeit* is a Berlin form of loudmouthed, *je m'en fiche* insolence, and it fits incongruously onto the image of the *jeune fille bien élevée*. Incidentally, Kenneth Tynan agreed with Dietrich about her lack of eroticism: "She dedicates herself to looking rather than being sexy," he wrote. How could he tell? Anyway, Sternberg chose her.

So they made *The Blue Angel*, which she despises ("It's enough to make you puke") and which made her famous. And then, indifferent to stardom and caring only about her daughter, Goethe, and cooking, she went to Hollywood, allowed herself to be made into a star, and cynically submitted to all the rites of stardom.

Schell chooses the clips from her Hollywood films with poetic justice—if that expression can mean doing justice to someone's poetry. There is a thrilling scene from Sternberg's *Dishonored* where Dietrich is about to be executed as a spy. The commander of the firing squad cannot bring himself to give the order to shoot, so a soldier is sent off to find a replacement: meanwhile Dietrich repairs her lipstick. What *Quatsch*, she comments, what *Kitsch*. "*Kitsch und Dreck*." The only thing she was interested in was getting her fall right. Should it be backward or forward? "Well, I didn't know, did I? I'd never been shot before." Another fib, actually: Fritz Kortner had already shot her in 1929 (the year of *The Blue Angel*) in Kurt Bernhardt's brilliant, sadistic, and witty silent, *Die Frau, nach der man sich sehnt*. Kortner played a monocled doctor obsessed with Dietrich. She herself radiated—not sex exactly, just radiance. It was quite an achievement in the spectacularly unbecoming clothes she had to wear. Anyway, what she is telling Schell is that the only thing that mattered to her was technique—being professional in her work. It is probably *Kitsch* to feel that Dietrich had a special affinity with the beautiful, brave, and intelligent spy in *Dishonored*, who declares that she is afraid of neither life nor death. To Schell Dietrich says that she does not fear death—it's life one ought to fear.

Among the rarities Schell has to show is a scene from Orson Welles's *Touch of Evil* (1958), in which Dietrich was only a guest star. She plays the madame of a Texas brothel, Welles a corrupt, alcoholic police chief on the skids. He comes into the brothel and finds her alone at a table in the hall.

> "You've been reading the cards, haven't you?" [he says].
> "I've been doing the accounts."
> "Come on, read the future for me."
> "You haven't got any."
> "Hm...what do you mean?"
> "Your future's all used up. Why don't you go home?"

Dietrich's voice is deadpan, but it breaks your heart all right with a Baudelairean sense of the pathos of human depravity, degradation, and doom.

Welles is falling apart. Schell, in spite of his evident admiration, seems bent on making Dietrich fall apart too. He gets nowhere, though, when he tries to draw her on the men in her life: Remarque, Hemingway, Welles, Gabin—up on their pedestals they disappear behind the smoke screen of her fervent admiration for their genius. About Hemingway she is quite specific: their relationship was on a plane way above sex. Having sex is what a woman does to keep her man—not for pleasure. Can it never be pleasurable? asks Schell. Oh well, she grumbles, sometimes maybe.

Burt Bacharach, the songwriter, orchestrator, and accompanist with whom she began her worldwide concert tours in 1953, is the only man about whom she uses the word "love": not in conversation with Schell, but on a tape of one of the concerts. She leads Bacharach to the footlights and declares her love for him (and her admiration, gratitude, etc.). There is a catch in her voice. But so there was right at the beginning of Schell's film, which opened with her farewell performance in Paris. She thanked the audience (in French) for being so wonderful. Dietrich was a mistress of the curtain call with tears choked back. We are watching a performance. And Schell, for his part, deliberately allows—and allows us to see—his film turning into a hide-and-seek between *Sein und Schein*, appearance and reality. "Then what is real here?" Anni Albers asks. "You'd better ask the author," replies the props girl.

Dietrich and Bacharach split up in 1964, but she went on with her concerts without him until well into the Seventies, by which time she was hobbling from various fractures. They did not stop her from being as shamelessly glamorous as ever, slinky and glittering with sequins from a fraction above the nipples to the floor, her hair swinging in a gold lamé curtain, the coils of her white fox cape ramping down into a long train so that she looks like a female Laocoön entwined with huge furry white caterpillars.

Eventually, against her wishes, Schell sneaks a video recorder into the Avenue Montaigne. But Dietrich refuses to watch her old films. Why? Because, says Schell:

> *Nessun maggior dolore*
> *Che ricordarsi del tempo felice*
> *Nella miseria.*

> (No greater pain than to remember
> happy times in times of misery.)

Dietrich's agent slipped him the Dante quotation. So after that, why can't he leave her alone?

WELL, OBVIOUSLY, he has to make his film. She gets more and more rattled. "You should go back to Mama Schell and learn some manners," she snaps. He hounds her about her deceptions. Why does she say she grew up an only child when there is a photograph of her with her sister who was only a year older? Why does she suppress Friedrich Holländer, who wrote the songs and played the piano in *The Blue Angel*, and was still writing and playing for her in 1948 in *A Foreign Affair*, Billy Wilder's film about postwar Berlin? Once more she was playing a ruthless nightclub entertainer, only now Lola-Lola was upgraded to Erika von Schlütow, an aristocrat down on her luck. Those were the days when Hollywood still preferred foreigners to be, if not peasants, then aristocrats like Boyer and Claudette Colbert in *Tovarich*. That preference seems the most likely reason for Dietrich's slight (and slapdash) upgrading of her origins. Even on the screen she never seriously went in for being a *grande dame* except when she played the German general's widow in *Judgment at Nuremberg*. She looked like a retired call girl who has married a well-to-do client and been sent by him to his mother's dressmaker. Her performance was phony, though much praised.

I think Alexander Walker gets it wrong when he sees her as the incarnation of the Prussian Junker spirit. What she represents is the spirit of Berlin, independent, streetwise, sophisticated, and *schnodderig*. Schell understands this and uses his knowledge of what is closest to her heart when he moves in for the kill. It is 1945; a camera flies over Berlin; acre upon acre of ruins fills the screen, limitless stretches of desolation. Meanwhile the city's prewar street songs creep stealthily onto the sound track. Dietrich begins to hum along, entranced by examples of Berlin humor in the lyrics. "*Himmlisch, nicht?*" (Divine, isn't it?), she half chuckles, half sobs. Her voice begins to go out of control; it weaves over the sound track like a drunk across the pavement.

Schell delivers the final thrust. He begins to recite a poem—a very bad poem by the nineteenth-century Ferdinand Freiligrath. It was Dietrich's mother's favorite, and Dietrich begins to chant it antiphonally with Schell:

> *O lieb, so lang du lieben kannst!*
> *O lieb, so lang du lieben magst!*
> *Die Stunde kommt, die Stunde kommt,*
> *Wo du an Gräbern stehst und klagst.*

("Oh love, while you can! Oh love, while you may! The hour will come, the hour will come, when you stand weeping over graves.")

They get to the verse:

> *Und hüte deine Zunge wohl!*
> *Bald ist ein böses Wort gesagt.*
> *O Gott, es war nicht bös gemeint—*
> *Der andere aber geht und klagt.*

("And guard your tongue! An unkind word is quickly said! Oh God, I did not mean to be unkind—but the other goes away weeping.")

Here Dietrich bursts into uncontrollable sobs. It makes an effective ending. Shocking. As shocking as a bullfight when the bull is old. It is not just another performance; not appearance, but reality.

Amelia Earhart

Originally published January 17, 1985, as a review of The Winged Gospel: America's Romance with Aviation, 1900–1950 *by Joseph J. Corn, Oxford University Press.*

GORE VIDAL

Love of Flying

I

I WAS TWICE FOOTNOTE to the history of aviation. On July 7, 1929, still on
the sunny side of four years old, I flew in the first commercially scheduled
airliner (a Ford trimotor) across the United States, from New York to Los
Angeles in forty-eight hours. Aviation was now so safe that even a little
child could fly in comfort. I remember only two things about the flight:
the lurid flames from the exhaust through the window; then a sudden loss
of altitude over Los Angeles, during which my eardrums burst. Always the
trouper, I was later posed, smiling, for the rotogravure sections of the newspapers, blood trickling from tiny lobes. Among my supporting cast that
day were my father, the assistant general manager of the company
(Transcontinental Air Transport), his great and good friend, as the never
great, never good *Time* magazine would say, Amelia Earhart, as well as
Anne Morrow Lindbergh, whose husband Charles was my pilot.[1] Both
Lindbergh and Amelia had been hired by the line's promoter, one C. M.
Keys (not even a footnote now but then known as the czar of aviation), to
publicize TAT, popularly known as "The Lindbergh Line."

My second moment of footnotehood occurred in the spring of 1936,
when I was—significantly—on the sunny side of eleven. I was picked up at
St. Albans School in Washington, DC, by my father, Eugene L. Vidal, director of the Bureau of Air Commerce (an appointee of one Franklin D.
Roosevelt, himself mere tinkling prelude to Reagan's heavenly choir). FDR
wanted to have a ministry of aviation like the European powers; and so the
Bureau of Air Commerce was created.

---

[1] A recent investigation of a certain newspaper of record shows that, contrary to
family tradition, I was *not* on the first flight. I made my first cross-country flight
a few months later, at the age of four. In any case, I am still a triumphant footnote: the first child ever to cross the country by air-rail.

ON HOT SPRING MORNINGS Washington's streets smelled of melting asphalt; and everything was a dull tropical green. The city was more like a Virginia county seat than a world capital. The men wore straw hats in summer; white suits. There was no air conditioning. People used palmetto fans. As we got into my implausibly handsome father's plausible Plymouth, he was mysterious, while I was delighted to be liberated from school. I wore short trousers and polo shirt, the standard costume of those obliged to pretend that they were children a half-century ago. What was up? I asked. My father said, You'll see. Since we were now on the familiar road to Bolling Field, I knew that whatever was up, it was probably going to be us. Ever since my father—known to all as Gene—had become director in 1933, we used to fly together nearly every weekend in the director's Stinson monoplane. Occasionally he'd let me take the controls. Otherwise, I was navigator. With a filling-station road map on my bony knees, I would look out the window for familiar landmarks. When in doubt, you followed a railroad line or a main highway. Period joke: a dumb pilot was told to follow the Super Chief no matter what; when the train entered a tunnel, so did the pilot. End of joke.

At Bolling Field, I recognized the so-called Hammond flivver plane. Gene had recently told the press that a plane had been developed so safe that anyone could fly it and so practical that anyone who could afford a flivver car could buy it—in mass production, that is. At present, there was only the prototype. But it was my father's dream to put everyone in the air, just as Henry Ford had put everyone on the road. Since 1933, miles of newsprint and celluloid had been devoted to Gene Vidal's dream—or was it folly?

We had been up in the Hammond plane before; and I suppose it really was almost "foolproof," as my father claimed. I forget the plane's range and speed but the speed was probably less than a hundred miles an hour. (One pleasure of flying then: sliding the window open and sticking out your hand, and feeling the wind smash against it.) As a boy, the actual flying of a plane was a lot simpler for me than building one of those model planes that the other lads were so adept at making and I all thumbs in the presence of balsa wood, paper, and glue—the Dionysiac properties of glue were hardly known then. But those were Depression years, and we Americans a serious people. That is how we beat Hitler, Mussolini, and Tojo.

Next to Hammond, there was a *Pathé* newsreel crew, presided over by the familiar figure of Floyd Gibbons, a dark patch covering the vacancy in his florid face where once there had been an eye that he had lost—it was rumored—as a correspondent in the war to make the world safe for democracy, and now for a flivver aircraft in every garage. Since my father appeared regularly in newsreels and *Marches of Time*, a newsreel crew was no novelty. At age seven, when asked what my father did, I said, He's in the newsreels. But now, since I had been taken so mysteriously out of class, could it be...? I felt a premonitory chill.

As we drove onto the runway (no nonsense in those days when the director came calling), Gene said, "Well, you want to be a movie actor. So here's your chance." He was, if nothing else, a superb salesman. Jaded when it came to flying, I was overwhelmed by the movies. Ever since Mickey Rooney played Puck in *A Midsummer Night's Dream*, I had wanted to be a star, too. What could Rooney do that I couldn't? Why was I at St. Albans, starting Latin, when I might be darting about the world, unconfined by either gravity or the director's Stinson? "I'll put a girdle round the earth in forty minutes!" Rooney had croaked. Now I was about to do the same.

As we parked, Gene explained that I was to take off, circle the field once, and land. After I got out of the plane, I would have to do some acting. Floyd Gibbons would ask me what it was like to fly the flivver plane, and I was to say it was just like driving a flivver car. The fact that I had never even tried to drive a car seemed to my father and me irrelevant as we prepared for my screen debut. As it turned out, I didn't learn to drive until I was twenty-five years old.

My earlier footnotehood was clear-cut. I was indeed the first child to cross the country by air. But now I was a challenger. In 1927, one Jack Chapman, aged eleven, had soloed. Since there had been so much public complaint (suppose he had gone and killed a cow?), my father's predecessor had made it the law that no one under sixteen years of age could solo. Now here I was a few months younger than Chapman had been in 1927, ready to break the prepubescent record. But the law said that I could not fly unattended. Ordinarily, my father—true pioneer—would have ignored this sort of law. But the director of the Air Commerce could not—at least in front of *Pathé News*—break a law that he was sworn to uphold.

As I stood by the door to the plane, staring glassy-eyed at the cobra-camera, a long discussion took place. How was I to solo (thus proving that the Hammond flivver was if not foolproof boyproof) and yet not break the 1927 law? Floyd Gibbons proposed that my father sit behind me. But Gene said no. He was already so familiar a figure in the Transluxes of the Republic that the audience would think that he had done the flying. Finally, Fred Geisse, an official of the bureau (and, like me, a nonpilot), got in first and crouched behind the pilot's seat. The cameras started to turn. With a slight but lovable Rooneyesque swagger, I climbed aboard.

RECENTLY, I SAW some footage from the newsreel. As I fasten my seat belt, I stare serenely off into space, not unlike Lindbergh-Earhart. I even looked a bit like the god and goddess of flight who, in turn, looked spookily like each other. I start up the engine. I am still serene. But as I watched the ancient footage, I recalled suddenly the terror that I was actually feeling. Terror not of flying but of the camera. This was my big chance to replace Mickey Rooney. But where was my script? My director? My talent? Thinking only of stardom, I took off. With Geisse behind me kindly suggesting that I keep into the wind (that is, opposite to the way that the lady's stocking on the flagpole was blowing), I circled the field not once but twice and landed with the sort of jolt that one of today's jet cowboys likes to bring to earth his DC-10.

The real terror began when I got out of the plane and stood, one hand on the doorknob, staring into the camera. Gibbons asked me about the flight. I said, Oh, it wasn't much, and it wasn't either. But I was now suffering from terminal stage fright. As my voice box began to shut down, the fingers on the door knob appeared to have a life of their own. I stammered incoherently. Finally, I gave what I thought was a puckish Rooneyesque grin which exploded onto the screen with all the sinister force of Peter Lorre's *M*. In that final ghastly frame, suddenly broken off as if edited by someone's teeth in the cutting room, my career as boy aviator was launched. I watched the newsreel twice in the Belasco Theater, built on the site of William Seward's Old Club House. Each time, I shuddered with horror at that demented leer which had cost me stardom. Yet, leer notwithstanding, I was summer famous; and my contemporaries knew loathing. The young Streckfus Persons (a.k.a. Truman Capote) knew of my exploit. "Among other things," Harper Lee writes of the boy she based on Capote, "he had been up in a mail plane seventeen times, he had been to Nova Scotia, he had seen an elephant, etc." In the Sixties, when I introduced Norman Mailer to my father, I was amazed how much Mailer knew of Gene's pioneering.

I record this trivia not to try to regain my forever-lost feetnotehood but to try to recall the spirit of the early days of aviation, a spirit itself now footnote to the vast air and aerospace industries of today. In Anthony Sampson's *Empires of the Sky*,[2] only a dozen pages are devoted to the first quarter-century of American aviation. There are also three times as many references to something called Freddie Laker as there are to Lindbergh. Well, *sic transit* was always the name of the game, even now when the focus is on space itself. Finally, I am put in mind of all this by a number of recent books on aviation, of which the most intriguing and original is *The Winged Gospel: America's Romance with Aviation, 1900–1950*, by Joseph J. Corn, in which the author recalls the quasi-religious fervor that Americans experienced when men took to the air and how for a time, there was "a gospel of flight," and Gene Vidal was its "high priest." Flight would make men near-angels, it was believed; and a peaceful world one.

---

[2] Random House, 1985.

II

EVER SINCE the development of the balloon in eighteenth-century France, so-called "lighter-than-air craft" were a reality. Heavier-than-air craft were considered mad inventors' dreams until the brothers Orville and Wilbur Wright created the first heavier-than-air plane and flew it at Kitty Hawk, North Carolina, on December 17, 1903. Curiously enough, it took five years before the press could figure out exactly *what* it was that they had done. At that time the world was full of inventors like the Wright brothers; but the others were either inventing lighter-than-air craft such as the dirigible, or experimenting with gliders. Only a few certified nuts believed in the practicality of heavier-than-air craft. One of these "crackpots" was Henry Adams's friend at the Smithsonian Institution, Dr. S. P. Langley; and he was on much the same theoretical tack as the Wright brothers. But they left earth first.

It was not until Orville Wright flew a plane at Fort Myer outside Washington in the presence of five thousand people that the world realized that man had indeed kicked gravity and that the sky was only the beginning of no known limit. Like so many of the early air-ship makers, the Wright brothers were bicycle mechanics. But then the bicycle itself had been a revolutionary machine, adding an inch or two to the world's population by making it possible for boys to wheel over to faraway villages where taller or shorter girls might be found. At least in the days when eugenics was a science that was the story. Other bicycle manufacturers soon got into the act, notably Glenn H. Curtiss, who was to be a major manufacturer of aircraft.

Although the first generation of flyers believed that airplanes would eventually make war unthinkable, the 1914–1918 war did develop a new glamorous sort of warfare, with Gary Cooper gallantly dueling Von Stroheim across the bright heavens. By 1918 the American government had an airmail service. In 1927 the twenty-five-year-old Lindbergh flew the Atlantic and became, overnight, the most famous man on earth, the air age beautifully incarnate. In 1928 Amelia Earhart flew the Atlantic; and took her place in the heavens as yin to Lindbergh's yang.

IT IS HARD to describe to later generations what it was like to live in a world dominated by two such shining youthful deities. Neither could appear in public without worshipers—no other word—storming them. Yet each was obliged to spend a lot of time not only publicizing and selling aircraft but encouraging air transport. Of the two, Lindbergh was the better paid. But, as a deity, the commercial aspect was nothing to him, he claimed, and the religion all. On the other hand, Earhart's husband, the publisher and publicist George Palmer Putnam (known as G. P.), worked her very hard indeed. The icons of the air age were big business.

Time magazine, September 28, 1931:

> To Charles Townsend Ludington, socialite of Philadelphia, $8,000 might be the price of a small cabin cruiser such as he sails on Biscayne Bay.... But the $8,073.61 profit which showed on a balance sheet upon [his] desk last week was as exciting to him as a great fortune. It was the first year's net earning of the Ludington Line, plane-per-hour passenger service between New York, Philadelphia and Washington.
>
> As practically sole financiers of the company [Nicholas and Charles Townsend] Ludington might well be proud. But they would be the first to insist that all credit go to two young men who sold them the plan and then made it work: brawny, handsome Gene Vidal, West Point halfback of 1916-1920, one time Army flyer; and squint-eyed, leathery Paul ("Dog") Collins, war pilot, old-time airmail pilot.

*Time*style still exerts its old magic, while *Time*checkers are, as always, a bit off—my father graduated from West Point in 1918. An all-American halfback, he also played quarterback. But he *was* one of the first army flyers; and the first instructor in aeronautics at West Point. Bored with peacetime army life and excited by aviation, he quit the army in 1926. Already married to the "beauteous" (*Time* epithet) Nina Gore, daughter of "blind solon" (ditto) Senator T. P. Gore, he had a year-old son for whom *Time* had yet to mint any of those Lucite epithets that, in time (where "All things shall come to pass," *Ecclesiastes*), they would.

NEW AIRLINES were cropping up all over the country. After 1918, anyone who could nail down a contract from the postmaster general to fly the mail was in business. Since this was the good old United States, there was corruption. Unkind gossips thought that an army flyer whose father-in-law was a senator would be well placed to get such a contract. But during the last years of President Hoover, Senator Gore was a Democrat; and during the first term of President Roosevelt, he was an enemy of the New Deal. Gore was no help at all to Gene. But anyone who could fly was automatically in demand at one or another of the small airlines that carried (or did not carry) the mail.

In 1929, C.M. Keys combined a couple of airlines and started Transcontinental Air Transport, or TAT. For a quarter million dollars cash, Keys hired, as a sort of consultant, Charles Lindbergh; he also gave the Lone Eagle shrewd advice on how to avoid income tax. Thus, TAT was dubbed "The Lindbergh Line." Keys was perhaps the first true hustler or robber baron in American aviation: "He had been an editor of the *Wall Street Journal* and had worked with Walter Hines Page on the old *World's Work*; Keys was also an important aviation promoter. He got into the manufacturing end of the industry during the war and eventually won control of Curtiss Aeroplane & Motor Company. . . ."[3] In other words, a businessman who "got control" of companies; who bought and sold them. TAT also acquired the ex–airmail flyer Paul Collins and Gene Vidal.

Like most of the early airlines, TAT was a combined air-rail service. Passenger planes did not fly at night; or over the turbulent Alleghenies. On a TAT transcontinental flight, the passengers left New York by rail in the evening; then, in Columbus, Ohio, they boarded a Ford trimotor (eight passengers maximum) and flew to Waynoka, Oklahoma. Here they transferred to the Santa Fe railroad for an overnight haul to Clovis, New Mexico, where another plane flew them into Los Angeles—or Burbank, to be precise. It is a tribute to the faith of the air-gospelers that they truly believed that this grueling two-day journey would, in time, be preferable to the comforts of a Pullman car. Interestingly enough, many descendants of the original railroad barons were immediately attracted to aviation, and names like Harriman and Whitney and Vanderbilt crop up on the boards of directors. These young men were prescient. By the end of the Second War, the railroads that had dominated American life since the Civil War, buying not only politicians but whole states, would be almost entirely superseded by civil aviation and the Teamsters Union. But the railroad lords suffered not all; they simply became airlords.

The transition was hardly overnight. In TAT's eighteen months of service, the line lost $2,750,000. There were simply not enough customers at sixteen cents a mile; also, more important, there was no mail contract.

TAT'S HEADQUARTERS were at St. Louis, and my only memory of the summer of 1929 (other than bleeding eardrums) was of city lights, as seen from a downtown hotel window. For anyone interested in period detail, there were almost no colored lights then. So, on a hot airless night in St. Louis,

3 Henry Ladd Smith, *Airways* (Knopf, 1942), p. 141.

the city had a weird white Arctic glow. Also, little did I suspect that as I
stared out over the tropical city with its icy blinking signs, a stone's throw
away, a youth of eighteen, as yet unknown to me and to the world,
Thomas Lanier Williams, was typing, typing, typing into the night while
across the dark fields of the Republic. . . .

Paul Collins describes the end of TAT (*Tales of an Old Air-Faring Man*):[4]

> About Christmastime 1929 all the St. Louis executives were called to a
> meeting in New York including Joseph Magee, the general manager; Gene
> Vidal, his assistant; Luke Harris, Jack Herlihy, and me. We were intro-
> duced in Mr. Keyes's [*sic*] office to one Jack Maddux, President of Mad-
> dux Airlines, an operation that flew from Los Angeles to San Francisco. . . .
> Mr. Keyes [*sic*] stated that a merger had been effected between TAT and
> Maddux.

The ineffable Keys then waited until the assembled management of TAT
had returned to St. Louis, where they were all fired.

Simultaneously, the Great Depression began. Small airlines either
merged or died. Since a contract to fly the mail was the key to survival, the
postmaster general, one Walter F. Brown, was, in effect, the most powerful
single figure in aviation. He was also a political spoils-man of considerable
energy. In principle, he wanted fewer airlines; and those beholden to him.
As of 1930, United Air Lines carried all transcontinental mail. But Brown
decided that, in this case, there should be two transcontinental carriers; one
would have the central New York–Los Angeles route; the second the southern Atlanta–Dallas–Los Angeles route. As befitted a Herbert Hoover socialist, Brown did not believe in competitive bidding. The southern route
would go to Brown-favored American Airlines and the central route to an
airline yet to be created but already titled Transcontinental and Western
Air, today's Trans World Airlines.

Brown then forced a merger between TAT (willing) and Western Air
Express (unwilling). But since neither flew the mail, Brown's promise of
a federal contract for the combined operation did the trick. Since Brown
was not above corporate troikism, a third airline, a shy mouse of a company called Pittsburgh Aviation Industries Corporation (PAIC), became
a member of the wedding. How on earth did such a mouse get involved
with two working airlines? Well, there were three Mellons on PAIC's board
of directors, of whom the most active was Richard, nephew of Andrew,
former secretary of the Treasury. The nobles missed few tricks in the early

[4] Foundation Press, University of Wisconsin–Stevens Point.

days of aviation. As it turned out, the first real boss of TWA was a PAIC man, Richard W. Robbins. And so, on August 25, 1930, TWA was awarded the central airmail route even though its competitor, United, had made a lower bid. There was outcry; but nothing more. After all, the chief radio engineer for TWA was the president's twenty-eight-year-old son, Herbert Hoover, Jr. In those days, Hoover socialism was total; and it was not until his successor, Franklin D. Roosevelt, that old-fashioned capitalism was restored.

DURING ALL THIS, Gene Vidal had retreated to Senator Gore's house in Rock Creek Park, Washington, DC. Certain that he had learned enough about the airline business to start one, he convinced the brothers Ludington that a regular New York–Philadelphia–Washington service was practical. He also came up with the revolutionary notion that the planes would fly "every hour on the hour": New York to Washington round trip was $23. When the Ludingtons insisted that costs be kept to a minimum, Gene, ever ingenious, said, "We'll operate at forty cents a mile, taking only a livable salary. Anything under forty cents, we'll agree to take in stock." The Ludingtons were charmed.

In September 1930, the Ludington Line began regular service. Tickets were sold in railway terminals. Gene personally built the first counter in Washington, using two crates with a board across. Everything was ad hoc. On one occasion, in Philadelphia, passengers from New York to Washington were stretching their legs while passengers from Washington to New York were doing the same. Then each group was shepherded into the wrong plane and the passengers to Washington went back to New York and those to New York back to Washington.

What to serve for lunch? My mother, always dieting, decided that consommé was bound to be popular. Fortunately, in those less litigious times, the first batch of badly scalded customers gallantly did not sue. Later, hard-boiled eggs and saltine crackers made the sort of lunch that stayed down longest. As the passengers dined, and the plane lurched, and the smell of exhaust filled the cabin, cylindrical cardboard ice-cream containers were tactfully passed around. The fact that what was supposed to contain ice-cream was used, instead, for vomit was my first metaphysical experience, an intimation of the skull beneath the skin. During the Second War, as first mate of an army ship in the Aleutians, I would grimly stuff our shaky passengers with crackers and hard-boiled eggs; and it is true: they do stay down longest.

At the end of the first year, the Ludington Line showed the profit duly noted by *Time*. As organizer and general manager, my father persuaded Amelia Earhart to become a vice-president; he also hired Felix Dupont to be the agent in Washington. He persuaded Herbert Hoover to light up the Washington monument at dusk because, sooner or later, a plane was bound to hit it. On the other hand, he ignored the mandatory fire drills at the Washington terminal on the sensible ground that "We have a real fire," as one of his mechanics put it, "most every day." Between New York and Washington, he put up twenty-four billboards. Slowpoke passengers on the Pennsylvania railroad could read, at regular intervals, "If you'd flown Ludington, you'd have been there." Were it not for Hoover socialism, so successful and busy a passenger airline would have got a mail contract. But Postmaster General Brown chose to give the franchise to Eastern Air Transport, who were eager to carry the mail at 89 cents a mile versus Ludington's 25 cents. But that has always been the American Way; who dares question it? The Ludingtons lost heart; and in February 1933 they sold out to Eastern. Even though Hoover socialism had been rejected at the polls, and there was now a new president, eager to restore prosperity with classic capitalistic measures.

Franklin Roosevelt was something of an aviation freak and, thanks in part to some backstage maneuvering on the part of Amelia Earhart and her friend Eleanor Roosevelt, Eugene L. Vidal became the director of the Bureau of Air Commerce at the age of thirty-eight. He was a popular figure not only in aviation circles but with the press. Henry Ladd Smith wrote: "Gene Vidal had fared so badly at the hands of Postmaster General Brown and the Republican administration that there was a certain poetic justice in his appointment...."[5] But Smith felt that there was more honor than power in the job. The bureau was divided into three parts and Vidal "had all the responsibilities that go with the title, but few of the powers. Unhappy Mr. Vidal took all the blame for mistakes, but he had to share credit with his two colleagues...." I don't think Gene felt all that powerless, although he certainly took a good deal of blame. Mainly he was concerned with, in Mr. Corn's words,

> the dream of wings for all...in November 1933 [he] announced that the government would soon spend half a million dollars to produce a "poor man's airplane." The machine would sell for $700.... He planned to launch the project with a grant from Harold Ickes's Public Works Admin-

[5] Smith, *Airways*, p. 283.

istration (PWA), one of the numerous government agencies established in
the depression to battle unemployment.

Although a lot of out-of-work engineers and craftsmen would be employed, Ickes saw nothing public in private planes; and Gene was obliged
to use his power to buy planes for the bureau's inspectors. He ordered five
experimental prototypes. The results were certainly unusual. There was
one plane whose wings could be folded up; and you could then drive it like
an automobile. Although nothing came of this hybrid, its overhead rotor
was the precursor of the helicopter, still worshipped as a god by the Vietnamese. Finally, there was the Hammond Y-1, which I was to fly.

Along with the glamour of flight, there was the grim fact that planes
often crashed and that the bodies of the passengers tended to be unpretty,
whether charred or simply in pieces strewn across the landscape. Knute
Rockne, Grace Moore, Carole Lombard died; and at least half of the people
I used to see in my childhood would, suddenly, one day, not be there.
"Crashed" was the word; and nothing more was said. As director, Gene was
obliged to visit the scenes of every major accident; and he had gruesome
tales to report. One survivor sued the bureau because the doctor at the
scene of the accident refused to replace in his scrotal sac the testicles that
lay nearby.

In 1934 the Democratic senator Hugo Black chaired a Senate committee to investigate the former Republican postmaster general Brown's deal-
ings with the airlines. Black's highly partisan committee painted Brown
even darker than he was. Yes, he had played favorites in awarding mail contracts but no one could prove that he—or the Grand Old Party—had in
any specific way profited. Nevertheless, Jim Farley, the new postmaster
general, charged Brown with "conspiracy and collusion" while the President, himself a man of truly superhuman vindictiveness, decided to punish
Brown, the Republican party, and the colluded-with airlines.

What could be more punitive—and dramatic—than the cancellation of
all US airmail contracts with private companies? Since the army had flown
the mail back in 1918, let them fly the mail now. The President consulted
the director of Air Commerce, who told him that army flyers did not have
the sort of skills needed to fly the mail. After all, he should know; he was
one. Undeterred, the President turned to General Foulois, the chief of the
air corps, who lusted for appropriations as all air corps chiefs do; and the
general said, of course, the air corps could fly the mail.

ON FEBRUARY 9, 1934, by executive order, the President canceled all airmail contracts; and the army flew the mail. At the end of the first week, five army pilots were dead; six critically injured; eight planes wrecked. One evening in mid-March, my father was called to the White House. As Gene pushed the President's wheelchair along the upstairs corridor, the President, his usual airy self, said, "Well, Brother Vidal, we seem to have a bit of a mess on our hands." Gene always said, "I found that 'we' pretty funny." But good soldiers covered up for their superiors. What, FDR wondered, should they do? Although my father had a deep and lifelong contempt for politicians in general ("They tell lies," he used to say with wonder, "even when they don't have to") and for Roosevelt's cheerful mendacities in particular, he did admire the President's resilience: "He was always ready to try something new. He was like a good athlete. Never worry about the last play. Only the next one." Unfortunately, before they could extricate the administration from the mess, Charles Lindbergh attacked the President; publically, the Lone Eagle held FDR responsible for the dead and injured army pilots.

Roosevelt never forgave Lindbergh. "After that," said Gene, "he would always refer to Slim as 'this man Lindbergh,' in that condescending voice of his. Or he'd say, '*your* friend Lindbergh,' which was worse." Although Roosevelt was convinced that Lindbergh's statement was entirely inspired by the airlines who wanted to get back their airmail contracts, he was too shrewd a politician to get in a shooting match with the world's most popular hero. Abruptly, on April 20, 1934, Postmaster General Farley let the airlines know that the Post Office was open to bids for mail contracts because, come May, the army would no longer fly the mail. It was, as one thoughtful observer put it, the same old crap game, with Farley not Brown as spoils-man.

In 1935, "lifelong bachelor" (as *Time* would say) Senator Bronson Cutting was killed in an air crash. He was a popular senator (survived to this day by his estimable sister, Iris Origo) and the Senate promptly investigated. My father was grilled at length.

> The bureau was accused of wasting time and money in a futile effort to develop a "flivver plane" for the masses.... Vidal himself did not fare so badly. The committee rebuked him mildly and reported that he appeared "lacking in iron," but since Vidal was hardly in the position to enforce orders, perhaps even this accusation was unfair.[6]

---

[6] Smith, *Airways*, p. 248.

My father's affection for politicians was not increased by the Senate hearings. But the real prince of darkness had now entered his life, Juan Trippe, and a lifelong struggle began. Even after I was grown, at the Maidstone Club in East Hampton I used to observe the two men, who never exactly *not* spoke to each other and yet never did speak.

JUAN TRIPPE WAS a smooth-looking man with very dark eyes. Grandson of a bank robber, as Gene liked to recall, Trippe had gone to Yale; got into the airline business in 1926, backed by two Yale friends, C. V. Whitney and William Rockefeller (what on earth do the rich *do* nowadays?). While Lindbergh was officially associated with my father and the Ludington Line, Slim was also being wooed by Trippe, who had acquired a small Florida-Cuba airline called Pan American. By 1931, Trippe had replaced Keys as the principal robber baron of the airways. Unlike Keys, he was wonderfully well connected socially and politically. For Pan American's original board, he managed to collect not only a Whitney but a Mellon son-in-law, David Bruce, and Robert Lehman. During Black's investigation of Brown, Trippe had been caught disguising his profits in what is now standard conglomerate procedure but in those sweet days was fraud; worse, Trippe was a Republican. But smoothness is all; and in due course, Trippe charmed Farley; and Gene; and for a time, the sly President.

Trippe's ambitions for Pan American were worldwide. He already had South America; he now wanted the Pacific and China; the Atlantic and Europe. But he would need considerable help from the administration to get the routes nailed securely down. Smoothly, he invited the director of the Bureau of Air Commerce to tour South America. A good time was had by all and, en route, Gene collected a number of exotic decorations from various exotic presidents. Then, back in Washington, Trippe presented Gene with a long list of requests. The guileless director explained to his recent host that the law required *competitive* bidding and that the United States, unlike old Europe, did not have "chosen instruments." Naturally, if Pan American wanted to enter in competition with other airlines. . . .

Trippe took his revenge. He went to his friend William Randolph Hearst—no longer a Roosevelt enthusiast—and together they orchestrated a press campaign against Gene Vidal, Jim Farley, and FDR—in that order. It is my impression that Lindbergh may have sided with Trippe. There is a curious photograph in *The Chosen Instrument*.[7] My father is at the center,

7 Marylin Bender and Selig Altschul, *The Chosen Instrument* (Simon and Schuster, 1982).

speaking into a microphone. Trippe is smoothly obsequious to his right while Igor Sikorky and Lindbergh are also present. The caption: "Attending the delivery of the Sikorsky S-42 in May 1934," followed by the names of all those present except for the director, whose endorsement was the point to the photograph. Thanks in part to Trippe's inspired press campaign, Gene quit the government in 1937; and the bureau was broken up. The Civil Aeronautics Board was then created; on January 1, 1985, it, too, ends, a victim of Reaganism.

Although Trippe got most of the world, he never forgave Gene. Some years later, when my father was put up for membership in Philadelphia's Racquet Club, Trippe tried to blackball him because Gene's father's name was Felix. "A *Jewish* name," said Juan smoothly. Those were racist days. When my father pointed out that in our section of Romano-Rhaetia, Felix is a common Christian name, he inadvertently revealed the family's darkest secret. Upon arrival (1848) in the Great Protestant Republic, the Roman Catholic Vidals had promptly turned Protestant. Obviously, during the Republic's high noon, no mass was worth exclusion from the Racquet Club against whose windows were pressed so many wistful Kennedy and Lee (born Levy) noses. Recently, a journalist told me that while interviewing Trippe, he noticed the old man was reading one of my books. When the journalist told him that the author was Gene Vidal's son, Trippe shook his head with wonder. "My, my," he said. "Hard to believe, isn't it?" Oh, they were real shits in those days.

III

I HAVE NO MEMORY of Lindbergh. But Amelia Earhart was very much a part of my life. She wrote poetry; and encouraged me to write, too. She had a beautiful speaking voice which I am sure I would have recognized during the war if she had really been, as certain fabulists believe, Tokyo Rose, a captive of the Japanese. Since she usually dressed as a boy, it was assumed that she had what were then called Sapphic tendencies. I have no idea whether or not she did but I do know that she wore trousers because she thought her legs were ugly; and if she were truly Sapphic, I doubt that she would have been so much in love with my father. She had milk-white eyelashes.

In the fall of 1936, Amelia, Gene, and I went to the Army-Navy game at West Point. On the way back, as her fans peered excitedly into our train compartment, she described how she planned to fly around the world, following, more or less, the equator. I asked her what part of the flight worried her the most. "Africa," she said. "If you got forced down in those jungles, they'd never find you." I said that the Pacific looked pretty large and wet to me. "Oh, there are always islands," she said. Then she asked Gene: "Wouldn't it be wonderful to just go off and live on a desert island?" He rather doubted it. Then they discussed just *how* you could survive; and what would you do if there was no water? and if there was no water, you would have to make a sun-still and extract salt from sea water and how was that done? As we approached Grand Central Station, I suddenly decided that I wanted a souvenir of Amelia. Shortly before she left on her flight around the world, she sent me the blue-and-white checked leather belt that she often wore. She gave my father her old watch. She also made a new will, as she usually did before a dangerous flight. She left Gene her California house, on condition that if he didn't want it (he didn't) he would give it to her mother, something she did not trust G. P., her husband, to do.[8]

ALTHOUGH MY FATHER was as fond of conspiracy theories as any other good American, he rejected most of the notions that still circulate about Amelia's last flight. Of course, he was at a disadvantage: he knew some-

---

[8] G. P. managed to suppress Amelia's final will; and my father didn't inherit the California property. I don't know what became of Amelia's mother.

thing about it. When Amelia's plane vanished July 2, 1937, somewhere between Lae, New Guinea, and Howland Island in the Pacific—where there are all those islands—the President sent the navy to look for her. He also asked Gene to help out, and act as a sort of coordinator. If Amelia had been on a spy mission for the American government, as is still believed in many quarters,[9] the commander in chief hadn't been told about it. Years later, Eleanor Roosevelt used to talk a lot about Amelia. When I asked her if she had ever been able to find out anything, she said no. More to the point, since Mrs. Roosevelt had been devoted to Amelia, if there *had* been a secret mission, Mrs. Roosevelt would have certainly revealed it after the war, and demanded all sorts of posthumous recognition for her friend. But Mrs. Roosevelt was certain that there had been no spy mission; on the other hand, she—like my father—thought there *was* something fishy about the whole business.

Shortly before Amelia left the States, she told my father that since she would have to take a navigator with her, she was going to hire Fred Noonan, formerly Pan American's chief navigator. Gene was alarmed: Noonan was a drunk. "Take anyone but Noonan," he said. "All right then," said Amelia, "why not you?" To Gene's surprise, she wasn't joking. Although Gene had recently divorced my mother and G. P. was simply Amelia's manager, Gene's affection for Amelia was not equal to her love for him."I'm not that good a navigator," he said. She then hired Noonan, who swore he was forever off the sauce. The flight began.

From India, Amelia rang G. P. and Gene together. She reported "personnel trouble": code for Noonan's drinking. Gene advised her to stop the flight. But she chose to keep on. Amelia rang again; this time from New Guinea. "Personnel trouble" had delayed her next hop—to Howland Island. This time both Gene and G. P. told her to abandon the flight. But she thought "personnel" might be improving. She was wrong. The night before they left Lae, Noonan was drunk; worse, he had had only forty-five minutes' sleep. When they took off, he was still drunk.

GENE'S THEORY of what happened is this: Amelia was going through a disagreeable early menopause; she deeply disliked her husband; she hated the publicness of her life and she was, at some romantic level, quite serious

---

9 For a gorgeously off-the-wall "search" for Amelia, read *Amelia Earhart Lives*, by Joe Klaas (McGraw-Hill, 1970). Apparently, in the Sixties, she was alive and well and living in New Bedford: she who had so deeply hated Rye.

about withdrawing to a desert island — symbolically if not literally. Years earlier, she had made a number of conditions when she allowed G. P. to marry her. The marriage was to be, as they called it then, "open." Also, "I may have to keep some place where I can go to be by myself now and then for I cannot guarantee to endure at all times the confinements of even an attractive cage." Finally, Gene thought it unlikely that even a navy so sublimely incompetent that, four years later, it would allow most of its fleet to be sunk at Pearl Harbor, would ever have engaged such a nervy lady to spy on Japan, while *she* would have pointed out that a pioneer circumnavigation of the globe was quite enough for one outing.

According to Gene, there were only two mysteries. One of Amelia's last radio messages was, "743 from KHAQQ: We must be on you but we cannot see you. Gas is running low. Been unable to reach you by radio. Flying at 1000 feet. One half-hour's gas left." Gene said that this was not a true report. She had a good deal more than a half-hour's gas left. Why did she lie? The second mystery was that of the radio frequency. Amelia's last message was at 8:46 AM: after that, some fourteen minutes passed with her frequency still coming in strong at what is known as "maximum 5." "Then," said Gene, "the frequency didn't break off, the way it does when you crash. Someone switched it off." So what happened? It was Gene's hunch that she had indeed found an island; and landed. "But what about Fred Noonan?" I asked. "He sounds even worse than G. P." Gene's response was grim. "If Amelia wanted to get rid of him, she'd have got rid of him. Hit him over the head with one of the bottles. She was like that."

Over the years, there were many stories of a white woman sighted on this or that island. The only intriguing one, according to G. P., was from a Russian sailor whose ship had passed a small island on which a white woman signaled them; she was wearing nothing except a man's drawers. "The funny thing is," said G. P. to my father, "she always wore my shorts when she flew, but I wore boxer shorts, and the sailor said this woman was wearing those new jockey shorts." Gene never told G. P. that for some years Amelia had been wearing Gene's "new jockey shorts." In any event the ship had not stopped; and no one ever followed up.

FOUR YEARS BEFORE Amelia's last flight, she and Gene started what is now Northeast airlines, with Paul Collins as president. Although Gene was never very active in the airline, he remained a director to the end of his life. According to Mr. Corn, Vidal never gave up his dream "of mass-produced personal planes, and in private life began experiments with molded plywood, a material he thought appropriate for the purpose." This is true enough, except that he also experimented, more successfully, with fibre-glass. But by the time he died in 1969, the world was far too full of people even to dream of filling the skies with private planes in competition with military aircraft and the planes of those airlines, three of which he had had a hand in founding. I do know that he found modern civil aviation deeply boring; and though he shared the general ecstasy when a man got to the moon, the gospel of flight that he and Lindbergh and Earhart preached was by then a blurred footnote to the space age where technology is all and, to the extent that there is a human aspect to space, it involves team players with the right stuff. Neil Armstrong first stepped on the moon but it was Werner von Braun and a cast of thousands who put him there. Mr. Armstrong did not fly to the moon; and for all his personal pluck and luck, he is perceived as a footnote, a name for Trivial Pursuit.

It was different on December 17, 1934, when my father asked all the nation's pilots "to take off at 10:30 in the morning and to stay in the air for half an hour. They would thus be aloft at the precise time at which, thirty-one years earlier, Orville Wright had also been airborne. The response to Vidal's call was impressive . . . an estimated 8,000 aircraft participated in the ritual."[10]

Today it is marvelous indeed to watch on television the rings of Saturn close; and to speculate on what we may yet find at galaxy's edge. But in the process, we have lost the human element; not to mention the high hope of those quaint days when flight would create "one world." Instead of one world, we have "star wars," and a future in which dumb dented human toys will drift mindlessly about the cosmos long after our small planet's dead.

[10] Corn, *The Winged Gospel*, p. 64.

*The Last Christmas of the War by Primo Levi was originally published January 30, 1986.
Copyright © 1981, 1985 by Guilio Einaudi editore s.P.a., Torino. English translation copyright © 1979, 1982, 1983, 1986 by Summit Books. Reprinted by permission of Summit Books,
a division of Simon & Schuster, Inc.*

PRIMO LEVI

Last Christmas of the War

IN MORE WAYS than one, Monowitz, a part of Auschwitz, was not a typical camp. The barrier that separated us from the world—symbolized by the double barbed-wire fence—was not hermetic, as elsewhere. Our work brought us into daily contact with people who were "free," or at least less slaves than we were: technicians, German engineers and foremen, Russian and Polish workers, English, American, French, and Italian prisoners of war. Officially they were forbidden to talk to us, the pariahs of KZ (*Konzentrations-Zentrum*), but the prohibition was constantly ignored, and what's more, news from the free world reached us through a thousand channels. In the factory trash bins we found copies of the daily papers (sometimes two or three days old and rain-soaked) and in them we read with trepidation the German bulletins: mutilated, censored, euphemistic, yet eloquent. The Allied POWs listened secretly to Radio London, and even more secretly brought us the news, and it was exhilarating. In December 1944 the Russians had entered Hungary and Poland, the English were in the Romagna, the Americans were heavily engaged in the Ardennes but were winning in the Pacific against Japan.

At any rate, there was no real need of news from far away to find out how the war was going. At night, when all the noises of the Camp had died down, we heard the thunder of the artillery coming closer and closer. The front was no more than a hundred kilometers away; a rumor spread that the Red Army was already in the West Carpathians. The enormous factory in which we worked had been bombed from the air several times with vicious and scientific precision: one bomb, only one, on the central power plant, putting it out of commission for two weeks; as soon as the damage was repaired and the stack began belching smoke again, another bomb and so on. It was clear that the Russians, or the Allies in concert with the Rus-

337

sians, intended to stop production but not destroy the plants. These they wanted to capture intact at the end of the war, as indeed they did; today that is Poland's largest synthetic rubber factory. Active anti-aircraft defense was nonexistent, no pursuing planes were to be seen; there were guns on the roofs but they didn't fire. Perhaps they no longer had ammunition.

In short, Germany was moribund, but the Germans didn't notice. After the attempt on Hitler in July, the country lived in a state of terror: a denunciation, an absence from work, an incautious word were sufficient to land you in the hands of the Gestapo as a defeatist. Therefore both soldiers and civilians fulfilled their tasks as usual, driven at once by fear and an innate sense of discipline. A fanatical and suicidal Germany terrorized a Germany that was by now discouraged and profoundly defeated.

A SHORT TIME before, toward the end of October, we'd had the opportunity to observe a close-up of a singular school of fanaticism, a typical example of Nazi training. On some unused land next to our camp, a *Hitlerjugend*— Hitler Youth—encampment had been set up. There were possibly two hundred adolescents, still almost children. In the mornings they practiced flag raising, sang belligerent hymns, and, armed with ancient muskets, were put through marching and shooting drills. We understood later that they were being prepared for enrollment in the *Volkssturm*, that ragtag army of old men and children that, according to the Führer's mad plans, was supposed to put up a last-ditch defense against the advancing Russians. But sometimes in the afternoon their instructors, who were SS veterans, would bring them to see us as we worked clearing away rubble from the bombings, or erecting slapdash and useless little protective walls of bricks or sandbags.

They led them among us on a "guided tour" and lectured them in loud voices, as if we had neither ears to hear nor the intelligence to understand. "These that you see are the enemies of the Reich, *your* enemies. Take a good look at them: would you call them men? They are *Untermenschen*, submen! They stink because they don't wash; they're in rags because they don't take care of themselves. What's more, many of them don't even understand German. They are subversives, bandits, street thieves from the four corners of Europe, but we have rendered them harmless; now they work for us, but they are good only for the most primitive work. Moreover, it is only right that they should repair the war damages; these are the people who wanted the war: the Jews, the Communists, and the agents of the plutocracies."

The child-soldiers listened, devout and dazed. Seen close up, they inspired both pain and horror. They were haggard and frightened, yet they looked at us with intense hatred. So we were the ones guilty for all the evils, the cities in ruins, the famine, their dead fathers on the Russian front. The Führer was stern but just, and it was just to serve him.

AT THAT TIME I worked as a "specialist" in a chemical laboratory inside the plant: these are things that I have written about elsewhere, but, strangely, with the passing of the years these memories do not fade, nor do they thin out. They become enriched with details I thought were forgotten, which sometimes acquire meaning in the light of other people's memories, from letters I receive or books I read.

It was snowing, it was very cold, and working in that laboratory was not easy. At times the heating system didn't work and at night, ice would form, bursting the phials of reagents and the big bottle of distilled water. Often we lacked the raw materials or reagents necessary for analyses, and it was necessary to improvise or to produce what was missing on the spot. There was no ethyl acetate for a colorimetric measurement. The laboratory head told me to prepare a liter of it and gave me the needed acetic acid and ethyl alcohol. It's a simple procedure; I had done it in Turin in my organic preparations course in 1941. Only three years before, but it seemed like three thousand.... Everything went smoothly up to the final distillation, but at that point suddenly the water stopped running.

This could have ended in a small disaster, because I was using a glass refrigerator. If the water returned, the refrigerating tube, which had been heated on the inside by the product's vapor, would certainly have shattered on contact with the icy water. I turned off the faucet, found a small pail, filled it with distilled water, and immersed it in the small pump of a Höppler thermostat. The pump pushed the water into the refrigerator, and the hot water fell into the pail as it came out. Everything went well for a few minutes, then I noticed that the ethyl acetate was no longer condensing; almost all of it was coming out of the pipe in the form of vapor. I had been able to find only a small amount of distilled water (there was no other) and by now it had become warm.

What to do? There was a lot of snow on the windowsills, so I made balls with it and put them into the pail one by one. While I was busy with my gray snowballs, Dr. Pannwitz, the German chemist who had subjected me to a singular "state examination" to determine whether my professional knowledge was sufficient, came into the lab. He was a fanatical Nazi. He

339

looked suspiciously at my makeshift installation and the murky water that could have damaged the precious pump, but said nothing and left.

A few days later, toward the middle of December, the basin of one of the suction hoods was blocked and the chief told me to unplug it. It seemed natural to him that the dirty job should fall to me and not to the lab technician, a girl named Frau Mayer, and actually it seemed natural to me too. I was the only one who could stretch out serenely on the floor without fear of getting dirty; my striped suit was already completely filthy....

I was getting up after having screwed the siphon back on when I noticed Frau Mayer standing close to me. She spoke to me in a whisper with a guilty air; she was the only one of the eight or ten girls in the lab—German, Polish, and Ukrainian—who showed no contempt for me. Since my hands were already dirty, she asked, could I fix her bicycle, which had a flat? She would, of course, give me something for my trouble.

This apparently neutral request was actually full of sociological implications. She had said "please" to me, which in itself represented an infraction of the upside-down code that regulated our relationships with the Germans. She had spoken to me for reasons not connected with work; she had made a kind of contract with me, and a contract is made between equals; and she had expressed, or at least implied, gratitude for the work I had done on the basin in her stead. However, the girl was also inviting me to break the rules, which could be very dangerous for me, since I was there as a chemist, and by repairing her bike I would be taking time away from my professional work. She was proposing, in other words, a kind of complicity, risky but potentially useful. Having a human relationship with someone "on the other side" involved danger, a social promotion, and more food for today and the day after. In a flash I did the algebraic sum of the three addends: hunger won by several lengths, and I accepted the proposal.

Frau Mayer held out the key to the padlock, saying that I should go and get the bicycle; it was in the courtyard. That was out of the question; I explained as best I could that she must go herself, or send someone else. "We" were by definition thieves and liars: if anybody saw me with a bicycle I'd really be in for it. Another problem arose when I saw the bicycle. In its tool bag there were pieces of rubber, rubber cement, and small irons to remove the tire, but there was no pump, and without a pump I couldn't locate the hole in the inner tube. I must explain, incidentally, that in those days bicycles and flat tires were much more common than they are now, and almost all Europeans, especially young ones, knew how to patch a tire. A pump?

No problem, said Frau Mayer; all I had to do was get Meister Grubach, her colleague next door, to lend me one. But this wasn't so simple. With some embarrassment I had to ask her to write and sign a note: "*Bitte um die Fahrradpumpe.*"

I made the repair, and Frau Mayer, in great secrecy, gave me a hard-boiled egg and four lumps of sugar. Don't misunderstand; given the situation and the going rates, it was a more than generous reward. As she furtively slipped me the packet, she whispered something that gave me a lot to think about: "Christmas will soon be here." Obvious words, absurd actually when addressed to a Jewish prisoner; certainly they were intended to mean something else, something no German at that time would have dared to put into words.

In telling this story after forty years, I'm not trying to make excuses for Nazi Germany. One human German does not whitewash the innumerable inhuman or indifferent ones, but it does have the merit of breaking a stereotype.

IT WAS A memorable Christmas for the world at war; memorable for me too, because it was marked by a miracle. At Auschwitz, the various categories of prisoners (political, common criminals, social misfits, homosexuals, etc.) were allowed to receive gift packages from home, but not the Jews. Anyway, from whom could the Jews have received them? From their families, exterminated or confined in the surviving ghettos? From the very few who had escaped the roundups, hidden in cellars, in attics, terrified and penniless? And who knew our address? For all the world knew, we were dead.

And yet a package did finally find its way to me, through a chain of friends, sent by my sister and my mother, who were hidden in Italy. The last link of that chain was Lorenzo Perrone, the bricklayer from Fossano, of whom I have spoken in *Survival in Auschwitz*, and whose heartbreaking end I have recounted here in "Lorenzo's Return."[*] The package contained ersatz chocolate, cookies, and powdered milk, but to describe its real value, the impact it had on me and on my friend Alberto, is beyond the powers of ordinary language. In the Camp, the terms eating, food, hunger had meanings totally different from their usual ones. That unexpected, improbable, impossible package was like a meteorite, a heavenly object, charged with symbols, immensely precious, and with an enormous momentum.

---

[*] *The New York Review*, November 7, 1985.

WE WERE NO LONGER alone: a link with the outside world had been established, and there were delicious things to eat for days and days. But there
were also serious practical problems to resolve immediately: we found ourselves in the situation of a passer-by who is handed a gold ingot in full view
of everyone. Where to put the food? How to keep it? How to protect it
from other people's greediness? How to invest it wisely? Our year-old
hunger kept pushing us toward the worst possible solution: eat it right then
and there. But we had to resist that temptation. Our weakened stomachs
could not have coped with the abuse; within an hour, it would have ended
in indigestion or worse.

We had no safe hiding places so we distributed the food in all the regular pockets in our clothes, and sewed secret pockets inside the backs of our
jackets so that even in case of a body search something could be saved. But
to have to take everything with us, to work, to the washhouse, to the la-
trine, was inconvenient and awkward. Alberto and I talked it over at length
in the evening after curfew. The two of us had made a pact: everything
either one of us managed to scrounge beyond our ration had to be divided
into two exactly equal parts. Alberto was always more successful than I in
these enterprises, and I often asked why he wanted to stay partners with
anyone as inefficient as I was. But he always replied: "You never know. I'm
faster but you're luckier." For once, he turned out to be right.

Alberto came up with an ingenious scheme. The cookies were the biggest
problem. We had them stored, a few here, a few there. I even had some in
the lining of my cap, and had to be careful not to crush them when I had
to yank it off fast to salute a passing SS. The cookies weren't all that good
but they looked nice. We could, he suggested, divide them into two packages and give them as gifts to the Kapo and the barracks Elder. According
to Alberto, that was the best investment. We would acquire prestige, and
the two big shots, even without a formal agreement, would reward us with
various favors. The rest of the food we could eat ourselves, in small, reasonable daily rations, and with the greatest possible precautions.

But in camp, the crowding, the total lack of privacy, the gossip and disorder were such that our secret quickly became an open one. In the space of
a few days we noticed that our companions and Kapos were looking at us
with different eyes. That's the point: they were looking at us, the way you
do at something or someone outside the norm, that no longer melts into
the background but stands out. According to how much they liked "the
two Italians," they looked at us with envy, with understanding, compla-
cency, or open desire. Mendi, a Slovakian rabbi friend of mine, winked at

me and said *"Mazel tov,"* the lovely Yiddish and Hebrew phrase used to congratulate someone on a happy event. Quite a few people knew or had guessed something, which made us both happy and uneasy; we would have to be on our guard. In any case, we decided by mutual consent to speed up the consumption: something eaten cannot be stolen.

On Christmas Day we worked as usual. As a matter of fact, since the laboratory was closed, I was sent along with the others to remove rubble and carry sacks of chemical products from a bombed warehouse to an undamaged one. When I got back to camp in the evening, I went to the washhouse. I still had quite a lot of chocolate and powdered milk in my pockets, so I waited until there was a free spot in the corner farthest from the entrance. I hung my jacket on a nail, right behind me; no one could have approached without my seeing him. I began to wash, when out of the corner of my eye I saw my jacket rising in the air. I turned but it was already too late. The jacket, with all its contents, and with my registration number sewed on the breast, was already out of reach. Someone had lowered a string and hook from the small window above the nail. I ran outside, half-undressed as I was, but no one was there. No one had seen anything, no one knew anything. Along with everything else, I was now without a jacket. I had to go to the barracks supply master to confess my "crime," because in the Camp being robbed was a crime. He gave me another jacket, but ordered me to find a needle and thread, never mind how, rip the registration number off my pants and sew it on the new jacket as quickly as possible. Otherwise *"bekommst du fünfundzwanzig"*: I'd get twenty-five whacks with a stick.

We divided up the contents of Alberto's pockets. He had remained unscathed, and he proceeded to display his finest philosophical resources. We two had eaten more than half the food, right? And the rest wasn't completely wasted. Some other famished man was celebrating Christmas at our expense, maybe even blessing us. And anyway, we could be sure of one thing: that this would be our last Christmas of war and imprisonment.

—translated by Ruth Feldman

Contributors

Gabriele Annan, who lives in London, is a book and film critic.

Hannah Arendt's books include *The Origins of Totalitarianism, The Human Condition, Eichmann in Jerusalem,* and *On Violence.* She died in 1975.

W. H. Auden died in 1973. Princeton University Press is publishing an eight-volume edition of his complete works.

Isaiah Berlin, formerly President of the British Academy, is the author of *The Hedgehog and the Fox, Russian Thinkers,* and *The Crooked Timber of Humanity,* among other works.

Pierre Boulez was formerly Director of the Institut de Recherche et Coordination Acoustique-Musique at the Centre Georges Pompidou in Paris. He is the author of *Boulez on Music Today, Notes of an Apprenticeship,* and *Gustave Mahler in Vienna,* in which the essay in this collection appeared in different form.

Joseph Brodsky, former Poet Laureate of the United States, won the Nobel Prize for Literature in 1987. He is Andrew Mellon Professor of English at Mount Holyoke College. Among his books are *A Part of Speech, To Urania,* and *Less Than One,* a collection of essays.

Bruce Chatwin's books include *In Patagonia, The Songlines, Utz,* and *What Am I Doing Here.* He died in 1989.

Joan Didion is the author of *Play It As It Lays, The White Album, Democracy, Miami,* and *After Henry.*

Richard Ellmann is the author of *James Joyce: A Biography, Yeats: The Man and the Masks,* and *Oscar Wilde.* He died in 1987.

Elizabeth Hardwick's books include *Bartleby in Manhattan and Other Essays, Seduction and Betrayal,* and the novel *Sleepless Nights.*

Robert Hughes is the art critic for *Time* and the author of *The Shock of the New, The Fatal Shore, Barcelona,* and *Culture of Complaint.*

Primo Levi's books include *The Periodic Table, If Not Now When?, Survival in Auschwitz, The Drowned and the Saved, The Monkey's Wrench,* and *Moments of Reprieve,* in which the essay in this anthology appeared. He died in 1987.

Jonathan Lieberson, who died in 1989, is the author of *Varieties.*

Robert Lowell won the Pulitzer Prize for Poetry for *Lord Weary's Castle* in 1946 and for *The Dolphin* in 1973. His *Collected Prose* was published in 1987. He died in 1977.

Dwight Macdonald's books include *Dwight Macdonald on Movies,* *Against the American Grain: Essays on Mass Culture,* and *Discriminations: Essays and Afterthoughts.* He died in 1982.

V. S. Pritchett is the author of many books of fiction and nonfiction. His *Complete Collected Stories* was published in 1991.

John Richardson is the author of books on Picasso, Braque, and Manet. He is currently at work on the second volume of *A Life of Picasso.*

Oliver Sacks is Professor of Neurology at the Albert Einstein College of Medicine. His books include *Migraine, Seeing Voices, Awakenings,* and *The Man Who Mistook His Wife for a Hat.* The essay in this anthology appeared in *A Leg to Stand On.*

Susan Sontag's books include *Against Interpretation, Styles of Radical Will, On Photography, AIDS and Its Metaphors, The Volcano Lover,* a novel, and *Alice in Bed.*

Andrei D. Sakharov died in 1989. His books include *Sakharov Speaks, The Politics of Human Rights,* and *My Country and the World.* He was awarded the Nobel Peace Prize in 1975.

Igor Stravinsky, in addition to his musical works, is the author of *Igor Stravinsky: An Autobiography* and of several volumes of conversations with Robert Craft. He died in 1971. Robert Craft is a conductor and the author of *Stravinsky: Chronicle of a Friendship* and several books of essays. He is also the editor, with Robert Gottlieb, of *Stravinsky: Selected Correspondence.*

Thich Nhat Hanh was exiled from Vietnam in 1966 and now lives in France. Among his many books are *Vietnam: Lotus in a Sea of Fire, The Miracle of Mindfulness,* and *Being Peace. Please Call Me by My True Names: The Collected Poems of Thich Nhat Hanh* and *Love in Action: Essays on Nonviolent Social Change* have just been published by Parallax Press.

Gore Vidal's most recent books include *Screening History, Live from Golgotha,* and *United States: Essays, 1952–1992.*